MULTICULTURAL ASSESSMENT IN COUNSELING AND CLINICAL PSYCHOLOGY

Buros-Nebraska Series
on
Measurement & Testing

Series Editor

JAMES C. IMPARA

Managing Editor
LINDA L. MURPHY

**Buros Institute of Mental Measurements
and
Department of Educational Psychology
University of Nebraska-Lincoln**

MULTICULTURAL ASSESSMENT IN COUNSELING AND CLINICAL PSYCHOLOGY

Edited by

GARGI ROYSIRCAR SODOWSKY
JAMES C. IMPARA
University of Nebraska-Lincoln

BUROS INSTITUTE OF MENTAL MEASUREMENTS
University of Nebraska-Lincoln

Buros Institute of Mental Measurements
135 Bancroft Hall
University of Nebraska-Lincoln
Lincoln, NE 68588-0348

The paper used in this publication meets the minimum requirements of American National Standard for Information Sciences—Permanence of Paper for Printed Library Materials, ANSI Z39.48-1984.

Buros-Nebraska Symposium on Measurement and Testing, 1993
Multicultural Assessment

ISBN 0-910674-41-8

Printed in the United States of America

Contents

Preface

This work evolved from the 1993 Buros-Nebraska Symposium on Testing and Measurement: Multicultural Assessment, held by the Buros Institute of Mental Measurements, Department of Educational Psychology, at the University of Nebraska-Lincoln. Among the symposium presenters, Stanley Sue, Juris Draguns, Guiseppe Costantino and Thomas Malgady, Janet Helms, Robert Carter, Sandra Choney and John Behrens, Joseph Ponterotto, Gargi Roysircar Sodowsky, and Donald Pope-Davis accepted the Buros Institute's invitation to contribute chapters to an envisioned multicultural assessment volume. The authors—some with the assistance of new collaborators—painstakingly revised their papers. They added measurement and statistical analyses that they have not previously published, advanced the theory-building of their respective topics, and wrote integrative literature reviews, thus providing substantive chapters for this book. With reference to the few multicultural and cross-cultural assessment books, book chapters, and journal reviews that are currently available in professional psychology, this book is an essential complement to them. Its uniqueness is that it responds to the paucity of measurement research in multicultural counseling. This collection might be characterized as recording multicultural assessment's empirical beginnings, a fairly unchartered territory.

Select multicultural instruments that are paper-and-pencil attitude and projective tests, developed recently and cited in refereed journals, are presented. New data are treated to multivariate statistics, exploratory and confirmatory factor analyses, structural equation modeling, cluster analyses, reliability estimation, and norm transformations. Tests are shown to be construct-related to multicultural theories and/or criterion-related to sociocultural variables. That is, instrument validity is supported through the theoretical groundedness of obtained results, through theory-building based on data interpretation, or through criterion predictions.

Test bias of mainstream instruments are discussed statistically as well as conceptually. Differences in test scores are given an interpretation different from the conclusion that deviant scores indicate deficits. Clinical judgement is shown to be subject to individual bias and to clinicians' immersion in their racial and cultural contexts and their inability to see their imposed bias. Decision trees, guidelines, and assessment reports are provided to illustrate qualitative methods for contextual diagnosis and integrative clinical judgement. Methods to identify social desirability in multicultural self-reports are discussed. Classical measurement theory is argued to overlook the multiplicity of person-environment reactivity that merits investigation in a multicultural society and in a majority-minority sociopolitical system.

Thus, this work represents empiricism, ideology, and applications, the scientist-practitioner hallmark of professional psychology. True to their professional training in applications, the authors' discourse, tables, and figures are reader- and consumer-friendly. The book has been designed to give counseling and clinical psychology students, researchers, and practitioners information that aims to make them multiculturally effective in their respective roles.

There are three sections, and each section is preceded by an introduction that highlights every chapter in the section. Finally, we invite you, as you read through the book, to ask yourself whether instruments can ever be developed that will provide appropriate clinical interpretations for anyone without regard to cultural, racial, and ethnic heritage. Our question reminds us of Standard 2.04(c) of the 1992 American Psychological Association's *Ethical Principles of Psychologists and Code of Conduct*, which states that on the basis of factors such as gender, age, race, ethnicity, national origin, religion, sexual orientation, disability, language, or socioeconomic status certain tests should not be used, or it may be necessary to adjust the interpretation of results on such tests.

Once again the Buros Institute tradition of being at the cutting edge of measurement concerns is continued by this book.

Gargi Roysircar Sodowsky
James C. Impara
Spring 1996
University of Nebraska-Lincoln

Section One

Test Bias, Multicultural Assessment Theory, and Multicultural Instrumentation

Gargi Roysircar Sodowsky

University of Nebraska-Lincoln

Stanley Sue in "Measurement, Testing, and Ethnic Bias: Can Solutions Be Found" addresses multicultural assessment and research with experienced wisdom and scientific inquiry. His tone is amicable, communicating a problem-solving attitude. Owing to its applicability, Sue's paper will appeal to a wide readership, with each reader finding a particular part especially meaningful. We find journalistic information on negligent diagnosis; a review of diagnostic studies; suggestions for new measurement methods to control for cultural bias in tests; analyses of a White prediction equation for the academic achievement of various Asians in the U.S.A.; ongoing research on MPPI-2 scores of diversely acculturated Asian Americans; hypotheses about Asian-American personality variables that influence responses to mainstream measures of psychopathology; and a discussion on institutional policy matters, something practitioners are rarely concerned about, but which is important to the advocacy of racial and ethnic equity.

One is introduced to what is minority group status, culture, ethnicity, and the overlap of the latter two. Sue cites research where substantial misdiagnosis of American ethnic minorities consists of both over- and underpathologizing, and where misdiagnosis may have resulted from the interaction of client-clinician racial/ethnic match and mismatch. The main point is that American ethnics are more likely to be misdiagnosed than White Americans. Sue notes that the two popular ways of identifying test bias in personality instruments are factor analysis and regression analysis (analysis of items within an instrument has been used particularly in achievement and aptitude tests [Sue, 1994, private communication]).

Sue addresses the nature and extent of bias when one group's regression equation is used as the standard. He summarizes a previous study that reports predictors of Asian academic achievement. A White regression equation both overpredicted and underpredicted various Asian groups. Sue and colleagues used Whites as the standard because prediction formulas established by universities are based primarily on the White-American majority group. Sue emphasizes (1994, private communication) that "over and underpredictions of GPA involving a difference of .17 is quite substantial, not only to student perceptions but also to admissions to graduate school. As one example, UCLA will not as a rule admit as graduate students undergraduates who have a cumulative GPA of under 3.00. You can imagine how many students receive GPAs between 2.83 and 3.00.... Finally, at some universities (such as UC Berkeley), there were attempts to increase the weight of SAT-Verbal over SAT-Math performance in admission. According to our findings, doing so would probably reduce the ability to identify the best Asian American students."

From Sue, a reader learns how culturally different decision-making abilities can be "conceptually equivalent"; how an assessor is also a measurement "instrument"; and how one does "back translation" and "parallel research." The response biases of Asian-American subjects to the MMPI-2 make Sue question the "metric equivalence" of the MMPI-2. He suggests using the Asian "loss of face" variable as a validity index to understand Asian response sets on measures of psychopathology. Thus, in Sue's chapter one encounters concepts that are unfamiliar to classical measurement theory.

Sue develops the view that people express distress in culturally acceptable ways, and thus symptoms may hold different meanings in different cultures. The implication is that assessment/diagnosis needs to focus on a deeper understanding (in addition to symptom enumeration or mental health status examination) of the client's phenomenology than is currently emphasized. From Sue one realizes that the clinician knows little about clients' history and etiology of problem.

Juris Draguns' "Multicultural and Cross-Cultural Assessment: Dilemmas and Decision" is rich in the breadth of its coverage;

development of arguments and counter arguments; presentation of assessment/diagnostic hypotheses and research ideas; and suggestions for ideal solutions to conflicts that inherently arise when assumptions are based on the contextualization of psychology. Draguns' ideas are scholarly, substantive, and complex.   The review of the psychodiagnostic literature and the reference list are excellent. This scholarly chapter is a "must" for graduate student researchers and cross-cultural/multicultural researchers.

Draguns draws a distinction between cross-cultural assessment and multicultural assessment. It is possible and worthy to compare anxiety responses, depression, schizophrenia, or coping responses to catastrophes across political, cultural, and geographic frontiers. Pluralistic localities in the U.S. provide similar opportunities for investigating the humanly universal and the culturally variable. This is the etic cross-cultural perspective. But not relevant to cross-cultural comparisons are disparities in interethnic comparisons in the U.S. such as the uneven distribution of power and privilege, the complex patterns of acculturation and ethnic identity in the U.S., multiple and overlapping group membership, and the difficulty of categorizing ethnic groups that have fuzzy intergroup boundaries. These latter challenging investigations have been taken up by the emic perspective of multicultural counseling. Draguns gives definitions of culture as it applies to psychology and makes the important point that the concept of culture should generate hypotheses rather than serve as a convenient source of post hoc explanations.

Like Sue, Draguns uses terms unfamiliar to classical measurement theory. Take, for example, his comparisons of "etic," John Berry's term "imposed etic," and his own version of "modified etic." Draguns illustrates how to integrate the contrasting options of emic-qualitative and etic-quantitative data in order to have a comprehensive understanding of psychopathology across all cultural borders. Draguns' examination of the acculturation and ethnic identity of American racial and ethnic minorities is useful because this is an important multicultural topic. Draguns references some important multicultural and cross-cultural assessment instruments.   He also provides an international dimension by referring to transcultural studies on depression and schizophrenia and to the epidemiological studies of the World Health Organization.

How does one compare equivalent stimuli that are not physically identical or that are physically identical but not equivalent? Draguns gives criteria for limiting such stimuli comparisons. He cautions against artificial matching as well as comparing samples that are widely divergent in relevant characteristics. In order to make sure that concepts carry constant meanings, Draguns suggests the systematic collection of empirical data on the equivalence of concepts, use of explicit rules of diagnosis and group assignment, and the employment of multimethods, serial studies, partial correlation, analysis of covariance, and mutivariate methods.

From the broad-based theoretical discourse of Stanley Sue and Juris Draguns, we turn to the presentation of a specific multicultural instrument. The TEMAS is being utilized with clinical populations in community mental health centers, and, unlike other multicultural instruments, it is commercially available. Giuseppe Costantino and Robert Malgady's "Development of The TEMAS, A Multicultural Thematic Apperception Test: Psychometric Properties and Clinical Utility" presents an interesting and viable projective test for Hispanic/Latino(a) and African-American children who live in urban pluralistic environments. A nonminority version is also available for urban White children. The authors have done several studies since the development of the TEMAS to investigate its psychometric properties and its validity. These studies have been conducted in New York and in settings in South America.

The primary theoretical difference between the Thematic Apperception Test (TAT) and the TEMAS could be that the basis of the TEMAS is in cognitive and ego psychology theories, whereas the TAT seeks to assess adjustment dynamics caused by intrapersonal needs and environmental presses. The TEMAS assesses three broad functions, Cognitive, Personality, and Affective. The authors have shown that pretherapy TEMAS scores can significantly predict posttherapy TEMAS outcome scores. Thus, the authors show how a newly researched multicultural instrument can also be clinically useful. The authors have studied the relationships of acculturation, ethnicity, and positive adjustment with the TEMAS. Their reference to such research fills what would otherwise be a gap in this book, which includes limited references to the assessment of acculturation adaptations. A particularly useful aspect of the Costantino and Malgady chapter is that it ends with samples of TEMAS client protocols and integrated assessment reports on three children who indicate body-image and self-identity problems, reality-testing problems, relationship difficulties with parental figures, aggression, and sexual molestation tendencies.

Costantino and Malgady, in addition to demonstrating the clinical utility of the TEMAS, also address psychometric definitions of bias. The authors provide five definitions of test bias. For example, they argue that even in the absence of compelling empirical evidence, assessment procedures ought not to be routinely generalized to different cultural groups, and that multicultural tests and assessments should be increasingly used. They explain that separate norms for mainstream instruments do not remove test bias because mean differences may be valid and minority populations may thus be underserved. Mean differences between an ethnic minority group and the White majority group perhaps suggest that the majority yardstick does not work for minorities, and so emic instruments may be needed.

Costantino and Malgady request research on face validity. Such research would reveal whether items in mainstream instruments or DSM criteria suspected of cultural bias are concordant or discordant with other items or diagnostic criteria considered beyond reproach. They encourage research that establishes the factor invariance of instruments across racial and ethnic groups because a difference between ethnic groups in number of factors, pattern of factor loadings, percentage of variance explained, or correlations among factors would constitute evidence of test bias.

MEASUREMENT, TESTING, AND ETHNIC BIAS: CAN SOLUTIONS BE FOUND?

Stanley Sue

University of California, Los Angeles

Assessment, evaluation, and diagnosis will gain increasing prominence as we head into the next century. Emphasis on managed care in the mental health system, well-being of individuals, job and work efficiency, personnel selection, upward promotions in one's career, admissions to institutions of higher education, etc., all require valid means of measurement and testing.

Several points are covered in this chapter. First, the assessment process involving ethnic minorities has many avenues by which bias can emerge. The biases can occur because of differences in culture or ethnicity as well as minority group status. Although culture has been defined in many different ways, it generally refers to the behavior patterns, symbols, institutions, values, and human products of a society (Banks, 1987). On the other hand, ethnicity can be used to describe a racial, national, or cultural group (Gordon, 1978). One's ethnicity typically conveys a social-psychological sense of "peoplehood" in which members of a group share a social and cultural heritage that is transmitted from one generation to another. Ethnic group members often feel an interdependence of fate with others in the group (Banks, 1987). In addition to culture and ethnicity,

The writing of this paper was supported in part by NIMH Grant number R01 MH44331.

members of ethnic minority groups also experience minority group status that involves a history of race or ethnic relations, a history that has affected interpersonal interactions, expectations, and performances. Thus to fully understand ethnic minority groups, their responses, and the assessment process, culture, ethnicity, and minority group status must be analyzed.

Second, concern with test and measurement bias is not simply a matter of being "politically correct" or of being perpetuated by ethnics who are disgruntled by their outcomes on various tests and measures. Bias does exist in many of our assessment instruments and procedures, and I shall try to demonstrate the range of biases using anecdotes and empirical evidence. Third, multiple steps should be taken to devise valid instruments and to understand the nature of cultural bias. Much of the research that will be cited involves Asian Americans; however, implications are drawn for ethnicity in general. Some anecdotal examples of sources of biases and consequences may more clearly indicate the importance of the issues to be presented.

Some Examples of Sources of Bias and Their Consequences

1.   In the development of the widely used *Diagnostic and Statistical Manual of Mental Disorders-III-R* (DSM-III-R) of the American Psychiatric Association (1987), Robert Spitzer contacted Arthur Kleinman, a prominent cross-cultural psychiatrist and anthropologist, for comments on cross-cultural issues. Kleinman (1991) wrote Spitzer a letter and was subsequently surprised to find that sections of his letter were compressed into two paragraphs of the introductory section of the DSM-III-R. He noted that considerations of the cultural limitations of the diagnostic system were too little, too late. Ethnicity and cross-cultural issues appeared more as an afterthought rather than a central variable. Fortunately, cross-cultural mental health researchers have been able to provide much more input into the recently published DSM-IV. Working groups were formed to offer recommendations concerning cross-cultural issues in diagnosis, and the DSM-IV has included discussions about cultural variations in symptoms of disorders as well as culture-bound syndromes. Although clearly an improvement over earlier versions, the DSM-IV still appears to lack a coherent approach to cross-cultural issues in psychopathology.

2.   A concrete example of the consequences of inattention to ethnicity in assessment is demonstrated in the following case of a Chinese American psychiatric patient, David Tom, as noted in the *Seattle Times* ("The forgotten," April 19, 1979):

The Cook County public guardian, Patrick T. Murphy, filed a $5 million suit yesterday against the Illinois director of mental health and his predecessors, charging that they kept a Chinese immigrant in custody for 27 years mainly because the man could not speak English.

The federal-court suit charged that the Illinois Department of Mental Health had never treated the patient...for any mental disorders and had found a Chinese-speaking psychologist to talk to him only after 25 years.

The suit said that David, who is in his 50s, was put in Oak Forest Hospital, then known as Oak Forest Tuberculosis Hospital, in 1952.

He was transferred to a state mental hospital where doctors conceded they could not give him a mental exam because he spoke little English. But they diagnosed him as psychotic anyway.

The suit said that in 1971 a doctor who spoke no Chinese said David answered questions in an "incoherent and unintelligible manner."

It was charged also that David was quiet and caused little trouble but was placed in restraints sometimes because he would wander to a nearby ward that housed the only other Chinese-speaking patient. (p. A5)

(Incidentally, the patient did win his suit against the state of Illinois.) Although the patient may well have been psychotic, confidence in arriving at such a diagnosis would have been greater had a bilingual and bicultural mental health professional been available.

3. Korchin (1980) argues that in interpreting research findings on members of ethnic minority groups, there is often an implicit assumption that such findings must be compared with those on White Americans—the standard for comparisons. Under this assumption, ethnic minority group phenomena are not considered very important. For example, Korchin submitted to a major journal a coauthored paper assessing the determinants of personality competence among two groups of African American men—namely, those demonstrating exceptional competence and those demonstrating average competence. One of the journal reviewers indicated that the study was "grievously flawed" because there was no White control group. Korchin noted that the purpose of the study was to analyze within-group differences and not to compare African Americans and Whites. He then raised some interesting questions: "What would happen, might we suppose, if someone submitted a study identical in all respects except that all subjects were White? Would it be criticized

because it lacked a Black control group?" (p. 263). I am not implying that ethnic comparisons—something that we often do in research—are inappropriate. Rather, my contention is that we must interpret the research in an appropriate context and that ethnic group research is important in and of itself.

4. Several years ago, the American Psychological Association's Committee on Psychological Tests and Assessment was reviewing guidelines on assessment. In attempting to see that assessment procedures would not be culturally biased against ethnic minorities, the Committee dealt with a proposal indicating that if clinicians were not competent to conduct a psychological evaluation of an ethnic minority client—presumably because of cultural unfamiliarity—or if the assessment instrument was not validated on these clients, they should avoid making an assessment. One can imagine a similar proposal that if clinicians' competence with ethnic clients is in question, then they should not provide clinical services. Obviously, it would be inappropriate to subject ethnic minority clients to inadequate assessments or services. On the other hand, if the proposal had been adopted, the question would arise as to who would conduct assessments with ethnics. In other words, mental health professionals have the responsibility not only to decline from providing services when they are not qualified, but also to see that services are available to all. By simply admonishing clinicians to stay within their own areas of expertise, issues concerning accessibility of services, training of multicultural competencies in all clinicians, and development of cross-culturally valid assessment instruments are ignored.

These examples illustrate our neglect of cultural influences, assumptions about the standards of comparison by which to evaluate findings, and inability to foresee consequences of actions in trying to address ethnic minority issues. It is not surprising that in the case of ethnic minority populations, assessment has had a very controversial history. The controversy is over possible biases that occur when assessing the status of ethnic minority group individuals. These possible biases have been discussed over a diverse set of assessment tasks such as the ability to make valid assessment during clinical interviews, attempts to render a diagnosis, evaluations of client outcomes, estimating prevalence rates of mental disorders, use of personality inventories, use of cognitive and performance tests, etc. It is easy to understand the controversial nature of assessment among ethnic minority groups. Cultural considerations of minorities have not traditionally played a central role in guiding our assessment and evaluation efforts.

DIFFICULTIES IN ASSESSMENT

In the assessment process, a number of problems can occur from a variety of sources in cross-cultural assessment. For example, Garcia (1981) argues that cross-cultural comparisons in IQ test performances fail to take into account possible cultural differences in motivation and task-relevant practice among test takers. Brislin (1993) takes issue with the equivalence of measures in cross-cultural assessment research: (a) translation equivalence, (b) conceptual equivalence, and (c) metric equivalence. Translation equivalence is a potential problem when questionnaires or instructions from one language group are used with another language group. It is based on the broader principle involving stimulus equivalence (e.g., whether a test item has the same meaning for different individuals). Translation equivalence exists when the descriptors and measures of psychological concepts can be translated well across languages. To test the translation equivalence of a measure that was developed in a particular culture, it is first translated by a bilingual expert to another language, then "back-translated" from the second language to the first by an independent bilingual translator. The two versions of the measure in the original language are then compared to discern which words or concepts seem to survive the translation procedures, with the assumption that the concepts that "survive" are translation equivalent. This procedure can be used to discover which psychological concepts appear to be culture-specific or culture-common.

Conceptual equivalence refers to the functional aspect of the construct that serves the same purpose in different cultures, although the specific behavior or thoughts used to measure the construct may be different. For example, one aspect of good decision making in the Western cultures may be typified by an ability to make a personal decision without being unduly influenced by others, whereas good decision making may be understood in Asian cultures as an ability to make a decision that is best for the group. These two different behaviors pertaining to making decisions are equivalent in that they comprise the very definition of the construct (good decision making) as used by individuals in the different cultures. Yet, the actual behaviors considered as good decision making are strikingly different.

Metric equivalence refers to the analysis of the same concept and the same measure across cultures, with the assumption that the scale of the measure can be directly compared across cultures. The assumption may be inaccurate. For example, a score of 100 on a certain scale or measure used with one population may not be equivalent to a score of 100 on the same measure when used with a different population or when translated into another language. The lack of metric equivalence is especially apparent when cutoff scores are derived from one culture and then applied to another. Let us suppose that in the United States, a score exceeding 50 on a measure of depression is associated with severe clinical depression. This does not necessarily mean that in another country scores exceeding 50 on the measure are indicative of severe clinical depression. Norms for clinical depression as well as response sets to the measure may differ from culture to culture. These affect metric equivalence.

Potential problems in translation, conceptual, and metric equivalence have been sufficiently great that some researchers even go so far as to refrain from making any inference from the results of quantitative comparisons of a given measure between subjects from two different cultures (e.g., Hui, 1988). However, it is highly unlikely that comparisons between different cultural groups will discontinue, which makes it all the more important to test for, or develop, equivalency.

The person who uses professional judgement in assessment or evaluation is also subject to bias. This person and his or her evaluation process may be considered as a measurement "instrument." The reliability and validity of the counselor or clinician's assessment can be tested. The clinician is essentially an observer or a stimulus to the client and collects verbal and nonverbal data from clients. The clinician then performs a series of tasks such as making clinical judgments, inferences, and interpretations—all of which are subject to human biases, stereotyping, and faulty processing of information.

EXISTENCE OF BIAS

Evidence has accumulated that suggests that assessments of individuals from culturally diverse populations are problematic (Jones & Thorne, 1987; Rogler, Malgady, & Rodriguez, 1989). Many investigators have suggested that cultural biases can affect therapists' interpretations of the psychological functioning of African Americans (Adebimpe, 1981; Mukherjee, Shukla, Woodle, Rosen, & Olarte, 1983; Neighbors, Jackson, Campbell, & Williams, 1989), American Indians (LaFromboise, 1988) Asian Americans (Li-Repac, 1980; Sue & Sue, 1987; Sue & Sue, 1991; Westermeyer, 1987), and Latinos (Good & Good, 1986; Lopez, 1989; Padilla & Salgado DeSnyder, 1985; Rogler et al., 1989). Because clinicians may not understand the cultural backgrounds or potential cultural response sets of ethnic minority clients, the validity of the clinical evaluations is open to questions.

In reviews of the literature, an overpathologizing bias (rating ethnic clients as being more disturbed than they actually are) was found by investigators who studied the validity of assessments of African American clients (Adebimpe, 1981; Neighbors et al., 1989). In one study, analysis of the records of 76 bipolar patients from different ethnic groups revealed that more than two-thirds of the clients had been previously diagnosed with schizophrenia (Mukherjee et al., 1983). The earlier diagnosis of schizophrenia was considered inaccurate because: (a) all patients demonstrated complete remission of psychotic symptoms without residual signs suggestive of schizophrenia; (b) the patients had been maintained on lithium, a drug commonly used to treat bipolar disorders, for an average of 3 years; and (c) not one patient's diagnosis was revised to schizophrenia. These data revealed that Latinos and African Americans were previously misdiagnosed with schizophrenia significantly more often than were White Americans.

It should be noted that overpathologizing is one direction of bias. Lopez (1989) has indicated that an underpathologizing bias (rating ethnic clients as being less disturbed than they actually are) can also occur. In his review of the literature, Lopez found that when instances of overpathologizing and underpathologizing are combined, substantial misdiagnosis of ethnics is found, and the evidence suggests that ethnic minority group individuals are more likely than are Whites to be assessed or diagnosed inaccurately.

Other studies have simply documented differences in evaluations as a function of ethnicity of therapists and clients. Li-Repac (1980) examined the influence of culture on the diagnostic approach of therapists. Five Chinese American and five White American male therapists rated the functioning of Chinese and White male clients during a videotaped interview. The results indicated that the ethnicity of both clients and therapists affected therapists' clinical judgments. Whereas White therapists rated Chinese American clients as anxious, awkward, confused, and nervous, Chinese therapists perceived the same clients as alert, ambitious, adaptable, honest, and friendly. White therapists rated White American clients as affectionate, adventurous, sincere, and easy-going, whereas Chinese therapists judged the same clients to be active, aggressive, rebellious, and outspoken. In addition, White therapists rated Chinese clients as more depressed, more inhibited, less socially poised, and having lower capacity for interpersonal relationships than did Chinese therapists. Chinese therapists rated White clients as more severely disturbed than did White therapists. These findings suggest that judgments about psychological functioning depend at least in part on whether or not therapists are of the same ethnic background as their clients.

We (D. Fujino, G. Russell, S. Sue, M. Cheung, & L. Snowden) have recently completed a study examining the relationship between ethnic matches or mismatches between therapists and clients and therapists' evaluations of the initial level of functioning of clients. The study involved thousands of clients entering the Los Angeles County Mental Health System. Initial level of functioning was assessed using the Global Assessment Scale (GAS; Spitzer, Gibbon, & Endicott, 1985) in which clinicians provide a subject rating of the level of functioning of clients. Results indicated that ethnically matched therapists judged clients to have higher psychological functioning than did mismatched therapists. This effect held for ethnic clients (African, Asian, and Mexican Americans), but not for Whites. When the effects of other variables, such as age, gender, marital status, socioeconomic class, referral source, therapist's discipline, diagnosis, and gender match, were controlled, the effects of therapist-client ethnic matching were maintained for clients of African and Asian descent. Ethnic match was found to be a strong predictor of admission GAS scores, second only to diagnosis, a variable expected to be highly related to psychological functioning. The results are, indeed, provocative. Why do therapists who are of the same ethnicity as their clients evaluate the clients as being higher in level of functioning than do therapists who are ethnically dissimilar to their clients? We are not in a position to indicate the veridicality of the evaluations or to explain the findings because we could not randomly assign clients to therapists. Perhaps the clients who see ethnically similar therapists are simply less disturbed. Another possibility, consistent with Li-Repac's (1980) experimental study, is that therapists tend to rate ethnically similar clients as being less disturbed. In any event, much more research should be addressed to these possibilities. The main point is that clinicians or raters themselves are subject to biases.

Finally, what is it about ethnicity that may affect clinical judgments? Many researchers argue that the cultural orientation of therapists guides the diagnostic approach employed. If therapists fail to understand the cultural values, behaviors, assumptions about normality, and symptom expression of those from different cultures, the probability of making diagnostic and assessment errors is increased (Brislin, 1993; Good & Good, 1986; Rogler et al., 1989; Takeuchi & Speechley, 1989). For example, Asian Americans have been found to report somatic symptoms more than do White Americans (Sue & Morishima, 1982). It may be that such symptoms are more acceptable in "face" oriented cultures, where having mental health disorders are quite stigmatizing and result in loss of face. Because people may learn to express distress in culturally acceptable ways, similar symptoms may hold different meanings in different cultures (Brislin, 1993). Thus, cultural modes of symptom expression can lead to misdiagnoses when clinicians do not understand the client's culture. Furthermore, it appears that the therapists' own sets of values and theoretical orientations influence their evaluations of client behavior (Rogler et al., 1989). For example, the Chinese and White clinicians in Li-Repac's study (1980) made different evaluations about the functioning of clients even though they viewed the same videotaped interviews.

Obviously, cultural factors may bias assessment and confound our interpretations. However, it is also possible that observed assessment differences between culturally different groups are real. For example, in a study by Keefe, Sue, Enomoto, Durvasula, and Chao (in press), the MMPI-2 performances were examined of Asian American and White students. Additionally, Asian Americans completed the Suinn-Lew Self-Identity Acculturation Scale (SL-ASIA; Suinn, Rickard-Figueroa, Lew, & Vigil, 1987). We divided the Asian Americans into those who were more acculturated and those who were less acculturated. The findings indicated that less acculturated Asian American students showed greater elevation on the Minnesota Multiphasic Personality Inventory-2 (MMPI-2; Hathaway, McKinley, & Butcher, 1989) profile than did more acculturated Asian American students or White students. Furthermore, more acculturated Asian American students had greater elevations than did their White counterparts. On individual MMPI-2 scales where differences were found, scale elevations were largely ordered in the following manner: Less acculturated Asian Americans > acculturated Asian Americans > Whites. (On the validity scales, the three groups did not significantly differ, except on the F Scale in which less acculturated Asians were higher than Whites.) The results can be interpreted in at least two ways. First, the results may suggest that Asian American students had more psychopathology than did Whites. Moreover, less acculturated Asian Americans were particularly high in disturbance. It could be argued that such findings reflect the fact that Asian Americans are under greater stress because of culture conflict, adjustment to a new environment, language problems, minority group status, and so forth. This may be especially true of the unacculturated.

Second, the ethnic differences may result from the metric nonequivalence of the scores or from response sets that vary from one cultural group to another. Response sets include acquiescence (e.g., tendency to agree with statements) and social desirability (i.e., answering in ways that are intended to create an appropriate or good impression on others). Thus, Asian Americans may not actually be more disturbed; rather, the assessment tool and the inferences drawn may not be equally valid for different groups. If this is the case, then the personality inventory must somehow be corrected or modified in order to provide an accurate assessment of Asian Americans. Without examining culture and cultural bias, finding an explanation for the results is problematic.

It should be noted that studies of bias are difficult to conduct in the mental health field because we often have no absolute criteria by which to unequivocally judge the accuracy of evaluations. In Li-Repac's experimental study (1980), evaluations of clients varied as a function of ethnicity of therapists and clients. However, this question remains unanswered: Which ethnic group therapists were more accurate in their judgements?

There are other means of assessing bias in tests, and two of the most popular include factor analysis and regression analysis. If the factor structures are different for different populations, the instrument is not tapping into the same phenomena for the populations. Regression analysis can be applied to see if the tests make similar, and similarly accurate, predictions between the tests and a criterion measure. If, for example, regression slopes for a test or evaluation procedure and a criterion differ for different groups, test bias exists. Such studies require that we have fairly clear-cut criteria on which to judge the adequacy of predictors. Although some researchers (Kaplan & Saccuzzo, 1982) believe that slope bias for ethnic minority groups has rarely been demonstrated in empirical studies, we found convincing evidence for slope bias in the case of Asian Americans. Let me now turn to some of our research on educational achievements among Asian Americans (Sue & Abe, 1988) in order to demonstrate some major biases in assessment.

PREDICTORS OF ACADEMIC ACHIEVEMENTS

In response to concerns over university admissions policies and criteria for admitting students, the University of California system collaborated with the College Board to investigate the validity of various predictors of academic achievement for Asian American students. Examined were Asian American students who enrolled as freshman in any of the eight University of California campuses during fall 1984. The campuses included Berkeley, Davis, Irvine, Los Angeles, Riverside, San Diego, Santa Barbara, and Santa Cruz. The purpose of the study was to determine how well certain variables such as high school grades and SAT scores predicted academic performance during the freshman year. The study was unique in that no other validity investigation had examined differences among various Asian American subgroups on these factors, nor had any other study reported on as many Asian American students.

In terms of the design, we examined the records of the 4,113 Asian domestic (nonforeign) freshman students who enrolled in any of the eight campuses and compared them with those of 1,000 randomly selected White students. Males constituted about 50% of the Asian Americans, whereas 49% of the White sample were males. The Asian American student numbers were, in descending order: Chinese 1,470, Filipinos 712, Japanese 643, Koreans 575, Other Asian Americans or those not members of the specific groups listed in this study 525, and Asian Indians/Pakistanis 170.

The criterion variable was the university freshman grade point average (GPA), which was the average of all grades received by a student during the academic year. Different predictor variables were used for the GPA. I shall only report on high school grade point average (HSGPA) calculated from courses and Scholastic Aptitude Test-Verbal and Scholastic Aptitude Test-Mathematics scores. HSGPA, SAT-V score, and SAT-M score were used as predictors of university grades. This set of variables has been widely employed in making admissions decisions and was of primary interest in this study. Regression analyses were performed for each Asian American group, all Asian American students combined, and Whites. Analyses were also made for all Asian Americans and Whites, according to sex and academic majors.

General Results

Let me briefly present the results. First, Asian American students were found to have superior high school grades compared to Whites. Considerable within group differences were found with Asian Indians/Pakistanis having the highest and Filipinos having the lowest mean HSGPA. With the exception of the Filipinos, all the Asian American subgroups exceeded the average HSGPA of Whites. Regardless of ethnicity, females had higher HSGPAs than did males. Second, consistent with previous studies, Asian Americans achieved higher average SAT-M scores than did Whites; they received lower average scores than did Whites on the SAT-V sections. For both Asian Americans and Whites, males had higher SAT-V and SAT-M scores than did females. Thus, although females exceeded males in high school grades, their average SAT scores, particularly on the mathematical portion, were lower than those of males. Large differences in SAT performances were found among the Asian American subgroups, with Asian Indians/Pakistanis having the highest SAT-V score, and Koreans having the lowest. On the SAT-M test, the Chinese scored the highest and Filipinos scored the lowest. Third, the university grade point averages for Asian American and White students were very similar. Whereas Asian American males and females were highly similar in GPA, White females tended to achieve higher grades than White males did. Within the Asian American student group, considerable ethnic differences in university GPA were found. In descending order, the mean GPAs for the groups were Chinese, Asian Indians/Pakistanis, Other Asians, Japanese, Koreans, and Filipinos.

High School Grades and SAT Scores as Predictors of University Grades

The most interesting results concern the ability of high school grades and SAT scores to predict university grades. Multiple correlations were used to note the contributions of the predictors to university grades. Let me summarize the findings. Whereas HSGPA made the largest contribution in the prediction of university grades for both Asian Americans and Whites, considerable differences were found in the contributions made by SAT performances. For Asian Americans the SAT-M score contributed more to the prediction of university grades than did SAT-V. For Whites the situation was reversed; SAT-V made a larger contribution to university grades than did SAT-M. Dividing the students by ethnicity and sex did not alter the findings. Some marked differences emerged when the various Asian American groups were compared. We also tried to analyze the ability of the SAT to predict grades within academic majors in order to find out if the superiority of math over verbal skills was specific to those students in quantitative fields. The overall results generally persisted in that regardless of majors, SAT-M tended to be a better predictor of grades for Asians than for Whites.

Another way of comparing ethnic differences in predictors of academic achievement is to examine the possible prediction bias that occurs when the regression equation derived from one group is applied to the other. In other words, is the regression equation generated by Whites accurate in predicting the performances of Asian American students? We wanted to use Whites because this population, rather than ethnic minority groups, is likely to be the standard of comparison. To derive the White regression equation, a standard least squares regression was performed. By entering into this equation the scores received by Asian American students on the predictor variables, we could compare the grades predicted by the White regression equation with those that were actually received by Asian American students. Asian Americans received actual grades that were .02 higher than the predicted grades. Thus, using the White regression equation for Asian Americans placed Asian Americans at a slight disadvantage. Some substantial differences occurred, however, when the prediction bias was examined for specific groups. The White regression equation severely underpredicted the performances of Chinese and Other Asian American students. For example, Chinese students were predicted to have a grade point average of 2.77, when they actually had an average of 2.89. Although GPA differences of .10 or .20 may seem slight, they are very important not only to the student but also to graduate programs which must often make difficult decisions about the students to admit. Serious overprediction occurred for Filipinos and Japanese. This means that the White regression equation was biased in either direction, depending on the particular Asian American group. Obviously, if the regression equation derived from the Chinese sample is used for other Asian groups (or for Whites), we would also find prediction bias. It is not surprising that the application of one sample's prediction equation to another sample results in decreased accuracy for the other sample.

The purpose of the study was to examine the validity of predictors of first-year university grades for Asian American and White students. The findings can be summarized as follows: (a) High school grades and SAT can, to a moderate degree, predict university freshman grades of Asian American and White students. (b) Consistent with findings from other studies, the best single predictor for all students was the high school grade point average. (c) For Asian American but not for White students, mathematics scores or quantitative skills are a better predictor of university grades than are verbal scores. This ethnic difference persisted even across academic majors declared by students. (d) No major sex differences emerged to contradict the *overall* ethnic differences that were found. (e) The various Asian American groups showed interethnic differences in the proportional contributions of high school grades and SAT scores in the prediction of university grades. (f) The White regression equation underpredicted or overpredicted the performances of Asian Americans, depending on the particular group.

The strength of this study was the inclusion of a large Asian American student sample broken down by particular ethnicity. However, there are some important limitations to consider. For example, it was not possible to examine other important variables such as the socioeconomic class of the students, which may substantially influence the validity of predictors. Also, the sole criterion of overall achievement was first-year university grades. Other criteria should be used, such as grades in certain courses, grades for more than just the freshman year, or nonacademic indices of achievement. These limitations suggest that further research is needed in order for us to understand the theoretical and policy-related issues involved in the academic achievement of Asian American students.

This study demonstrates that in something as important as prediction of university grades, substantial ethnic differences exist in predictor-criterion relationships. The use of a regression found for one ethnic group may present a seriously biased picture for members of another ethnic group. The problem is that in practice a single prediction equation may be used, based on the dominant or majority group, which then reduces the validity of the prediction for members of minority groups. Assuming that one major goal of admissions criteria is to enroll the best students, it is interesting to note that I know of no university that has tried to use group specific regression equations in the selection of Asian American students. I am not arguing that English verbal skills are unimportant. Rather, if we want to select the best students—at least in terms of freshman grades—then mathematics scores should be weighed more heavily than verbal skills among many Asian American groups.

ADDRESSING ASSESSMENT BIAS

Given that tests and measurements of ethnic minority group populations are problematic and subject to bias, the question arises regarding what can be done. Several tasks should be considered. Let me briefly outline six major tasks, discussing in more detail the last three in which my colleagues and I have been involved.

Devise New Tests and Measures

New psychological tests and measures that are appropriate for ethnic minority populations need to be developed. I can think of three areas where new tests and measures would be very helpful. First, alternative measures for assessing attitudes, personality, and behaviors are a potentially fruitful area of investigation. Two decades ago, Robert Williams (1974) attempted to establish the Black Intelligence Test of Cultural Homogeneity, a intelligence test that is heavily loaded on items that are more specific and familiar to African Americans than to Whites. Although the validity of the test for predicting intellectual functioning has been controversial, Williams' work highlighted the importance of culture in influencing performance in at least some of the items typically used in IQ tests. Mercer (Mercer & Lewis, 1979) has also established the System of Multicultural Pluralistic Assessment, which is another attempt to take into consideration cultural elements in intellectual performance. Such efforts should continue because they bring into the forefront issues concerning the nature of what we examine (e.g., what is IQ?) and the impact of culture in the tests. New tests should be devised as alternatives to what is available.

Second, assessment of concepts that are pertinent to cross-cultural concerns are also important to assess. For example, researchers have been trying to develop means of measuring acculturation (Cuellar, Harris, & Jasso, 1980; Sodowsky & Plake, 1991; Suinn et al., 1987), ethnic or racial identity (Helms, 1990; Helms & Carter, 1991; Mendoza, 1989; Phinney, 1992), or multicultural competence and the elements comprising competence in counseling (see Ottavi, Pope-Davis, & Dings, 1994; Ponterotto & Casas, 1991; Sodowsky, Taffe, Gutkin, & Wise, 1994). The research is significant because the findings provide important knowledge of the similarities and differences within and between ethnic groups, social development associated with cultural practices, self-esteem and well-being, and cross-cultural competencies. In these areas, cross-cultural and ethnic minority researchers can provide special expertise.

Third, we should develop new measures that evaluate important values or traits that have salience especially for ethnics. As an illustration, let us examine personality assessment. In the United States, researchers have unearthed five orthogonal personality factors, called the "Big Five" (Goldberg, 1981), that include characteristics such as agreeableness, conscientiousness, and emotional stability. It is likely that these five factors have importance to a greater or lesser degree across different cultures (Yang & Bond, 1990). Nevertheless, the question remains of whether for certain ethnics other characteristics may be more salient or important than the Big Five as personality dimensions. One of my colleagues, Nolan Zane, is trying to address this issue with Asian Americans. He believes that one significant personality attribute that affects interpersonal interactions is "face." Loss of face (defined as the threat or loss of one's social integrity) has been identified as a key and often dominant interpersonal dynamic in Asian social relations, particularly when the relationship involves help-seeking issues among Asian and White students. Many individuals fear the loss of face or their social integrity, particularly Asian Americans who come from face cultures. Zane (1991) has developed a loss of face measure (LOF). The 21-item measure reflects four face-threatening areas involving social status, ethical behavior, social propriety, and self-discipline. Preliminary finding indicate that the measure has good reliability and validity. It correlated positively with other-directedness, self-consciousness, and social anxiety and negatively with extraversion and acculturation level of Asian Americans. Asian Americans also score higher on the measure than do Whites. LOF appears to be able to predict, independently of social desirability, certain behaviors such as assertiveness and help-seeking behaviors. Zane suggests that certain personal constructs may be more culturally salient for some groups than others.

Evaluate Tests and Revise to Make Them Cross-Culturally Valid

Most research on assessment with ethnic minority groups has examined the use of existing instruments. Many studies have tried to determine the validity of instruments, derived in the West, when used with members of ethnic minority groups or cross national populations. Intelligence tests (e.g., the Wechsler Adult Intelligence Scale [WAIS]), personality inventories (e.g., MMPI-2), and survey instruments (e.g., Diagnostic Interview Schedule) have been employed in the study of ethnic minorities or cross-national groups. Rogler, Malgady, and Rodriguez (1989) indicate that common problems include not only translation equivalence and item familiarity but also assumptions concerning the meaning of responses to items. With respect to meaning of responses, they note that in Puerto Rican culture spiritualism is practiced and that answering affirmatively to MMPI items, such as "Evil spirits possess me at times," may not be indicative of pathology. Under such circumstances, the instruments can be modified in order to enhance their validity or local norms can be established with different populations. Such efforts are important in that they provide a standard by which to compare different groups and yield insights into what aspects or items of a measure are cross-culturally appropriate or inappropriate and what modifications may be necessary in order to strengthen validity and to more accurately interpret test results.

Advocate for Cross-Cultural Considerations and Policies

We have certain roles to perform as assessment researchers and practitioners. Involvement in our professions should also include participation in the formulation of policies and practices, if we are to have an impact on assessment. We should caution others about the difficulties in conducting assessments of members of ethnic minority groups and advocate for the integration of cross-cultural considerations in research, theory, and assessment practice. After all, psychology and the social sciences involve the study of human beings and not of a particular group. In order to affect assessment policies and practices, cross-cultural assessment experts should be included in all boards, committees, policy-making groups in organizations such as the American Psychological Association, American Psychiatric Association, American Educational Research Association, and American Evaluation Association, as well as in state and local governmental agencies that deal with assessment. They should also have strong input into all policies concerning the use of assessment tools and the appropriateness of assessment procedures.

Adopt New Assessment Research Paradigms

A variety of research strategies have been used in cross-cultural psychology. The strategies can be classified as (a) point research, (b) linear research, and (c) parallel research (Sue & Sue, 1987; Zane & Sue, 1986). Each progressively helps to uncover the meaning of assessment in cross-cultural comparisons.

Point research. Point research simply compares the performance of one cultural group with another. It is the most frequently used cross-cultural approach. In most cases, an assessment instrument developed in one culture is used in another culture. Often, the scores on the instruments are compared between the different cultures and interpreted from the norms developed from one culture. Because of the relatively long history of psychology in Western societies, many of the instruments are of American or Western European origin, frequently requiring language translations for use with non-English-speaking groups. For example, we (Chu, Lubin, & Sue, 1984) have translated the Depression Adjective Checklist and studied the reliability and validity of the instrument for Chinese in Taiwan. The use of measures developed in one culture and applied in another culture runs the risk of perpetuating an imposed emic in assessment. That is, taking an emic (culturally specific) assessment scale and using it as if it were etic (universally applicable) in nature can be a serious problem. Researchers are increasingly aware of potential problems caused by an imposed emic, but for many cross-cultural investigators, more safeguards should be used.

As mentioned earlier, several assumptions underlie the development of a cross-cultural measure. It is assumed that the concept as measured by the instrument exists in both cultures, that the concept is equivalently operationalized, and that there is scalar or metric equivalence of the instrument. Violation of these assumptions frequently occurs in cross-cultural research (Hui & Triandis, 1985). Other cultures may not have the concept under investigation or may define it differently (Dohrenwend & Dohrenwend, 1969). In using the Beck Depression Inventory among Vietnamese populations, Kinzie, Manson, Vinh, Tolan, Anh, and Pho (1982) found that the Beck Depression Inventory was not reliable or valid in the diagnosis of depression. This may be the result of cultural differences in conceptualization of depression or in symptom manifestations of the same disorder. Investigators (Kleinman, 1977; Sue, Wagner, Ja, Margullis, & Lew, 1976; White, 1984) have found that some constructs derived from the Western perspective are conceptualized differently or do not exist in other cultures. The difficulty involved in translating words used on assessment devices may be an indication that the concepts may not be equivalent. In view of these potential problems, the mere fact that different cultural groups exhibit differences on a particular assessment measure suggests that the groups *may* differ. Point research should be supplemented by linear research in order to more firmly establish that the differences found in point research are real.

Linear and multimethod models. In trying to validate measures, researchers often see if the measure relates well to other measures or indices of the construct under investigation or if the measure is a good predictor of the phenomenon being studied. For example, if an intelligence or cognitive measure, which was originally developed and validated in the United States, is a valid indicator of intellectual functioning in Japan, we would expect the measure to: (a) correlate well with other measures of intelligence among Japanese, and (b) predict the future performance of Japanese, for instance, in academic performance. If the measure shows little concurrent or predictive validity among Japanese, then it may be poorly suited for cross-cultural use.

Linear research is intended to examine the validity of an instrument. Whereas point research establishes that two cultural groups differ on a measure, linear research tries to establish whether the differences are real or an emic artifact of the measure. A series of studies using different measures of a construct can be used with two or more culturally distinct groups, or different measures can be used in a single study. For example, Sue, Ino, and Sue (1983) wanted to study assertiveness among Asian American and Whites and used a multimethod strategy. In this study, individuals were administered paper-and-pencil tests, typically used in studies of White Americans, as well as behavioral measures of assertiveness. The self-report, paper-and-pencil measure supported the notion that Asian Americans are less assertive than their White counterparts. However, no overall differences on behavioral measures were found. The finding that Asian Americans could behave as assertively as their comparison group raises questions about the validity of the paper-and-pencil measure.

Another example of the linear approach can be seen in the series of studies reported by Dohrenwend and Dohrenwend (1969). The investigators wanted to study the prevalence of psychopathology among different ethnic groups in the United States. The strategy employed was based on point research in which different cultural groups are compared on a measure. After administering the Midtown 22-item symptom questionnaire, they did find ethnic differences: Puerto Ricans scored higher in psychological disturbance than did Jewish, Irish, or Black respondents in New York City. But how did they know if the Puerto Ricans were actually more disturbed or if the findings were simply an artifact of the measure? That is, the findings may simply indicate that the instrument failed to have cross-cultural validity. Fortunately, the Dohrenwends then adopted a linear research strategy to test whether the higher score among Puerto Ricans indicated higher actual rates of disorders. In a subsequent study, they matched patients from each ethnic group in terms of psychiatric disorders and administered the same questionnaires as before (i.e., the Midtown 22-item symptom questionnaire). Because patients were matched on type and presumably severity of disorders, one would expect no differences in symptom scores. However, Puerto Ricans again scored higher than the other groups. Dohrenwend and Dohrenwend argued that the higher scores for Puerto Ricans probably reflected a response set or a cultural means of expressing distress on the questionnaire rather than actual rates of disturbance. Their conclusions were based on a series of studies trying to ferret out cultural factors from actual psychopathology in the analysis of the measure.

Parallel Research. Unlike the point approach in which differences between ethnic groups are examined on a particular measure, and the linear approach in which researchers try to establish if observed group differences are real, the parallel research strategy is intended to explain any real differences that are found. Explanations for behaviors often differ from one culture to another. In parallel research, the task is to develop means of conceptualizing the behavioral phenomena from the different cultures in question. A parallel design is essentially two linear approaches, each based upon its own cultural viewpoint. Previously, I discussed the issue of decision making. If we constructed a Western measure of decision making, individuals from nonWestern cultures might reliably differ on the measure and appear to have deficits. Only by adopting each cultural explanation can we truly understand that in some Western cultures good decision making involves making independent judgments whereas in some Eastern cultures good decision making is associated with doing what is best for the group. The advantage of this design is that the framework or perspective from one cultural group is not imposed on another. In this way, similarities and differences of the construct or concept under investigation can be determined. This can be illustrated in research on depression among Asian Americans.

Clinical folklore among researchers and practitioners suggests that Asian Americans may express depressive symptoms differently from White Americans. Asians often seem to manifest somatic symptoms rather than strict depressive symptomatology, such as self-reports of sadness or dejection (Sue & Morishima, 1982). Thus, it is unclear if measures of depression, used in the United States, can be appropriately applied to Asian Americans. Kleinman (1977) believes that depression is conceptualized differently by certain Asian groups and that attempts to study depression in other cultures by using Western-derived criteria such as those listed in the *Diagnostic and Statistical Manual* of the American Psychiatric Association may be misleading. Given the uncertain validity of depression measures and possible cultural differences in the expression and conceptualization of depression, Kinzie et al. (1982) adopted a research approach much like the parallel research strategy described above, in developing a depression scale for Vietnamese. In the United States, relatively much research has been conducted on the assessment and measurement of depression, and the symptoms and syndromes associated with depression among White Americans have been identified. However, this is not the case with Asian American groups such as Vietnamese Americans. Therefore, a parallel strategy would entail the development and validation of a depression measure based on indigenous (i.e., Vietnamese) conceptualizations of the disorder and the analysis of the reasons why White and Vietnamese Americans may differ in the disorder or its manifestations.

To begin the task, four bilingual mental health workers, who worked independently, generated a list of Vietnamese words that were related to depression in the areas of thinking, feeling, and behavior (items associated with DSM III criteria for depression were given consideration). The adjectives were then compared and revised in terms of lexicon and grammar. Interestingly, the investigators used a 3-point rather than 5-point Likert scale because they found that Vietnamese felt that five rating levels would not be sensible to their cultural group. The items were then translated into English and back-translated into Vietnamese to check semantic integrity. They were then administered to a small group of Vietnamese as a pretest to test for sensibility and appropriateness. Any items that needed explanation and that proved to be inappropriate were revised. To validate the scale, scores on the scale from a depressed Vietnamese clinic sample were compared with those from a demographically matched community sample of Vietnamese adults. The comparisons showed that the depressed clinic sample and the control sample differed significantly on the majority of items (27 of 45). Surprisingly, only 4 out of the 27 items that were statistically significant between the depressed and control groups were similar to those in the DSM III (these were psychophysiological symptoms). The other 23 were from Vietnamese descriptions of cognitive, affective, and somatic indicators of depression.

The symptoms of depression that were common in Vietnamese and Western cultures were primarily somatic, or psychophysiological, in nature: Poor appetite, headache, poor concentration, and exhaustion. However, those items indicative of moods, such as "sad and bothered," "low spirited and bored," and "downhearted and low spirited," were more difficult to interpret. These phrases were not overlapping (i.e., not much commonality was found in Vietnamese and Western cultures). About two-thirds of the items were unrelated to items often associated with the Western conception of depression, including,"being angry," "feeling shameful and dishonored (not guilt)," "feeling desperate," and "having a feeling of going crazy." The results demonstrated that conceptualizations of disorders do differ among different cultural groups. Kinzie and his colleagues reported difficulty in translating many of the Vietnamese concepts and stated that "the lack of one-to-one correspondence also suggests that the meanings of particular Vietnamese thoughts, feelings, and behaviors may be different from our own, are implicated, and cannot be adequately conceptualized apart from a broader semantic network" (p. 1280). In summary, the results of the work by Kinzie and his associates indicate that there is some overlap in the symptoms reported by both Western and Vietnamese cultures. However, the nature of differences may indicate that the symptoms do not reflect the same construct. Responses to assessment measures may then vary according to culture and can be explained by different cultural construals of depression.

Study the Nature of Bias

One research area that has been largely ignored in cross-cultural assessment is that of bias. Although many scholars have discussed the nature of bias and have offered conceptual analyses of it, we lack empirical research into the origins of bias. Let me explain our research in this area. Our research program is intended to study the response sets or cultural dimensions that may operate when Asian Americans are administered measures of psychopathology developed in Western societies. The ultimate goal of the research is to understand cultural processes that influence responses to assessment instruments and, with this understanding, to increase the validity of the instruments for Asian American populations. The research was undertaken for several reasons. First, current assessment tools that are widely used in the United States have been criticized for not taking into account cultural factors that may bias evaluations for ethnic populations in general and Asian Americans in particular. Second, although research and clinical assessment instruments are continually being revised and modified in order to achieve greater reliability and validity, the adequacy of the instruments is rarely examined for Asian American populations because they are relatively small in numbers. When validation studies for Asian Americans are conducted, they tend to occur many years after an assessment tool is developed. By that time, new instruments have been devised and Asian American researchers are then studying the validity of an "old" instrument. Third, validation studies simply tell us whether or not an instrument is appropriate for a given population. If the instrument is inappropriate, the reasons and underlying processes for the lack of validity are a matter of speculation. Finally, although the obvious solution would be to design a valid assessment tool specifically for Asian Americans, there are many practical problems in devising a culture-specific measure, and such a measure would not allow comparisons to be made with non-Asian populations. A culture-specific measure may be appropriate and helpful in some situations, as mentioned earlier. However, our research plan is to gain insight into the processes underlying Asian American responses to assessment instruments—processes and principles that may have generality across different assessment tools.

The proposed pilot research is important in discovering sources of bias and means of correcting the bias. The findings can be used to evaluate all inventories, because underlying dimensions or processes are identified. In turn, the validity of measures for clinical and epidemiological use with Asian American populations will improve, because the identified biases can be controlled. This means that researchers can *continue* to use existing, mainstream, and traditional measures with Asian Americans. Rather than to abolish such measures or construct some measures that are specific to Asian Americans, one simply needs to control for identified biases in existing instruments. For example, the development of a social desirability measure has enabled researchers to control for socially desirable responses on existing personality and psychopathology measures.

At a more basic or theoretical level, the research can lead to a greater understanding of the factors that influence responses on measures of psychopathology, especially cultural-based ones. In the past, researchers have suggested that factors such as cultural differences in shame and stigma, response sets such as social desirability, concepts of mental illness, etc., have hindered an accurate assessment of various ethnic minority groups including Asian Americans. Our task has been to see if ethnic differences in responding can be predicted by cultural response sets (or cultural dimensions). We want to see if certain cultural dimensions (such as shame and stigma, tolerance for symptoms, and cultural familiarity with symptoms), which some investigators have proposed as being important for Asian Americans, can predict performances on certain measures. Our study has several steps:

1. *Identify cultural dimensions that differentiate responses of Asian Americans and Whites on self-reported measures of psychopathology.* Researchers have often speculated that Asian Americans and Whites differ in cultural variables (e.g., shame and stigma and self-disclosure) or response sets (e.g., social desirability) that may influence responses to personality or psychiatric inventories. The project empirically examines how Asians and Whites differ on their evaluations of individual questionnaire items in terms of stigma, cultural familiarity, etc. Using this method, those items or sets of items on questionnaires that are likely to demonstrate ethnic differences on the basis of cultural response sets can be identified. We can also determine which instruments are heavily loaded on cultural response sets and likely to give biased findings.

2. *Use the identified dimensions to construct scales in a major study that can be used to control for bias in order to increase cross-cultural validity.* Once dimensions have been identified as being important, scales can be developed to represent the dimensions. The scales can then be used to control for cultural bias. For example, if Asian Americans tend to underreport symptoms that arouse feelings of shame, and a particular questionnaire is

heavily loaded on items involving shame, a shame scale can be constructed and used to control for the underreporting.

The proposed research program investigates the effects of cultural factors on responses to assessment instruments. It seeks to identify cultural orientations that affect assessment instruments. Once cultural factors are identified, it will be possible to evaluate any measure as to the extent of bias on these factors and to attempt to control bias and increase validity of instruments. Therefore, existing instruments can still be used while controlling for the identified cultural factors.

The research is guided by several assumptions. First, Asian Americans may evaluate items on measures of psychopathology differently from Whites. These evaluations may be based on cultural factors such as social desirability, shame and stigma, familiarity with specific test items, defensiveness, conceptions of mental health, etc. Indeed, intra-Asian group differences may also exist. The task is to identify dimensions in which group differences are exhibited. Second, the validity of measures is threatened when evaluations significantly differ from one group to another. Cultural factors may suppress or enhance one's responses to assessment instruments. The task is to identify which cultural evaluations tend to influence responses to questionnaires. Third, once confounding cultural factors have been identified, it is possible to improve the validity of assessment instruments. The task is to make improvements in validity by "correcting" for bias or by constructing tests in which ethnic differences no longer exist on the identified dimensions. For example, let us assume that Asians are less likely than Whites to endorse a personality inventory item such as, "I have unusual sex practices." Let us also assume that Asians tend to give higher ratings of shame and stigma to the item. The ethnic differences in the endorsement of the item can be attributed to actual ethnic differences on the item *or* to differences on shame and stigma. Greater validity can be achieved by controlling for shame and stigma (by statistical means or by procedures similar to those used on the K-correction scale of the MMPI) or by constructing a test with items equally loaded for shame and stigma among different ethnic groups (similar to procedures on the Edwards Personal Preference Schedule [Edwards, 1959] in which respondents chose between items that are equated for social desirability).

The first study compared Asians and Whites in their performance on a measure of psychopathology, MMPI-2, in order to identify clinical scales in which group differences occur. As mentioned earlier, Asians reported more symptoms than Whites. In addition, less acculturated Asians reported more symptoms than more acculturated

Asians or Whites. The second study examines the influence of three hypothesized cultural dimensions on responses to the MMPI-2. Shame, symptom tolerance (i.e., whether the symptom is bothersome), and cultural familiarity (i.e., whether the symptom is common or frequent in the particular cultural group) were identified as important cultural dimensions for Asian Americans based on the past literature (e.g., Kim, 1978; Kitano, 1976; Sue & Morishima, 1982). The second study focused on whether ehnic differences in performance on the MMPI-2 can be explained by the cultural evaluations of the MMPI-2 items. Subjects are asked to rate the degree of shame, symptom tolerance, and cultural familiarity associated with each item of the MMPI-2. The data collection has been completed. In order to increase the generalizability of the findings, the data have been gathered from other universities across the U.S. as well as from UCLA. Once the important cultural dimensions are identified from the pilot studies, major studies will be proposed to develop scales that can control for the cultural biases.

Assessment

The final point is addressed to practitioners. As noted earlier, skepticism has been voiced over assessment because of possible biases in the nosological systems; in the use of cognitive, personality, and psychopathology measures; and in making clinical inferences. Despite the skepticism, psychologists are frequently required to make evaluations in schools, mental health agencies, and courtrooms. What procedures can be used in such circumstances? Although issues of reliability and validity are involved, perhaps it is wise to distinguish two aspects, as noted in a previous paper of mine (Sue, 1988). The first deals with assessment procedures in general. The second includes special procedures that may be necessary with ethnic minority groups.

In any assessment task, the first step is to specify what one is interested in measuring (the referral question). The second step is to select the most appropriate inventory or test. Although factors such as the ease of administration, cost, degree of expertise required, etc., are often considered, reliability and validity of the measure for the characteristic of interest are the most important factors. Test manuals should include information on reliability and validity, as well as norms and samples upon which the norms are based. Of course, many assessment tools have not been adequately developed for different ethnic minority populations. With ethnic minority populations, there are some guidelines that are important to consider. These guidelines are not new. Nevertheless, they are important to reiterate.

1. Find tests that can be linguistically understood by clients. Also important is to determine the stimulus (linguistic) and conceptual equivalence of measures that are translated for the clients.

2. See if the test or assessment instrument has been standardized and normed on the particular ethnic minority group of the client. Increasingly, test developers are aware of the need to sample and validate tests and measures with different ethnic populations. For larger ethnic group populations, especially African Americans and Latino Americans, some measures have been standardized and normed. In the case of smaller populations, such as American Indians and Asian Americans, this is less likely to be the case.

3. If the test has not been standardized and normed on the group, exercise caution in interpreting the results. Tests and measures can still be useful, even if they have not been validated with a population. They provide samples of behaviors under standardized conditions. The primary issue is how to interpret findings. If the validity of a measure is uncertain, psychologists should exercise great care in interpreting the findings.

4. Test findings should be used to generate hypotheses for further testing. Although this is sound practice in general, this procedure is especially important in assessing members of ethnic minority groups because many assessment instruments may not have been validated with these groups.

5. Use multiple measures or multimethod procedures to see if tests provide convergent results. Before drawing conclusions, it is important to confirm findings from one instrument. This confirmation process should involve the administration of several different measures or different methods (e.g., behavioral ratings as well as self-reports) in order to see if the results are consistent.

6. Try to understand the cultural background of the client, in order to place test results in a proper context. Ethnic minority groups exhibit significant heterogeneity and individual differences. Individual differences exist in country of origin, language spoken and English proficiency, level of acculturation, ethnic identity, family structure, cultural values, history, etc. These differences have important implications for the ideal selection and interpretation of test results.

7. Enlist the aid of consultants who are familiar with the client's background and culture. It is difficult to know the cultures of

all the different ethnic groups in our society. Because cultural background has a major effect on assessment outcomes, the assistance of ethnic consultants is important. The consultants can help to place test findings in a proper cultural context.

Because of the growing multiethnic nature of our society and the increasing importance of assessment in all phases of life, there is an urgent need to direct our attention to the issues facing ethnic minority populations. A relatively small amount of research effort has been devoted to the valid assessment of these populations. The time is ripe for us to expend substantial efforts to address cross-cultural assessment issues.

REFERENCES

Adebimpe, V. (1981). Overview: White norms and psychiatric diagnosis of black patients. *American Journal of Psychiatry, 138*, 279-285.

American Psychiatric Association. (1987). *Diagnostic and statistical manual of mental disorders* (3rd ed., rev.). Washington, DC: Author.

Banks, J. A . (1987). *Teaching strategies for ethnic studies*. Boston: Allyn and Bacon.

Brislin, R. W. (1993). *Understanding culture's influence on behavior*. New York: Harcourt Brace Jovanovich.

Chu, C., Lubin, B., & Sue, S. (1984). Reliability and validity of the Chinese Depression Adjective Checklist. *Journal of Clinical Psychology, 40*, 1409-1413.

Cuellar, I., Harris, L., & Jasso, R. (1980). An acculturation scale for Mexican American normal and clinical populations. *Hispanic Journal of Behavioral Sciences, 2*, 199-217.

Dohrenwend, B. P., & Dohrenwend, B. S. (1969). *Social status and psychological disorder*. New York: Wiley.

Edwards, A. L. (1959). Edwards Personal Preference Schedule. San Antonio, TX: The Psychological Corporation.

The forgotten: Chinese, lacking English, confined for 27 years. (1979, April 19). *Seattle Times*, p. A5.

Garcia, J. (1981). The logic and limits of mental aptitude testing. *American Psychologist, 36,* 1172-1180.

Goldberg, L. R. (1981). Language and individual differences: The search for universals in personality lexicons. In L. Wheeler (Ed.), *Reviews of personality and social psychology* (vol. 2, pp. 141-165). Beverly Hills, CA: Sage.

Good, B. J., & Good, M. D. (1986). The cultural context of diagnosis and therapy: A view from medical anthropology. In M. R. Miranda & H. H. L. Kitano (Eds.), *Mental health research & practice in minority communities: Development of culturally sensitive programs* (pp. 1-27). Rockville, MD: National Institute of Mental Health.

Gordon, M. M. (1978) *Human nature, class, and ethnicity.* New York: Oxford University Press.

Hathaway, S. R., McKinley, J. C., & Butcher, J. N. (1989). Minnesota Multiphasic Personality Inventory-2. Minneapolis: University of Minnesota Press.

Helms, J. E. (1990). *Black and white racial identity.* Westport, CT: Greenwood Press.

Helms, J. E., & Carter, R. T. (1991). Relationships of White and Black racial identity attitudes and demographic similarity to counselor preferences. *Journal of Counseling Psychology, 38,* 446-457.

Hui, C. H. (1988). Measurement of individualism-collectivism. *Journal of Research in Personality, 22,* 17-36.

Hui, C. H., & Triandis, H. C. (1985). Measurement in cross-cultural counseling: A review and comparison of strategies. *Journal of Cross Cultural Psychology, 16,* 131-152.

Jones, E. E., & Thorne, A. (1987). Rediscovery of the subject: Intercultural approaches to clinical assessment. *Journal of Consulting and Clinical Psychology, 55,* 488-495.

Kaplan, R. M., & Saccuzzo, D. P. (1982). *Psychological testing: Principles, applications, and issues.* Monterey, CA: Brooks/Cole.

Keefe, K., Sue, S., Enomoto, K., Durvasula, R., & Chao, R. (in press). Asian American and White College Students' Performance on the MMPI-2. In J. N. Butcher (Ed.), *Handbook of international MMPI-2 research.* NY: Oxford University Press.

Kim, B. L. C. (1978). *The Asian-Americans: Changing patterns, changing needs.* Montclair, NJ: Association of Korean Christian Scholars in North America.

Kinzie, J. D., Manson, S. M., Vinh, D. T., Tolan, N. T., Anh, B., & Pho, R. N. (1982). Development and validation of a Vietnamese-language depression rating scale. *American Journal of Psychiatry, 139,* 1276-1281.

Kitano, H. H. L. (1976). *Japanese-Americans: The evaluation of a subculture.* Englewood Cliffs, NJ: Prentice-Hall.

Kleinman, A. M. (1977). Depression, somatization, and the new cross-cultural psychiatry. *Social Science and Medicine, 11,* 3-10.

Kleinman, A. (1991, April). *Culture and DSM-IV: Recommendations for the introduction and for the overall structure.* Paper presented at the Conference on Culture and DSM-IV, Pittsburgh.

Korchin, S. J. (1980). Clinical psychology and minority problems. *American Psychologist, 35,* 262-269.

LaFromboise, T. D. (1988). American Indian mental health policy. *American Psychologist, 43*, 388-397.

Li-Repac, D. (1980). Cultural influences on clinical perception: A comparison between Caucasian and Chinese-American therapists. *Journal of Cross-Cultural Psychology, 11*, 327-342.

Lopez, S. R. (1989). Patient variable biases in clinical judgment: Conceptual overview and methodological considerations. *Psychological Bulletin, 106*, 184-204.

Mendoza, R. H. (1989). An empirical scale to measure type and degree of acculturation in Mexican-American adolescents and adults. *Journal of Cross-Cultural Psychology, 20*, 372-385.

Mercer, J. R., & Lewis, J. R. (1979). *System of Multi-Cultural Pluralistic Assessment: Conceptual and technical manual.* San Antonio, TX: The Psychological Corporation.

Mukherjee, S., Shukla, S., Woodle, J., Rosen, A. M., & Olarte, S. (1983). Misdiagnosis of schizophrenia in bipolar patients: A multiethnic comparison. *American Journal of Psychiatry, 140*, 1571-1574.

Neighbors, H. W., Jackson, J. S., Campbell, L., & Williams, D. (1989). The influence of racial factors on psychiatric diagnosis: A review and suggestions for research. *Community Mental Health Journal, 25*(4), 301-311.

Ottavi, T. M., Pope-Davis, D. B., & Dings, J. G. (1994). Relationship between white racial identity attitudes and self-reported multicultural counseling competencies. *Journal of Counseling Psychology, 41*, 149-154.

Padilla, A. M., & Salgado DeSnyder, N. (1985). Counseling Hispanics: Strategies for effective intervention. In P. Pedersen (Ed.), *Handbook of cross-cultural counseling and therapy* (pp. 157-164). Westport, CT: Greenwood Press.

Phinney, J. S. (1992). The multigroup ethnic identity measure: A new scale for use with diverse groups. *Journal of Adolescent Research, 7*, 156-176.

Ponterotto, J. G., & Casas, J. M. (1991). *Handbook of racial/ethnic minority counseling research.* Springfield, IL: Charles C. Thomas.

Rogler, L. H., Malgady, R. G., & Rodriguez, O. (1989). *Hispanics and mental health: A framework for research.* Malabar, FL: Krieger Publishing Company.

Sodowsky, G. R., & Plake, B. S. (1991). Psychometric properties of the American-International Relations Scale. *Educational and Psychological Measurement, 51*, 207-216.

Sodowsky, G. R., Taffe, R. C., Gutkin, T. B., & Wise, S. L. (1994). Development of the Multicultural Counseling Inventory: A self-report measure of multicultural competencies. *Journal of Counseling Psychology, 41,* 137-148.

Spitzer, R. L., Gibbon, M., & Endicott, J. (1985). Global Assessment Scale. New York: Department of Research Assessment and Training, New York State Psychiatric Institute.

Sue, D., Ino, S., & Sue, D. M. (1983). Nonassertiveness of Asian Americans: An inaccurate assumption? *Journal of Counseling Psychology, 30,* 581-588.

Sue, D., & Sue, S. (1987). Cultural factors in the clinical assessment of Asian Americans. *Journal of Consulting and Clinical Psychology. 55*(4) 479-487.

Sue, D. W., & Sue, D. (1991). *Counseling the culturally different: Theory and practice.* New York: Wiley.

Sue, S. (1988). *Sociocultural issues in the assessment and classroom teaching of language minority students.* Crosscultural Special Education Series, V.3. Sacramento: California State Department of Education.

Sue, S., & Abe, J. (1988). *Predictors of academic achievement among Asian American and White students.* New York: The College Board.

Sue, S., & Morishima, J. (1982). *The mental health of Asian Americans.* San Francisco: Jossey-Bass Publishers.

Sue, S., Wagner, N. N., Ja, D., Margullis, C., & Lew, L. (1976). Conceptions of mental illness among Asian and Caucasian American students. *Psychological Reports, 38,* 703-708.

Suinn, R., Rickard-Figueroa, K., Lew, S., & Vigil, P. (1987). The Suinn-Lew Asian Self-Identity Acculturation Scale: An initial report. *Educational and Psychological Measurement, 47,* 401-407.

Takeuchi, D., & Speechley, K. N. (1989). Ethnic differences in the marital status and psychological distress relationship. *Social Psychiatry and Psychiatric Epidemiology, 24,* 288-294.

Westermeyer, J. (1987). Cultural factors in clinical assessment. *Journal of Consulting and Clinical Psychology, 55*(4), 471-478.

White, J. L. (1984). *The psychology of blacks: An Afro-American perspective.* Englewood Cliffs, NJ: Prentice Hall.

Williams, R. L. (1974). Scientific racism and IQ: The silent mugging of the Black community. *Psychology Today, 7,* 32-41.

Yang, K. S., & Bond, M. H. (1990). Exploring implicit personality theories with indigenous or imported constructs: The Chinese case. *Journal of Personality and Social Psychology, 58,* 1087-1095.

Zane, N., & Sue, S. (1986). Reappraisal of ethnic minority issues: Research alternatives. In E. Seidman & J. Rappaport (Eds.), *Redefining social problems* (pp. 289-304). New York: Plenum.

Zane, N. (1991, August). *An empirical examination of loss of face among Asian Americans.* Paper prsented at the annual meeting of the American Psychological Association, San Francisco.

MULTICULTURAL AND CROSS-CULTURAL ASSESSMENT: DILEMMAS AND DECISIONS

Juris G. Draguns

The Pennsylvania State University

Cross-cultural psychologists aspire to scientific objectivity and cultural sensitivity. These two objectives are pursued simultaneously, yet they often exercise a pull in divergent directions. If the investigator's concepts, instruments, and procedures are designed to maximize cultural appropriateness, they may not be usable within other cultures. If, however, comparability is the principal consideration, sensitivity to the unique culture that is being investigated may be compromised.

The assessment of disturbed behavior across cultures is not exempt from these two pressures. In this chapter, four objectives are pursued. First an attempt is made to take stock of the present state of multicultural assessment. Second, the choices that are open to the contemporary investigator and practitioner of cultural assessment of psychological disturbance are articulated. Third, some preliminary suggestions are proposed for dealing with the challenge of simultaneously achieving cross-cultural comparability and cultural sensitivity. Fourth, proceeding from this proposal, generalizations are formulated about the culturally distinctive components of the experience and expression of psychological disorder and about their integration in the course of assessment. All of this information is brought to bear upon the practical issues of assessing distressed and/or disabled individuals in culturally diverse environments. Before this body of accumulated relevant findings is applied in multicultural assessment, a number of complications must be identified and, if possible, resolved.

Because the activities of culturally oriented assessment have potent consequences for better or worse, those engaged in this enterprise should be warned against dangers and pitfalls, such as equating different and unfamiliar behavior with the bizarre and the dysfunctional. It should also be emphatically pointed out that the comparison of complex and meaningful behaviors across cultures does *not* imply the superiority or inferiority of any group at either pole on any psychological dimension. The history of the last 30 years of cumulative, organized research in cross-cultural psychology (Berry, Poortinga, Segall, & Dasen, 1992; Brislin, 1983; Kagitcibasi & Berry, 1989; Segall, 1986) decisively demonstrates that socially relevant behavior can be compared realistically and sensitively, without the investigators either extolling or devaluing any of its culturally characteristic variants. Thus, the unfortunate and long history of comparisons of intelligence across racial, ethnic, and cultural lines has, so far, not been repeated by the contributors to the modern enterprise of cross-cultural psychology. Moreover, cross-cultural psychologists have by and large been successful in avoiding the pitfall of equating cultural differences with deficits (cf., Cole & Bruner, 1972). Time may now be ripe for applying the results of the culturally oriented assessment effort to the solution of practical problems in community, educational, psychiatric, and other settings. To this end, however, certain specifications and distinctions must be introduced.

SETTINGS, CONCEPTS, AND METHODS: INITIAL AND TENTATIVE SPECIFICATIONS

Cross-Cultural and Multicultural Settings

Cultural barriers are encountered and, in the fortunate case, overcome in two contexts. First, there is the worldwide panorama of psychiatric symptoms across political and cultural frontiers and geographic obstacles and distances. It is possible and worthwhile to compare the anxiety responses of the Inuit of the Arctic with those of the urban Canadians of Metropolitan Toronto or the symptoms of the hospitalized depressives in Germany and in Japan or the coping responses under conditions of extreme stress during the earthquakes in Mexico in 1985 and in India in 1993. Second, the ethnocultural diversity of many localities in the United States provides both challenges and opportunities for the recording, comparison, and investigation of the humanly universal and the culturally variable aspects of psychological disturbance. Moreover, cultural diversity is not unique to the United States. Ethnocultural groups share their habitat in Canada, Brazil, India, Singapore, Australia, Kenya, and Nigeria, to name but a few of the multicultural nations. Although culturally homogeneous nation states do exist, as exemplified by Japan, Korea, and Iceland, voluntary and forced population movements of the past few decades have contributed to making monocultural nations the exceptions to the worldwide trend of an ever greater degree of interethnic mingling in residential and working environments.

There are then two kinds of cultural challenges to be considered: across national frontiers, geographical, and physical barriers and within the multicultural microcosm of many contemporary communities in North America and elsewhere. The problems faced by the investigators of these two kinds of diversity are in some respects similar, although important distinctions should also be kept in mind. Members of several ethnic groups within a region or city are seemingly easier to compare than people who live thousands of miles apart, speak different languages, and stake out their livelihood by radically different means. Yet hidden disparities in interethnic comparisons within a region or city should not be overlooked. The first and foremost among them is the uneven distribution of power, privilege, and opportunity, both as a current condition and as a historical memory (cf., King, 1978; Sue, Sue, & Sue, 1981). The second challenge is posed by the interactive and complex influences to which the several ethnic groupings of a multicultural society are exposed. These influences reverberate within the members of these ethnic groupings to produce complex patterns of acculturation and identity. Compounding this complexity, there is the problem of multiple and overlapping group membership and the difficulty of converting the naturally fuzzy intergroup boundaries into clearly delineated categorical entities. In the prototypical case, nothing appears to be easier than deciding whether a person is Japanese, Portuguese, or Finnish. The task calls for a binary, either-or, inclusion-exclusion judgment. However, in the multiethnic environment of the United States and Canada as well as many other sites, the seemingly straightforward activity of assigning an ethnic or cultural label to an individual becomes exceedingly complex. Thus, there are the several criteria of ethnic group membership to be considered, similar but not identical in the typical case, yet exercising a subtle and simultaneous pull into a number of directions. These topics are discussed at greater length in another section of this chapter. (See *Identity, Acculturation, Biculturalism*.).

One of the distinctive dangers in assessment across culture lines is to equate the deviant with the disturbed and "to blame the victim" in the process of assigning responsibility for his or her problems and entanglements. Another ubiquitous pitfall is stereotyping for which the blatantly prejudiced persons are not the only ones at risk. Closely related to it is the potentially distorting effect of pre-existing attitudes and expectations; again, these variables need not be negative or derogatory to obscure or confuse the observer's view. Later in this chapter (see *Diagnosis as Social Interaction*) opportunities are provided for immersion into these complexities. For the time being, the priorities of this undertaking should be spelled out. The present chapter draws upon both multicultural and cross-cultural sources. Its thrust, however, is to disentangle the assessment issues as they apply to a geographically delimited, but culturally diverse environment, as exemplified by, but not restricted to, the contemporary population composition of the United States.

Culture Around and Within Us

Herskovits (1949, p. 9) defined culture as the human-made part of the environment, implicitly encompassing within this statement both artifacts and ideas. LeVine (1984) made this inclusion explicit by referring to culture as "a shared organization of ideas that includes the intellectual, moral, and aesthetic standards prevalent in a community and the meanings of communicative actions" (p. 67). Triandis (1972) introduced the concept of subjective culture and identified a great many subtle and complex indicators of its operation. In particular, subjective culture comes into play in determining interrelationships between concepts, in tying together concepts, roles, and behaviors, and in articulating implicit cognitive assumptions that underlie various actions in everyday life. Generically, subjective culture can be equated with the fund of knowledge, attitudes, and beliefs shared within a cultural milieu. Its tenets are silently assumed rather than articulated by its members while engaging in social interaction and representing it cognitively. Thus conceived, subjective culture becomes a potentially important mediator of meanings and behaviors within a cultural milieu and a possible determinant of both adaptive and dysfunctional patterns of experience and action.

At a more abstract level, culture remains a complex concept several steps removed from the observable. It is yet to be unpackaged. The progression which the field of assessment has begun to traverse is from culture as a variable "which makes things happen" or, retrospectively, as an entity that is invoked after its putative effects have been observed. Instead, the question to be answered is: "What about the culture is responsible for various characteristic behaviors among its members?" Thus reformulated, the concept of culture could generate meaningful hypotheses, instead of serving as a convenient source of post hoc explanations. Betancourt and López (1993) have pointed out that cross-cultural investigators have often neglected to specify the characteristics of culture that are crucial for influencing behavior. Thus, little is learned about the components of culture that have contributed to its relationship with behavioral variables. According to these authors, the optimal course of action is to incorporate culture into the research design prospectively and explicitly rather than invoke cultural influences as explanation for the results obtained on a post hoc basis. This recommendation is equally applicable to both basic and applied research. Its implementation "would result in instruments and interventions that are more sensitive to the reality and cultural diversity of society and the world" (Betancourt & López, 1993, p. 636). As an example, López, Hurwicz, Karno, and Telles (1992) were able to trace the greater frequency of hallucinations among Mexican American patients, as compared to their Anglo counterparts, to the intense religiosity in the Mexican culture which tolerates and explains supernatural experiences.

Assessment, Diagnosis, and Measurement

Assessment is an inclusive term that encompasses the appraisal of a person's characteristics in quantitative and/or qualitative terms. Measurement constitutes the quantitative aspect of assessment and is embodied in a multiplicity of tests and scales. At this point, the field of cross-cultural and multicultural assessment of psychological disturbance largely relies upon qualitative procedures. It has not reached the point of thorough and consistent quantification of its observations, judgments, and inferences. Its data are typically couched in qualitative terms of which the diagnostic activity of clinical practitioners of assessment provides a prominent example. To be sure, there are scales, tests, and other measures of specific aspects of psychological disturbance, exemplified by the multiple measures of depression. In cross-cultural usage, however, these instruments remain in an auxiliary role. They provide valuable and important information that contributes to, but does not by itself determine decisions concerning diagnostic formulations or treatment and intervention, which constitute the most important justification for assessment.

Assessment is often focused upon diagnosis. In the restrictive sense, diagnosis refers to the assignment of individuals to qualitatively distinct categories of mental disorder. In its broader meaning, diagnosis extends beyond categorization and labeling and encompasses all the information that is relevant for therapeutic intervention. The current official diagnostic and statistical manual, DSM-IV (American Psychiatric Association, 1994), attempts to fulfill this objective. It includes five axes, which both divide and amplify the task of diagnosis, and supplement it with the appraisal of stress imposed and of demonstrated adaptive assets at the person's disposal. Assessment then is often geared toward diagnosis; diagnosis is one of its goals, although virtually never its sole concern.

Psychological Disturbance by Many Names: Its Current Conception.

The objective of assessment for the purposes of this chapter is variously referred to as psychopathology, psychological disturbance, or mental disorder. It roughly corresponds to the scope of the syndromes included in DSM-IV, the current version of the official American diagnostic manual. The fundamental criteria for inclusion of a behavior pattern in DSM-IV are *distress* and *disability*. The criteria of mental disorder are described by the authors of DSM-IV (American Psychiatric Association, 1994) as follows:

> In DSM-IV each of the mental disorders is conceptualized as a clinically significant behavioral or psychological syndrome or pattern that occurs in a person and that is associated with present distress (a painful symptom) or disability (impairment in one or more important areas of functioning) or with a significantly increased risk of suffering death, pain, disability, or an important loss of freedom. In addition, this syndrome or pattern must not be merely an expectable response to a particular event, e.g., the death of a loved one. Whatever its original cause, it must currently be considered a manifestation of a behavioral, psychological, or biological dysfunction in the individual. Neither deviant behavior, e.g., political, religious, or sexual, nor conflicts that are primarily between the individual and society are mental disorders unless the deviance or conflict is a symptom of a dysfunction in the person, as described above. (pp. xxi—xxii)

This statement articulates another important distinction; it sharply differentiates mental disorder from social deviance. This difference is crucial in the application of DSM-IV to ethnically and culturally diverse populations (cf. Good, 1993).

The immediate predecessor of the current manual, DSM-III-R, has generally received positive evaluations for its markedly increased reliability by comparison with the earlier versions of DSM. DSM-III-R has also been praised for reducing the ethnocentric bias toward the mainstream Anglo-American culture of these early documents, although it has not eliminated misdiagnosis of culturally atypical individuals (cf. Good, 1993). In DSM-IV, several further steps have been taken toward incorporating cultural sensitivity into the diagnostic process. Specifically, its authors have listed and described several points that are essential for the diagnostician to consider in arriving at a culturally sensitive formulation and in assessing the impact of the individual's cultural context. This listing includes: (a) the cultural identity of the individual, (b) the cultural explanations of the individual's illness, (c) the cultural factors that may be related to the individual's psychosocial environment and his or her levels of functioning, (d) the cultural elements of the relationship between the individual and the clinician, and (e) an overall cultural assessment for both diagnosis and intervention. Moreover, the cultural ramifications of diagnosis have been addressed on the conceptual plane in the introductory portion of the manual. Another novel feature included in DSM-IV is a glossary of culture-bound syndromes. Even though most of these conditions, exemplified by *Amok*, *Koro*, and *Susto*, are not likely to be encountered within the clientele of most North American clinicians, this roster should sensitize the users of the DSM-IV to the possibility of unusual symptom patterns by culturally atypical clients. The authors of DSM-IV recognize that culture-bound syndromes can be fitted into the existing nosological grid with difficulty, if at all. Cultures just have not shaped their patterns of maladaptation with the available slots of DSM-IV in mind! The final culturally sensitive innovation in DSM-IV pertains to Axis 5, which is concerned with the assessment of the adequacy of person's global functioning. On this axis, DSM-IV has incorporated a provision for culturally patterned modes of functioning.

These modifications go a long way toward making the diagnostic process and its results more culturally sensitive and informative. However, it would be hasty to conclude that all of the psychometric, clinical, and cultural limitations of the diagnostic system have thereby been overcome. There is no doubt that DSM-IV will be critically and searchingly scrutinized, last but not least for its adequacy in assessing mental disorder and maladaptation in a culturally diverse environment.

Anticipating these critiques, Fabrega (1992) entertained the possibility of incorporating an additional axis into the future version of DSM. This axis would assess the extent of the influence of cultural factors upon the patient's clinical condition and his or her accessibility to treatment. Somewhat similarly, Eisenbruch (1992) emphasized the inadequacy of the existing DSM categories such as post-traumatic stress syndrome in providing information relevant for intervention with patients from other cultures. The cultural bereavement of Cambodian refugees, for example, defies being fitted into the preexisting DSM diagnostic grid. More important, it does not allow for the recognition of indigenous, within-culture distinctions, which are taken into account by traditional Cambodian healers in choosing among the several available intervention strategies. In Eisenbruch's view, a cross-culturally applicable nosology must strive toward capturing the cultural meaning of the patients' suffering and its incorporation into diagnosis. It is difficult to envisage how this objective would be accomplished within the concrete framework of future DSMs. In any case, an important threshold has been crossed in acknowledging the relevance of cultural factors in diagnosis. The dialectic interplay between biological and social components of human distress continues to pose a challenge to diagnosticians and assessors in multicultural milieus. The further course of making diagnosis both factually based and clinically sensitive is envisaged as an open-ended or, in Fabrega's (1992, p. 6) words, an "interminable" progression.

Beyond these critiques, however, an important unsolved problem, inherited from the preceding versions of the manual, remains to be addressed: that of the fuzzy outward boundaries of DSM-IV. At what point does disorder stop and normal functioning begin? At what point are distress and/or disability so slight, fleeting, or self-corrective as to pass unnoticed by the outside observers or fall below the implicit threshold of disturbance? Clues to these answers may be sought in the context of diagnostic criteria for the several specific disorders; no generic set of decision rules has been formulated that could be applied across all of the diagnostic entities. Thus, as the authors of DSM-IV explicitly recognize, diagnostic decisions continue to be based on clinical judgment. The other limitations of DSM-IV pertain to its applicability beyond the milieu for which it was constructed: the socially and culturally diverse, contemporary United States. Conceivably, even within the United States the DSM-IV may not provide sufficient guidance and may misdirect the diagnostic process in the case of atypical, and isolated cultural groups, outside of the social mainstream of modern North America, despite the culturally sensitive features introduced into the manual. Certainly, there is no assumption that DSM-IV provides a universal diagnostic framework, to be used anywhere around the world. Rather, everything that is known about the manifestation of psychological disturbance strongly suggests that this is not the case. Although some diagnostic entities, as will be seen, approximate worldwide distribution, it would be extraordinary if a compendium of disorders and rules for diagnoses developed by a committee of American psychiatrists in the late twentieth century—with inputs from a number of their international colleagues—were valid across time and space in all cultures.

ASSESSMENT PROCESS AS A SERIES OF CHOICES AND DECISIONS

The conceptions that guide this chapter are organized around a series of choice points and decisions with which the investigator or practitioner of assessment across cultures is faced. Schematically, these choices are represented in Table 1. It concentrates on the

Table 1. Cultural Research in Psychopathology: Contrasting Options

Conceptual Orientations:

Emic (culturally indigenous)	Etic (universal, cross-culturally comparable)
Idiographic	Nomothetic
Cultural Uniqueness and Sensitivity	Objectivity, Comparability

Research Objective:

Description	Comparison

Characteristic Types of Studies:

Anthropological Descriptions	Epidemiological Studies (WHO)
Indigenous Concepts & Explanations	Multicultural Comparisons
Culture-Bound Syndromes	Archival Studies
Native Healers	Bicultural Comparisons
Within Culture Relationships	Traditional Transcultural Studies of Depression, Schizophrenia, etc.

Resulting Information and Knowledge:

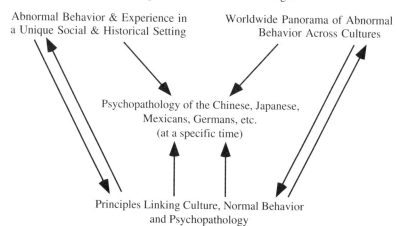

Abnormal Behavior & Experience in a Unique Social & Historical Setting

Worldwide Panorama of Abnormal Behavior Across Cultures

Psychopathology of the Chinese, Japanese, Mexicans, Germans, etc. (at a specific time)

Principles Linking Culture, Normal Behavior and Psychopathology diverging paths taken historically by the investigators who have worked in this area and represents options open to the practitioner of assessment. It represents the several steps in the research program, from its conception through the accumulation of observations to its implementation in a case-centered assessment.

Briefly restated, the investigator and/or assessor starts out with the choice between a universal (etic) *or* an indigenous (emic) orientation. There is a point of contact here, as Clark (1987) has recognized, with the idiographic versus nomothetic dichotomy in personality theory and research: the attempt to capture a phenomenon's unique qualities *versus* the endeavor to place it in relation to all other comparable phenomena regardless of their context of occurrence. These two conceptions are then bolstered by arrays of observations and data, which elucidate respectively their relationships to antecedents, concomitants, and consequents within a unique cultural milieu or place them in reference to a variety of norms collected at various localities and periods. These two sources of information are then respectively brought to bear upon the assessment of an individual. In the ideal case, an integration of these two perspectives is accomplished. However, this objective is ambitious and difficult to attain. At this point, it represents an ideal to be pursued more than a standard that is routinely met in practice.

The Emic-Etic Distinction

Pike (1967), a prominent linguist, coined the terms emic and etic to describe two traditions of inquiry, applicable across a variety of cultural fields and disciplines. *Emic* refers to an inside perspective and is derived from the word phonemic. Its prototype then is the study of the sound systems within a language. *Etic* is a contraction of phonetic and it signifies a comparative investigation, of sounds or any other phenomena, across several languages. Within cross-cultural psychology, especially of abnormal behavior, the emic tradition of inquiry capitalizes upon the description of occurrences within their culturally unique context. The point of departure may be an indigenous concept such as *Latah*, *Windigo*, or *Amok*, to mention but three of the indigenous names for the culture-bound syndromes that have been reported to occur at various sites around the world (in the case of these three, in Malaysia, among the Algonquin Indians, and in the Philippines and elsewhere in South East Asia, respectively). The manifestations of these disorders have been described within the contexts of their occurrence (cf. Pfeiffer, 1994; Simons & Hughes, 1985). Once these initial data have been gathered, the road is clear for the collection of information on the distribution of these disorders, treatment techniques for dealing with them, positive, negative, and mixed outcomes for them, as well as the prevailing explanations of their causes. In general, emically oriented investigators stay within the universe of the culture they are investigating. Kleinman (1982, 1986, 1988a, 1988b) in a series of studies that were focused upon the experience of distress in Mainland China discovered the prevalence of fatigue and ill-being which approximated the old and discarded Western diagnostic category of neurasthenia. This symptom pattern, however, exhibited many points of contact with depression, a point on which Kleinman found himself in disagreement with the official consensus of Chinese psychiatrists. In the Chinese psychiatrists' view, neurasthenic symptoms in the form of chronic fatigue and general malaise were *sui generis*; from Kleinman's perspective, they represented a cultural idiom of distress for communicating depression. Although the concepts he employed are not purely emic, Kleinman's focus upon the phenomena and experiences *within* a culture is in keeping with the emic tradition of inquiry. Thus, a rich, culturally unique tapestry of interrelationships is woven around a locally observed and conceptualized phenomenon. These results lend themselves to generalization across cultures and populations only with difficulty, and the data of such studies defy incorporation into formal multicultural or bicultural research designs, precisely because of their culturally shaped, unique, and incomparable nature.

In another context, Kinzie, Manson, Vinh, Tolan, Anh, and Pho (1982) were faced with the need for developing a depression scale for Vietnamese refugees in the United States. They started out by translating the widely used Beck Depression Inventory (BDI) (cf. Beck, Steer, & Garbin, 1988) into Vietnamese, but supplemented this procedure by adding and discarding items based on their perceived meaningfulness and appropriateness for Vietnamese clients. Particular attention was paid to generating statements pertaining to somatic and behavioral changes that could be attributed to depression. The list of items so generated was pretested with a small group of Vietnamese adults. Upon the completion of all of these preliminary steps, Kinzie et al. constructed a 45-item scale that was then submitted to validation in a depressed group and to a matched community sample. The resulting set of 42 differentiating items constituted the Vietnamese Depression Scale (VDS). It was later reduced to a 15-item list that collectively accounted for a very high share of the total variance.

It is noteworthy that only four of the 42 statements retained were from the BDI. An entirely new instrument was developed through the several steps of transformation described above. Kinzie et al. then classified the symptoms tapped by the VDS into three groups pertaining to physical states, depressed or sad mood, and those not related to either lowered mood or the Western concept of depression, as exemplified by "being angry, feeling shameful and dishonored, feeling desperate, and having a feeling of going crazy" (Kinzie et al., 1982, p. 1279).

A similar procedure was followed by the research team of Zeldine et al. (1975) in Senegal who found that they had to discard one-third of the original items of the Hamilton (1967) Depression Scale because of their irrelevance in the Senegalese context. Local informants were consulted and several new items were added that reflected the locally prevalent complaints and manifestations. Thus, the object of study remained constant, but the operational measure changed beyond recognition. Neither Kinzie et al. nor Zeldine et al. proceeded in a purely emic manner, but both of their studies illustrate the willingness of contemporary, culturally sensitive investigators to walk an extra mile to arrive at an understanding of the culture's internal frame of reference and to discard a lot of the imported concepts and measures in the process.

The difficulties experienced and overcome by these investigators should not overshadow the observations of those researchers who have used the translated and adapted versions of the BDI closer to its home base. In at least four Western countries (Canada, France, Germany, and Spain), and in three languages (French, German, and Spanish), no difficulties were reported in translating or validating the scale and no changes other than minimal ones were found to be necessary (Bourque & Beaudette, 1982; Conde, Esteban, & Useros, 1976; Delay, Pichot, Lemperiere, & Mirouze, 1963; Kammer, 1983). On a subtler level, a series of studies in Hawaii with Caucasian, Japanese American, and Chinese American students (Marsella, Kinzie, & Gordon, 1973) revealed ethnocultural differences in depressive experiences related to the body and the self. Two reports of multinational comparisons of the Self-rating Depression Scale (SDS) by Zung (1969, 1972) demonstrate the cross-cultural applicability of this instrument. In the first study, Zung (1969) found that the SDS scores were comparable in samples of depressive patients in seven countries: Australia, Czechoslovakia, England, Germany, Japan, Switzerland, and the United States. Moreover, at all of these sites, SDS scores were higher for depressed than nondepressed psychiatric patients. These scores also were positively correlated with other depression rating scales and were useful for predicting patients' response to therapeutic interventions. In the second study, Zung (1972) succeeded in demonstrating a reasonably close correspondence between the average SDS scores of normal nondepressed groups of persons in six countries (Czechoslovakia, England, Germany, Spain, Sweden, and the United States) and the suicide rates of the same nations. It is of interest to note that this report, with its thrust on etic comparability, also uncovered ethnic nuances in the experience of depression. Upon principal factor analysis, the first factor was labeled dissatisfaction in Czechoslovakia, hopelessness in England, emptiness in Germany, fatigue in Spain, and confusion in Sweden. All of these results should be replicated and extended before they are accepted as definitive. Even in their present state, these findings suggest that self-reports of depressive symptoms are comparable across a fairly wide range of cultures, and that these indicators reveal cultural differences in both baselines of depression and in its preferred modes of expression.

These examples can be contrasted with the etic investigation of an overlapping phenomenon. The World Health Organization (1983) has been involved in a series of investigations of depression in various regions of the world. Their samples consisted of hospitalized depressed patients in Switzerland, Canada, Iran, and Japan. These studies yielded findings on the most cross-culturally constant symptoms of depression. This is a finding that no series of emic investigations could have conclusively and objectively produced. Important as it is, especially if it is replicated in other countries by similar cross-national investigations, it conveys little of the "local color" of the experience of depression in Geneva, Montreal, Teheran, or Nagasaki. To be sure, some of these features can be recaptured by shifting focus upon the specific sites of the investigation, as has been done in the case of Japan (Radford, 1989).

Neither the emic nor the etic perspective is inherently superior or inferior. The etic approach, as exemplified *par excellence* by the World Health Organization's multi-country projects on schizophrenia and depression and by a host of studies organized on the basis of conceptions that have originated in the investigator's cultural framework (i.e., are broadly Western), provides an unsurpassed panoramic view, somewhat akin to viewing Paris from the top of the Eiffel Tower, but offers no substitute for the immersion into the hustle and bustle of street life, normal or disturbed, within a specific milieu.

Both the etic and emic frameworks then have their respective places in the research enterprise and also in individual assessment. However, bridges between them can also be built, as has been shown in a classical article by Berry (1969). Berry's acknowledged preference was for a "radically emic" approach (Berry, 1972). He recognized the unavoidable necessity of transporting the prevalent concepts from one's own culture and employing them provisionally across cultural lines as though they were etic. In the process of further study, this, the so-called "imposed etic" is gradually modified and eventually discarded in the course of obtaining more data, until a true etic (i.e., a concept genuinely relevant to and applicable across cultures) can finally emerge.

And, of course, there are no arguments against the sequential investigation of the phenomena of interest—except for the very real considerations of cost, time, and commitment. In practice, studies with a shifting emic or etic focus are exceedingly difficult to implement. A practitioner, however, may have more flexibility in shifting from a within-culture to across-cultures orientation and, finally, incorporating both perspectives into his or her appraisal of the person.

In the end, both perspectives merge in producing an integrated body of pertinent information that can be brought to bear upon a specific culture and can be applied toward formulating the general principles linking cultural factors with the experience and manifestation of psychological disorder.

POPULATIONS TO BE STUDIED: ANOTHER LOOK

Cultural and Ethnic Categories

What are the limits of a cultural group? How is the pool of subjects to be delimited and defined? Some anthropologists (Naroll, 1970) insist upon a rigorous, narrow definition of a cultural group, as exemplified by traditional tribes such as the Navajo or the Kwakiutl. For better or worse, investigators of psychopathological variables have rarely chosen to be so restrictive. Practical interest has dictated the choice of more inclusive groupings, largely corresponding to ethnic, national, and related categories used in popular discourse. Many of the concepts of ethnic groups are implicitly based upon a prototypical case with extremely fuzzy outside boundaries. Thus, the complexities of casting the net too broadly are readily apparent. It is relatively easy to start with the prototype of a German American. Such a person would have strong personal and cultural ties to his or her country of origin, would practice and observe many German customs, and be proficient in the German language. But does this category encompass the Amish farmers of Pennsylvania who cling to a German dialect, but have lost virtually all contact to their ancestral country (Hostetler, 1980), the descendants of nineteenth-century German immigrants who are monolingual in English, and the recently arrived bilingual university graduates from Germany (Billigmeier, 1974; Winawer-Steiner & Wetzel, 1982)? In an even more complex manner, the term Hispanic refers to a supraordinate administrative category that includes persons whose descent is traceable to Mexico, Puerto Rico, Cuba, Dominican Republic, Colombia, and many other countries (Bernal, 1982; Casas & Vasquez, 1989; Falicov, 1982; Garcia-Preto, 1982; Rivera-Ramos, 1984). For psychological purposes it is hardly meaningful to include all of these in one group; dealing with Hispanics as a homogeneous category runs the risk of producing a lot of error variance. Trimble and Fleming (1989) have warned against glib generalizations about American Indians and have emphasized the tremendous variety in background, outlook, and adaptive strategies within the inclusive American Indian population. Most investigators are in agreement that targeting research operations upon a reasonably homogeneous group in ethnic descent and membership is preferable to a vague and overinclusive criterion.

In cross-national research, culture is all too often equated with country. Little thought is given to the ever increasing pluralism within most national borders. Another important category to consider is the regional differences which, in the case of Italy for example, have the reputation of being a lot more numerous, pervasive, and intense than they appear to be in the United States.

Identity, Acculturation, Biculturalism

Finally, in reference to both national and international samples, the person's cultural identity may be important to ascertain. This point marks the transition of ethnic or cultural membership from a categorical to a continuous variable. How Australian, for example, is this specific person who was not born in but resides in Australia? This question can be answered on the basis of an empirically validated Australianism scale (Taft, 1977). In multicultural settings, acculturation scales provide useful data. Their use and interpretation, however, is complicated by the existence of several kinds of acculturation. Berry (1990) identified four varieties of acculturative experience: integration, assimilation, separation, and marginalization. Contemporary investigators of acculturation, committed as they are to multiculturalism, tend to favor integration over the other three options. As yet, however, there is little evidence for any clear-cut advantage, in relation to vulnerability to disorder, of integration over either assimilation or ethnic encapsulation. There is no question though that the remaining quadrant in this fourfold table, that of marginalization, is associated with susceptibility to mental health problems.

There are three established ways of determining a person's ethnicity (Isajiw, 1974). First, a person's ethnic self-designation can be ascertained; the individual is then assigned to the ethnic category of his or her own choosing. Second, ascriptive and concrete criteria can be used as a basis for ethnic categorization, such as the person's own or parental birthplace, family name, skin color, other physical characteristics, etc. Third, ethnicity can be determined on the basis of consensus, by either in-group or out-group members or both.

Recent trends, however, have focused upon behavioral and lifestyle indicators of ethnicity (Phinney, 1990; Sodowsky, Kwan, & Pannu, 1995). Thus, ethnic group membership can be inferred from a person's participation in activities and rituals, membership in organizations, preferences and aversions, language use, and other choices and decisions. This approach is consonant with the shift from external and concrete to internal and subtle criteria of ethnicity (cf. Isajiw, 1990). The complexity and ambiguity of which criteria to use, what weights to assign to them, and how to incorporate them into some kind of a composite or global score or judgment are as yet not resolved, but the rationale of current ethnic identity determination is clearly moving away from ascriptive and toward psychological indicators.

This development is epitomized by a host of acculturation scales (e.g., Szapocznik, Scopetta, Kurtines, & Aranalde, 1978) which have been typically applied to populations of immigrants and their descendants. Where a person stands in relation to several possible group memberships is assessed by a host of such instruments. Usually, these instruments capitalize upon the identification with a specific group, and it is difficult to envisage a generic acculturation measure. Hence, these instruments have to be adapted and revised, often radically, as they are extended beyond their original target population. Recently, however, steps have been taken toward developing a generally applicable measure of acculturation (Sodowsky, Lai, & Plake, 1991; Sodowsky & Plake, 1991). This scale was originally designed for studying international students. It was then modified for use with members of minority groups, such as Hispanic and Asian Americans. Data on the construct validity of this instrument are promising. There is the prospect then of an instrument by means of which groups of normal and/or disturbed subjects of different provenance and ethnicity could be compared in the degree and nature of their acculturation. In assessing psychological disturbance in culturally diverse populations, it is desirable to go beyond the categorical labels of ethnic or cultural membership and to include a standardized and quantitative indicator of the person's adaptive functioning within his or her original cultural milieu and in various culturally pluralistic host-culture settings.

The obverse of acculturation scales is constituted by various instruments that tap retention of the culture of origin. In combination, these two kinds of measures provide indicators of a person's stand in relation to both his or her culture of descent and that of current residence. From these data, various combinations result that have given rise to Berry's (1990) fourfold typology composed of integration of elements from the cultures of origin and adoption, assimilation into the host culture, isolation in the community of one's compatriots, and marginalization, which is tantamount to the inadequate mastery of skills necessary for functioning in either of the two settings.

In a culturally diverse and dynamic social structure like that of the contemporary United States an even more complex situation is encountered. Sodowsky et al. (1995) have conceptualized the process of maintaining or changing ethnic identity in a host culture as a conflict that can be resolved in four ways corresponding to Berry's options of integration, assimilation, isolation, and marginalization. Shifts to and from any one of these four reference points are possible and indecision, tension, and erratic changes are also accommodated within this model. Along similar lines, Szapocznik and Kurtines (1993) have addressed the problems of Cuban American adolescents who are pulled in several directions by the family, their peers, and the larger society, with each of them representing somewhat different cultural frameworks. According to these authors, the simultaneous operation of these forces generates opportunities for conceptualization, investigation, and application of the several value orientations. As yet no instruments have emerged to quantify and objectify these variables. Szapocznik and Kurtines have proposed the concept of embeddedness to encompass the simultaneous membership of several interacting groupings. This notion is exemplified by the research undertaken by Szapocznik and Kurtines, which involves the study of the person within the family context while the family is embedded in its cultural milieu. Potentially, the construct of embeddedness can be applied to the situation of the bicultural or multicultural person trying to reconcile and integrate several strands of ethnic or cultural influence (e.g., from the mainstream or majority culture, ethnically homogeneous or mixed peers, and a traditional ethnic family).

Psychological Disturbance and Its Indicators

How is the presence and degree of disturbance determined in a person? The identification of criterion groups is essential for the development of indicators of mental disorder and related characteristics. Such identification is also indispensable for the investigation of the interplay between psychopathology and the culture in which it occurs. Several research strategies have been applied to this end.

The first of these approaches has been to start with extreme populations that are usually hospitalized for psychiatric reasons, especially in developed countries with a fully developed network of psychiatric services. This was the research strategy of the World Health Organization (WHO) investigators in their landmark cross-national projects on schizophrenia (WHO, 1979) and depression (WHO, 1983). This mode of data collection yields valuable data; it also has the advantage of starting out with populations whose behavior patterns are observable on a continuous basis. Problems of cross-cultural comparability, however, ensue as the criteria for hospitalization at the various participating research sites are considered. Disparities in reasons for voluntary or involuntary hospitalization may have accounted for the often cited finding of the WHO (1979) investigators of the *inverse* relationships between socioeconomic and educational status of schizophrenic patients and their favorable prognosis in two developing countries, Nigeria and India. This finding is exactly the opposite of that reported consistently in technologically and economically developed countries (Dohrenwend & Dohrenwend, 1969). A possible explanation that may be explored in any future attempts to replicate this finding is that only the most serious and chronic cases of schizophrenia of higher occupational and educational status would be found in public institutions of developing countries. At this point, the idea has the status of an alternative hypothesis, which remains to be scrutinized in light of any pertinent future data. This unexpected and, at first glance, counterintuitive result serves to illustrate the complexities and ambiguities of the relationship between psychopathology and culture. It also provides a note of caution lest the results of formal cross-cultural psychopathology research be mechanically and automatically applied to assessment at the case level.

The second strategy is essentially based on self-definition and self-referral. It encompasses ambulatory clients who have sought mental health services on their own initiative or have been referred for them, but who have in any case exercised their judgment in establishing and maintaining clinical contacts. It is generally recognized that geographically separate cultures and spatially proximate ethnocultural groups differ in access to and patterns of utilization of mental health services. Studies based on these populations are open to criticisms because of the disparities at the point of entry into the system.

An even greater share of information on the role of ethnic and cultural variables is contributed by the third category of studies, which concentrate on patients with a uniform diagnosis. Even though the disorder may be identically labeled, the bases for the label may interact with the culturally determined modes of self and distress presentation and with the diagnosticians' biases and selective perceptions, especially when there is ethnic or cultural disparity between the patient and the diagnostician.

Finally, the fourth solution to the selection and criteria/problem is invariably costly and large-scale. One may envisage an epidemiological study with identical selection criteria and information-gathering techniques at several culturally removed sites. On the basis of these data, individuals identically diagnosed would be selected for further cross-cultural comparisons. Even more ambitiously, one could imagine within the context of this hypothetical investigation conclusive cross-cultural or cross-ethnic comparisons of the incidence of various mental disorders. Such a task, however, has so far not been undertaken.

One can imagine the size of the subject pools that would be necessary for carrying out this utopian project. Even the World Health Organization has not attempted anything comparable to this scale! It is, however, possible to realize some of these objectives in the microcosm of ethnically diverse communities, such as in Hawaii (Katz, Sanborn, Lowery, & Ching, 1978) or in California (López, Hurwicz, Karno, & Telles, 1992) and/or in a sequential series of studies rather than in a comprehensive giant undertaking. In the absence of such findings, however, it behooves the culturally sensitive practitioner to keep in mind the available, piecemeal, and fragmentary results despite their inevitable major methodological limitations. Thus, it can be concluded that there are genuine cultural differences in the modes of expression in psychopathology. This conclusion has remained valid from the earliest (cf. Draguns, 1973, 1980) to the most recent (López et al., 1992) studies. At the same time, it should be emphasized that the exact nature and extent of these differences remains uncertain. In many cases, they have to be "purged" of various distortions that are traceable to hidden disparities between samples of even identically diagnosed patients of different cultures or ethnicities. These impurities for the most part are broadly social, without being specifically cultural. An example would be an ethnic difference in symptom expression, which turns out to be traceable to discrepancies in socioeconomic status, age distribution, or gender composition of the two populations. A definitive resolution of the issues raised must await the replacement of the samples of convenience and opportunity with those based on representativeness and randomness. In the meantime, the interested practitioner of mental health services is well advised to retain the proverbial grain of salt.

CLINICAL SENSITIVITY VERSUS THE OBSERVER'S BIAS: THE DUAL CONTRIBUTION OF THE CLINICIAN

Diagnosis as Social Interaction

Contemporary theorists (e.g., Kleinman, 1986) conceptualize the experience of psychopathology as a transaction during which distress is communicated through multiple channels and is subjected to several obstacles, distortions, and disguises. All of these consideration come into play in disentangling the intricacies of interaction between the diagnostician and the patient across an ethnocultural gulf. Such encounters are a daily occurrence in the multicultural settings in the United States and many other countries.

DeHoyos and DeHoyos (1965) were among the first to document the tendency of white American "mainstream" clinicians to record fewer subtle, less visible, affective symptoms in their African American patients and to note a greater number of conspicuous manifestations of disorder often related to violence and aggression in that population.

The other finding contributed by DeHoyos and DeHoyos (1965) pertained to the significantly smaller number of symptoms recorded for African American patients as compared with their majority group white counterparts. Quite likely, these two trends are related; if fewer symptoms are noticed, they are probably among the most extreme, bizarre, and dramatic. Since then, these findings have been corroborated in several investigations and extended to a variety of other ethnic and minority groups. Good (1993) concluded that "evidence continues to cumulate that misdiagnosis is higher among minority patient populations in the United States than among patients from the majority population. Given the potential consequences of misdiagnosis— inappropriate use of medication, labeling, and mistaken treatment within mental health services—this pattern should be viewed with great concern" (pp. 430–431). This statement reverberates with Adebimpe's (1981, 1984) conclusion that African American psychiatric patients are at greater risk for error in diagnosis and assessment than are their majority group counterparts. Moreover, Adebimpe's reviews recapitulate the observations by earlier authors that African Americans are more likely to receive the diagnosis of schizophrenia and less likely to be diagnosed as suffering from affective disorder. These tendencies are not confined to one major minority group. Findings on Hispanics, American Indians, and Asian Americans also substantiate nonrandom diagnostic errors; their nature and direction parallel in some respects and diverge in others from those observed for African Americans (cf. Good, 1993; López, 1989; Mukherjee, Shukla, Woodle, Rosen, & Olarte, 1983).

Not all of these errors, however, point in the same direction. In a sample of 118 licensed mental health professionals in California, López and Hernandez (1992) documented a tendency to underestimate, rather than to overestimate, the severity of psychopathology in their minority-group clients. Moreover, this bias occurred in a group of diagnosticians who reported a high degree of awareness of the importance of cultural factors in clinical intervention. López and Hernandez (1992) warned that "clinicians may be at risk to dismiss psychopathology as being representative of culturally normative behavior" (p. 605). The antidote that they recommend is the clinicians' sensitivity to the heterogeneity that exists within most minority groups and their recognition of the limitations of the relevant empirical literature.

It is easy and tempting to attribute many of the diagnostic errors to prejudice and racism, but these phenomena are both more frequent and complex. Instances of blatant prejudice and virulent hostility toward minority groups are probably rare among the contemporary members of mental health professions, yet diagnostic biases remain widespread. As Ridley (1989) noted in a different context, "prejudiced people stereotype, but people who stereotype are not necessarily prejudiced" (p. 59). López (1989) concluded that "evidence that therapists err in their judgments of patients from groups who are not traditionally subject to discrimination supports the notion that errors based on patient variables are the results of selective information processing rather than of the previously assumed prejudicial sentiments" (p. 193). Other evaluators of this research evidence (Adebimpe, 1981, 1984; DeHoyos & DeHoyos, 1965; Good, 1993) have arrived at similar conclusions. In fact, there appears to be a consensus among the experts in this area that systematic diagnostic errors cannot be reduced to prejudicial and rejecting attitudes on the part of the diagnosticians. Practical implications can be drawn from this recognition. López (1989) contrasted the old, traditional model designed to promote reduction and elimination of prejudice with the new conceptualization that is focused upon more efficient and effective problem-solving strategies. To quote López (1989):

> This conceptual framework has several implications for future research. First of all, systematic errors in judgment based on patient variables may pertain to all clinicians and not just to those clinicians

with prejudicial attitudes. This suggests that less emphasis should be placed on therapists' social values and more emphasis should be placed on the general processes that lead to judgment error. Second, investigators should give careful consideration to the symptoms or disorders used as their clinical stimuli, at least among studies of gender and racial/ethnic bias. Third, if there is evidence for bias with the present conceptualization, then the implications for training clinicians to prevent such biases will differ greatly from the original model. Although never addressed, the training implication of the old model was to change attitudes or values. The present conceptualization suggests that clinicians can be trained to improve the way in which they process information. (p. 194)

An alternative explanation of the diagnosticians' biases would take into account the expectations of the clinicians based on their personal experience with their own cultural group and other ethnic categories. The complex results of these processes are illustrated in a study by Li-Ripac (1980) who documented the divergent perceptions of Chinese-American and majority group clinicians of their Chinese and Caucasian clients. These results demonstrate a greater readiness to understand a client of one's own ethnicity and a more realistic view of his/her presenting problems. Generally, Caucasian therapists rated their Chinese clients as more depressed and inhibited and less socially poised by comparison with the ratings of the Chinese-American colleagues. Conversely, Chinese-American therapists assigned higher ratings of disturbance to Caucasian clients than did their white counterparts. Similarly, Berman (1979) reported that African American counselors emphasized the social character of their African American clients' problems, whereas the Caucasian counselors were inclined to see intrapsychic sources of the African American clients' difficulties. There is no ready way of establishing who was "right" and who was "wrong" in these two cases. The only conclusion that can be drawn is that mental health professionals proceed from their specific perspective, which is rooted in part in their cultural experience, and react to the social reality from their socially determined vantage point. This process results in partially veridical and partially incomplete or even distorted perception.

Empathy and Social Distance in the Diagnostic Process

To take an additional inferential step, one may relate diagnostic sensitivity to the clinician's affective distance from the client. Within the context of the above formulation, accurate perception and judgment of internal distress, prominently exemplified by depression, is facilitated by the experience of empathy. To tune in to another person's subjective affective state, however, is more easily accomplished in cases of low social distance (i.e., in interacting with individuals in similar and familiar social categories). Perhaps that is why depression and other expressions of distress often remain unheard when they are uttered across a social gulf, whether it be determined by age, socioeconomic status, culture, or ethnicity. Overlooking of the subjective and subtle depressive manifestations and capitalizing upon the more readily visible expressions of schizophrenia in a group with which personal and reciprocal contacts may have been few may be conceptualized as an instance of this principle. As stated elsewhere (Draguns, 1973):

> Across the cultural barrier, the observer tends to see the patients as though he were viewing them from afar. Consequently, he may selectively perceive conspicuous or dramatic symptoms and may miss some of the subtler expressions of disorder. Empirically these effects have been demonstrated to occur even across subcultures, as in the case of a white psychiatrist interviewing a Black patient in the United States. These findings suggest that the clinician's prized tools—his empathy and sensitivity—suffer impairment as they are applied outside his cultural domain. As a consequence, the record obtained runs the risk of being quantitatively and qualitatively impoverished. (p. 13)

Future work may put these expectations to a test by studying the relationship of empathy and diagnostic sensitivity in patient-diagnostician dyads of different ethnicities and by investigating the effect of increased social contact across ethnic lines upon the reduction of diagnostic errors, especially as they pertain to affective disorders.

National and Cultural Tendencies

Apart from social distance, social baselines are germane to cultural styles and tendencies toward diagnostic assignment. The results of the U.S.-U.K. comparison of the diagnostic operations of the psychiatrists of these two countries are well known (Cooper, Kendell, Gurland, Sharpe, Copeland, & Simon, 1972). Briefly, British psychiatrists were found to diagnose depression much more readily than their American colleagues, whereas the Americans displayed, in the DSM-II era, a penchant for the diagnosis of schizophrenia. Other, less firmly substantiated differences among diagnosticians across national boundaries have also been recorded. These findings may be explained on the basis of cultural differences in sensitivity to various psychological symptoms. Cultures then may set different markers in establishing the minimal standards of acceptable social behavior. In

England, the general public may have a lower "threshold" for taking notice of and action in depression than in the United States; the opposite pattern of socially consensual reaction may obtain for instances of bizarre and visibly "crazy" behavior that may result in the eventual imposition of the diagnosis of schizophrenia in the United States and in the United Kingdom. It is, however, not immediately clear why in England the diagnosticians should be selectively sensitized to depression, which, apparently, as an affect is widely experienced and accepted in that country, and why the socially deviant behavior exemplified in schizophrenia should be so poorly tolerated in the United States and especially in its socially heterogeneous and impersonal cities. Although the explanations advanced above on a post hoc basis carry a certain plausibility, the opposite pattern of results could conceivably be explained equally well by recourse to the same arguments and observations. The fact remains, however, that mental health professionals in their diagnostic capacity remain the guardians of the social limits of eccentricity. This is a state of affairs that radical critics of mental health practices and concepts such as Szasz (1961) bemoan. Many mainstream mental health professionals would accept this social function as legitimate. However, there is no denying that the confounding of the "technical" aspects of diagnosis with social judgment (Phillips & Draguns, 1971) greatly complicates the attainment of diagnostic comparability across ethnicity and culture.

Body versus Mind as a Cultural Medium of Distress

One of the major themes in the cross-cultural literature on psychopathology is the frequency of bodily complaints among the patients referred for psychological and psychiatric problems from several culturally distinct groups, especially Asian (Sue & Sue, 1987). Kleinman's (1986, 1988a, 1988b) observations of the prevalence of neurasthenia in mainland China have already been briefly mentioned. These and other findings raise the question of the locus and meaning of somatic symptoms in states of psychological dysfunction and distress. As White (1982), Kirmayer (1984), and Kleinman (1986) point out, it may be ethnocentric to dismiss these manifestations simply as a result of a lack of "psychological mindedness." Rather, culture may foster a selective sensitivity to either psychological or physiological processes that are both components of the experience of stress. "Psychologization" of stressful experiences may be the modal reaction in certain segments of the population in various European and American settings. Similarly, experience and communication of distress in China and in various other cultures may be focused upon bodily sensations and reactions, which may then be reported in greater specificity and, perhaps, with greater sensitivity and accuracy. Thus somatization, in culturally or ethnically different clients should not be dismissed as a deficit of psychological sophistication; it can be construed as a genuine skill in attending to and reporting somatic processes.

In a thorough clinical investigation of over 200 outpatients in an internal medicine clinic in Nanjing, China, Ots (1990) blended concepts drawn from Chinese traditional medicine with Western phenomenological methods of inquiry. He was able to establish connections between intense, but verbally unexpressed emotions and bodily symptoms. Thus, liver was implicated in the experience of anger, heart in anxiety, and spleen in depression. Among heart patients, 85% were found to experience anxiety and insecurity, often brought on by a threatening event, such as a challenging promotion, difficult examination, or prospect of loss of status or position.

Moreover, the contextual aspects of symptom presentation should be considered, especially as they occur across cultural lines. Encounters between a mental health professional who represents the mainstream American culture and a patient of a different cultural background may be conducted across a gap or even a chasm that many culturally different help seekers find difficult to cross. Under these circumstances, bodily distress becomes an easily communicated and perhaps a readily relieved component of a vague tangle of adverse experiences that defy being put into words to a stranger and in an imperfectly mastered language.

This is especially likely to happen if in the patient's culture somatic distress customarily evokes sympathy and concern, whereas verbal communications of aversive personal reactions are often overlooked. Such a situation has been described in China (cf. Kleinman, 1986), but may also exist in many other cultures. The Western clinician should keep in mind the prominence of the somatic channel for experiencing aspects of psychic distress in his or her clients of a different cultural provenance. In such instances, hasty referral outside of the range of personal counseling and mental health services for exclusively biomedical treatment should be avoided.

Equating Extreme Deviance with Disturbance: A Dangerous Trend

Episodic information from a variety of sources has been accumulating of instances in which conspicuous nonconformity and/or defiant disregard of social norms are all too readily assimilated into the category of psychological disturbance, usually in its most extreme varieties, often as schizophrenia. Behavior is torn from its cultural context and is quickly absorbed into the preexisting notions of a mental disorder. It will be recalled that DSM-IV explicitly cautions against this danger in its definition of mental disorder. Nonetheless, the risk of such misdiagnosis has not been removed once and for all. Two of its manifestations must now be addressed.

The most extreme instances of this distortion involve the misattribution of normal behavior patterns of an unfamiliar and highly different social group to mental disorder. This diagnostic error presupposes lack of familiarity with the potential patient's culture, a high level of cultural and social naiveté, and perhaps, inadequate conceptual understanding of diagnostic rationale, apart from gross stereotyping and, quite likely, prejudice. With the increase in cultural sophistication and diagnostic skill, it is expected that these gross diagnostic misattribution errors will decline in frequency and perhaps disappear. In any case, they should be increasingly amenable to being prevented, spotted, reversed, and corrected. Still, there are occasional shocking reports of such malfeasance in the media, one of which is recapitulated by Sue in the present volume. Another documented case study in the professional literature (Jewel, 1952) describes the hospitalization of a male Navajo for 11 months as a catatonic schizo-phrenic—just because the man was speaking his native language, which no one on the hospital staff was able to understand. In Trimble and Fleming's (1989) words, "it's not a pleasant article to read" (p. 177). It is indeed difficult to construe these cases of misdiagnosis and of the resulting mistreatment other than as instances of gross incom-petence, negligence, and irresponsibility on the part of the clinical staff. They are only mentioned here as the factually verified extreme of the consequences of cultural insensitivity and the ultimate tragic result of equating strangeness with disturbance.

Much more insidious and frequent are the instances of misdiagnosis, usually in the direction of greater chronicity or disturbance, on the basis of the interactive, and very likely multiplicative, effects of conspicuous social deviance and ab-normality. In Pennsylvania, the Amish have long had the reputation among some of the local psychiatrists to be suscep-tible to schizophrenia (Egeland, Hostetter, & Eshleman, 1983). Thorough and conclusive epidemiological research conducted as part of the search for the genetic source of affective disorder (Egeland & Hostetter, 1983; Hostetter, Egeland, & Endicott, 1983; Egeland, Hostetter, & Eshleman, 1983) has decisively dispelled this impression and has established instead the pres-ence of bipolar affective disorder. Yet, in light of explicit and reliable Research Diagnostic Criteria (Spitzer, Endicott, & Robins, 1977), manic-depressive disturbance among the Amish was misdiagnosed by experienced and qualified local diagnosticians as schizophrenic in 22 out of 28 cases. The reason for these errors, as some of the practitioners admitted on interview, was the conviction of the existence of a strong link between social deviance and schizophrenia and the inability to distinguish the two sources of disturbance. Egeland et al. (1983) quoted one of the local psychiatrists as saying: "I know the diagnosis immediately, all our Amish patients are schizophrenic" (p. 68). The tendency to overdiagnose schizophrenia in members of minority groups, as recapitulated earlier in this chapter, may be another case in point. It remains to be demonstrated that the symptoms of minority group patients were by some objective standard more socially extreme or conspicuous than those of the majority group or mainstream patients.

Interim Conclusions

Perhaps the principal conclusion from the findings summarized in this section is the recognition that the assessment operations of clinicians are susceptible to errors that can be traced to cultural barriers and disparities. This inference, however, should not be overgeneralized; numerous culturally atypical clients are realistically diagnosed by mainstream professionals, and the clinicians involved in cultural and ethnic assessment should be warned against adopting a position of extreme cultural relativism. Good (1993) concluded: "It takes a great deal of naiveté, plus a very selective reading of the literature to argue for extreme cultural relativism in the study of psychopathology. Anthropological efforts to reduce psychopathology to cultural psychology are as mistaken as psychiatry's reduction of suffering to disordered physiology" (p. 430). The cross-national surveys of schizophrenia (WHO, 1979) and depression (WHO, 1983) referred to earlier in the chapter were successful in documenting constant core symptoms of these two disorders. The cumulative results of cross-cultural research on psychological disorder provide no comfort for the proponents of radical relativist (e.g., Benedict, 1934) positions. As Good (1993) put it, "One crucial area in which research should be pursued is in investigating the cross-cultural validity in diagnostic categories, specific differences in diagnostic criteria cross-culturally, and the role of culture in the diagnostic process" (p. 430). In the remaining portions of this chapter, the reader will be guided through the succession of the available choices in this enterprise.

CONCEPTUAL AND METHODOLOGICAL OPTIONS IN CROSS-
CULTURAL RESEARCH AND ASSESSMENT: NUMEROUS AND
IMPERFECT

Equivalence: An Abiding Concern

Cross-cultural psychologists have refined and differentiated the
concept of equivalence. They have not as yet proposed a definitive
solution to this thorny and persistent problem. Table 2 presents a
condensation of the array of choices open to the investigator of cross-
cultural assessment issues. In the ideal case, the stimuli to be investigated or applied should, in several cultures, be identical physically
and semantically, stand in the same relationship to the concepts from
which they were derived, display the same functional relationship to
key behavioral variables, and have the same metric properties.

This ideal is never attained in the real world. Thus, the investigator is left to his or her choice regarding which of the above aspects
of equivalence are to be emphasized and which are to be de-empha-
sized. Although much has been written about the psychological
equivalence of stimuli that are physically nonidentical, there have as
yet been no studies in which equivalent, but physically different
stimuli have been used in the same research design. For example, the
meaning of a specific item on a verbal scale may vary across cultures.
Yet it would be rash to substitute an item equivalent in meaning, but
discrepant in content, and to use it in cross-cultural comparisons as
though it were textually identical at both sites of the investigation.

The situation is somewhat different in case-oriented assessment.
The Minnesota Multiphasic Personality Inventory (MMPI), for example, has been extensively revalidated outside of the United States
and is in use in numerous languages around the world (Butcher &
Clark, 1979). It broadly fulfills the same purpose in these settings of
providing diagnostically oriented assessment information. Its
revalidation around the world, however, has inevitably introduced
modifications in the context of its items and in their relationship to
scales. Such modifications have been deliberately kept at a minimum
in order to preserve as much as possible the relationship between the
MMPI scores and the various characteristics of the instrument. The
evaluators of this effort (Butcher & Clark, 1979) have concluded that
in its translated versions, the MMPI continues to perform its assessment function well, although invariably to different degrees, depending on the version, the country, and the specific purpose. General
trends have also been noted. By and large, the so-called psychotic
tetrad composed of elevations of Scales 6, 7, 8, and 9 has remained

Table 2. Conceptual and Methodological Problems Relevant to Cross-Cultural Assessment of Abnormal Behavior

---

Equivalence of stimuli and instruments:
       (1) physical
       (2) conceptual
       (3) contextual

Problem: Comparing equivalent stimuli that are not physically identical and physically identical stimuli that are not equivalent.
Solution: Limit comparisons to stimuli meeting criteria of (1), (2), and (3).
Cost: Restriction of range of the stimuli compared.

Comparability of samples and populations:
       (1) in distress and disability (DSM-IV-R definition of mental disorder)
       (2) in diagnosis
       (3) in demographic and social characteristics
       (4) in (premorbid) personality characteristics
       (5) in nonpersonality variables (e.g., intelligence)
       (6) in the manner of recruiting

Problem: Comparing samples/groups widely divergent in relevant characteristics.
Solution: Concentrate on (reasonably) comparable samples, use appropriate statistics (e.g., partial correlation, analysis of covariance, multivariate methods), record and note remaining discrepancies.
Caution: Avoid artificial matching.
Cost: Restriction of the scope of comparisons, limitations of generalizations.

Comparability (or identity) of concepts
       (1) diagnostic (e.g., schizophrenia, agoraphobia)
       (2) affective-motivational (e.g., anxiety, depression)

Problem: Making sure that identical words carry constant meanings.
Solution: Obtain systematic empirical data on the equivalence of concepts, use explicit rules of diagnosis and group assignment, use objective measures if valid and appropriate; employ a multimethod approach and conduct a series of studies.
Cost: Incomplete understanding of the meaning, context, and social consequences of the concepts employed.

Special Problems:
       (1) Translation of verbal materials:
           (a) back-translation
           (b) decentering
       (2) Constancy of demand characteristics and contextual variables:
           (a) verbal questionnaires
           (b) brass instrument experimentation
           (c) personal interview (intrusion)
       (3) Observer's/tester's demand characteristics:
           (a) in behavior
           (b) in subjects'/testees' perception

reasonably constant throughout translations and revalidations and can be interpreted in a convergent fashion; the neurotic triad made up of Scales 1 through 3 has shown a moderate degree of fluctuation in various cultures, which is probably traceable to a joint effect of test and person variables; and Scale 3, which measures depression, has displayed a general tendency toward elevation in translated versions by comparison to the original MMPI. None of these trends have as yet been noted on the recently revalidated MMPI-2 on the basis of the cumulative translation, adaptation, and revalidation effort, which is too new to have been applied and researched in other language areas. A network of closely related tests based on the original MMPI has been created which, however, are textually and otherwise nonidentical. In light of information on the psychometric properties of these translated and revalidated versions of the MMPI, they are capable of performing highly similar functions at their respective sites of adoption. Empirical comparisons of these cross-national adaptations, however, are frustrated by the problem of "adding apples and oranges"; even though the scales are identically numbered and labeled, they are based on highly overlapping, yet inevitably and invariably somewhat different pools of items. Thus, they can only provide the "raw materials" for comparisons on the inferential and interpretive, and hence inescapably speculative, level.

The example of the use of the MMPI across cultures and languages illustrates a problem that defies being overcome, that of physical or, in the case of verbal stimuli, textual equivalence. The other more sophisticated aspects of equivalence can and often are accommodated, but only by means of subtraction and eliminations of the questionable stimuli or items that have failed to meet the test of equivalence.

Several possible solutions to this dilemma come to mind. The investigators may construct specially designed stimuli for the purpose of a specific cross-cultural research project that would be acceptable and appropriate at the several research sites. As an alternative, simple face and/or content valid stimulus materials may be selected that would not require adaptation or revalidation at new and culturally different locations. Finally, one may envisage the simultaneous development and validity of measures at several points across cultures and their subsequent application at the several research sites. Instances of the first two methods are legion in the modern cross-cultural literature. As a rule, however, these research reports do not lead to sequential, continued, and cumulative use. They tend to remain isolated and discrete instances of application of their specially designed stimuli. The symmetrical multicultural approach of constructing stimuli of equal relevance and applicability for all the cultures to be compared has been repeatedly recommended (e.g., Draguns, 1977, 1982), but as yet has not been fully implemented in relation to the assessment of maladaptation or disturbance. Apparently, intractable practical issues stand in the way of converting this ambitious objective into reality. The available solution remains, as indicated in Table 2 (i.e., to start out with a pool of items selected at a specific point in space and time). This set of items would correspond to what Berry (1969) called the imposed etic. Its adaptation would largely entail elimination of those items that would fail to meet the criteria of nonphysical equivalence: conceptual, functional, and metric. These would be replaced by more culturally appropriate items that would also be closer to the original in the three additional criteria of equivalence. These modifications would enhance the validity and sensitivity of the instrument in the new locale; they would not, however, benefit cross-cultural research application.

MMPI in American Minority Groups: An Illustration

At this point, the present account will digress to consider an issue of practical importance in clinical assessment. The MMPI, in its original and now in its revalidated version, constitutes in the United States the most widely used self-report measure centered upon diagnostic variables. For several decades (cf., Gynther, 1972) its validity, sensitivity, and utility for use with ethnocultural minority groups, especially African Americans, has been the subject of considerable debate and argument. Gynther (1972) argued that it amounts to a prescription for discrimination to rely mechanically for diagnostic purposes with African Americans on the original MMPI, which was validated on an unrepresentative majority group sample in Minnesota in the 1930s. Pritchard and Rosenblatt (1980) countered this argument by contending that the increase of false positives (i.e., instances of misdiagnosing of African Americans free of psychological impairment) has never been demonstrated for this population. A comprehensive review by Greene (1987) has been conducted of all MMPI research involving four major American minorities: African Americans, Hispanics, American Indians, and Asian Americans. The results of this exhaustive analysis have put to rest at least some of the legitimate apprehensions concerning the use of the MMPI with minority clients. Greene's (1987) conclusions deserve to be presented in his own words:

> First, the failure to find a consistent pattern of scale differences between any two ethnic groups suggests that it is very premature to begin to develop new norms for ethnic groups. It appears that

moderator variables, such as socioeconomic status, education, and intelligence, as well as profile validity, are more important determinants of MMPI performance than ethnic status. Definitely, research is needed that examines the role of identified cultural factors on MMPI performance when appropriate controls are instituted for the multitude of factors that can affect the results. (p. 509)

Thus the conclusion of Greene's definitive review dispels the notion that the MMPI is an inherently misleading tool of diagnostic assessment for members of minority groups. It does not close the books on the issue of its appropriateness and sensitivity for minority group members or for various sections of these populations. In fact, Greene specified several urgent problems in need of research-based resolution. In keeping with a point made earlier in this chapter, he called for the assessment of subjects' identification with their ethnic group. Other suggestions include the incorporation of moderator variables, such as socioeconomic status, education, and intelligence; the identification of empirical correlates of any interethnic differences that may be established; and the extension of comparative ethnic research beyond the standard clinical scales of the MMPI to various special scales that have been designed for this instrument.

It is well worth emphasizing that these conclusions apply to the MMPI before its recently completed revision. However, because the standardization sample for MMPI-2 includes proportionate numbers of members of several prominent minority groups, it is unlikely that the problems examined in Greene's review have become more severe. Specifically, 12.5% of the subjects in the revalidation sample were African American, 3% Hispanic, 3% Native American (Butcher, 1990; Butcher, Dahlstrom, Graham, Tellegen, & Kaemmer, 1989; Graham, 1993). These figures suggest statistically proportionate representation for African American and Native Americans. It could be argued that Hispanics as well as Asians, who constitute two of the most rapidly growing ethnic groups in the United States, continue to be underrepresented. Moreover, given their rapid increase through immigration, the norms obtained may not be valid in the future. Butcher et al. (1989) have provided normative information for the four minority groups in an appendix to the MMPI-2 manual. The results that have trickled in suggest that the gap on clinical scales between African Americans and Caucasians has narrowed but not disappeared (Shondrick, Ben-Porath, & Stafford, 1992). Analogous findings have been obtained for Hispanics (Velasquez & Callahan, 1990); no relevant findings have as yet appeared for Asian or Native Americans. However, unresolved issues remain, even though steps in the right direction have been taken with MMPI-2. Greene's (1987) lead of exploring specific and limited effects of ethnicity rather than their broad overall impact has not been systematically pursued with MMPI-2. Dahlstrom, Lachar, and Dahlstrom (1986) asserted that not all interethnic differences are artifactual; this admonition should be kept in mind by users and investigators of MMPI-2.

The conclusion is still justified that the MMPI is a usable, but imperfect, tool of appraisal within the multicultural American setting, especially for the limited purpose for which it was originally designed (i.e., as a diagnostic aid). This point is well worth making in order to help steer clear of the extremes of skepticism that eventually result in psychometric nihilism and rejection of any and all tests for persons who are culturally atypical. In the case of the MMPI there appears to be no justification for this extreme course of action nor is there need for a less extreme but laborious remedy, that of developing separate norms for each minority group. However, it should also be recognized that the MMPI-2 does not as yet address the complex problems of culture by psychopathology interaction. Continuous, systematic, and sequential research remains a necessity.

THE ISSUE OF COMPARABILITY: A REPRISE

Populations and Samples

It is necessary at this point to go over the ground that has already been covered in the earlier portions of this chapter. The problem to which we now return is that of comparing members of populations that are discrepant in social and cultural background and that may be located in different habitats. In Table 2, six moderator or control variables are listed, which in the ideal case, should be equated in validational and other research across cultural boundaries. Yet, just as in the case of stimulus equivalence, this lofty goal remains beyond the range of realistic attainment. The investigator is faced with the need for spelling out priorities and deciding which of these several factors to consider important enough to control and which to disregard. There is no absolute a priori basis for this determination; the researcher is free to use his or her judgment on the basis of the needs and requirements of the research project and subjective curiosities and preferences. The ultimate test of the "correctness" of the researcher's choices would be the plausibility of alternative hypotheses that could be invoked in reference to those variables that have been left uncontrolled. In the complex and imperfect world in which, of necessity, cross-cultural research is conducted, progress toward eliminating or at least reducing the obtrusive disparities can probably only be achieved in a gradual fashion by conducting a series of studies while controlling successively for the several variables. This procedure would still leave any possible interaction effects unexplored, such as those that were revealed in the mosaic on ethnic research on the MMPI. It would, however, help the observers of the field and the users of the research findings to move closer to the objective of untangling the culture's relationships with possible moderator variables in determining the manifestations of psychological disturbance.

More comprehensive solutions can be envisaged in the form of using representative samples, as is done in modern epidemiological studies. Unfortunately, cross-cultural study of psychopathology has not yet moved beyond the reliance, dictated by circumstances, upon samples of opportunity and convenience, with all the pitfalls of haphazard selection that this mode of research implies.

Virtually all the writers on this subject are in agreement with the avoidance of artificial, individual matching across culture lines (Brislin, 1977; Brislin, Lonner, & Thorndike, 1973; Campbell & Naroll, 1972; Draguns, 1977, 1982; Guthrie & Lonner, 1985; Malpass & Poortinga, 1986). This is a seemingly rigorous technique that increases the danger of Type 2 errors while it lessens the risk of Type 1 errors. In the process, however, it generates a host of intractable problems of conceptualization and interpretation. Prominent among these is the virtual impossibility of generalizing beyond the artificially constructed samples, especially when the discrepancies between these two groups are major. Let us suppose that a match must be found for an American divorcée who, moreover, is a college graduate, professionally employed, and the mother of two young children. Let us further imagine that this woman's counterpart is sought in a hypothetical society in which divorce is exceedingly rare, women's educational opportunities are limited, and professional employment for them is virtually unknown. The result of matching, if successful, would pair a fairly typical member of the contemporary United States society with a person of exceptional opportunities and achievement in another culture. To whom could the results of such a comparison be generalized? Thus, a lot of painstaking effort often results, especially if it is applied to milieus with widely different social indicators, in findings that are virtually inapplicable to any populations within one or both settings. There is the risk, however, that the atypical, laboriously chosen subjects at one or both of the sites of the comparison will be overlooked and the results will be mindlessly extended to the typical and representative members of the two populations.

What other expedients exist for intergroup comparison? Brislin and Baumgardner (1971) proposed a simple and straightforward solution that has remained relevant to this day. They advocated the comparison of samples in their existing state, with all the discrepancies in their demographic indicators. However, they also counseled the investigators to record carefully and completely these characteristics for purposes of more refined comparisons or replications in the future. Although this suggestion continues to be viable, the development of flexible and sophisticated statistical techniques provides potential alternatives for isolating, partialing out, or otherwise reducing and perhaps eliminating disparities between samples.

Diagnostic Concepts

Little remains to be said about the operational definitions of diagnostic concepts, such as schizophrenia or depression.

The advent of rule-based diagnosis, together with computerized conversion of symptoms into diagnostic categories, has opened new avenues for checking and controlling the subjectivity and the fallibility of the clinician as well as the culturally determined slants and biases. This development has contributed to making these distortions objects of research rather than sources of uncontrollable error. The objectification of diagnostic judgments is a tremendous advance for the entire diagnostic enterprise. For culturally sensitive assessment, it has created the possibility of research-based objective diagnosis and of identifying its culturally characteristic features.

In the past, national diagnostic systems differed in the scope, nomenclature, and defining features of diagnostic entities. Thus, identical terms often masked differences in manifestations and identical symptom patterns were encompassed within differently named entities (cf. Draguns, 1980). The different modes of expression for and the diverging connotations of depression across cultures are a case in point (cf. Marsella, 1980). These effects have been shown to operate within the professional mental health community and in the lay public (cf. Tanaka-Matsumi & Marsella, 1976), sometimes in a parallel manner (cf. Townsend, 1975).

Verbal Instruments

The procedures for assuring the equivalence of verbal scales and tests across language (Brislin, 1970, 1976) are well known and widely practiced and scarcely need to be reiterated at this point. They hinge on the pivot of independent back-translation as the indispensable safeguard for textual equivalence across language. This problem can be considered to have been technically solved. A still open issue concerns the connotations of specific words, phrases, and terms and their affective valence, not only across languages, but also across cultural and ethnic groups within the same linguistic community. In the case of bilinguals, the connotations of words and statements in their first language, which often persists as the means of communication of subjective and affective experience, remain to be systematically investigated. As yet, there are no bases for recommending a specific course of action in these situations for the clinicians involved in assessment.

Formats and Contexts of Investigation

Interviewers and examiners immersed in their professional activity may assume intercultural uniformity in the prevailing modes and formats of assessment. In particular, the limited-option group format of testing has long been a fixture of the United States educational system and of personnel and employment settings. It is all too easy to overlook the culture-bound character of these activities. Boesch (1971) in Germany has made the point that self-disclosure is a worldwide phenomenon, but its expression through the true-false, forced-choice, or Likert-scale format is a development that originated and spread at a specific point in time and space. As yet, there are no systematic comparisons of reactions and attitudes to this mode of testing across cultures. Episodic observations and anecdotal evidence suggest that both normal volunteers and hospitalized psychiatric patients in continental European countries (e.g., Germany) are a lot more resistant to responding to biographical and personal inquiry by the objective, limited-options methods than are their counterparts in North America. Conceivably, similar ambivalence and reluctance may also be experienced by members of some ethnic groups within the United States. This phenomenon appears to be worth exploring, the more so since the worldwide trend toward automatization and computerization may cause it to wane and eventually to disappear. Even then, however, there may remain culturally mediated differences in readiness to share personal information with nobody in particular, on somebody else's terms.

A striking, if isolated, demonstration from Japan by Lazarus, Tomita, Opton, and Kodama (1966) points to the global affective effects of testing overriding the valence of specific arousing stimuli. Japanese subjects showed increased skin conductance across all conditions of the experiment, in contrast to Americans who displayed the expected variations to arousing vs. neutral stimuli. Lazarus et al. tentatively interpreted this finding as indicative of the Japanese subjects' increased sensitivity to the global experimental situation. This finding needs to be extended and replicated before any conclusions are drawn concerning the interplay of cultural and social factors that have produced it. At this point, it only suggests the possibility of culturally variable meanings of the formats and contexts of assessments.

Social Climate or Atmosphere: The Examiner's or Observer's Contribution.

Diaz-Guerrero and Diaz-Loving (1990) recently have called attention to a hitherto neglected source of cross-cultural variation to the assessment enterprise. In a comparison of personality characteristics of school children in Mexico City and Austin, Texas (Holtzman, Diaz-Guerrero, & Swartz, 1975), examiners were found to display strikingly different demeanor, even though they were identically trained to administer the project measures. In the words of Diaz-Guerrero and Diaz-Loving (1990),

> The American tester was detached and, to the Mexican observers, cold. The American child was absorbed, challenged, and involved with the tasks. He/she gave to most of the observers the impression of competing with the tester. The noise level and commotion were minimal. The Mexican tester was vehement and expressive—to the American observers, overly warm. The Mexican child was responsive and involved in the interpersonal relation; it seemed that he/she wanted to please the tester with good answers to the tests. The noise level and commotion seemed high to the American observers. (p. 491)

Holtzman et al. (1975) decided to accept these divergent interactions as components of the cultures they were studying. Another option, open to future investigators, is to incorporate these variations into the research design and to establish their impact upon the subjects' responses. As yet, this step has not been taken. Once the contribution of the examiner to the social climate of the assessment experience is established, interviewers and testers could accommodate to the culturally based expectations of their clients and thereby facilitate optimal responsiveness and self-expression.

CONCLUSIONS

The field of cross-cultural assessment of psychological disturbance is in a state of flux and precarious balance. It is torn between the imperative of equivalence and the ideal of sensitivity. Simultaneously, culturally oriented researchers strive to both capture personal experience in its culturally unique richness and complexity while they try to fit these observations into some kind of a universally comparable mold. All too often, however, they find that the pursuit of these two goals cannot be easily reconciled. The partial solution to this dilemma that comes to mind combines rigor in the research phases of this undertaking with flexibility in its application in a practical service context. Precision and objectivity are called for in determining the person's relationship to both his or her original and host cultures, and the field of cross-cultural assessment has made a significant spurt toward developing empirically based and practically applicable instruments to that end. Diagnostic instruments and scales have moved considerably from their intuitive, subjective and often culture-bound beginnings. Most important, the new diagnostic system, embodied in DSM-IV, has incorporated cultural considerations into its rationale and has recognized the relevance of cultural information for diagnostic activities. Moreover, the advent of objectified and explicit rules of diagnosis represents a tremendous advance in research determination of psychological disorder. Yet it is at the very least incautious to apply such rules in a practical context in which decisions about living persons are involved. The mindless use of cutoff scores of tests in educational, mental health, personnel, and counseling contexts is to be avoided, especially with a multicultural clientele. The impact of culture upon adaptation is best conceived as a dynamic interplay of forces rather than as a static and finite entity that affects the person's functioning once and for all.

Starting out as the younger sibling of the better developed field of the cross-cultural assessment of cognitive and other abilities, the assessment of psychological disturbance has made inconspicuous and undramatic, but still perceptible progress over the last 30 years. One has only to compare the impressionistic and semi-intuitive pronouncements of the post-World War II culture-and-personality era and the confounding of evidence, inference, and speculation that characterized that period of time with the methodological and conceptual self-consciousness and sophistication that have by now emerged in research and practice. Cross-cultural assessment of psychological disorder has experienced nothing like the advance that the related and more inclusive field of cross-cultural measurement of aptitudes and abilities has achieved. There is nothing in it to compare with the two landmark conferences on mental tests and cultural adaptation (Cronbach & Drenth, 1972) and human assessment and cultural factors (Irvine & Berry, 1983). Nonetheless, there has been accretion of sound data, development of new methods, and evolution of more fitting concepts (Draguns, 1990a, 1990b). The future of the field, to the extent that it can be discerned, is likely to be characterized by a flexible reliance on a multimethod and multiperspective approach, with the prospect of a definitive integration into a multifaceted and complex cognitive structure of facts, concepts, and their interrelationships. Recognition has been gaining currency that cross-cultural assessment is difficult, yet possible to implement.

In evaluating the results of a major conference on human assessment and cultural factors, Cronbach (1983) suggested that "the search for universal relationships is self-defeating" (p. VIII). As I understand his statement, Cronbach voiced skepticism concerning the prospect of discovery of main effects of culture upon behavior and experience that would be simple to formulate and easy to assess. The search for such universals on the planes of both conceptualization and assessment is reminiscent of the quest for culture-free or at least culture-fair tests of intelligence about 50 years ago. By now the hope of ever constructing such a generally applicable instrument has been largely abandoned. Instead, investigators in the field have redirected their efforts toward designing measures of intelligence for specific populations at their respective sites and contexts. Similarly, the agenda for the cross-cultural assessment of adaptive and maladaptive patterns of behavior calls for a multitude of piecemeal efforts toward describing the predicament of human beings as they struggle with their frustrations and challenges in their specific cultural milieus. To this end, the clinician should be on guard against two major and grievous cognitive errors. One of them involves pigeonholing clients into their respective standard diagnostic rubrics and the other entails stereotyping persons on the basis of their culture or ethnicity. Especially ominous is the conjunction of these two tendencies which, in their extreme form, results in equating social deviance with psychological disturbance. The danger of glossing over individual differences within cultural and/or diagnostic category must ever be kept in mind and the possibility of reciprocal, interacting, and dynamic influences linking culture and psychopathology should not be overlooked. Moreover, a sensitive assessment effort would involve both ability and readiness on the part of theoreticians, researchers, and practitioners to shuttle their perspectives between the emic and the etic, the quantitative and the qualitative, the categorical and the continuous, and the personal and the contextual. If such flexibility is attained and maintained, there is reason to hope that culturally specific and humanly universal facets of a complex human structure will be disentangled. Such a development has the potential of elucidating the process of coping with challenges of adaptation on the basis of individual resources, cultural assets, and general human potential. How these threads intertwine is a story that is gradually unfolding as information is accumulated about people of different cultural backgrounds coping with their aspirations, stresses, and problems.

REFERENCES

Adebimpe, V. R. (1981). Overview: White norms and psychiatric diagnosis of Black patients. *American Journal of Psychiatry, 138*, 279-285.

Adebimpe, V. R. (1984). American Blacks and psychiatry. *Transcultural Psychiatric Research Review, 21*, 81-111.

American Psychiatric Association. (1994). *Diagnostic and statistical manual of mental disorders* (4th ed.). Washington, DC: American Psychiatric Association.

Beck, A. T., Steer, R. A., & Garbin, M. (1988). Psychometric properties of the Beck Depression Inventory: Twenty-five years of evaluation. *Clinical Psychology Review, 8*, 77-100.

Benedict, R. (1934). Culture and the abnormal. *Journal of General Psychology, 10*, 59-82.

Berman, J. (1979). Individual versus societal focus in problem diagnosis of black and white male and female counselors. *Journal of Cross-Cultural Psychology, 10*, 497-507.

Bernal, G. (1982). Cuban families. In M. McGoldrick, J. K. Pearce, & J. Giordano (Eds.), *Ethnicity and family therapy* (pp. 187-207). New York: Guilford Press.

Berry, J. W. (1969). On cross-cultural comparability. *International Journal of Psychology, 4*, 119-128.

Berry, J. W. (1972). Radical cultural relativism and the concept of intelligence. In L. J. Cronbach & P. J. D. Drenth (Eds.), *Mental tests and cultural adaptation* (pp. 77-88). The Hague, Netherlands: Mouton.

Berry, J. W. (1990). Psychology of acculturation. In J. J. Berman (Ed.), *Nebraska Symposium on Motivation 1989* (pp. 201-234). Lincoln: University of Nebraska Press.

Berry, J. W., Poortinga, Y. H., Segall, M. H., & Dasen, P. R. (1992). *Cross-cultural psychology*. New York: Cambridge University Press.

Betancourt, H., & López, S. R. (1993). The study of culture, ethnicity, and race in American psychology. *American Psychologist, 48*, 629-637.

Billigmeier, K. H. (1974). *Americans from Germany: A study in cultural diversity*. Belmont, CA: Wadsworth.

Boesch, E. E. (1971). *Zwischen zwei Wirklichkeiten (Between two realities)*. Berne: Huber.

Bourque, P., & Beaudette, D. (1982). Étude psychométrique du questionnaire de dépression de Beck aupres d'un echantillon d'étudiants univesitaires francophones. *Canadian Journal of Behavioural Science, 14,* 211-218.

Brislin, R. W. (1970). Back-translation for cross-cultural research. *Journal of Cross-Cultural Psychology, 1,* 185-216.

Brislin, R. W. (1976). *Translation: Application and research.* New York: Garden Press.

Brislin, R. W. (1977). Methodology of cognitive studies. In G. Kearney & D. McElwain (Eds.), *Aboriginal cognition* (pp. 29-53). Canberra: Australia Institute for Aboriginal Studies.

Brislin, R. W. (1983). Cross-cultural research in psychology. *Annual Review of Psychology, 34,* 363-400.

Brislin, R. W., & Baumgardner, S. R. (1971). Non-random sampling of individuals in cross-cultural research. *Journal of Cross-Cultural Psychology, 2,* 397-400.

Brislin, R. W., Lonner, W. J., & Thorndike, R. M. (1973). *Cross-cultural research methods.* New York: Wiley.

Butcher, J. (1990). *Assessing patients in psychotherapy: Use of the MMPI-2 for treatment planning.* New York: Oxford University Press.

Butcher, J. N., & Clark, L. A. (1979). Recent trends in cross-cultural MMPI research. In J. N. Butcher (Ed.), *New developments in the use of the MMPI* (pp. 69-112). Minneapolis: University of Minnesota Press.

Butcher, J. N., Dahlstrom, W. G., Graham, J. R., Tellegen, A., & Kaemmer, B. (1989). *Minnesota Multiphasic Personality Inventory—2 (MMPI-2): Manual for administration and scoring.* Minneapolis: University of Minnesota Press.

Campbell, D. T., & Naroll, R. (1972). The mutual methodological relevance of anthropology and psychology. In F. L. K. Hsu (Ed.), *Psychological anthropology* (new ed.) (pp. 435-468). Cambridge, MA: Schenkman.

Casas, J. M., & Vasquez, M. J. T. (1989). Counseling the Hispanic client: A theoretical and applied perspective. In P. B. Pedersen, J. G. Draguns, W. J. Lonner, & J. E. Trimble (Eds.), *Counseling across cultures* (3rd ed.) (pp. 153-176). Honolulu: University Press of Hawaii.

Clark, L. A. (1987). Mutual relevance of mainstream and cross-cultural psychology. *Journal of Consulting and Clinical Psychology, 55,* 461-470.

Cole, M., & Bruner, J. S. (1972). Cultural differences and inferences about psychological processes. *American Psychologist, 26,* 867-876.

Conde, V., Esteban, T., & Useros, E. (1976). Revisión critica de la adoptación castellana del cuestionario de Beck. *Revista de Psicología General y Aplicada, 31,* 469-491.

Cooper, J. E., Kendell, R. E., Gurland, B. J., Sharpe, L., Copeland, J. R. M., & Simon, R. (1972). *Psychiatric diagnosis in New York and London*. New York: Oxford University Press.

Cronbach, L. J. (1983). Foreword. In S. H. Irvine & J. W. Berry (Eds.), *Human assessment and cultural factors* (p. vii-ix). New York: Plenum Press.

Cronbach, L. J., & Drenth, P. J. (Eds.), (1972). *Mental tests and cultural adaptation*. The Hague: Mouton.

Dahlstrom, W. G., Lachar, D., & Dahlstrom, L. E. (1986). *MMPI patterns of American minorities*. Minnesota: University of Minnesota Press.

DeHoyos, A., & DeHoyos, G. (1965). Symptomatology differentials between Negro and white schizophrenics. *International Journal of Social Psychiatry, 11*, 245-255.

Delay, J., Pichot, P., Lemperiere, T., & Mirouze, R. (1963). La nosologie des états dépressifs. Rapports entre étiologie et la sémiologie, Résultats du Questionnaire de Beck. *Encéphale, 52*, 497-505.

Diaz-Guerrero, R., & Diaz-Loving, R. (1990). Interpretation in cross-cultural personality assessment. In C. R. Reynolds & R. W. Kamphaus (Eds.), *Handbook of psychological and educational assessment of children: Personality, behavior, and context* (pp. 491-523). New York: Guilford.

Dohrenwend, B. P., & Dohrenwend, B. S. (1969). *Social status and psychological disorder: A causal inquiry*. New York: Wiley.

Draguns, J. G. (1973). Comparisons of psychopathology across cultures: Issues, findings, directions. *Journal of Cross-Cultural Psychology, 4*, 9-47.

Draguns, J. G. (1977). Advances in methodology of cross-cultural psychiatric assessment. *Transcultural Psychiatric Research Review, 14*, 125-143.

Draguns, J. G. (1980). Disorders of clinical severity. In H. C. Triandis & J. G. Draguns (Eds.), *Handbook of cross-cultural psychology: Psychopathology* (vol. 6) (pp. 99-174). Boston: Allyn & Bacon.

Draguns, J. G. (1982). Methodology in cross-cultural psychopathology. In I. Al-Issa (Ed.), *Culture and psychopathology* (pp. 33-70). Baltimore: University Park Press.

Draguns, J. G. (1990a). Applications of cross-cultural psychology in the field of mental health. In R. W. Brislin (Ed.), *Applied cross-cultural psychology* (pp. 302-324). Newbury Park, CA: Sage.

Draguns, J. G. (1990b). Culture and psychopathology: Toward specifying the nature of the relationship. In J. Berman (Ed.), *Cross-cultural perspectives: Nebraska Symposium on Motivation 1989* (pp. 235-277). Lincoln: University of Nebraska.

Egeland, J. A., & Hostetter, A. M. (1983). Amish study I: Affective disorder among the Amish, 1976-1980. *American Journal of Psychiatry, 140*, 56-61.

Egeland, J. A., Hostetter, A. M., & Eshleman, S. K. (1983). Amish study III: The impact of cultural factor on diagnosis of bipolar illness. *American Journal of Psychiatry, 140*, 67-71.

Eisenbruch, M. (1992). Toward a culturally sensitive DSM: Cultural bereavement in Cambodian refugees and the traditional healer as a taxonomist. *Journal of Nervous and Mental Disease, 180*, 8-10.

Falicov, C. J. (1982). Mexican families. In M. McGoldrick, J. K. Pearce, & J. Giordano (Eds.), *Ethnicity and family therapy* (pp. 134-163). New York: Guilford Press.

Fabrega, J., Jr. (1992). Diagnosis interminable: Toward a culturally sensitive DSM-IV. *Journal of Nervous and Mental Disease, 180*, 5-7.

Garcia-Preto, N. (1982). Puerto Rican families. In M. McGoldrick, J. K. Pearce, & J. Giordano (Eds.), *Ethnicity and family therapy* (pp. 164-186). New York: Guilford Press.

Good, B. J. (1993). Culture, diagnosis, and comorbidity. *Culture, Medicine, and Psychiatry, 16*, 427-446.

Graham, J. R. (1993). *MMPI-2: Assessing personality and psychopathology* (2nd ed.). New York: Oxford University Press.

Greene, R. L. (1987). Ethnicity and MMPI performance: A review. *Journal of Consulting and Clinical Psychology, 55*, 497-512.

Guthrie, G. M., & Lonner, W. J. (1985). Assessment of personality and psychopathology. In W. J. Lonner & J. W. Berry (Eds.), *Field methods in cross-cultural research* (pp. 231-264). Beverly Hills: Sage Publications.

Gynther, M. (1972). White norms and black MMPI's: A prescription for discrimination? *Psychological Bulletin, 78*, 386-402.

Hamilton, M. (1967). Development of a rating scale for primary depressive illness. *British Journal of Social and Clinical Psychology, 6*, 278-296.

Herskovits, M. J. (1949). *Man and his works: The science of cultural anthropology.* New York: Knopf.

Holtzman, W. H., Diaz-Guerrero, R., & Swartz, J. D. (1975). *Personality development in two cultures.* Austin: University of Texas Press.

Hostetter, J. A. (1980). *The Amish society* (3rd ed.). Baltimore: John Hopkins University Press.

Hostetter, A. M., Egeland, J. A., & Endicott, J. (1983). Amish study II: Consensus diagnoses and reliability results. *American Journal of Psychiatry, 140*, 62-66.

Irvine, S. H., & Berry, J. W. (1983). *Human assessment and cultural factors.* New York: Plenum Press.

Isajiw, W. (1974). Definitions of ethnicity. *Ethnicity, 1*, 111-124.

Isajiw, W. W. (1990). Ethnic identity retention. In R. Breton, W. W. Isajiw, W. E. Kalbach, & J. G. Reitz (Eds.), *Ethnic identity and equality* (pp. 34-91). Toronto: University of Toronto Press.

Jewel, D. P. (1952). A case of a psychotic Navaho Indian male. *Human Organization, 11*(11), 32-36.

Kagitcibasi, C., & Berry, J. W. (1989). Cross-cultural psychology: Current research and trends. *Annual Review of Psychology, 40*, 493-531.

Kammer, D. (1983). Eine Untersuchung der psychometrischen Eigenschaften des deutschen Depression Fragebogens von Beck. *Diagnostica, 29*, 48-60.

Katz, M. M., Sanborn, K. O., Lowery, H. A., & Ching, J. (1978). Ethnic studies in Hawaii: On psychopathology and social deviance. In L. C. Wynne, R. L. Cromwell, & S. Mathysse (Eds.), *The nature of schizophrenia: New approaches to research and treatment.* (pp. 572-585). New York: Wiley.

King, L. M. (1978). Social and cultural influences upon psychopathology. *Annual Review of Psychology, 29*, 405-434.

Kinzie, J. D., Manson, S. M., Vinh, D. T., Tolan, N. T., Anh, B., & Pho, T. N. (1982). Development and validation of a Vietnamese-language depression rating scale. *American Journal of Psychiatry, 139*, 1276-1281.

Kirmayer, L. (1984). Culture, affect, and somatization: Parts 1 and 2. *Transcultural Psychiatric Research Review, 21*, 159-188 & 237-262.

Kleinman, A. (1982). Neurasthenia and depression: A study of somatization and culture in China. *Culture, Medicine, and Psychiatry, 6*, 117-190.

Kleinman, A. (1986). *Social origins in distress and disease.* New Haven: Yale University Press.

Kleinman, A. (1988a). *Rethinking psychiatry: From cultural category to personal experience.* New York: Free Press.

Kleinman, A. (1988b). *The illness narratives: Suffering, healing, and the human condition.* New York: Basic Books.

Lazarus, R. S., Tomita, M., Opton, E., & Kodama, M. (1966). A cross-cultural study of stress-reaction patterns in Japan. *Journal of Personality and Social Psychology, 4*, 622-633.

LeVine, R. A. (1984). Properties of culture: An ethnographic view. In R. Shweder & R. A. LeVine (Eds.), *Culture theory: Essays in mind, theory, and emotion.* (pp. 67-87). Cambridge: Cambridge University Press.

Li-Ripac, D. (1980). Cultural influences on clinical perception: A comparison of Caucasian and Chinese American therapists. *Journal of Cross-Cultural Psychology, 11*, 327-342.

López, S. R. (1989). Patient variable biases in clinical judgment: Conceptual overview and methodological considerations. *Psychological Bulletin, 106*, 184-203.

López, S. R., & Hernandez, P. (1992). How culture is considered in evaluations of psychopathology. *Journal of Nervous and Mental Disease, 176*, 598-606.

López, S. R., Hurwicz, M., Karno, M., & Telles, C. A. (1992). *Schizophrenic and manic symptoms in a community smple: A sociocultural analysis.* Unpublished manuscript. (Cited in Betancourt & López, 1993.)

Malpass, R. S., & Poortinga, Y. H. (1986). Strategies for design and analysis. In. W. J. Lonner & J. W. Berry (Eds.), *Field methods in cross-cultural research* (pp. 47-84). Beverly Hills, CA: Sage Publications.

Marsella, A. (1980). Depressive experience and disorder across cultures. In H. C. Triandis & J. G. Draguns (Eds.), *Handbook of cross-cultural psychology* (vol. 6) (pp. 237-290). Boston: Allyn & Bacon.

Marsella, A. J., Kinzie, D., & Gordon, P. (1973). Ethnic variations in the expression of depression. *Journal of Cross-Cultural Psychology, 4*, 435-458.

Mukherjee, S., Shukla, S., Woodle, J., Rosen, A. M., & Olarte, S. (1983). Misdiagnosis of schizophrenia in bipolar patients: A multiethnic comparison. *American Journal of Psychiatry, 140*, 1571-1574.

Naroll, R. (1970). The culture bearing unit in cross-cultural surveys. In R. Naroll & R. Cohen (Eds.), *Handbook of method in cultural anthropology* (pp. 721-765). New York: Natural History Press.

Ots, T. (1990). The angry liver, the anxious heart and the melancholy spleen: The phenomenology of perceptions in Chinese culture. *Culture, Medicine and Psychiatry, 14*, 21-58.

Pfeiffer, W. (1994). *Transkulturelle Psychiatrie.* (2nd ed.). Stuttgart: Thieme.

Phillips, L., & Draguns, J. G. (1971). Classification of the behavior disorders. *Annual Review of Psychology, 22*, 447-482.

Pike, K. L. (1967). *Language in relation to a unified theory of the structure of human behavior.* The Hague, Netherlands: Mouton.

Phinney, J. S. (1990). Ethnic identity in adolescence and adulthood: A review of research. *Psychological Bulletin, 108*, 499-544.

Pritchard, D. A., & Rosenblatt, A. (1980). Reply to Gynther and Green. *Journal of Consulting and Clinical Psychology, 48*, 273-274.

Radford, M. H. B. (1989). *Culture, depression, and decision making behaviour: A study with Japanese and Australian clinical and non-clinical populations.* Unpublished doctoral dissertation, Flinders University of South Australia.

Ridley, C. R. (1989). Racism in counseling as an aversive behavioral process. In P. B. Pedersen, J. G. Draguns, W. J. Lonner, & J. E. Trimble (Eds.), *Counseling across cultures* (3rd ed.) (pp. 55-78). Honolulu: University of Hawaii Press.

Rivera Ramos, A. N. (1984). *Hacia una psicoterapia para el puertoriqueño.* San Juan, Puerto Rico: Centro para el Estudio y Desarollo de la personalidad puertoriqueña.

Segall, M. H. (1986). Culture and behavior: Psychology in global perspective. *Annual Review of Psychology, 37,* 523-564.

Shondrick, D. D., Ben-Porath, Y. S., & Stafford, K. P. (1992, May) *Forensic applications of MMPI-2.* Paper presented at the 27th Annual Symposium on Recent Developments in the Use of the MMPI (MMPI-2 and MMPI-A). Minneapolis, MN.

Simons, R. C., & Hughes, C. S. (Eds.). (1985). *The culture-bound syndromes: Folk illnesses of psychiatric and anthropological interest.* Dordrecht, Holland: D. Reidel.

Sodowsky, G. R., Lai, E. W. M., & Plake, B. (1991). Moderating effects of sociocultural variables on acculturation attitudes of Hispanics and Asian Americans. [Special issue. Multiculturalism as a fourth force.] *Journal of Counseling and Development. 70,* 194-204.

Sodowsky, G. R., & Plake, B. (1991). Psychometric properties of the American-International Relational Scale. *Educational and Psychological Measurement, 51,* 207-216.

Sodowsky, G. R., Kwan, K. L., & Pannu, R. (1995). Ethnic identity of Asians in the United States. In J. G. Ponterotto, M. Casas, L. Suzuki, & C. Alexander (Eds.). *Handbook of multicultural counseling* (pp 123-154). Thousand Oaks, CA: Sage.

Spitzer, R., Endicott, J., & Robins, E. (1977). *Research diagnostic criteria (RDC) for a selected group of functional disorders* (3rd Ed.). New York: New York State Psychiatric Institute Biometrics Research.

Sue, D., Sue, D. W., & Sue, S. (1981). *Understanding abnormal behavior.* Boston: Houghton Mifflin.

Sue, D., & Sue, S. (1987). Cultural factors in the clinical assessment of Asian Americans. *Journal of Consulting and Clinical Psychology, 55,* 479-487.

Szapocznik, J., & Kurtines, W. M. (1993). Family psychology and cultural diversity. Opportunities for theory, research, and application. *American Psychologist, 48,* 400-407.

Szapocznik, J., Scopetta, M., Kurtines, W., & Aranalde, M. (1978). Theory and measurement of acculturation. *International Journal of Psychology, 12*, 113-130.

Szasz, T. S. (1961). *The myth of mental illness: Foundations of a theory of personal conduct.* New York: Harper & Row.

Taft, R. (1977). Coping with unfamiliar cultures. In N. Warren (Ed.), *Studies in cross-cultural psychology* (vol. 1) (pp. 121-151). London: Academic Press.

Tanaka-Matsumi, J., & Marsella, A. J. (1976). Cross-cultural variations in the phenomenological experience of depression: Part I, Word association studies. *Journal of Cross-Cultural Psychology, 7,* 379-396.

Townsend, J. M. (1975). Cultural conceptions and mental illness: A controlled comparison of Germany and America. *Journal of Nervous and Mental Disease, 160,* 409-421.

Triandis, H. C. (1972). *The analysis of subjective culture.* New York: Wiley.

Trimble, J. E., & Fleming, C. M. (1989). Providing counseling services for Native American Indians: Clients, counselor, and community characteristics. In P. B. Pedersen, J. G. Draguns, W. J. Lonner & J. E. Trimble (Eds.), *Counseling across cultures* (3rd ed.). Honolulu: University of Hawaii Press.

Velasquez, R. J., & Callahan, W. J. (1990). MMPI comparisons of Hispanic-and White-American veterans seeking treatment for alcoholism. *Psychological Reports, 67,* 95-98.

White, G. (1982). The role of cultural explanations in "somatization" and "psychologization." *Social Science and Medicine, 16,* 1519-1530.

Winawer-Steiner, H., & Wetzel, N. A. (1982). German families. In M. McGoldrick, J. K. Pearce, & J. Giordano (Eds.), *Ethnicity and family therapy* (pp. 247-268). New York: Guilford Press.

World Health Organization. (1979). *Schizophrenia: An international follow-up study.* New York: Wiley.

World Health Organization. (1983). *Depressive disorders in different cultures: Report on the WHO collaborative study on standardized assessment of depressive disorders.* Geneva: World Health Organization.

Zeldine, G., Ahvi, R., Leuckx, R., Boussat, M., Saibou, A., Haanck, C., Collignon, R., Tourame, G., & Collomb, H. (1975). A propos de l'utilisation d'une échelle d'évaluation en psychiatrie transculturelle. *Encéphale, NS, 1,* 133-145.

Zung, W. W. K. (1969). A cross-cultural survey of symptoms in depression. *Archives of General Psychiatry, 126,* 116-121.

Zung, W. W. K. (1972). A cross-cultural survey of depressive symptomatology in normal adults. *Journal of Cross-Cultural Psychology, 3,* 177-184.

DEVELOPMENT OF TEMAS, A MULTICULTURAL THEMATIC APPERCEPTION TEST: PSYCHOMETRIC PROPERTIES AND CLINICAL UTILITY

Giuseppe Costantino

Lutheran Medical Center & Fordham University

Robert G. Malgady

New York University

INTRODUCTION

The propriety of administering psychological tests standardized on nonminority, middle-class, and English-speaking populations to examinees who are not fluent in English or are from culturally or demographically diverse backgrounds has been a controversial topic for over five decades (Dana, 1993b; Olmedo, 1981). Although the controversy originally surrounded intelligence testing of Blacks, similar allegations of bias toward Hispanics have been raised in the

Parts of this chapter were published in Costantino, G., Malgady, R., & Rogler, L. (1988). *TEMAS (Tell-Me-A-Story) Manual*, Western Psychological Services, Los Angeles, CA. The authors would like to thank Drs. Jean Bailey, Mark Rand, Robert Steneir (Sunset Park Mental Health Center of Lutheran Medical Center) and Robert Lopez (San John's University) for contributing test results and clinical protocols for Case Studies 2 and 3 in this chapter.

context of personality testing and diagnostic evaluation, a topic which is our present focus. The prevailing view is that in the absence of empirical evidence to the contrary, standard mental health evaluation procedures are considered unbiased (e.g., Lopez, 1988). The other side of the polemic argues that clients' variations in English-language proficiency, cultural background, or demographic profile pose potential sources of bias for standard assessment and diagnostic practices (e.g., Dana, 1993b; Malgady, Rogler, & Costantino, 1987). That is, behavior recorded in an assessment situation—whether by symptom rating scale, projective test or face-to-face psychiatric interview—may present a distorted image of the attributes the assessment process is intended to reveal. Even in the absence of compelling empirical evidence, we argue that assessment procedures ought not to be routinely generalized to different cultural groups, and multicultural tests and assessments should be increasingly used (Costantino, 1992; 1993; Malgady, 1990, 1996).

This chapter first presents a review of selected literature on the topic of multicultural assessment. This literature is organized according to a variety of definitions of test bias in accordance with psychometric tradition: face and content validity, mean differences, factor invariance, differential validity/prediction, and measurement equivalence. We then turn to a specific effort to develop a "culturally sensitive" psychological assessment technique for pluralistic groups: the TEMAS ("Tell-Me-A-Story") test. Developmental and psychometric research on this test has been conducted on Hispanic children and adolescents, as well as Blacks and Whites. Finally, the clinical utility of the TEMAS test is illustrated through the presentation of three case studies.

PSYCHOMETRIC DEFINITIONS OF BIAS

Face and Content Validity

At the most rudimentary level, polemics persist about apparent bias in the nature of symptom indicators and diagnostic criteria defining psychopathology in the context of mainstream American society. Some items in widely used assessment devices such as the Minnesota Multiphasic Personality Inventory (MMPI) refer to culturally patterned behaviors, beliefs, and feelings that are not pathological in certain Hispanic subcultures (Padilla & Ruiz, 1975). For example, Rogler and Hollingshead's (1985) discussion of the salience of spiritualistic beliefs in traditional Puerto Rican culture, such as mental illness being caused by the invasion of evil spirits, challenges the apparent validity of test items or interview questions inferring pathology from spiritualistic responses. Others in cross-cultural psychiatry have raised similar concerns about the danger of ethnocentrism in defining psychopathology, that is taking an "etic" perspective rather than an "emic" view from within the culture of concern (Dana, 1993b; Kleinman & Good, 1985). Without belaboring this point, such challenges are tantamount to psychometric questions of face validity: Does the test or psychiatric interview elicit an *ostensibly* valid assessment in the context of the client's culture? Two observations emerge in attempting to answer this question.

First, many of the allegations of apparent invalid assessment of minorities are largely impelled by argument from counter-examples; to our knowledge no research has attempted to shed empirical light on face validity. To do so, research on face validity might address whether or not items suspected of bias on commonly used psychological scales or suspect psychodiagnostic criteria provide an assessment that is concordant or discordant with other items or diagnostic criteria that are beyond reproach. Such research would reveal not only the extent to which particular measures or diagnoses appear biased, but also would suggest whether differential clinical assessments are obtained with and without the suspect items or criteria.

The second observation is that, if face validity concerns are consequential to assessment and diagnosis, research needs to disentangle culturally patterned behavior from pathological behavior. It is probably safe to assume that there are some Hispanics and culturally diverse individuals who feel possessed by spirits because of their cultural predisposition to interpret symptomatology in this manner, as well as others who report being possessed because they are schizophrenic. Awareness of culturally patterned behavior is well intentioned, but does not imply that behavioral signals associated with dysfunction in the mainstream culture should be disregarded just because they may have mainstream cultural roots. Research is needed that not only identifies which behaviors are of questionable mental health significance for cultural reasons, but also provides empirical evidence of how cultural and pathological behavior can be discriminated in minority clients. As Lopez and Hernandez (1987) suggested, there is a lack of attention to cultural nuances in standard diagnostic criteria, such as the *Diagnostic and Statistical Manual of Mental Disorders* (DSM-III-R). In the absence of guidelines for how to take culture into account in diagnosis, Lopez and Hernandez found that clinicians tend to develop their own notions of how cultural information is considered in a diagnostic situation. Unfortunately, uninformed clinicians may be disregarding their client's culture, and misinformed clinicians may be indiscriminately applying cultural stereotypes to culturally diverse people, who may differ substantially in language proficiency, acculturation, and demographic background.

The face validity issue clearly affects a related issue of content validity. If standardized test items or DSM-IV criteria that are suspected or eventually known to be biased were discarded, the remaining content could well represent an inadequate sample of the behavioral domain, which is the intention of measurement or diagnosis. Thus, efforts to refine current assessment procedures cannot be merely reductionistic. They must also be reconstructive to ensure that key elements of minority clients' cultures are not lost in the definition of psychopathology. There is a need to define which symptom indicators and diagnostic criteria cross cultures and which are unique to a given cultural context.

Thus, the available evidence on bias in face and content validity is *qualitative*. Cross-cultural research is needed that examines *quantitative* formulations of the face and content validity of diagnosis and measurement of pathological behavior among Hispanic populations. Bias in face and content validity has been argued exhaustively, but empirical research on measurement outcomes is still lacking.

Mean Differences Between Populations

A second way in which bias is psychometrically defined is in terms of different normative profiles between ethnic or cultural groups. Psychological assessment conventionally implies a comparison of an individual's behavior or performance with that of a norm group. The issue of differential normative performance and the attendant question of whether ethnic-specific norms need to be developed are prominent in the minority assessment literature (e.g., Rogler, Malgady, & Rodriguez, 1989). Even in unstructured situations, such as routine psychiatric interviews where clinicians do not explicitly refer to normative data, a minority client is implicitly compared with the clinician's Anglo-American perception of pathology. Although it is debatable whether or not Hispanics have higher psychiatric prevalence and symptomatology rates than other ethnic groups (Lopez, 1988; Malgady, Rogler, & Costantino, 1988), when epidemiological studies have reported higher prevalence rates and higher levels of symptomatology among Hispanics, such findings have been questioned on the basis that they reflect biases of the Anglo-American culture (e.g., Good & Good, 1986).

Using the Hispanic Health and Nutrition Examination Survey (HANES), Moscicki, Rae, Regier, and Locke (1987) reported higher rates of depression, as measured by the CES-D, among Puerto Ricans in comparison to Mexican- and Cuban-Americans, as well as White norms. Canino et al. (1987) estimated DSM-III-R prevalence rates, based upon the Diagnostic Interview Schedule (DIS), among Puerto Rican islanders, finding few differences from White mainland norms. The major ethnic group differences consisted of higher Puerto Rican rates of cognitive impairment, somatization, and alcohol abuse/dependence. Malgady et al. (1987) reviewed 37 studies of the MMPI involving cross-cultural comparisons of Blacks, Hispanics, and Whites. Of seven studies pertaining to Hispanics, six reported Hispanic-White or Hispanic-Black differences on select MMPI scales. More recently, Shrout et al. (1992) compared native Puerto Ricans, Mexican-Americans, and non-Hispanic Whites on five DSM-III disorders, as measured by the DIS. They found Mexican-Americans to be at high risk for affective disorder and alcohol abuse/dependence, whereas Puerto Ricans were at the highest risk for somatization disorder.

Thus, unlike the first definition of test bias, there is considerable empirical research, though some equivocal, on normative differences between ethnic populations. However, regardless of the weight of evidence favoring a mainstream versus ethnic-specific frame of reference, the presence of mean differences between populations—whether in terms of test norms or epidemiological prevalence rates—is inconclusive evidence of bias. Demands for separate test norms or culturally oriented diagnostic criteria implicitly reflect an underlying assumption that one ethnic population is not more disordered than another. Hence the assumption is that the norms of one group must be biased against the other group. If mean differences between ethnic populations represent valid differences in pathology—and this remains unknown—the development of separate norms would be a disservice to the ethnic minority community: Disordered individuals would then tend to be underdiagnosed and would be less likely to receive therapeutic intervention. The presence of mean differences between an ethnic minority group and the majority group only suggests that the majority yardstick may not be appropriate for the minority or that actual differences may exist in a particular domain. Further inquiry is required to examine the reasons for population differences, which may or may not be valid differences in the construct being measured.

Invariance of Factor Structure

The issue of bias in measurement has also been defined by comparing the internal or latent factor structure of tests across different populations. The term "factor invariance" refers specifically to the congruence of factor structures or factor loadings across populations (Mulaik, 1973). Technically, a difference between ethnic groups in number of factors, pattern of factor loadings, percentage of variance explained, or correlations among factors would constitute evidence of test bias.

Estimation of factor invariance among White, Black, and Hispanic children has appeared in the intelligence testing literature (e.g., Gutkin & Reynolds, 1981a, 1981b), but little is known about cross-cultural variations in factor structure of personality tests or symptom scales. One exception is the Center for Epidemiological Studies Depression Scale (CES-D), which has been found to display similar factor structures among White, Black, and Mexican-American groups (Aneshensel, Clark, & Frerichs, 1981; Roberts, 1980). Factor analytic research on the MMPI has produced more ambiguous findings. Differences in both the number and composition (i.e., loadings) of MMPI factors among Whites, Blacks, and Mexican-Americans have been reported (Holland, 1979), whereas other studies have not found such differences (Prewitt-Diaz, Nogueras, & Draguns, 1984).

Thus, the empirical findings of factor invariance across ethnic populations are limited in scope and equivocal. There are also technical psychometric problems with this research. Olmedo (1981) has called attention to problems in determining the congruence of factors across ethnic groups, and recommended confirmatory factor analysis to determine how well the factor structure extracted in one population fits the factor structure of another population. Another approach is offered by Mulaik (1973), who detailed the assumptions and procedures necessary and sufficient to establish factor invariance. Both Olmedo's and Mulaik's approaches have been largely ignored in cross-cultural factor analysis research.

The consequences of differential latent structure in a test depend upon the manner in which scores are profiled. A test that offers a profile of multiple scales derived from factor analysis is of questionable utility if the items do not coalesce into the same factors with minority examinees as with majority examinees. In this case, differential factor structure in the minority group would suggest that another arrangement of items into different scale scores is warranted, and at the very least would attenuate reliability. On the other hand, if different factor structures underlie a total test score, the considerations raised in discussing differences in normative performance apply to this situation as well. Mere observation of different factor structures does not in itself verify test bias, unless it is shown that ethnic minorities are being evaluated unfairly by the test in question.

Assuming that overall reliability is not substantially affected, and that only the number or composition of factors varies, the test may be measuring different constructs or different dimensions of the same construct cross-culturally. Variations in the internal properties of a test across cultures invite research to determine whether there are accompanying variations in the test's external properties or construct validity.

To the best of our knowledge, the issue of whether factor structures of symptomatology patterns are variant or invariant cross-culturally has not been examined in regard to psychiatric diagnosis. Even in nonminority psychiatric research, DSM-III-R diagnostic categories bear little resemblance to the symptom clusters that emerge from factor analytic studies of psychopathology (Mirowsky & Ross, 1989). Thus, it is hardly surprising that cross-cultural differences in the factor structure of symptom indicators have largely been ignored.

Differential Validity/Prediction/Measurement Equivalence

Other definitions of bias refer to population differences in the manner in which test scores relate to an external criterion-related measure. Differential validity is a question of equivalence across populations in terms of validity (correlation) coefficients (Cole, 1981). Differential prediction is a question of equivalence of the accompanying regression equations (Drasgow, 1982). If a test's correlation with a criterion-related measure varies cross-culturally, individuals from different cultures with the same test score have different predicted scores on the criterion variable.

The personality testing literature reveals a general neglect of differential validity and prediction with culturally diverse populations. Evidence that the criterion-related validity of standardized personality profiles or symptom scales is substantially lower for Hispanics and Blacks than Whites would constitute strong evidence of test bias, implying that test scores would be less relevant to the clinical disposition of Hispanic and Black clients. Independent of validity, evidence of differential regression equations would suggest that test bias takes the form of under- or overprediction of a criterion-related variable, implying that unfair clinical disposition of Black and Hispanic clients is likely to occur systematically.

An analogous problem arises in diagnostic situations when we inquire about how cultural factors might influence the validity of clinical judgments about Hispanic and Black clients. Some research specific to Hispanics suggests that greater psychopathology is inferred when clients are interviewed in Spanish than in English (Del

Castillo, 1970; Price & Cuellar, 1981). Yet other studies have reached the opposite conclusion (Marcos, Alpert, Urcuyo et al., 1973; Marcos, Urcuyo, Kesselman et al., 1973). Although this literature has been critically reviewed elsewhere (Vazquez, 1982), there is still no resolution of this important issue, which can be framed in terms of a psychometric question of whether or not cultural and language factors bias the criterion-related validity of psychiatric diagnosis.

A highly refined definition of test bias concerns the concept of measurement equivalence, which refers to the relationship between observed measurements and underlying latent traits of examinees from different populations (Drasgow, 1982, 1984). When measurements are not equivalent across ethnic groups, bias occurs because individuals from different cultures with the same underlying symptom or severity receive different observed test scores or diagnoses. In other words, numerical test scores or nosological classifications have a different functional meaning across ethnic groups. Needless to say, there are very few applications of this measurement technique in personality or psychiatric research, and none has been cross-culturally oriented.

Drasgow (1982) reviewed the literature on ability and aptitude testing in light of the ubiquitous finding that for most performance tests there is little evidence of bias in terms of differential validity. His own simulation of differential validity for two groups of equal latent ability showed that, if measurement equivalence is not satisfied, statistical significance tests are insensitive to true differences between validity coefficients. Because statistical power drops to near zero when measurement equivalence is lacking, studies of bias are incapable of detecting validity differences under this condition. Drasgow concluded, therefore, that unless prerequisite measurement equivalence is established, the failure to observe significant differences in validity coefficients should not be taken as evidence that tests are fair to ethnic minority groups.

INTRODUCTION TO THE TEMAS

The theme emergent from the research we have discussed is that traditional psychological testing and psychiatric diagnostic practices have been challenged with regard to propriety for Hispanics and other ethnic/racial minority groups, according to a variety of psychometric definitions of bias. Nevertheless, despite several decades of rhetoric and scattered research efforts, there is some empirical consensus, depending upon the particular definition of test bias, that cultural factors do indeed impact on the outcomes of standardized testing and psychiatric diagnosis. There is a need, therefore, to develop culturally sensitive psychological tests for reliable and valid diagnosis and personality assessment of culturally and linguistically diverse children and adults. In the next section, we consider developmental and psychometric research on a thematic apperception test (TEMAS) that was developed in response to criticisms of standardized tests, as discussed in the preceding section. The TEMAS test was developed for Hispanic children and adolescents, and later expanded to include Blacks and Whites.

BACKGROUND: PROJECTIVE TESTS

Thematic apperception techniques and other traditional projective tests are based on the psychodynamic assumption that an individual projects onto ambiguous stimuli unconscious drives, which are ordinarily repressed (Murray, 1951). Early clinicians tended to place strong emphasis on the content analysis of the Thematic Apperception Test (TAT) stories in order to understand personality dynamics. However, with the advent of ego psychology, clinicians began to refocus their attention from the content of the *id* to the structure of the *ego*. *Ego* psychology posited that, whereas the *id* provided the energy to motivate behavior, the *ego* structure was responsible for the nature and direction of behavior. Consequently, there was a parallel shift in the analysis of TAT stories. The new emphasis focused primarily on the structure of the theme (how the story was told), and secondarily on the symbolic content of the story (what was told) (Bellak, 1954).

The highly cognitive nature of TAT stories was recognized in the early 1960s. Holt (1960a, 1960b), for example, argued that TAT stories are not fantasies or products of primary processes, but are, rather, cognition or products of conscious cognitive processes. Although he labeled TAT productions "fantasies," Kagan (1956) emphasized the importance of analyzing the *ego* defenses of the stories in addition to their symbolic content. Even earlier, Bellak (1954) had pointed out that TAT stories needed to be analyzed for both content and structure.

The emphasis on cognitive processes in projective testing was the natural progression of the theoretical development of behaviorism, which converged into the cognitive theories of the 1970s. There has been an impetus among some cognitive-behavioral psychologists to integrate the basic assumptions of *ego* psychology and cognitive psychology in the application of projective analyses (Anderson, 1981; Forgus & Shulman, 1979; Singer & Pope, 1978; Sobel, 1981). Interest in projective tests has been growing dramatically even among the cognitive psychologists. In fact, Sobel (1981) proposed the development of a "projective-cognitive" instrument to assess an individual's problem-solving strategies, coping skills, and self-instructional styles.

Traditionally in clinicians' analyses of responses to projective personality tests, Hispanic and Black children have been evaluated as being less verbally fluent, less behaviorally mature, and more psychopathological than their nonminority counterparts (Ames & August, 1966; Booth, 1966; Durret & Kim, 1973). This is a particular problem because it has been widely acknowledged that the validity of projective techniques is impugned when administered to examinees who are verbally inarticulate (Anderson & Anderson, 1955; Reuman, Alwin, & Veroff, 1983). In contrast, minority children are articulate when tested with culturally sensitive instruments (Bailey & Green, 1977; Costantino & Malgady, 1983; Costantino, Malgady, & Vazquez, 1981; Thompson, 1949).

Nonetheless, projective tests have not fared equally well even with white children. Urging the development of new valid instruments, Gallager (1979) lamented that "We often curse the quality of the tools we have. But we are trapped by them." The research literature has also emphasized the need to develop psychological tests for reliable and valid diagnosis and personality assessment of minority children (Padilla, 1979) and to create culture-specific norms for projective tests (Dana, 1986a; Exner & Weiner, 1982).

Projective techniques, especially the Rorschach and the TAT, have been used to probe the cognitive, affective, and personality functioning of individuals from different cultural backgrounds. From early cross-cultural investigations using projective tests in the 1940s, it was observed that the TAT (Murray, 1943) stimuli had limited relevance to individuals of different cultures; hence, culturally sensitive TAT stimuli were developed to study such groups as Mexican Indians, Ojibwa Indians, Southwest Africans, and South Pacific Micronesians (Henry, 1955). However, such early efforts to provide a culture-specific and sensitive interpretive TAT framework have not been eagerly pursued by psychometricians (Dana, 1986a, 1986b).

More recently, the work of Monopoli (1984, cited in Dana, 1986a) indicated that culture-specific stimuli were necessary for personality assessment of unacculturated Hopi and Zuni Indians, whereas the Murray TAT was deemed more useful with acculturated individuals. Avila-Espada (1986) found that, following the development of an objective scoring system and norms, the standard TAT seems to have only a modest clinical utility for personality assessment of European Spaniards. Dana (1993b), moreover, strongly emphasizes that most personality tests are assumed to be genuine etic or culture general and universal in their assessment. Consequently, the use of an etic orientation with multicultural groups has erroneously minimized cultural differences and hence has generated inappropriate inferences using Anglo-American personality constructs, thus creating unfavorable psychological test results and unfair clinical dispositions (Costantino, 1992, 1993; Dana, 1993a; Malgady, 1990, 1996). Dana (1993a) further emphasizes that a correct etic orientation needs to be used in order to demonstrate multicultural construct validity. He evaluates the TEMAS test, which was "developed to salvage the Thematic Apperception Test... as a landmark event for multicultural assessment because it provides a picture-story test that has psychometric credibility" (p. 10). In the same vein, Ritzler (1993) writes that TEMAS "represents a milestone in personality assessment. It also represents the first time a thematic apperception assessment technique has been published in the United States with the initial expressed purpose of providing valid personality assessment of minority subjects" (p. 381).

DEVELOPMENT OF TEMAS

Based on these considerations, the TEMAS test (which in English is an acronym for *Tell-Me-a-Story*, and in Spanish means *themes*) was developed as a multicultural thematic apperception test for use with Puerto Rican, other Hispanic, Black, and White children. TEMAS is different from previous thematic apperception tests in a number of ways: (1) The test was specifically developed for use with children and adolescents; (2) it has two parallel sets of stimulus cards, one set for minorities and another for nonminorities; (3) it has extensive normative data for both minorities and nonminorities; (4) it has an objective scoring system of both thematic content and structure; and (5) the TEMAS pictures embody the following features: (a) structured stimuli and diminished ambiguity to pull for specific personality functions; (b) chromatically attractive, ethnically and racially relevant and contemporary stimuli to elicit diagnostically meaningful protocols; and (c) representation of both negative and positive intrapersonal and interpersonal functions in the form of conflicts that require a solution (resolution of conflict or problem solving) (Costantino, 1987; Costantino, Malgady, & Rogler, 1988).

THEORETICAL FRAMEWORK

The principal rationale for the development of TEMAS was the acknowledged need for a psychometrically sound and multicultural thematic apperception test designed specifically for use with children and adolescents. It can be used normatively with children and adolescents aged 5 to 13 and used clinically with children and adolescents aged 5 to 18.

The theory underlying TEMAS incorporates the dynamic-cognitive framework, which states that personality development occurs

within a sociocultural system. Within this system, individuals internal-
ize the cultural values and beliefs of family and society (Bandura &
Walters, 1967). Personality functions are learned initially through modeling (Bandura, 1977) and are then developed through verbal and
imaginal processes (Paivio, 1971; Piaget & Inhelder, 1971). When a test's
projective stimuli are similar to the circumstances in which the personality functions were originally learned, these functions are readily transferred to the testing situation and are projected into the thematic stories
(Auld, 1954). Moreover, personality is a structure comprising a constel-
lation of motives that are learned and internalized dispositions and that
interact with environmental stimuli to determine overt behavior in
specific situations. Because these dispositions are not directly observable
in clinical evaluation, projective techniques prove to be useful instruments in probing beneath the overt structure or "phenotype" of the
personality, thereby arousing the latent motives imbedded in the personality "genotype." Hence it is assumed that projective tests assess
relatively stable individual differences in the strength of underlying
motives, which are expressed in narrative or storytelling. Atkinson
(1981) emphasizes that the analysis of narrative (thematic content) has a
more solid theoretical foundation than ever before and "remains the
most important and virtually untapped resource we have for developing
our understanding of the behavior of an animal distinguished by its
unique competence in language and use of symbols" (p. 127).

THE STIMULUS CARDS

The settings, characters, and themes were created by Costantino
(1978), and the art work was rendered by Phil Jacobs, an artist who
worked closely with the author. Several hundred pictures were
drawn before the 23 standardized pictures were selected (see section
on Standardization).

There are two parallel versions of TEMAS pictures: the minority
version consisting of pictures featuring predominantly Hispanic and
African-American characters in an urban environment, and the
nonminority version consisting of corresponding pictures showing
predominantly White characters in an urban environment. The
various personality functions depicted in the two parallel sets of
pictures present identical themes.

Both the minority and nonminority versions have a Short Form
comprising 9 cards from the 23-card Long Form. Of the 9 Short Form
cards, 4 are administered to both genders and 5 are gender-specific.
Of the 23 Long Form cards, 12 are for both genders, 11 are gender-
specific, and 1 is age-specific. Furthermore, there are 4 cards with

pluralistic characters, which can be used interchangeably for both the minority and nonminority versions (Cards 15, 16, 20, and 21).

THE TEMAS MEASURES

Cognitive Functions. There are 18 Cognitive Functions that can be scored for each TEMAS protocol:

Reaction Time (RT); *Total Time* (TT); *Fluency* (FL); *Total Omissions* (OM); *Main Character Omissions* (MCO); *Secondary Character Omissions* (SCO); *Event Omissions*(EO); *Setting Omissions* (SO); *Total Transformations* (TRANS); *Main Character Transformations* (MCT); *Secondary Character Transformations* (SCT); *Event Transformations* (ET); *Setting Transformations* (ST); *Inquiries* (INQ); *Relationships* (REL); *Imagination* (IMAG); *Sequencing* (SEQ); and *Conflict* (CON).

Personality Functions. Nine Personality Functions are also assessed by TEMAS. Each stimulus card pulls for at least one of the following Personality Functions:

Interpersonal Relations (IR); *Aggression* (AGG); *Anxiety/Depression* (A/D); *Achievement Motivation* (AM); *Delay of Gratification* (DG); *Self-Concept* (SC); *Sexual Identity* (SEX); *Moral Judgment* (MJ); *Reality Testing* (REAL).

Affective Functions. Finally, the TEMAS scoring system evaluates seven Affective Functions:

Happy (HAP); *Sad* (SAD); *Angry* (ANG); *Fearful* (FEAR); *Neutral* (NEUT); *Ambivalent* (AMB); *Inappropriate Affect* (IA).

EXAMINER QUALIFICATIONS

In testing culturally, linguistically, and ethnically/racially diverse children, examiners should be fluent in the language in which the examinee is dominant and should have knowledge of the cultural and ethnic/racial heritage of the youngster being tested (Costantino, Malgady, & Rogler, 1988; Dana, 1993; Fuchs, 1986).

Administration

The TEMAS test is administered individually. The examiner reads the same instructions and inquiries to all children. After having initiated a working relationship with the child, the examiner says:

"I would like you to tell me a story. I have several interesting pictures that I'm going to show you. Please look carefully at the people and the places in the pictures and then tell me a complete story about each picture—a story that has a beginning and an end."

Two types of instructions may be used by the examiner: Temporal Sequencing and Structured Inquiries.

Temporal Sequencing

The examiner shows the first picture to the child and says: "Please tell me a complete story about this picture and all the other pictures I will show you. The story should answer three questions:

1. What is happening in the picture now?
2. What happened before?
3. What will happen in the future?

Following these instructions, the child engages in spontaneous storytelling, during which the examiner may ask clarifying questions which are not part of the structured inquiries.

Structured Inquiries

Once the child has ended his/her spontaneous storytelling, the examiner makes any of the following inquiries for information that is missing from the narrative.

Inquiry 1.	a)	Who are these people?
	b)	Do they know each other?
Inquiry 2.	a)	Where are these people?
	b)	Where is this person?
Inquiry 3.	a)	What are these people doing and saying?
	b)	What is this person doing and saying?
Inquiry 4.	a)	What were these people doing before?
	b)	What was this person doing before?
Inquiry 5.	a)	What will these people do next?
	b)	What will this person do next?
Inquiry 6.	a)	What is this person (main character) thinking?
	b)	What is this person (main character) feeling?

Recording Time

A stopwatch (or digital watch) is needed for recording administration time accurately. Normative data have been collected on *reaction time (RT)* (latency time between the handing of the card to the child and the beginning of the story) and *total time (TT)* (the time the child has taken to complete the story, including the time taken by the examiner to make the structured inquiries). The examiner may record *spontaneous time (ST)*, which is the time during which the child has told the story spontaneously, just before the structured inquiries.

SCORING

TEMAS protocols are scored on a detailed record booklet; each story is scored separately for cognitive, affective, personality functions. The 18 Cognitive Functions are scored in the following way: *Reaction Time* is scored in seconds; *Total Time* in minutes and seconds; *Fluency* is indicated by the number of words per story; *Conflict* is scored 1 if it is not recognized and blank if it is recognized; *Sequencing* is scored 1 if it is omitted and blank if it is recognized; *Imagination* is scored 1 if the narrative is stimulus bound and blank if it abstracts beyond the stimulus; *Relationships* is scored 1 if it is recognized and blank if it is not recognized; *Inquiries* are scored 1 if they are unanswered and blank if they are all answered; *Omissions* and *Transformations* are scored in accordance with the number of omissions and transformations of *Main Character, Secondary Character, Event,* and *Setting.*

All affective functions (e.g., *Happy, Sad, Angry*) are scored 1 if they are present in the narrative and left blank if they are not mentioned. (Please note that the 1/0 values are dichotomous scores.) Personality functions are scored on a Likert-type 4-point rating scale, with "1" representing the most maladaptive resolution of the conflict and "4" the most adaptive. A personality function is scored as "N" when the particular function it represents cannot be scored. In accordance with the Sullivanian construct of *selective inattention* (Sullivan, 1953), this N-scoring has been found to discriminate between attention deficit disordered children (Costantino, Malgady, Rogler, & Tsui, 1988; Costantino, Malgady, Colon-Malgady, & Bailey, 1992).

A score of "1" for any personality function indicates a highly maladaptive resolution for a particular card. For example, references to murder, rape, and assault are scored "1" for *Interpersonal Relations, Aggression,* and *Moral Judgment.* A suicidal theme earns a "1" under the *Anxiety/Depression* function. The decision to drop out of school or steal rather than work results in a "1" for *Achievement Motivation* and *Delay of Gratification.* The anticipation of complete failure and concomitant refusal to attempt a given task results in a "1" for *Self Concept of Competence.* A character who changes gender or rejects his or her gender earns a "1" in *Sexual Identity.* Scores of "1" in *Moral Judgment* reflect a total lack of regard for the consequences of antisocial behavior. Severely impaired reality testing would be scored only for the most bizarre and impossible resolutions (e.g., inanimate objects come alive and kill; a child causes harmful events to occur by a strange power of the mind). A score of "2" for any personality function reflects a moderately maladaptive resolution. Examples of such resolutions are: children cheat and get away with it; a conflict is resolved by fighting; money is squandered rather than saved; homework is avoided in favor of play; a child runs away from home and never returns; the monster in a dream could also be in the backyard. A score of "3" represents a partially adaptive resolution. Examples of such resolutions are: children who cheat are caught and punished; fighting ceases in favor of compromise; money is saved for a time and then spent; homework is grudgingly completed; a runaway child returns home. A score of "4" represents a highly adaptive resolution. The child must perceive the intended conflict and solve the problem in a mature, age-appropriate manner. A score of "4" implies a striving for the greater good, a sense of responsibility, and an intrinsic motivation. Examples of such resolutions are: a child rejects the notion of cheating as contrary to learning; conflicts are discussed and a compromise is reached; money is saved for the future; home work is completed because good grades are valued; a child decides to talk to parents rather than run away; dreams are never real.

STANDARDIZATION

Standardization Sample

TEMAS was standardized on a sample of 642 children (281 males and 361 females) from public schools in the New York City area. These children ranged in age from 5 to 13 years, with a mean age of 8.9 years (SD = 1.9). The total sample represented four ethnic/racial groups: Puerto Ricans and other Hispanics, Blacks, and Whites.

Data on the socioeconomic status (SES) of the standardization sample indicate that these subjects were from predominantly lower- and middle-income families.

ADMINISTRATION PROCEDURES FOR INSTRUMENT STANDARDIZATION

TEMAS was administered to each subject, with 23 cards presented in random order by an examiner of the same ethnic/racial background as the examinee. All subjects were tested individually by graduate psychology students in sessions conducted in the public schools. After developing a rapport with each child, the examiner administered the TEMAS according to the instructions described above. Examinees subsequently responded by telling a story about each picture for typically 2 to 5 minutes; the responses were recorded verbatim by the examiner. Hispanic examinees were tested by bilin-gual Hispanic examiners in the examinee's dominant language. In the case of Hispanic examinees who responded in Spanish, stories were translated into English for scoring. Protocols were scored according to administration instructions. Black examinees were tested by Black examiners, and White examinees by White examiners.

QUANTITATIVE SCALES AND QUALITATIVE INDICATORS

The nature of the distribution of some TEMAS functions made it impractical to convert them to standard scores, because scores other than zero were rare in the standardization sample. These functions were designated "Qualitative Indicators." The TEMAS functions that had relatively normal distributions were designated "Quantitative Scales."

STRATIFICATION OF THE STANDARDIZATION SAMPLE

In the standardization sample, significant correlations of low magnitude were found between age and many of the TEMAS func-tions. Correlations ranged from .01 to -.52 (see Table 1). Although these correlations are small, it is believed that they reflect real devel-opmental trends in children's cognitive, affective, and personality functioning. Thus, in order to accommodate the effects of these trends, while still retaining respectable sample sizes, age was col-lapsed into three age-range groups: 5-to-7-year-olds, 8-to-10-year-olds, and 11-to-13-year-olds.

For each of the 17 Quantitative Scales, three-way analyses of variance (ANOVAs) were computed by age, ethnic/racial background, and gender of the standardization sample. The three-way interaction terms were not significant for any of the quantitative functions. The two-way interactions between gender and age were also nonsignifi-cant for these scales. However, the two-way interaction of sex and ethnic/racial background was significant for one of the 17 Quantita-tive Scales—(*Sexual Identity*). However, given the number of hypoth-eses tested, this result may be attributable to chance.

There were no significant main effects of gender for any of these functions. This result is consistent with the results of other studies that have investigated the effects of gender on TEMAS functions.

Short Form. Means and standard deviations for the Short Form were derived by extracting the scores of the 9 cards from the 23-card protocols of the standardization sample. The correlations between the 23-card Long Form of TEMAS and the 9-card Short Form for each function were computed separately for the total sample and for each ethnic/racial group (see Table 2). The correlation between the Long

Table 1. Correlations of TEMAS Indices with Age.

	Hispanic	Black
Cognitive Function		
Reaction Time	.00	.22
Total Time	.11	.01
Fluency	.18	.20
Total Omissions	-.23	-.11
Total Transformations	-.17	-.52*
Inquiries	-.13	-.25
Main Character Omissions	-.17	-.19
Main Character Transformations	-.14	-.35*
Secondary Character Omissions	-.01	-.24
Secondary Character Transformations	-.12	-.40*
Event Omissions	-.13	-.11
Event Transformations	-.05	—
Setting Omissions	-.31*	.00
Setting Transformations	-.19	-.37*
Conflict	-.21	-.18
Sequencing	-.11	-.38*
Imagination	-.14	-.31*
Relationships	-.20	-.39*
Personality Function		
Interpersonal Relations	-.21	.17
Aggression	-.26*	.02
Anxiety/Depression	-.18	.34*
Achievement Motivation	.02	.23
Delay of Gratification	.07	.20
Self-Concept	-.05	.10
Sexual Identity	-.34*	.29
Moral Judgment	.05	.12
Reality Testing	-.10	.18
Affective Function		
Happy	.16	-.12
Sad	-.28*	.08
Angry	.08	.13
Fearful	.12	.04
Neutral	.00	-.29
Ambivalent	.00	.12
Inappropriate Affect	-.09	-.05

[a] $n = 115$ (73 Hispanics, 42 Blacks).
[b] Father SES, $n = 54$ Hispanics, 27 Blacks.
[c] Mother SES, $n = 69$ Hispanics, 39 Blacks.
*$p<.05$.

Table 2. Correlation Between TEMAS Long and Short Forms

Function	White Sample N	r	Puerto Rican Sample N	r	Other Hispanic Sample N	r	Black Sample N	r
Quantitative Scale								
Reaction Time	87	.95	117	.95	84	.94	113	.96
Total Time	124	.97	122	.98	84	.97	114	.99
Fluency	123	.98	125	.97	86	.97	113	.97
Total Omissions	172	.72	164	.70	93	.81	206	.74
Interpersonal Relations	143	.95	164	.87	45	.99	206	.91
Aggression	136	.92	164	.96	38	.99	206	.95
Anxiety/Depression	171	.90	151	.84	100	.83	206	.89
Achievement Motivation	172	.79	163	.79	100	.81	203	.88
Delay of Gratification	163	.89	161	.87	84	.82	203	.96
Self-Concept	166	.82	155	.70	98	.77	193	.82
Sexual Identity	145	.69	76	.86	86	.80	127	.90
Moral Judgment	158	.81	163	.78	90	.64	197	.73
Reality Testing	171	.75	125	.84	100	.66	206	.83
Happy	172	.87	163	.81	94	.96	206	.71
Sad	172	.82	163	.79	94	.94	206	.72
Angry	172	.77	163	.84	94	.87	206	.77
Fearful	171	.88	163	.83	94	.88	206	.80
Qualitative Indicator								
Neutral	171	.86	163	.86	94	.86	206	.91
Ambivalent	171	.72	163	.61	94	.79	206	.94
Inappropriate Affect	171	.77	163	.39	94	.86	206	.74
Conflict	172	.77	163	.80	100	.82	206	.91
Sequencing	172	.82	163	.57	100	.79	206	.57
Imagination	172	.82	163	.97	96	.84	206	.65
Relationships	172	.62	163	.76	94	.75	206	.59
Total Transformations	172	.76	164	.80	96	.72	206	.71
Inquiries	172	.87	162	.04	98	.66	206	.72
Main Character Omissions	172	.64	164	.82	95	.79	206	.95
Secondary Character Omissions	172	.78	164	.75	98	.78	206	.80
Setting Omissions	172	.69	164	.65	100	.60	206	.64
Event Omissions	172	.68	164	.66	100	.87	206	.63
Main Character Transformations	172	.47	164	.57	96	.63	206	.55
Secondary Character Transformations	172	.60	164	.68	100	.65	206	.34
Setting Transformations	172	.66	164	.94	100	.76	206	.61
Event Transformations	172	.83	164	.73	100	.72	206	.70

Form and the Short Form was uniformly high across samples. The median correlation between forms was .81 for the Total Sample, .82 for Whites, .80 for Blacks, .80 for Puerto Ricans, and .81 for other Hispanics.

DERIVATION OF STANDARD SCORES

To enable users to directly compare scores within a single protocol, and to facilitate comparisons with the performance of the standardization sample, raw scores of Quantitative Scales were converted to normalized *T*-scores. To minimize irregularities in the raw score distribution, an analytic smoothing technique was also used (Cureton & Tukey, 1951).

Because it was inappropriate to transform raw scores of the Qualitative Indicators to standard scores, critical levels based on the raw score distributions have been developed, based on expert clinical opinion. Because the critical levels are based on expert clinical evaluation, the Qualitative Indicators should be named Clinical Indicators.

RELIABILITY

Internal Consistency

In this context, internal consistency refers to the degree to which individual TEMAS cards are interrelated in measuring particular functions.

Long Form. Internal consistency reliabilities of the TEMAS functions were derived using a sample of 73 Hispanic and 42 Black children (see Table 3). The internal consistency reliability coefficients for the Hispanic sample ranged from .41 for *Ambivalent,* an affective function, to .98 for *Fluency,* a cognitive function, and had a median value of .73. For the Black sample, coefficients ranged from .31 for *Setting Transformations* to .97 for *Fluency,* with a median of .62.

Reaction Time, Fluency, and *Total Time* demonstrated high levels of internal consistency in both the Hispanic and Black samples. However, in general, *Omissions* and *Transformations* of perceptual details (*Main Character, Secondary Character, Event,* and *Setting*) had lower magnitudes of internal consistency than other TEMAS functions in both samples. This may be attributable to the fact that these two functions, being clinical scales, tend to occur less frequently, in nonclinical children (Costantino, Colon-Malgady, Malgady, & Perez, 1991). The internal consistency reliabilities for *Omissions* and *Transformations* were uniformly lower for Blacks than for Hispanics.

Conflict, Imagination, and *Relationships* demonstrated moderate-to-high internal consistency reliability in both ethnic/racial groups. The alpha coefficient for *Sequencing,* a cognitive function, was moderately high in the Hispanic sample but low in the Black sample. With respect to affective functions, reliability estimates in the Hispanic sample were highest for *Happy, Sad, Angry,* and *Fearful,* whereas in the Black sample, the highest reliability was evident for *Sad, Angry, Neutral,* and *Ambivalent.*

With respect to personality, pictures pulling for *Interpersonal Relations, Aggression,* and *Moral Judgment* showed the highest levels of internal consistency in the Hispanic sample, whereas *Anxiety/Depression, Achievement Motivation, Delay of Gratification, Self-Concept, Sexual Identity,* and *Reality Testing* had low-to-moderate reliability. For Blacks, alphas were again uniformly lower than for Hispanics, with the highest reliabilities associated with Aggression and Moral Judgment. Low reliabilities for the personality functions may be due partially to the fact that personality function scores are based on relatively few TEMAS cards.

The coefficient alphas for the standardization sample, differentiated by ethnic/racial group membership for the Long Form, were, for the most part, in the moderate range, with a median alpha of .83 for the Quantitative Scales for the Total Sample. On these functions, the median reliability ranged from .80 for Black children to .69 for other Hispanic children. On the Short Form, alphas were generally lower, with a median reliability of .68 for the Total Sample on the Quantitative Scales. Reliability coefficients for ethnic/racial groups on these functions ranged from a median coefficient of .65 for the White sample to .54 for the Black sample. Reliability coefficients on the Qualitative Indicators were lower, due, in large part, to the nonmetric nature of the scoring system used with these scales.

TEST-RETEST RELIABILITY (SHORT FORM)

Test-retest stability of the TEMAS functions was computed for the Short Form by correlating the results of two administrations, separated by an 18-week interval. The sample used in this study consisted of 51 subjects chosen at random from the 210 Puerto Rican students screened for behavior problems. Results indicated that TEMAS functions exhibited low-to-moderate stability over an 18-week period (see Table 3). The eight TEMAS functions with significant test-retest correlations were *Fluency, Event Transformations, Conflict, Relationships, Happy, Ambivalent, Anxiety/Depression,* and *Sexual Identity.* Two explanations for the generally low level of test-retest reliability have been proposed. First, test-retest correlations may be lower-bound estimates of reliability in this case because different raters were

Table 3. Internal Consistency (Alpha) Reliability and Test-Retest (r)
Reliability over 18-week Interval.

	Hispanic	Black	N	r
Cognitive Function				
Reaction Time	.95	.92	50	.17
Total Time	.98	.97	50	.06
Fluency	.98	.97	50	.45
Total Omissions	.80	.75	50	.13
Total Transformations	.64	.45	51	.05
Inquiries	.82	.51	51	.27
Main Character Omissions	.76	.59	51	.04
Main Character Transformations	.52	—	51	-.05
Secondary Character Omissions	.65	.56	51	-.06
Secondary Character Transformations	.77	.36	51	-.07
Event Omissions	.74	.72	51	.27
Event Transformations	.48	—	51	.46
Setting Omissions	.75	.60	51	.15
Setting Transformation	.55	.31	51	-.08
Conflict	.69	.83	51	.53
Sequencing	.82	.46	51	-.01
Imagination	.98	.75	51	.11
Relationships	.75	.68	51	.39
Personality Function[2]				
Interpersonal Relations (16)	.92	.62	50	.24
Aggression (8)	.84	.78	50	.16
Anxiety/Depression	.50	.49	50	.45
Achievement Motivation	.65	.52	48	.11
Delay of Gratification (4)	.45	.45	50	.17
Self-Concept (4)	.59	.45	45	-.07
Sexual Identity (3)	.58	.63	33	.38
Moral Judgment	.72	.70	49	.07
Reality Testing	.56	.44	49	.21
Affective Function				
Happy	.86	.67	51	.35
Sad	.89	.79	51	.15
Angry	.76	.77	51	-.04
Fearful	.82	.50	51	.25
Neutral	.50	.84	51	-.03
Ambivalent	.41	.77	51	.45
Inappropriate Affect	—	—	—	

[2]The number of pictures pulling each function is indicated in parenthesis.

employed at pre- and post-testing. Therefore, they include error variance due to interrater reliability. Second, the indicators of this instrument have limited range and hence, the correlation may be attenuated.

INTERRATER RELIABILITY

The protocols of 27 Hispanic and 26 Black children were drawn at random from the sample of 73 Hispanics and 42 Blacks described previously in the section on internal consistency of the Long Form. Each protocol was scored independently by two raters. These scores were then correlated to estimate the degree to which the two raters agreed in their scoring of a particular picture for a given TEMAS Personality Function.

Interrater reliabilities in scoring *Total Omissions* and *Transformations* are generally moderate-to-high for both the Hispanic and the Black protocols (see Table 4). Little difference is evident as a function of ethnic/racial group. Raters generally showed greater agreement in scoring Omissions than Transformations. Although illogical synthesis and integration of ideas regarding resolution of *Conflict, Sequencing, Imagination,* and *Relationships* generally occurred rarely in both samples, available estimates of correlations are suggestive of moderate-to-high interrater agreement.

For the Affective Functions, the pattern of correlation between raters is generally high, with no substantive differences between the Hispanic and Black samples. With respect to the Personality Functions, correlations are low-to-moderate for Reality Testing and Sexual Identity in the Hispanic sample and substantially higher for the remaining functions. Contrary to the pattern of internal consistency reliability estimates, the interrater reliabilities obtained for Hispanics are generally higher than for the Black sample.

Interrater reliability was also estimated in a recent study of the nonminority version of the TEMAS Short Form (Costantino, Malgady, Casullo, & Castillo, 1991). Two experienced clinical psychologists (one with extensive training in scoring TEMAS and the other a newly trained scorer) independently rated 20 protocols. The results of this study indicated a high interrater agreement in scoring protocols for Personality Functions, ranging from 75%–95%. The mean level of interrater agreement was 81%, and in no cases were the two independent ratings different by more than one-rating scale-point.

It is important to clarify that whereas the interrater agreement for Personality Functions in the first interrater reliability study ranged from 31%–100%, in the recent study, the interrater agreement ranged

Table 4. Interrater Reliabilities For Hispanic and Black Samples ($N = 27$) across 23 TEMAS Cards.

Function	Hispanic Sample		Black Sample	
	Range r	Median r	Range r	Median r
Cognitive				
Omissions	.54–1.00	.82	.33–1.00	.87
Transformations	.32–.95	.69	.37–1.00	.80
Congruence	.47–1.00	.80	.42–1.00	.69
Affective				
Happy	.70–1.00	.87	.70–1.00	.92
Sad	.70–1.00	.85	.65–1.00	.85
Angry	.55 –1.00	.85	.46–1.00	.85
Fearful	.61–1.00	1.00	.40–1.00	.78
Neutral	.30–1.00	.84	.40–1.00	.75
Ambivalent	.55–1.00	.75	.68–1.00	.78
Personality				
Interpersonal Relations	.27–.80	.63	.40–.88	.62
Aggression	.35–.81	.50	.54–.87	.73
Anxiety/Depression	.43–.73	.52	.33–.85	.58
Achievement Motivation	.20–.65	.51	.41–.80	.59
Delay Gratification	.53–.58	.56	.40–.87	.54
Self Concept	.59–.84	.65	.38–.73	.59
Sexual Identity	.32–.36	.34	.66–.87	.76
Moral Judgment	.44–1.00	.80	.31–1.00	.69
Reality Testing	.32–.60	.39	.74–.83	.75

from 75%–95%. The explanation for this discrepancy is that during the first study, which was conducted in 1983, the TEMAS scoring system was still undergoing changes, whereas in the second study, which was conducted in 1987, the scoring system and the instructions were completely formulated.

CONTENT VALIDITY

TEMAS pictures were designed to "pull" for specific Personality Functions based upon the nature of the psychological conflict represented in each picture. As previously described in the "Scoring" section, all TEMAS pictures are scored for at least two and not more than four Personality Functions. A study was conducted to assess the concordance among a sample of practicing school ($N = 8$) and clinical

($N = 6$) psychologists regarding the pulls of each TEMAS picture for specific Personality Functions. Six of the psychologists were at the doctorate level and eight had received their Master's degrees; they ranged in age from 24 to 54 ($M = 36.57, SD = 7.53$). They had a mean of 8.64 years ($SD = 6.53$) of experience in testing and/or counseling minorities, and a mean of 7.79 years ($SD = 5.36$) of experience with projective techniques. With respect to ethnicity, seven were White, one was Black, and six were Hispanic. The clinical orientations of the psychologists in this sample included eclectic, psychoanalytic, cognitive, and ego psychology.

The psychologists were presented the TEMAS pictures in random order and were asked individually to indicate which, if any, of the nine functions were pulled by each picture. The percentage of agreement among the 14 clinicians revealed surprisingly high agreement (71%–100%) across the pictures, thus confirming the pulls scored for specific Personality Functions.

RELATIONSHIP TO OTHER MEASURES

A group of 210 Puerto Rican children screened for behavior problems were administered a number of measures along with the TEMAS, and their adaptive behavior in experimental role-playing situations was observed and rated by psychological examiners. The measures administered included: the Sentence Completion Test of Ego Development (SCT; Loevinger & Wessler, 1970) or its Spanish version (Brenes-Jette, 1987); the Trait Anxiety Scale of the State-Trait Anxiety Inventory for Children (STAIC; Spielberger, Edwards, Lushene, Montuori, & Platzek, 1973) or its Spanish version, *Inventario de Ansiedad Rasgo-Estado Para Niños* (Villamil, 1973); the Teacher Behavior Rating scale (TBR: Costantino, 1980) (described in subject screening), and the parallel Mother Behavior Rating Scale (MBR: Costantino, 1980) in both English and Spanish. Finally, the children participated in four experimental role-playing situations, designed to elicit adaptive behavior.

Results of the regression analyses indicated that TEMAS profiles significantly predicted ego development (SCT), $R=.39, p<.05$; teachers' behavior ratings (TBR), $R=.49$, $p<.05$; delay of gratification (DG), $R=.32, p<.05$; self-concept of competence (SCC), $R=.50, p<.05$; disruptive behavior (DIS), $R=.51$, $p<.05$; and aggressive behavior (AGG), $R=.32, p<.05$. However, the multiple correlation for predicting trait anxiety was not significant. TEMAS functions accounted for between 10% (for DG and AGG) and 26% (for DIS) of the variability in scores on the criterion measures.

Predictive validity was established using hierarchial multiple regression analysis to assess the utility of TEMAS profiles for predicting post-therapy scores ($N = 123$) on the criterion measures, independent of pretherapy scores. In the first step of the hierarchy, the pretherapy score on a given criterion measure was entered into the regression equation, followed in the second step by a complete TEMAS pretherapy profile. Results of these analyses showed that pretherapy TEMAS profiles significantly predicted all therapeutic outcomes, ranging from 6% to 22% variance increments, except for observation of *Self-Concept of Competence*. Outcome measures were the Sentence Completion Test of Ego Development (14%); Trait Anxiety Inventory for Children (22%); Conner's Behavior Rating Scale (6%); and observational tasks measuring delay gratification (20%); disruptive behavior (17%); and aggression (14%).

PSYCHOMETRIC STUDIES

Several other studies have been conducted on TEMAS; here we summarize the most prominent ones. The first study of the TEMAS research (Costantino, Malgady, & Vazquez, 1981) was conducted in 1980 with 72 Hispanic children in fourth and fifth grades attending public schools in New York City. This study assessed the responsiveness of the Hispanic examinees to TAT and TEMAS. Results indicated that the examinees were more verbally fluent to TEMAS pictures than TAT pictures, and this effect was more pronounced for females than males. Furthermore, the children were more likely to respond in Spanish to TEMAS and to switch from English on the TAT to Spanish on TEMAS. Results supported earlier findings of increased responsiveness of minority children to culturally relevant stimuli, and also suggested a promising instrument for assessment of Hispanic children.

The second study (Costantino & Malgady, 1983) compared Hispanic, Black, and White children on the TAT and TEMAS. Seventy-two Hispanic, 41 Black, and 43 White examinees in grades K-6 were administered the minority version of TEMAS (depicting Hispanic and Black characters), the nonminority version of TEMAS (depicting White characters), and the TAT. Results indicated that females were more fluent than males; Hispanics and Blacks were more verbally fluent on both TEMAS tests compared to the TAT; but only Hispanics were less fluent than Whites on the TAT. Attending to effect size, however, the pattern of standardized differences suggested small convergent and discriminant effects, as ethnic minorities were more fluent on the minority version of TEMAS, whereas Whites were more fluent on the nonminority version of TEMAS.

The third study investigated the psychometric properties of TEMAS (Minority version) (Malgady, Costantino, & Rogler, 1984). The TEMAS test was administered to 73 public school and 210 clinical Puerto Rican children of low socioeconomic status in grades K–6. TEMAS protocols were scored for personality, cognitive, and affective functions. Results indicated internal consistency and interrater reliability in scoring TEMAS stories, and TEMAS indices significantly discriminated between public school and clinical samples.

The fourth study investigated the clinical utility of TEMAS by discriminating public school and clinical Hispanic and Black children (Costantino, Malgady, Rogler, & Tsui, 1988). The examinees were 100 outpatients at psychiatric centers and 373 public school students, all from low SES, inner-city families. All subjects were tested individually by examiners of their same ethnicity. Results indicated that TEMAS profiles significantly ($p < .001$) discriminated the two groups and explained 21% of the variance independent of ethnicity, age, and SES. Classification accuracy, based on the discriminant function, was 89%. The TEMAS profiles interacted with ethnicity; better discrimination was evident for Hispanics than African-Americans.

The fifth study endeavored to assess attention deficit by utilizing the scores of selective attention (Costantino, Colon-Malgady, & Perez, 1991). Attention deficit-hyperactivity disorder (AD-HD) is regarded as being relatively common among school-age children, but the literature reveals a number of confounding factors with standard assessment techniques of the disorder. Using TEMAS to measure attention to pictorial stimuli depicting characters, events, settings, and covert psychological conflicts, a study was conducted with 152 normal and 95 clinical Hispanic, Black, and White school-age children. Results revealed that the AD-HD children were significantly more likely than normal children to omit information in the stimuli about characters, events, settings, and psychological conflicts. Differences between the groups were large and persistent in the presence of structured inquiries made by the test examiners. Results suggested the potential utility of structured thematic apperception techniques for the assessment of AD-HD, eventually to facilitate DSM-III-R diagnosis, but users are also invited to give closer scrutiny in carefully controlled validity studies.

The focus of a sixth study was the cross-cultural standardization of TEMAS in three Hispanic cultures (Costantino, Malgady, Casullo, & Castillo, 1991). This research compared the normative profiles, the reliability, and the criterion-related validity of TEMAS with school and clinical children from three different Hispanic cultures: Puerto Ricans in New York City; natives of San Juan, Puerto Rico; and South

Americans in Buenos Aires, Argentina. Children in New York and
Puerto Rico were administered 23 minority TEMAS cards, the Spielberger
Trait-Anxiety Scale for Children, and the Piers-Harris Children's Self-
Concept Scale. Argentinean children were administered 10 TEMAS
cards (the nonminority short form) and the Piers-Harris scale. Results of
the study supported the use of TEMAS with examinees in the three
cultures. However, it also indicated that the original card 15 (depicting
"a policeman awarding a group of PAL baseball players and a policeman
arresting a group of three boys and one girl who have broken a window
and stolen merchandise") was biased towards the Argentinean children.
These children scored lower than the other two Hispanic groups in *Moral
Judgment* in this card, for they tended to perceive the baseball players as
having also stolen the awards. Analysis of the results indicated that the
Argentinean children tended to attribute wrong doing to the baseball
players because of the presence of the policeman, who apparently was
perceived as a punitive agent because of the experience of these children
during the military regime. (The study was conducted in 1984-85.) In
addition, the card was perceived as culturally relevant because soccer
and not baseball is the national sport in Argentina. (Card 15 in the
nonminority version has been modified to show a coach giving awards
to a group of soccer players.)

The focus of the seventh study (Costantino, Malgady, Colon-Malgady,
& Bailey, 1992) was to investigate the validity of the nonminority version
by discriminating between public school ($n = 49$) and outpatient ($n = 36$)
samples of White examinees from inner city, low to lower middle SES,
largely female-headed households. Results indicated that TEMAS profiles significantly discriminated between the normal functioning and
clinical groups ($p < .001$), with 86% classification accuracy.

The aim of the eighth study, which is still in progress, was to
establish the clinical utility of TEMAS in relation to predicting DSM-
III-R. Hispanic school-age children are affected by low SES, cultural
adjustment issues, and bilingualism, which place them at high risk for
special education; however, their overrepresentation in special education classrooms appears to be also associated with biased cognitive
and clinical assessments and biased intelligence and personality tests.
Preliminary data analyses conducted with 45 (of the 80) Hispanic
school-age children attending two major mental health centers showed
levels of agreement ranging from .73 to .92 between TEMAS scores
and classification of clinical examinees into their target diagnostic
categories (Costantino & Malgady, 1993).

The ninth study endeavored to assess the cultural sensitivity of
TEMAS (Bernal, 1991). Research assessing the appropriateness of

projective instruments utilized with ethnic minority populations is scarce and traditionally such research has overlooked acculturation issues. The purpose of the study was to describe the relationship between acculturation level and two popular thematic tests: the Robert's Apperception Test for Children (RAT-C) and TEMAS. Participants were 40 (24 females and 16 males) Mexican-American and Anglo-American children in grades 4 through 7 who were between the ages of 10 and 12. This study utilized a nonexperimental cross-sectional design to test seven research hypotheses. The Vineland Adaptive Behavior Scales Survey Form or Classroom Edition was utilized to define examinee well-adjustment, and the System of Multicultural Pluralistic Assessment (SOMPA) Urban Acculturation Scale was utilized to define acculturation level. Results pointed out that whereas the TEMAS seemed to be a more culturally sensitive instrument in assessing Mexican-Americans than the RAT-C, both the RAT-C and the TEMAS seemed to be valid instruments for assessing personality functioning among Anglo-American children.

The tenth study constitutes a pioneer attempt to use the TEMAS projective test as therapeutic stimuli, thus linking assessment to treatment. Hispanic children were treated in this study by a culturally sensitive storytelling intervention. Inner-city, 9-13 year olds ($N = 90$) were screened for symptomatology by structured interview (Child Assessment Schedule-CAS), randomly assigned to an 8-week TEMAS intervention or attention-control group, and pre- and post-tested with standardized instruments (CED and STAIC). (The TEMAS test in this study was used *only* as therapeutic stimuli, not as an assessment instrument.) Results indicated significant improvement in anxiety, depression and phobic symptomatology, and school conduct based on the use of TEMAS pictures as therapeutic stimuli (Costantino, Malgady, & Rogler, 1994).

The next section presents three case studies that illustrate the clinical application of the TEMAS test in school and clinic settings. The cases presented include presenting problem, family history, results of TEMAS and other psychological evaluations, how TEMAS facilitated the assessment, and some exemplary stories told by the children.

CLINICAL UTILITY: CASE STUDIES

Case Study 1

The first (school) case illustrates the utility of TEMAS, which was administered together with WISC-III, the Bender-Gestalt Test, and the H-T-P test, in assessing the strengths and weaknesses of a 6-

year-old Hispanic student. Referred for possible placement in Special Education classes, the student was recommended to remain in regular classes, following positive results on both the WISC-III and TEMAS.

Psychological Testing Report

Name: Roberto   Language Dominance: English/Spanish
DOB: 11/11/86   Testing Language: English/Spanish
DOT: 4/30/93   Grade: 1st

Reason for Referral

Roberto is a 6-year-5-month-old Hispanic student who is attending first grade in regular classes. According to his teacher's report, he was experiencing academic problems and, at times, exhibited inappropriate classroom behavior. An evaluation was requested to assess his cognitive, intellectual, and emotional functioning as well as school achievement to determine his need for Special Education Services.

Tests Administered

- Wechsler Intelligence Scale for Children-III (WISC-III)
- The Bender Gestalt Test
- The House-Tree-Person (H-T-P)
- TEMAS (Tell-Me-A-Story) Thematic Apperception Test (Minority Version)

Brief Family and Development History

Roberto lives with his mother, who takes care of the household, his father who works as an auto mechanic, and three sisters and one brother. Roberto is the oldest of the siblings. According to the psychosocial report, he was born full term following a normal pregnancy. He achieved his developmental milestones with some delay. He walked at the age of 3 years and began to speak by the age of 3 years. He is left handed. No history of major medical problems or hospitalizations was reported. However, the child developed asthma by the age of 10 months and continues to experience occasional asthma attacks. He exhibited some sibling rivalry and showed strong attachment to his parents. He did not attend kindergarten and entered school at the first grade level. During the first and second quarters of the school year, "he exhibited poor reading and math skills, was very quiet and failed to participate in classroom activities." However, according to his teacher, "starting with the third quarter, the child began to be more active in the classroom and to show some improvement in both reading and math, especially in the latter subject." In general, he got along well with his parents and played with his siblings. He watched television for several hours a day.

Test Results

WISC-III

On the WISC-III Roberto achieved a Verbal Score within the average range, a Performance Score within the low average range, and a Full Scale Score within the average range; thus his overall Intellectual Functioning fell within the average category. However, if his intra- and intertest scatter, bilingualism, and psychosocial environment are taken into consideration, it can be assumed that he had the potential to function within the upper end of the average category to the high average category. It is of importance to note that his Verbal Scores were higher than his Performance Scores, which is unusual for a Hispanic, bilingual student, indicating that his psychomotor functioning lags behind. (His limits were tested in order to assess his learning potential.)

BENDER MOTOR GESTALT TEST

On the Bender, Roberto achieved a score of "6" (according to the Koppitz scoring system), indicating some delay in visual motor coordination maturation and grapho-motor skills.

TEMAS

On the TEMAS test, when compared with Hispanic youngsters of his age, Roberto scored within low average to high average range in the Cognitive Functions. More specifically, he scored within the Average range in Reaction Time, indicating the ability to transform visual stimuli into meaningful stories; within high average range in Storytelling Time, for his stories were lengthy; and within high average range in Verbal Fluency, thus showing good story-telling verbal ability. Furthermore, he showed good imagination, but tended to show a somewhat poor understanding of the depicted psychological conflicts in several cards, as well as thematic perseveration in several cards.

In the Personality Functions, he scored within the low to average range overall. More specifically, he scored within the low to average range in interpersonal relations with parental figures, for he tends "to be sometimes obedient towards the maternal figure." However, he perceives his mother as insensitive when she doesn't allow him to play with his friend and punitive when he doesn't want to take a bath. He also perceives "the father as demanding, punitive and not listening to the other members of the family." The boy scored within low to average range in interpersonal relations with siblings because he tends to engage with his siblings in mischievous behavior; and he scored within average range in interpersonal relations with peers because he relates with them in a conflict-free manner. Roberto scored within the low to average range in ability to delay gratification because he tends to gratify his immediate oral needs and, at the same time, "he wants to buy a bike, but feels sad because he doesn't have enough money." Roberto scored within low to average range in ability to cope with anxiety/depression provoking situations because he does not recover from scary situations and continues to experience high anxiety even when the stressful situation is over. He scored within low to average range in control of aggressive impulses because he tends to relate to aggressive situations; however, "he tends to be a spectator instead of the aggressor." He achieved a score within low average range in school achievement motivation because "he is afraid that he is not going to do well in the test and the teacher won't give him a prize." He scored within the low average range in self-sexual identity (body image) because "he thinks he has a wrong body and a wrong face which make him fall down... and perceives his body as being awkward just like a strange dog, which has a tail on his head and a head on his tail." Furthermore, he "tends to identify the wrong face as his mother's who pushes him in the bathtub to take a bath when he doesn't like to take a bath, thus making him bang his head against the bathtub." Roberto scored within the low average range in moral judgment because, "although he knows right from wrong, he constantly tells lies and even accuses his mother of wrong-doing." Furthermore, he scored within the low to average range in his ability to distinguish reality from fantasy. In the Affective Functions, he showed a restricted range of feelings, with an elevated score in "Sad."

Summary and Recommendations

Roberto is a 6-year-5-month-old Hispanic male youngster of average height and average weight for his age; he is attending first grade in regular classes. A complete initial evaluation was requested to determine his need for special education classes. On the WISC-III, he achieved a Verbal Score within the average range; a Performance Score within the low average range; and a Full Scale within the average range. However, there were indications showing the potential to function within the upper end of the average to the high average category.

Analysis of the projective tests revealed that Roberto presented strengths in certain cognitive functions such as reaction time (average range), storytelling time, verbal fluency (above average range), and imagination (average range). He showed weaknesses in the recognition of psychological conflicts and in thematic perseveration from card to card. In the personality functions, he showed strength in the areas of interpersonal relations with peers; and relative strengths in the areas of interpersonal relations with parental figures and siblings, delay of gratification, control of aggressive impulses, coping with anxiety and depression, and reality testing. Roberto showed weaknesses in the areas of moral judgment and self-identity/body image. Emotional expression was restricted with an elevated score in "Sad." Emotional indicators fell within the low to adaptive level, indicating the need for individual and group psychotherapy in a clinical setting. Parental involvement is also recommended.

Based on the psychological test results, the following tentative recommendations are suggested so that an appropriate determination can be made.

- Consideration for Resource Room Services in order to remediate Roberto's academic deficits. Instruction in this setting should be provided with continuous reinforcement in order to foster more adaptive attention span and to develop appropriate classroom behavior. His storytelling ability should be utilized to foster more adequate reading, writing, and comprehension skills through the technique of Language Experience Chart Method. Moreover, he should be offered training to develop more adaptive grapho-motor skills.
- Referral for ESL classes to foster English fluency.
- Possible referral for individual and group therapy to work out his emotional problems. Parental involvement is also recommended.

In order to obtain a clearer picture of Roberto, a card-by-card sequential and content analysis was made. This analysis confirmed the TEMAS results with respect to Roberto's poor body image and self-identity (his concern with his clumsiness), possible physical abuse by his mother, and his "feelings of getting even with his mother." To illustrate those dynamics, we are enclosing three stories.

Card No. 7. An angry mother is watching her son and daughter arguing over a broken lamp. (Evaluated to pull for *Interpersonal Relations, Aggression,* and *Moral Judgment*).

R.T.:4" The boy and the girl are blaming the mother because she broke the lamp and the boy and the girl did not like it, because it's their lamp. (?) And they didn't want it to be broken. It was on the table and the kids were running down the stairs real fast and the mother run too fast.

1. Brother and Sister.
2. At home.
4. Running downstairs.
5. They're going to clean it up. Anyway they lied to their mother that she broke the lamp because they did and that they were going to clean it up; and they didn't. She's going to clean it up.
6a. They lied that the mother broke the lamp.
6b. The boy feels sad (?) because she broke his lamp. The girl also feels sad. The mother feels angry because she thinks that the kids did it.

T.T.:4'50"
F: 130

Card 21-M. A youth in bed is dreaming of a monster eating and of a monster threatening. (Evaluated to pull for *Aggression, Anxiety/ Depression,* and *Reality Testing.*)

R.T. 4" First he's dreaming about a nightmare and then he saw a good dragon; and then he put his hand on his eyes, because he doesn't like the nightmare; but he continues to see the nightmare and he's scared of the bad nightmare.
1. He's the boy, when he could not play with his friends.
2. In his bed.
4. He took the money from the piggy bank and that's why he has a nightmare. (?) Because he didn't buy the bike.
5. He's going to tell his mother that he wants to buy the bike. His mother will say, "No," because the bike is too big. (?) He wanted the sandwich and the milk but couldn't get it because of the wrong nightmare.
6b. Scared (?) because he didn't like the nightmare part.

T.T.: 6'15"
F: 124

(Examiner: "Do you have any nightmares?")
(Participant: "I dream of a monster, a very scary monster; I dream of a dog which has the tail on his head and the head on his tail.")

Card 22B-M. A boy is standing on a stool and looking at the bathroom mirror, imagining his face reflected in the mirror with attributes of both sexes. (Evaluated to pull for *Anxiety/Depression, Sexual Identity,* and *Reality Testing.*)

R.T.: 6"   The boy went to wash his hands and he sees the wrong
              face and the wrong body. And he couldn't wash his
              hands. (?) Because the wrong body and wrong head is
              bothering him. (?) He falls down the chair because the
              wrong head and the wrong body pushed him out of the
              chair.

   1.   9 years old.
   2.   In the bathroom.
   3.   "What Am I."
   4.   He saw the wrong face.
   5.   The face pushed him in the sink (?) His mother's face.
   6.   He feels real sad (?) because his mother pushed him
          and he hurt his head.

T.T.: 3'55"
F: 94

              (Examiner: "Is your mother also pushing you in the
              sink?")
              (Participant: "Yes, because I don't like to take a bath
              and I don't like to go into the water, my mother pushes
              me into the sink (bathtub), and I bang my head.)

CLINICAL UTILITY: CASE STUDIES

Case Study 2

The second (clinical) case illustrates the utility of TEMAS, which
was administered together with WISC-III, the Bender Gestalt Test,
and the H-T-P test, in assessing the strengths and weaknesses of a 6-
year-11-month-old White student. The child, who was undergoing
psychotherapy at the time of the testing, was referred for evaluation
in order to assess her intellectual potential and clarify the underlying
dynamics of her emotional problems.

Name: Cathy   School: Catholic school
Age: 6 years 11 months   Grade: 1st
Ethnic Background: White

Reason for Referral

Cathy is a 6-year-11-month-old White child who is presently attending first grade in a parochial school. She was referred to the mental health
center by her mother because of her poor school achievement.

Family Background

Cathy is an only child born in an intact family. Her parents were
formerly divorced. Her father did not have children from his previous

marriage; however, her mother had three adult daughters who live outside the household and whom Cathy calls as aunts. According to the mother, she is spoiled by the father. The father is a businessman and the mother works in a hospital setting.

Provisional Diagnosis: Oppositional Behavior. r/o Attention Deficit Disorder.

Therapeutic Intervention

Cathy began individual play therapy with a female therapist who set therapeutic goals of having Cathy improve her school achievement and develop more adaptive interpersonal relationship with peers, especially female, because she is antagonistic towards other girls, and oppositional with both her father and mother.

After 3 months of therapy intervention, the therapist referred Cathy for psychological testing in order to assess her intellectual potential and to clarify underlying motives. The child had made very little therapeutic progress during this treatment period.

Psychological Testing

Cathy was administered the WISC-III and the TEMAS. On the WISC-III, she achieved a Verbal Scale Score within the low average range, a Performance Scale Score within the Borderline Range, and a Full Scale Score within the Borderline Range. There was significant intra- and intertest scatter, indicating that the child had the potential to function at higher intellectual level. Her serious weaknesses were in the visual-motor organization areas.

On the TEMAS, when compared with White children of her age, Cathy scored within the low to average range in the cognitive functions. More specifically, she scored within the low average range in reaction time, thus indicating cognitive impulsivity; within average range in storytelling time and within average range in verbal fluency. Furthermore, she showed adequate imagination, but inadequate understanding of the psychological conflicts. In the Personality functions, she scored within the low average range in all nine personality functions: interpersonal relations with parental figures and peers, aggressive impulse control, coping with anxiety and depression, delay of gratification, self-concept, sexual identity, moral judgment, and reality testing. Her lowest scores were in reality testing, interpersonal relationship with parental and peer figures, aggression, and body image. Her affective function was restricted with an elevated score in "Sad."

Interpretation of Results (Projective Content Analysis)

Content Analysis of the following two stories indicated a strong preoccupation with "wanting a baby brother" and homicidal feelings towards her parents, whom she perceived as unloving and unwilling to give her a baby brother...and rejecting because she was switched at birth..." These feelings are projected in the following two stories.

Card No. 7. An angry mother is watching her son and daughter arguing over a broken lamp. (Designed to pull for Interpersonal Relations, Aggression, and Moral Judgment.)

R.T.: 2" The mother is pregnant and they are fighting over the mother for the baby. Once the mother says, "Yes, I'm pregnant..." The kids get into a fight. They're saying, "No, you said it first..." "No, you said it first..." That's it.

1. The Adams Family.
2. Scary. (Where are these people?). In the House, it's spooky.
4. I don't know.
5. I don't know.
6a. I don't know.
6b. How should I know?

T.T.: 2' 50"

F: 54

Card 22G. A girl is standing on a stool and looking at the bathroom mirror, imagining her face reflected in the mirror with attributes of both sexes. (Evaluated to pull for *Anxiety/Depression, Sexual Identity,* and *Reality Testing.*)

R.T.: 3" Her hair is different, she is all grown up in the mirror; but she is only 8 years old; she's the same child as in the other picture (also in the yellow dress); but maybe they are sisters. That's it.

2. In her house, alone.
3. She killed them; the mother and the father was murdered by her. (?) I don't know maybe she didn't love them.
4. She didn't want to tell her mother and father her feelings. (How come?) That's it; that's all. Show me another picture.
5. Maybe she's going to be a murderer, a killer.
6a. She's thinking that she loves her father and mother, but she's mistaken; she didn't know, she was switched when she was a baby.
6b. Sad.

T.T.: 3' 55"

F.: 124

Summary: Follow-up and Recommendations

Cathy was a 6-year-11-month-old White child of average height and weight for her age. She was referred for psychological testing because of poor school achievement, maladaptive interpersonal skills, and poor therapy outcome.

The results of the psychological tests with emphasis on WISC-III and TEMAS were shared with the therapist, who in turn discussed the results with Cathy's parents.

In order to remediate poor school achievement, the therapist will recommend Resource Room Services (remedial reading and writing, and math) for the student. There were indications that the student's learning potential was within the average range of intellectual functioning and that her emotional problems strongly interfered with her cognitive/intellectual functioning and thus school achievement.

The TEMAS results pointed out some cognitive strengths and clarified the child's underlying motives and needs; thus relating her school and emotional and psychosocial problems to high anxiety and not to attention deficit disorder. More specifically, the TEMAS results revealed the child's constant preoccupation and high anxiety for not "having a baby brother." and for "feeling rejected by ... and un-wanted by her parents ...," Although her therapist was aware of the child's preoccupation, the therapist did not perceive that the child's preoccupation bordered on obsession and psychotic behavior. The constant preoccupation with "having a baby brother" coupled with the high degree of anxiety of feeling rejected and abandoned by her parents interfered with her attentional processes both in school and at home; thus precipitating an attentional deficit disorder, low school achievement, and maladaptive behavior. Moreover, the therapist was unaware that Cathy had such strong angry feelings toward both her parents. The TEMAS test results and interpretation reveled new underlying motives and clarified her dysfunctional behavior and poor school achievement. Consequently, the therapist modified the Individual Treatment Plan (ITP) as follows.

- Both parents were involved in filial therapy sessions, for having Cathy realize and experience that her parents loved her even if they were not going to have another child.
- Cathy's strong preoccupation with having a baby brother was addressed in individual session by utilizing the storytelling technique, whereby the main character in the stories was "a happy only child...who had the undivided parental affection ..."

- Brief pharmacotherapy (low dosage of Mellaril) in order to alleviate her high anxiety associated with her unmet needs, and thus increase her attention span and interest in school work.
- Follow-up with group psychotherapy in order to foster more adaptive psychosocial and interpersonal skills.

Cathy began to show some improvement in school and at home 2 months after the modified ITP's goals and objectives were implemented.

CASE STUDY 3

The third (clinical) case illustrates the utility of TEMAS, which was administered together with WISC-III, the Bender Gestalt Test, and the H-T-P, and other tests in assessing the strengths and weaknesses of a 14-year-7-month-old Black (Haitian) student. The student, who was referred to the Project Second Try (a special program for juvenile sexual offenders), was tested as part of the intake evaluation to assess cognitive intellectual functions and personality functions in order to help develop the Initial Treatment Plan and set up goals and objectives.

Name: Roger
Age: 14 years old
Ethnic Background: Black (Haitian)
Grade: 8—regular

Referral

Roger was referred by Family Court following allegations of sexual abuse that he had forced anal and oral sex upon his 6-year-old nephew. There is no known history of sexual victimization or perpetration outside of this single reported incident. No history of prior psychiatric disturbance or treatment is indicated in the history provided by the family.

Background

Roger was born to Haitian parents living in Brooklyn, NY. He is the youngest of six siblings from an intact marriage, with the older siblings ranging in age from 22 to 34. Psychiatric history of family members reflects only a brief period of counseling for one sibling secondary to behavior problems during school-age.

Neither parent is presently working. The father is semi-retired and is supported by social security income; the mother is receiving disability income because of a medical condition that is interfering with her usual employment as a hotel room attendant. The oldest sibling, Gauchos, lives with the family and appears to function in a parental role with Roger. Sibling conflict is described among several of the older siblings, but Roger is not depicted as a party to any family conflict. The family presents an idealized view of Roger's functioning and behavior that makes the reported sexual misconduct appear to be an isolated and inexplicable occurrence. However, the psychological test results to be reported shortly suggest considerable underlying disturbance to be present.

Roger attends 8th grade, regular education classes, in a Brooklyn public school where he is making adequate progress. He reports mild peer difficulties in the form of being readily teased by peers. No other history of school-related difficulties is presented.

Behavioral Observations

Roger presented as a large-boned, somewhat overweight 14-year-old Black male with a lumbering appearance. He related in a pleasant manner and remained fully cooperative throughout a lengthy testing session. His affect seemed mildly dysphoric and he stated that he felt ashamed when asked about the circumstances of his referral to his treatment program, preferring not to discuss them. He was fully fluent in English despite a bilingual background in which the primary language of the home was Creole.

The sustained cooperation and interpersonal warmth was in marked contrast to the unusually and intensely aggressive content evident in the projective test protocols.

Battery of Instruments Utilized

Parent Report Measure: *Johnson Child Sexual Behavior Checklist.* *Child Measures: WISC-III; Bender-Gestalt Test; TEMAS; Kinetic Family Drawings; Piers-Harris Children's Self-Concept Scale.*

Parent Report Findings

The information obtained from the parent report measure is limited because of the mother's poor English and the unavailability of a Haitian Creole interpreter. Mother responded to the Johnson Child Sexual Behavior Checklist to the best of her ability. She indicated that the family home contained no sources through which Roger might have been exposed to sexually explicit materials or the viewing of sexual behaviors. She noted that he socialized with peers of the same age. She indicated that he bathed alone and independently. She denied that he was ever sexually victimized.

Mother acknowledged the single incident of anal sodomy that led to Roger's referral to this treatment program. She does not acknowledge awareness of any other inappropriate sexual conduct or concerns.

Roger obtained scores on the WISC-III that fall within the low end of the average category. A Full Scale Score of 93 was obtained with a Verbal Score of 89 and a Performance Score of 99. The test behavior supported optimal demonstration of abilities. Adequate attention span was sustained for the duration of the testing session. Effective rapport was maintained and no anxiety was observed. Failure on specific items was generally tolerated without discomfort. A pattern of sharp cognitive drop-off was noted, wherein the last item answered correctly on a particular subtest would be of a high quality, followed by a sudden reduction in ability. This suggests that the test was accurately measuring the true limit of intellectual potential. Roger displayed considerable achievement motivation, often persisting toward task completion well beyond the standard time frames, without much frustration or diminution of interest.

The pattern of scaled scores suggested mild weakness in academically loaded subtests such as arithmetic and vocabulary, but solid performance in tasks that are purer measures of aptitude. Mild weakness was observed on tasks measuring visual motor coordination and organization and grapho-motor skills, although the index score for processing psychomotor speed still fell within the average range. However, performance on the Bender-Gestalt Test revealed an age-appropriate ability for visual-motor organization and coordination maturation and grapho motor.

Of importance in light of the nature of the referral was the relative strength (scaled score of 11) on the subtest measuring social comprehension. It was apparent that Roger was capable of understanding social cues and responding with effective judgments and behavior. The lapse in judgment leading to this sexual perpetration warranted explanation.

Emotional Functioning

TEMAS, projective stimuli, and the Piers-Harris Children's Self-Concept Scale were utilized to assess personality and emotional functioning. However, the following interpretations and analyses are based primarily on the TEMAS protocols. (The TEMAS test results are analyzed clinically because there are no norms for 14-year-old-youngsters.)

The results were very striking in light of the compliant, cooperative, and well-related nature of Roger's observed interaction style. The profile depicted an extremely poor psychosocial status containing several notable features that appeared, in conjunction with one another, to suggest pronounced disturbance and explain the propensity to act out violently. Probably most striking of these was Roger's extreme aggressive ideation and the insufficiency of his defenses to reduce the intensity or volume of the ideation. In contrast, however, Roger apparently could utilize controls to delimit his overt aggression in the vast majority of instances. Intellectualization, denial, reaction-formation, and projection were the defenses favored to maintain his control.

A second feature evident in the profile was Roger's pronounced self-image and sexual identity disturbances. Self-Concept was bound up in a highly anxious orientation containing a strong wish for approval and relying extensively upon extrinsic reinforcement. Self-image appeared to comprise an extrinsically derived perception of negations by others and to exist largely in the absence of any peer group identity. Identity confusion was a pervasive feature with apparent preoccupation with issues related to both sexual and racial identity. He displayed an identity diffusion and appeared to have been supplied with very inadequate parental role-models as aids to stable identity formation.

A third factor related to an apparently inadequately developed moral reasoning that was evidenced in the extremity of aggressive ideation, with intense and expansive expression. Once the aggression was provoked, no one was safe from it. Bullets sprayed indiscriminately from a "rifle with a sensitive trigger." "Police killed children and children killed police ... a brother shot his sister ... a boy killed his girlfriend's father ... parents were repeatedly murdered." These responses were not without evidence of guilt and remorse, expressed in stories in which the storyteller was the inadvertent victim of his own aggression. But the undermodulation of control over aggressive ideation appeared to reflect an incomplete moral reasoning for evaluation of behavior.

The fourth factor related to the vulnerability to *ego* disintegration and the concomitant disruption in reality-testing and inadequacy of insight. This was suggested primarily by the frequent transformation of stimuli and the apparent dissociation of his self-concept from his own aggressiveness. Further, his affective identifications appeared to be quite variant from the content of his ideation.

Some additional observations based on the TEMAS results are supplied:

First, there were notable strengths. Roger displayed considerable motivation for school achievement and the capacity to delay gratification in pursuit of this achievement. The impulse-control required for this delay was, however, greatly intruded upon by the underlying aggression when it was triggered. An additional strength was the high quality of Roger's verbal expressive ability. This capacity, as evidenced in the story-telling, exceeded the ability inferred from the verbal scaled scores on the WISC-III.

Second, the emotional dynamics could be elucidated further. There was evidence that Roger harbored extreme feelings of vulnerability and a need for protection. He seemed to experience an underlying sense of futility and a vulnerability to the intensity of his own impulses, particularly his aggression. A huge amount of rage was evoked in relationship to father figures in the TEMAS stimuli. He repeatedly evoked images of a hostile father and created scenes of violent retribution against these characters. This dynamic appeared to be bound up with an enormous amount of underlying anxiety, which similarly to the aggression, was dissociated from the self-perception. Roger appeared to be left with a more consciously expressed fear of recrimination over the outcome of his rage. Pervading the thematic material were the ideas of "lost innocence," vulnerability to loss, need for protection, and the inevitability of violence. A sense of helplessness and futility around the wish for safe sanctuary would be the best summary statement to encapsulate this dynamic.

A final note based on the results of the Piers-Harris Children's Self-Concept Scale is supplied:

The global self-concept score (T-38; 10th percentile) was comprised two normal range subscales (Behavior and Anxiety) and three subscales reflecting very significantly diminished self-concept ratings (Intellectual and School Status, Physical Appearance and Attributes, Happiness and Satisfaction). This test often produces inflated scores as the effect of youngsters' wishes to appear in a socially desirable light. As such, Roger's very low subscales were quite striking, the latter three falling at or below the 2nd percentile. Of further note, Roger's two normal range subscores were in areas already suggested to be readily dissociated from conscious awareness, particularly anxiety, which was so apparent on the projective assessment. The combination of the TEMAS and Piers-Harris results added weight to the concern over greatly impaired self-esteem.

Summary

Roger was a young adolescent referred by Family Court because of a serious sexual assault against a younger male cousin, an apparently isolated behavior within a general pattern of normative conduct. His psychological test results conveyed a sense of very serious underlying emotional disturbance in contrast to his observable behavior style of cooperation and conformity.

Intellectual assessment found generally average functioning with mild deficits in verbal processing, although the rich and fluent TEMAS stories clearly demonstrated the strength of his expressive language capability.

Personality assessment revealed significant maladaptation in the areas of aggression, anxiety and depression, self-concept, and sexual identity. A vulnerability to loss of reality testing and *ego* disintegration was indicated, although he could utilize defenses rather effectively in support of behavioral control in the vast majority of instances. Dynamics uncovered included a strongly sensed vulnerability to a sense of lack of an effective paternal or maternal role model, an ethnic-cultural loss and a sense of alienation from the mainstream culture, and a tendency to dissociate aggression and anxiety from his self-perception.

Roger may require intensive treatment in order to address the underlying aspects of his personality disturbance and before he can begin to develop a more adaptive self-identity and adaptive psychosocial skills. He will benefit from individual and group therapy whereby he can develop a more adaptive self-identity, more adaptive defenses to deal with depression and aggressive impulses, and more adaptive psychosocial and interpersonal skills. Roger appears to have limited insight, at this point, to understand and explore the maladaptive nature of his sexual misconduct due to the intensity of his affects and the extent of his reliance upon dysfunctional defenses to maintain control over these affects. Therefore, the initial goal of treatment should be in fostering his insight and awareness.

Diagnosis: Undersocialized Conduct Disorder, (solitary) aggressive type.

The following TEMAS stories show a narrative illustration of his dynamics.

Card 4-M. A father is threatening the wife and his children. A young woman is in bed covering her face with her hands. (Evaluated to pull for *Interpersonal Relations, Aggression, Anxiety/Depression*, and *Moral Judgment*.)

    R.T.: 10" That's the same family. The little baby grew up. There was the same father where the mother took the children out and the little son ran into the room to tell the father they were back. When the boy got in the room he saw the father in bed with another woman. And the boy ran back to the mother and told her the father was in bed with another woman. The father yelled at the son. And when the mother went into the room, she saw the lady in the bed. The mother said that she's gonna really divorce the father and she did. And she gave the family the ring back. And the children stayed with the mother and the mother got married again. And the children threatened the father that one day he'll be sorry. And the children were right. The father got shot 3 days later after the divorce. He got shot 3 times, twice in the chest and once in the head because the woman in the bed was his best friend's wife. His best friend hired a hit man to kill him.

6A - boy - That if he was the mother, he'd hit the father.

6b - little boy - He felt sorry for his mom. He didn't know his father would do that. Cheat on his wife. He felt like punching father in the face (angry).

T.T.: 7'

F: 230

Card 20-M. A youth is in bed dreaming of a scene with a horse on a precipice, a river, and a castle. (Evaluated to pull for *Anxiety/ Depression*.)

R.T.: 5"   Oh!

There was this girl. She had a dream that she was flying on a gold unicorn. The unicorn lived in a castle with only a king but no queen. The unicorn took the girl to the king. The king was the girl's boyfriend and they got married. Had 12 children (it's the first time I've had to stop and think of something).

And the girl took the flying unicorn and went shopping for clothes for her children and shoes and the children grew up and had kids of their own. The end.

6a - girl on awakening - She wished that this was true.

6b - same - felt that really did happen. Happy.

T.T.: 4' 59"

F: 109

Card 22B-M. A boy is standing on a stool and looking at the bathroom mirror, imagining his face reflected in the mirror with attributes of both sexes. (Evaluated to pull for *Anxiety/Depression, Sexual Identity*, and *Reality Testing*.)

R.T.: 5'   There was a man who went into the bathroom and he looked into the mirror and saw half of his face and half of his dead wife's face. When he saw his dead wife's face he started to sneeze and to throw up. After he went into the living room and he saw that same wife washing the dishes and cooking food. And he went crazy again and went to the bathroom and filled the tub with water and went into the tub and felt somebody massaging his shoulders. And when he looked it was his dead wife again. And from all this craziness he died, right in the tub. And his children came into the bathroom and saw the father laying there in the tub. They called the grandmother and the aunt and told them that the father died in the tub. The end.

(How she died?) - She had a heart attack in the hospital right after she got hit by a car.

T.T.: 5' 30"

F: 161

Card 5. A youth is in bed dreaming of a scene of a picnic with a girlfriend and of a scene of a youth sleeping while an individual enters the bedroom from a window. (Evaluated to pull for *Interpersonal Relations* and *Aggression*.)

R.T.: 5"   This is a young girl.

There was this little girl who had a dream that she got out of her house and went out with her boyfriend. They went to the woods and her boyfriend picked out some flowers for her. That same night, she had another dream, that her father saw her with that boy and her father starting shooting at the boy. He was lucky that the bullets from the father's gun didn't hit him. So, another night she had the same dream, but this time the father got hit with his own bullet because there was this bulletproof tree, it was chain-saw proof and dynamite proof. And then the father died because the bullet hit him in the head. They had a funeral for the father and the girl's boyfriend came to the funeral and the father came back to life and killed the boy, took him with him because he had a grenade in his hand.

6a - Girl upon awakening: She saw her father wake her up. She ran and hugged her father and kissed him and said thank God that he's alive. Then she saw her boyfriend and said Thank God, he's alive also.

6b - Girl upon awakening: That she's happy that she has a father and a boyfriend. That she doesn't want neither of them to die. That the father likes the boy and he's hoping that they get married.

T.T.: 6' 55"

F: 236

REFERENCES

Ames, L. B., & August, J. (1966). Rorschach responses of Negro and white 5 to 10-year-olds. *Journal of Genetic Psychology, 10,* 297-309.

Anderson, H., & Anderson, G. (1955). *An introduction to projective techniques.* New York: Prentice-Hall.

Anderson, M. P. (1981). Assessment of imaginal processes: Approaches and issues. In T. Merluzzi, C. Glass, & M. Genest (Eds.), *Cognitive assessment.* New York: Guilford Press.

Aneshensel, C .S., Clark, V. A., & Frerichs, R. R. (1981). Race, ethnicity and depression: A confirmatory analysis. *Journal of Personality and Social Behavior, 22,* 385-398.

Atkinson, H. W. (1981). Studying personality in the context of advanced motivational psychology. *American Psychologist, 36,* 117-128.

Auld, F. (1954). Contribution of behavior theory to projective testing. *Journal of Projective Techniques, 18,* 129-142.

Avila-Espada, A. (1986). *Manual operativo para el Test de Apercepcion Tematica.* Madrid: Ediciones Piramide, S.A.

Bailey, B. E., & Green, J., III. (1977). Black thematic apperception test stimulus material. *Journal of Personality Assessment, 4*(1), 25-30.

Bandura, A. (1977). *Social learning theory.* Englewood Cliffs, NJ: Prentice-Hall.

Bandura, A., & Walters, R. H. (1967). *Social learning and personality development.* New York: Holt, Rinehart & Winston.

Bellak, L. (1954). A study of limitations and "failures": Toward an ego psychology of projective techniques. *Journal of Projective Techniques, 10,* 279-293.

Bernal, I. (1991). *The relationship between level of acculturation, The Robert's Apperception Test for Children, and the TEMAS (Tell-Me-A-Story Test).* Dissertation, Los Angeles, California School of Professional Psychology.

Booth, L. J. (1966). A normative comparison of the responses of Latin American and Anglo American children to the Children's Apperception Test. In M. R. Haworth (Ed.), *The CAT: Facts about fantasy.* New York: Grune & Stratton.

Brenes-Jette, C. (1987). *Mother's contribution to an early intervention program for Hispanic children.* Unpublished dissertation, New York University, New York City.

Canino, G. J., Bird, H. R., Shrout, P. E., Rubio-Stipec, M., Bravo, M., Martinez, R., Sesman, M., & Guevara, L. M. (1987). The prevalence of specific psychiatric disorders in Puerto Rico. *Archives of General Psychiatry, 44,* 727-735.

Cole, N .S. (1981). Bias in testing. *American Psychologist, 36,* 1067-1077.

Costantino, G. (1978, November). *TEMAS, a new thematic apperception test to measure ego functions and development in urban Black and Hispanic children.* Paper presented at the Second Annual Conference on Fantasy and the Imaging Process. Chicago, IL.

Costantino, G. (1980). *The use of folktales as a new therapy modality to effect change in Hispanic children and their families.* (National Institute of Mental Health Grant 1-RO1-MH33711). Rockville, MD: NIMH.

Costantino, G. (1987). *TEMAS (Tell-Me-A-Story) Pictures.* Los Angeles, CA: Western Psychological Services.

Costantino, G. (1992). Overcoming bias in educational assessment of Hispanic students. In K. F. Geisinger (Ed.), *Psychological testing of Hispanics* (pp. 89-98). Washington, DC: APA.

Costantino, G. (1993). School dysfunctions in Hispanic children. In E. H. Wender (Ed.), *School dysfunctions in children and youth* (pp. 206-112). Report of the 24th Ross Roundtable on Critical Approaches to Common Pediatric Problems. Columbus, OH: Ross Product Division.

Costantino, G., Colon-Malgady, G., Malgady, R. G., & Perez, A. (1991). Assessment of attention deficit disorder using a thematic apperception technique. *Journal of Personality Assessment, 57,* 87-95.

Costantino, G., & Malgady, R. G. (1983). Verbal fluency of Hispanic, Black and White children on TAT and TEMAS, a new thematic apperception test. *Hispanic Journal of Behavioral Sciences, 5,* 199-206.

Costantino, G., & Malgady, R. G. (1993, August). *Overcoming bias in clinical assessment of Hispanic school-age children.* Paper presented at the 101th Convention of the American Psychological Association, Toronto, Ontario, Canada.

Costantino, G., Malgady, R., Casullo, M. M., & Castillo, A. (1991). Cross-cultural standardization of TEMAS in three Hispanic subcultures. *Hispanic Journal of Behavioral Sciences, 13,* 48-62.

Costantino, G., Malgady, R. G., Colon-Malgady, G., & Bailey, J. (1992). Clinical utility of the TEMAS with non-minority children. *Journal of Personality Assessment, 59,* 433-438.

Costantino, G., Malgady, R., & Rogler, L. (1988). *TEMAS (Tell-Me-A-Story).* Los Angeles, CA: Western Psychological Services.

Costantino, G., Malgady, R .G., & Rogler, L. H. (1994). Storytelling through pictures: Culturally sensitive psychotherapy for Hispanic children and adolescents. *Journal of Clinical Child Psychology. 23,* 13-20.

Costantino, G., Malgady, R. G., Rogler, L. H., & Tsui, E. (1988). Discriminant analysis of clinical outpatients and public school children by TEMAS: A thematic apperception test for Hispanics and Blacks. *Journal of Personality Assessment, 52,* 670-678.

Costantino, G., Malgady, R. G., & Vazquez, C. (1981). A comparison of the Murray TAT and a new thematic apperception test for urban Hispanic children. *Hispanic Journal of Behavioral Sciences, 3*, 291-300.

Cureton, E. E., & Tukey, J. W. (1951). Smoothing frequency distribution, equating tests, and preparing norms. *American Psychologist, 6*, 404-410.

Dana, R. H. (1986a). Personality assessment and native Americans. *Journal of Personality Assessment, 50*, 480-500.

Dana, R. H. (1986b). Thematic Apperception Test used with adolescents. In A. I. Rabin (Ed.), *Projective techniques for children and adolescents* (pp.14-36). New York: Springer.

Dana, R. H. (1993a, July). *Cross-cultural personality assessment: A model for practice.* Paper presented at the 14th International Congress of the Rorschach and other projective methods, Lisbon, Portugal.

Dana, R. H. (1993b). *Multicultural assessment perspectives for professional psychology.* Boston: Allyn & Bacon.

Del Castillo, J. (1970). The influence of language upon symptomatology in foreign born patients. *American Journal of Psychiatry, 127*, 242-244.

Drasgow, F. (1982). Biased test items and differential validity. *Psychological Bulletin, 92*, 526-531.

Drasgow, F. (1984). Scrutinizing psychological tests: Measurement equivalence and equivalent relations with external variables are the central issues. *Psychological Bulletin, 95*, 134-135.

Durret, M. E., & Kim, C. C. (1973). A comparative study of behavioral maturity in Mexican American and Anglo preschool children. *Journal of Genetic Psychology, 123*, 55-62.

Exner, J. E., & Weiner, I. B. (1982). *The Rorschach: A comprehensive system: Vol.3. Assessment of children and adolescents.* New York: John Wiley & Sons.

Forgus, R., & Shulman, B. (1979). *Personality: A cognitive view.* Englewood Cliffs, NJ: Prentice-Hall.

Fuchs, D. (1986, August). *You can take a test out of a situation, but you cannot take the situation out of a test: Bias in minority assessment.* Paper presented at the 94th Annual Convention of the American Psychological Association, Washington, DC.

Gallager, J. J. (1979). Research centers and social policy. *American Psychologist, 34*, 997-1000.

Good, B. J., & Good, M. J. (1986). The cultural context of diagnosis and therapy: A view from medical anthropology. In M. R. Miranda & H. H. Kitano, (Eds.), *Mental health research and practice in minority communities* (pp. 1-27). Washington, DC: NIMH, Minority Research Resources Branch, Division of Biometry and Applied Sciences.

Gutkin, T. B., & Reynolds, C. R. (1981a). Factorial similarity of the WISC-R for Anglos and Chicanos referred for psychological services. *Journal of School Psychology, 18*, 34-39.

Gutkin, T. B., & Reynolds, C. R. (1981b). Factorial similarity of the WISC-R for white and black children from the standardization sample. *Journal of Educational Psychology, 73*, 227-231.

Henry, E. W. (1955). The Thematic Apperception Technique in the study of group and cultural problems.In H. H. Anderson & G. L. Anderson (Eds.), *An introduction to projective techniques and other devices for understanding the dynamics of human behavior* (pp. 230-278). New York: Prentice-Hall.

Holland, T. R. (1979). Ethnic group differences in MMPI profile pattern and factorial structure among adult offenders. *Journal of Personality Assessment, 43*, 72-77.

Holt, R. R. (1960a). Cognitive controls and primary processes. *Journal of Psychological Researches, 4*, 105-112.

Holt, R. R. (1960b). Recent developments in psychoanalytic ego psychology and their implications for diagnostic testing. *Journal of Projective Techniques, 24*, 251-266.

Kagan, J. (1956). The measurement of overt aggression from fantasy. *Journal of Abnormal Social Psychology, 52*, 390-393.

Kleinman, A., & Good, B. (1985). *Culture and depression.* Berkeley: University of California Press.

Loevinger, J., & Wessler, R. (1970). *Measuring ego development 1. Construction and use of a sentence completion test.* San Francisco: Jossey-Bass.

Lopez, S. R. (1988). Empirical basis of ethnocultural and linguistic bias in mental health evaluations of Hispanics. *American Psychologist, 43*, 1095-1097.

Lopez, S. R., & Hernandez, P. (1987). When culture is considered in the evaluation and treatment of Hispanic patients. *Psychotherapy, 24*, 120-126.

Malgady, R. G. (1990, May). *Overcoming obstacles in minority research: Issues of bias assessment.* Paper presented at the meeting of the American Psychiatric Association, New York City.

Malgady, R. G. (1996). The question of cultural bias in assessment and diagnosis of ethnic minority clients: Let's reject the null hypothesis. *Professional Psychology: Research and Practice, 27*, 101-105.

Malgady, R. G., Costantino, G., & Rogler, L. H. (1984). Development of a Thematic Apperception Test (TEMAS) for urban Hispanic children. *Journal of Consulting and Clinical Psychology, 52*, 886-896.

Malgady, R. G., Rogler, L. H., & Costantino, G. (1987). Ethnocultural and linguistic bias in mental health evaluation of Hispanics. *American Psychologist, 42*, 228-234.

Malgady, R. G., Rogler, L. H., & Costantino, G. (1988). Reply to the empirical basis for ethnocultural and linguistic bias in mental health evaluations of Hispanics. *American Psychologist*, *43*, 1097.

Marcos, L. R., Alpert, M., Urcuyo, L., & Kesselman, M. (1973). The effect of interview language on the evaluation of psychopathology in Spanish-American schizophrenic patients. *American Journal of Psychiatry*, *130*, 549-553.

Marcos, L. R., Urcuyo, L., Kesselman, M., & Alpert, M. (1973). The language barrier in evaluating Spanish-American patients. *Archives of General Psychiatry*, *29*, 655-659.

Mirowsky, J., & Ross, C. E. (1989). Psychiatric diagnosis as reified measurement. *Journal of Health and Social Behavior*, *30*, 11-25.

Monopoli, J. (1984). *A culture-specific interpretation of thematic test protocols for American Indians*. Unpublished master's thesis, University of Arkansas, Fayetteville.

Moscicki, E. K., Rae, D., Regier, D. A., & Locke, B. Z. (1987). The Hispanic health and nutrition examination survey: Depression among Mexican-Americans, Cuban Americans, Puerto Ricans. In M. Gaviria & J. D. Arana (Eds.), *Health behavior: Research agenda for Hispanics* (pp. 145-149). Chicago: University of Illinois at Chicago Circle (Simon Bolivar Research Monograph No. 1).

Mulaik, S. (1973). *The foundations of factor analysis*. New York, McGraw Hill.

Murray, H. A. (1943). *The Thematic Apperception Test*. Cambridge, MA: Harvard University Press.

Murray, H. A. (1951). Uses of the Thematic Apperception Test. *American Journal of Psychiatry*, *107*, 577-581.

Olmedo, E. L. (1981). Testing linguistic minorities. *American Psychologist*, *36*, 1078-1085.

Padilla, A. M. (1979). Critical factors in the testing of Hispanic Americans: A review and some suggestions for the future. In R. Tyler & S. White (Eds.), *Testing, teaching and learning: Report of a conference on testing* (pp. 219-243). Washington, DC: National Institute of Education.

Padilla, A. M., & Ruiz, R. A. (1975). Personality assessment and test interpretation of Mexican Americans: A critique. *Journal of Personality Assessment*, *39*, 103-109.

Paivio, A. (1971). *Imagery and verbal processes*. New York: Holt, Rinehart & Winston.

Piaget, J., & Inhelder, B. (1971). *Mental imagery in the child*. New York: Basic Books.

Prewitt-Diaz, J. O., Nogueras, J. A., & Draguns, J. (1984). MMPI (Spanish translation) in Puerto Rican adolescents: Preliminary data on reliability and validity. *Hispanic Journal of Behavioral Science, 6*, 179-190.

Price, C., & Cuellar, I. (1981). Effects of language and related variables on the expression of psychopathology in Mexican American psychiatric patients. *Hispanic Journal of Behavioral Science, 3*, 145-160.

Reuman, D. A., Alwin, D. F., & Veroff, J. (1983, August) *Measurement models for thematic apperceptive measure of achievement motive.* American Psychological Convention, Anaheim, CA.

Ritzler, B. (1993).   TEMAS (Tell-Me-A-Story).   *Journal of Psychoeducational Assessment, 11*, 381-389.

Roberts, R. E. (1980). Reliability of the CES-D scale in different ethnic contexts. *Psychiatry Research, 2*, 125-134.

Rogler, L. H., & Hollingshead, A. B. (1985). *Trapped: Puerto Rican families and schizophrenia.* Maplewood, NJ: Waterfront Press.

Rogler, L. H., Malgady, R. G., & Rodriguez, O. (1989). *Hispanics and mental health: A framework for research.* Malabar, FL: Krieger.

Shrout, P. E., Canino, G. J., Bird, H. R., Rubio-Stipec, M., Bravo, M., & Burnam, M. A. (1992). Mental health status among Puerto Ricans, Mexican Americans, and non-Hispanic whites. *American Journal of Community Psychology, 20*, 729-752.

Singer, J. L., & Pope, K. (Eds.).   (1978). *The power of human imagination: New methods in psychotherapy.* New York: Plenum Press.

Sobel, J. J. (1981). Projective methods of cognitive analysis. In T. Merluzzi, G. Glass, & M. Genest (Eds.), *Cognitive assessment* (pp. 127-148). New York: Garfield Press.

Spielberger, C. D., Edwards, C. D., Lushene, R. E., Montuori, J., & Platzek, D. (1973). *Preliminary test manual for the State-Trait Anxiety Inventory for Children.* Palo Alto, CA: Consulting Psychologist Press.

Sullivan, H. S. (1953). *Interpersonal theory of psychiatry.* New York: W. W. Norton.

Thompson, C. E. (1949). The Thompson modification of the Thematic Apperception Test. *Journal of Projective Techniques, 17*, 469-478.

Vazquez, C. (1982). Research on the psychiatric evaluation of the bilingual patient: A methodological critique. *Hispanic Journal of Behavioral Science, 4*, 75-80.

Villamil, B. (1973). *Desarrollo del Inventario de Ansiedad Estado y Rasgo para niños.* (Development of the State-Trait Anxiety Inventory for children). Unpublished master's thesis, University of Puerto Rico.

Section Two
New Developments in the Theories and Measurement of White and Black Racial Attitudes

Gargi Roysircar Sodowsky

University of Nebraska-Lincoln

Janet Helms in "Toward a Methodology for Measuring and Assessing Racial as Distinguished from Ethnic Identity" proposes (a) theoretical advancements in the Black and White racial identity models, (b) a nontraditional psychometric understanding of the White Racial Identity Attitudes Scale (WRIAS), and (c) assumptive differences in the constructs of racial identity and ethnic identity.   Helms has introduced new concepts, such as, "sociorace," "racial assignment," "societally defined racial classification system" and "societally regulated racial group," to argue that one cannot classify people in the U.S. according to genetic origins and phenotypes. Rather, race-defining characteristics are chosen by the White dominant group, the group that holds the political power. Thus, race is sociopolitically defined, and racial identity of an individual is the internalized consequence of imposed societal categories.

Originally Helms had conceptualized racial identity as a linear, hierarchical developmental process. She used the construct of "stages" to describe the respective processes of U.S. Blacks and Whites who progress from negative and hateful attitudes to positive and healthy attitudes towards both the Black and the White racial groups. Helms has now suggested that "ego statuses" be used instead of "stages" when understanding a person's "racial self-conception."

An intrapsychic status process is caused by a person-environment reactivity. But statuses are hypothetical constructs, which cannot be measured. What can be measured is the individual's information-processing strategy, as related to one's currently predominant status. However, different information-processing strategies may underlie each status. Thus, two individuals governed by the same status may actually express themselves through different information-processing strategies (for example, in the Black Preencounter status, denial by one and individualism in another). One cannot conclude that any single sample of race-related behavior, as indicated by scale responses, reveals all of the statuses that are potentially accessible to a person. That is, because a status has differentiated to some extent in the person's ego does not mean it will govern all of the person's responses on a measure. Helms uses a circular diagram to represent the status profile of a person. The circle is used to emphasize that racial identity statuses are not hierarchical, in the sense that the use of one status does not preclude the use of another.

These ideographic and dynamic aspects of racial identity have challenged Helms to rethink how to use her objective, Likert-type scales. Helms argues that the basic tenets of classical measurement theory (e.g., items need to be linearly related as in the case of internal consistency reliability) are probably not directly applicable to the measurement of racial identity statuses. Helms says that relationships among items may be underrepresented if one uses unadjusted linear methodologies to evaluate such relationships.

Helms says racial identity profiles rather than single scores should be used to describe the individual. She has used the standard error of the difference between two subscale scores to determine by how many points subscale raw scores must differ in order to be significantly different from one another. This method of developing individual profiles is meaningful in comparison to just showing group differences, as has been suggested by research to understand significantly different scores between verbal and performance tests on the WISC-R, and by Sodowsky and collaborators' use of a critical difference score between two subscales to show differences in the worldviews of individual Chinese subjects. Helms gives a norm table that shows the minimum number of points by which each pair of adjacent subscales must differ from each other to demonstrate high difference, very high difference, or no difference. According to Helms, reliance on untransformed raw score comparisons may contribute to misleading conclusions.

Helms has relabeled the Black Racial Identity Attitudes (BRIAS) subscales by using a combination of Atkinson's minority identity development (MID) model and Cross' Black racial identity labels. Helms has also relabeled her Black racial identity model as Black and other People of Color identity, meaning that the Black identity processes can be applied to "visible racial and ethnic groups" who have internalized reactions to their respective assignments in the sociopolitical power system. What was previously an oppression-driven, race-specific White-and-Black emic model is now generalized to other U.S. racial and ethnic minority groups who have historically not experienced slavery. Prior to Helms, Atkinson had already made the case for an etic or universal minority identity development model (MID), and Sue and Sue had proposed the racial/cultural identity development model. So could this mean that there is now a meeting of two theoretically different models, the MID model and the Black racial identity model?

Helms suggests that identity models be considered racial if they describe reaction to racial oppression, and identity models be considered "ethnic" if the constructs of ethnicity and common cultural socialization as the source interconnectedness among group members are basic to them. Helms adds that in U.S. society, acknowledgement of ethnicity is "largely voluntary," whereas race is not, and ethnicity typically is "permitted" to adapt itself across generations. Therefore, Helms describes her racial identity measures as process measures which, she says, cannot be evaluated by classical measurement theory. On the other hand,she argues, classical measurement theory can be used to construct the content-specific homogeneous constructs of ethnic identity measures. Helms' differentiation of racial and ethnic identity models may not be supported by Bernal, Phinney, Isajiw, Smith, Sodowsky and Kwan, and Derald Wing Sue and Stanley Sue, all of whom refer to the effects of the White group's domination on an ethnic person, and some of whom also refer to different implicit ethnic identity aspects that require internal processing.

Robert T. Carter in "Exploring the Complexity of Racial Identity Attitude Measures" examines the scale constructions of the WRIAS and BRIAS and illuminates (a) various subscales and (b) the use of percentile scores versus raw scores. The objective of Carter's research appears to be to keep pace with Helms' recent theory development of racial identity. Through content analysis, Carter groups 11 factors, factor themes, items, and the factor loadings of the WRIAS into two primary dimensions that he labels Racial Distance/Discomfort and Racial Awareness/Acceptance. Subsequently, Carter reports findings of a cluster analysis. A two-cluster solution for the five White racial identity subscales represented the best fit in terms of proportion of cases in two groups. Thus, Carter argues that Helms' White racial identity constructs of "abandoning racism" and "developing a nonracist White identity" are discernible.

Carter advocates the use of transformed percentile scores from his norm tables presented in this chapter. He reminds us of Helms' warning that local racial climates might influence the racial identity of subjects and volunteer participants, which may, in fact, explain the low subscale reliabilities of the WRIAS and BRIAS and the varying scale scores across samples. To justify his point, Carter transformed the two clusters' rank-ordered WRIAS subscale mean raw scores into percentiles, using the WRIAS norm table. When considering the rank-ordered raw scores instead of percentile scores, the relative influence of the subscales is less apparent.

Carter also reports a cluster analysis of the BRIAS. A three-cluster solution best fit the data, which, according to Carter, suggests three underlying dimensions to Black racial identity: Pro-White, Racial Confusion, and Racial Pride. These domains approximate Helms' previous understanding of the properties of the BRIAS. At first glance at the raw scores, the three clusters do not appear to be distinct from each other, with Clusters 2 and 3 having the same rankings of mean subscale scores. However, by using percentiles from the BRIAS norm table, the rankings change, suggesting distinct profiles within each cluster. Surprisingly, the pro-White cluster has its strongest influence from Preencounter (anti-Black and pro-White attitudes), followed by Immersion-Emersion (pro-Black and anti-White attitudes). Carter explains that both these subscales involve stereotypical perspectives of Blacks, which might have jointly influenced the cluster.

The first half of the chapter provides updated definitions of the White and Black racial identity attitudes. There is a comprehensive review of empirical research, showing how each subscale of the WRIAS and BRIAS, respectively, has differently predicted psychological, social, and personal attributes across samples and environments in several studies by diverse researchers. This section and its references will be very beneficial for future researchers of racial identity.

Sandra Choney and John Behrens[1] in "Development of the Oklahoma Racial Attitudes Scale Preliminary Form (ORAS-P)" first acknowledge Janet Helms' leadership in urging researchers to investigate the racial orientation of Whites as it may affect White-non-White interactions. Then Choney and Behrens proceed to show that the ORAS-P is different from Helms and Carter's WRIAS in (a) theory and (b) instrument development and analyses. They end by responding to Helms and Carter's conclusion regarding the "factorial complexity" of the WRIAS. Choney and Behrens emphasize that validity is demonstrated by an extensive instrument development process, such as their envisioned

---

[1]Choney and Behrens' theoretical collaborators are Wayne Rowe and Donald Atkinson who are referenced in the chapter.

undertaking for the ORAS-P, and that there is a presumption that the WRIAS has a level of validity in Helms and Carter's argument that their measure is factorially complex. Thus one of Choney and Behrens' objectives in presenting the ORAS-P is to demonstrate that its factor structure is not different from that proposed by their theory.

Choney and Behrens explain that Helms' White racial identity development theory uses an "oppression-adaptation" construct which is more appropriate to explain the reactions of U.S. racial and ethnic minorities who experience oppression than to explain White racial attitudes. It provides "developmental interpretations." Finally, it uses the "abstraction" identity.

Calling their own model "pragmatic," Choney and Behrens say that White racial consciousness is characterized by the "significance of being White." The "types" of attitudes that embody the significance of being White reflect ethnocentrism and privilege in White relationships with minorities. Although Helms observes that Phinney fails to distinguish between racial identity and ethnic identity, Choney and Behrens have applied Phinney's ethnic identity concepts to understand White ethnocentrism. Despite such theoretical differences, it appears that the idea of "oppression" may be shared by both White racial consciousness and White racial identity. Also, although Choney and Behrens do not propose a developmental model, they have utilized Phinney's and Marcia's concepts of "achieved" and "unachieved" statuses which have developmental underpinnings.

Choney and Behrens explain attitude change from Bandura's social learning/cognitive theory. When there is dissonance between currently held racial attitudes and recent experiences in the environment, this cognition-environment mismatch may lead to changes in types of racial attitudes. The unique nature of the "dissonant" type is that its experience is available to all types, and it is a necessary transition experience. The central position of dissonance is indicated by a circumplex diagram, which shows that the four "achieved" types are blocked from each other, except when there is movement through dissonance. The racial consciousness in the "avoidant" and "dependent" unachieved types is low because movement between each other does not need a dissonance experience. This stated assumption about dissonance by Choney and Behrens makes their conceptualization about changes in White racial attitudes different from that conceptualized by Helms and Carter. However, it appears the White individual in both models is practicing "adaptation" in attitudes, in one case through a differentiating ego, and in the other through conscious learning.

Thus, we now have two models of White racial attitudes, each accompanied by its own measure. The significant contribution of the two models to multicultural assessment is that their respective instruments permit scientific inquiry and debate, unlike many other multicultural concepts and positions that cannot be measured.

Choney and Behrens state that their objective for constructing the ORAS-P was to provide empirical validation for their proposition of types. They employed the deductive approach, with items designed to measure seven predetermined constructs. Seven administrations of the ORAS-P over a 3-year period permitted the study of individual item performance, univariate and bivariate distribution of subscale scores, and internal consistency reliabilities. Items were modified, substituted, or newly introduced with each administration and analyzed.

Although there are relatively few items per type, with the avoidant type having only three items, the internal consistency reliabilities of the subscales are moderately high. Test-retest reliabilities are similar to those of most trait instruments. Confirmatory factor analysis (CFA) results reported in this chapter indicate relatively strong loadings for a majority of the items and acceptable values for select goodness-of-fit indexes. When the subscales for the four achieved types were collapsed into two bipolar subscales (combined "dominitive"/"integrative" and combined "reactive"/"conflictive"), the CFA fit for the five-factor model was worse than the original seven-factor model. Nonetheless, Choney and Behrens agree that their future item refinement will need to focus on further distinction of dominitive and integrative subscales as well as the reactive and conflictive subscales. The authors' explanation about their CFA methods and understanding of obtained results are useful information for researchers who use factor analytic methods.

Although Choney and Behrens show that interfactor correlations and their directions make conceptual sense, some correlations are moderately high, raising the definitional argument of whether trait instruments are multidimensional or unidimensional or have overarching higher order factors that have not been psychometrically ruled out. The authors may not have empirically shown that their constructs' "unachieved" and "achieved" statuses are the moorings for the various White racial consciousness types. However, given Choney and Behrens' laudable empirical ambitions of "developing" rather than "establishing" the ORAS-P, one expects future refinements to address various questions. While we await new developments, the ORAS-P's initial psychometric properties are promising.

TOWARD A METHODOLOGY FOR MEASURING AND ASSESSING RACIAL AS DISTINGUISHED FROM ETHNIC IDENTITY

Janet E. Helms

University of Maryland at College Park

In the 1970s, as an offshoot of the civil rights movements of that era, applied psychologists began to grapple with the issues of how to measure racial and ethnic identity. Given the increased emphasis on improving the life circumstances of disenfranchised peoples in the United States, practitioners and applied social and behavioral scientists sought pragmatic strategies for determining how best to intervene in the environments primarily of peoples of color in order to contribute to positive mental health outcomes for them as well as society more inclusively (Sue, 1992).

However, as Helms (1990a) noted, the sophistication of theoretical models and formulations used to explain the psychological effects of being socialized in racially oppressed and culturally distinct social groups far outstripped efforts to develop strategies for assessing the relevant psychological aspects of racism and ethnocentricism. Thus, in her overviews of existing theoretical models that purported to address aspects of racial or ethnic identity, Helms (1990a, 1990b) located 11 models for African Americans, six for White Americans, two for Asian Americans, two for Latino/Hispanic Americans, and four for Native Americans. She also noted that some of the theorists that she reviewed considered that they had developed models of "ethnic" or "cultural" identity, whereas others contended that they had developed models of "racial" identity, although each seemed to be addressing aspects of the same societal dynamics of in-group/out-group oppression. In general, it seemed to be the case that theorists who believed that their own discomfort with race or ethnicity was due to racism and the resulting racial discord developed theories of racial identity, whereas theorists who felt that their societal disempowerment was due to cultural mismatch of some sort developed theories of ethnic identity.

However, problems with this language of convenience are that it helped to perpetuate the imprecision in terminology in psychological research when matters of race, ethnicity, or culture are discussed. Furthermore, such imprecise usage makes it difficult to operationally define any of the relevant constructs. Consequently, Helms (1994a, 1994b) recommended that identity models be considered "racial" models if they describe reactions to societal dynamics of "racial" oppression (i.e., domination or subjugation based on racial or ethnic physical characteristics commonly *assumed* to be racial or genetic in nature). She suggested that identity models be considered "ethnic" models if acquisition or maintenance of cultural characteristics (e.g., language, religious expression) are defining principles.

Each of the models that Helms summarized had in common the underlying assumption that an in-group racial or ethnic identity was formed by contrasting oneself and one's societally ascribed racial or ethnic group against the dominant White group if one was a Person of Color or the Black group if one was White. Each of the models also assumed that societal stereotypes and attributions about one's racial or ethnic group are internalized by each person, and influence his or her responses to racial or ethnic stimuli. Yet some of the theories emphasized the intrapsychic processes by which the ingroup/outgroup comparisons occurred (e.g., stages of development), whereas others emphasized the outcomes of differential socialization (e.g., personality types). Since Helms's original reviews, the number of theoretical models for describing the racial identity of each of the racial groups (e.g., Sabnani, Ponterotto, & Borodovsky, 1991) as well as various ethnic groups (e.g., Hutnik, 1991; Phinney, 1990) has continued to proliferate.

However, it is more difficult to count the number of measures of racial or ethnic identity primarily because there is no clear conceptualization of what constitutes "measurement" of racial or ethnic identity, or for that matter, what is meant by "racial" or "ethnic" identity. In addition, measurement efforts have been hampered by a variety of other problems. Perhaps the most important of the measurement dilemmas are the absence of an articulated model for measuring and assessing processes of identity as distinguished from outcomes, and the lack of common measurement approaches for measuring processes in which person-by-environment interactions are considered to be critical aspects of the process. As a result, researchers have attempted to force processes that are conceptualized as operating on an individual person-environment level to conform to group-level measurement principles (Helms, 1989).

Often the incongruence between conceptual models of racial identity and the measurement models by which they are operationally defined has resulted in the misinterpretation or misapplication of classical measurement theory in addressing certain types of measurement issues common to process-identity measures. The primary purpose of this paper is to discuss each of these issues as they pertain to measurement of racial identity as distinguished from ethnic identity.

A second purpose is to propose strategies for increasing the pragmatism of existing racial identity measures. The issue of pragmatism with respect to racial and ethnic identity measures has been virtually ignored, even though assessment of identity was the issue that originally fueled theorists' (e.g., Cross, 1971; Vontress, 1971; Milliones, 1980) efforts to describe racial and ethnic identity in applied psychology. Pragmatism refers to usage of such measures to intervene in and/or assist the assessed person to make decisions about his or her life.

To make this latter point, it is necessary to distinguish "measurement" from "assessment." Aftanas (1994) makes the following distinction: "Assessment is the process of obtaining information that may be prenumerical, such as identifying that one has more of something than another person has. There are many different instruments in psychology that give us this information, including human judgment. When an appropriate method can be found to convert this information into numerical information, then we can conclude that measurement has occurred" (Aftanas, 1994, p. 889). Graham and Lily (1984), who consider the use of standardized tests a part of the assessment process, further stipulate that assessment ought to provide information that enables the assessor to make and communicate inferences or predictions about the person being assessed. Although neither explicitly says so, assessment usually is intended to occur at the individual level, that is, to have implications for individuals. Nevertheless, viable racial or ethnic identity strategies for assessing individuals either do not presently exist, or are not widely known.

Definitions

Adequate measurement or assessment of either racial or ethnic identity requires a clear definition of the constructs that one intends to measure. Helms (1994a, 1994b) noted that in psychological research, part of the difficulty in operationally defining racial factors in particular is the ambiguous language used to discuss "racial" and "race-related" (e.g., ethnic groups, culture) constructs. With respect to racial and ethnic identity, the measurement problems are further complicated by the nebulous meaning of "identity." Therefore, it seems necessary to propose some terminology by which racial and cultural matters in conjunction with identity might be discussed. Nevertheless, the proposed terminology is not necessarily intended to convey the message that there is only one right way to discuss such matters, because the contemporary lexicon of race and culture-focused language is in such disarray that the only correct usages are those on which one can obtain some consensus at the time. Thus, the subsequent definitions are Helms's (1994a) attempt to begin the discourse concerning development of terminology that is less equivocal. She contends that reduction in the confusion with respect to terminology will make it possible to increase the conceptual clarity in the research process where issues of racial and ethnic identity measurement and assessment are concerned.

Prior to Helms's (1994a) observations about the lack of meaningfulness to scientists of commonly used "racial" terms, several authors (e.g., Betancourt & Lopez, 1993; Johnson, 1987; Yee, Fairchild, Weizmann, & Wyatt, 1993; Shibutani & Kwan, 1965) had noted the tendency of researchers to collude with society in using concepts such as race, ethnicity or ethnic group, and culture as though they have a clear common meaning and are interchangeable. Of this triad, the concept that is most important for racial identity theory and measurement is the notion of "race" as a psychological construct, whereas for ethnic identity measurement the constructs of "ethnicity" and "culture" are more germane.

Race

According to Gordon (1976), "Race, technically, refers to differential concentrations of gene frequencies responsible for traits which, so far as we know, are confined to physical manifestations [phenotypes] such as skin color or hair form; it *has no intrinsic connection with cultural patterns and institutions*" (p. 32, italics added). The obvious implication of Gordon's definition is that societal racial categories are biologically or genetically defined. However, many scholars (e.g., Spikard, 1992; Zuckerman, 1990) have advised that if different biologically determined racial groups exist anywhere in the world (a doubtful premise at best), it is not in the United States where a long history of involuntary and voluntary cross-group miscegenation has resulted in so-called mutually exclusive "racial" groups, which share biological and genetic ancestry in typically unassessed amounts.

In anthropological, psychological, and medical research as well as lay society, a person's "racial" category typically has been "measured" by means of crude indicators of phenotypes or physical appearance (Helms, 1994a; Jackson, 1992; Yee et al., 1993). As is true of society more generally, preferred indicators in the social and behavioral sciences have included imprecise "empirical" criteria such as perceived skincolor, self-reported racial classifications, and researcher racial designations. However, Scarr (1981) notes that phenotypes reveal virtually nothing about a person's underlying "racial" genetic composition. Offspring of the same set of parents may demonstrate different phenotypes (e.g., skincolor), whereas offspring of different parents may exhibit similar phenotypes (e.g., skincolor). People of the same racial classification may exhibit different phenotypes, whereas people of different racial classifications may exhibit similar phenotypes (Zuckerman, 1990). Moreover, Jackson (1992) contends that existing anthropological models have never been adequate for demonstrating the presence of biologically defined racial differences worldwide, given their frequent assumption that geographic locations differentiate racial populations from one another.

One consequence of the crudeness of measurement of race is that people who possibly are genetically similar are treated as though they are different. In other words, racial categories that have no known valid inclusion criteria (other than legally defined standards and social custom) become the definers of who is permitted access to societal resources and define the manner in which such access can occur (Gotunda, 1991; Takaki, 1993). Helms (1994a) proposes that the term "sociorace" replace "race" in acknowledgement of the fact that typically the only criteria used to assign people to racial groups in this country are socially defined and arbitrary. In other words, racial classifications are imposed. Be that as it may, at an individual level, a person's ascribed status in the society initially depends upon the location on the racial hierarchy of her or his outwardly defined group (Spikard, 1992).

Racial identity may be broadly defined as the psychological or internalized consequences of being socialized in a racially oppressive environment and the characteristics of self that develop in response to or in synchrony with either benefitting from or suffering under such oppression. Some theorists (e.g., Vontress, 1971) conceptualize the characteristics as stable personality "types," whereas others (Hardiman, 1982; Helms, 1986, 1990a, 1995) describe them as "stages," "worldviews," or "ego statuses." The primary focus of this paper is the racial identity perspectives that purport to examine dynamic processes such as stages or statuses rather than static personality traits or types. Given the foregoing definition, then the relevant measurement and assessment tasks are to construct measurement devices for quantifying differential levels or amounts of relevant internalized oppression-related characteristics, and adapting them for usage at the individual or person level.

Ethnic Group and Ethnicity

In an effort to overcome the research limitations that result from the reification of race as a biological construct, some theorists have attempted to resolve conceptual ambiguities by substituting the terms "ethnic group" or "ethnicity" for "race" (e.g., Gordon, 1976; Johnson, 1987). However, this linguistic compromise ignores the importance of ethnicity as a distinct construct. Ethnicity implies membership in a particular group. According to The *American Heritage Dictionary*, *ethnic* is defined as "Of or pertaining to a social group within a cultural and social system that claims or is accorded special status on the basis of complex, often variable traits including religious, linguistic, ancestral, or physical characteristics" (Morris, 1975, p. 450).

It should be noted that although "physical characteristics" is included in the definition, in fact, one does not have to share the same physical attributes to belong to an ethnic group. For example, Casas (1984) notes that Latinos/Hispanics can be of any racial classification, even though they may share Spanish cultural heritage. Also, Spikard (1992) has observed that members of the African-American ethnic group historically only have needed 1/32 (i.e., "a drop") of presumed African ancestry in order to be classified as "black."

Moreover, inclusion of presumably visible physical characteristics as a definer of ethnicity rather than race belies the fact that historically such information was used to identify people as belonging to different "racial" groups (see Spikard, 1992; Takaki, 1993). For example, in this regard, Takaki has noted that for most of their history in this country, Asian Indians were classified by society as "Caucasian" but not of the White race. Although ethnic groups may exhibit physical manifestations of their group-specific culture (e.g., clothing, symbols), these markers typically are not permanent. In most cases, when they are removed, the person is assumed to be of and is treated by outgroups as though he or she belongs to the socioracial group he or she most resembles.

Betancourt and Lopez (1993) recommend that "ethnicity [be] used in reference to groups that are characterized in terms of common nationality [tribe, community, or geographical region], culture, or language [of one's original ancestors in this country]" and share an "ethnic quality or [group] affiliation ... which is normally characterized in terms of culture" (p. 631). Thus, the critical ingredients in their conceptualization of ethnicity is culture. Consequently, from their perspective, "ethnic group" implies a group whose members are identifiable because of shared cultural characteristics which can transcend societal racial categories.

Gordon (1976) subsumed a variety of racial and cultural (e.g., language, religion) groups under the generic label of "ethnicity." His justification for doing so was that due to historical experience, each group shares with the others "a sense of peoplehood" and this group kinship is recognized in the American lay public's often interchangeable use of racial and cultural terms. However, it can be argued that not only do people have different internal representations of their various potential types of groupness or peoplehood, that is, social categories, but also that these various representations differentially influence their covert and overt behavior.

With respect to racial identity, for example, the inner sense of interconnectedness presumably results from the historical circumstances of racial domination or subordination, whereas with respect to ethnic identity, common cultural socialization is assumed to be the source of interconnectedness. Thus, presumably, even if societal racial oppression no longer existed, multiple ethnic groups still might exist to the extent that different cultural socialization was needed to insure a people's survival and/or the members of the ethnic group continued to value their own culture.

Moreover, it can be argued that American society conceptualizes race and ethnicity differently. Hypothetically, ethnicity is something to be abandoned or blended into a common societal or "American" melting pot. Therefore, acknowledgement of ethnicity is largely voluntary, whereas race is not. For example, governmental agencies such as the Census Bureau only include ethnic-group classifications if they are requested to do so vociferously enough by the groups who intend to use the categories (e.g., Takaki, 1993).

Ethnic classifications rarely have differential long-term implications for national social and political policy in and of themselves, unless specific phenotypes also accompany them. Furthermore, ethnicity typically is permitted to adapt itself across generations to conform to environmental conditions. However, race is valued or devalued according to which group one belongs to, and is considered to be deep-rooted and life-long, although the number and names of the groups may change to reflect societal sensitivities. For example, the "mulatto" and "coloreds" group designations in the 1870 Census became "blacks" in later censuses (Spikard, 1992).

Be that as it may, in order to measure or assess ethnicity, the researcher must measure cultural manifestations in some manner. Thus, the critical measurement and assessment issues for ethnic identity theorists are to (a) operationally define the group-specific culture (i.e., ethnicity) in a manner that visibly distinguishes it from reactions to racial oppression, and (b) determine the extent to which the identified culture has been absorbed. Otherwise, ethnicity and race are merely redundant. Table 1 summarizes the dimensions that are proposed to differentiate (socio)race from ethnicity.

Culture

Psychological or internalized culture might be defined as those beliefs, values, customs, traditions, and rituals that are transmitted in

Table 1. Summary of Characteristics That Distinguish Sociorace From Ethnicity

Characteristics	
Sociorace	Ethnicity
Defines group members' position in a societal hierarchy	Does not define a definite place in a societal hierarchy
For most people, it is not mutable	It is mutable for all people
Does not define a single culture	Defines a single culture
Implies knowledge of racism and own-group racial stereotypes	Implies knowledge of own-group culture
Determined by law and custom	Determined by in-group desires
For most people, it lasts across generations	For most people, it virtually disappears after three generations
Can generally be recognized by out-group members	Can rarely be recognized by out-group members
Does not require the person to do anything to belong	Requires some familiarity with group's culture to belong
Does not require infusion of immigrants or visits to homeland to persist	Requires an ongoing infusion of immigrants or sojourns to a homeland to persist

some form across successive generations of a group, are present during critical eras of a person's lifespan socialization, and become a part of the person's inner psychological experience. Triandis (1994) distinguishes between subjective culture (e.g., values), meaning those aspects of culture that a person learns or incorporates as a part of oneself; and objective culture, meaning the products (e.g., art work) that typify a particular cultural group. Also, Helms (1994a) distinguishes between metacultures and cultures. Thus, she suggests that the dominant culture, that is, the culture to which everyone in a society is expected to conform, is a metaculture, whereas cultures are the customs of smaller social groups and communities within the society such as ethnic groups. In the United States, contemporary Anglo-Saxon culture is the metaculture (see Alba, 1990; Feagin, 1984; Katz, 1985).

Presumably, familiarity with and competence in one's subjective culture(s) is the substance of ethnic identity and its measurement. However, knowledge of or capacity to express a particular culture is not the essence of racial identity or its measurement, although attitudes and feelings toward or evaluations of group-specific cultures might be relevant content. In other words, racial identity theorists usually hypothesize that a person might choose to embrace or reject a culture assumed to typify one's societally ascribed racial group, even if he or she has inaccurate knowledge about and/or is not competent in the culture(s) involved.

Identity

Racial and ethnic identity measurement problems are compounded by the fact that the term identity has no clear conceptual meaning. Erikson (1963, 1968) is generally considered to be the personality theorist who not only made the term identity a watchword in psychology, but also explicitly incorporated the notion of collective identities (e.g., occupational, gender, religious) into a theoretical formulation. Thus, he described a developmental process by which a person could integrate most of his or her various social group memberships into a healthy personality configuration.

Briefly, Erikson proposed that in general, psychosocial identity development is characterized by the following four-stage developmental sequence: (a) foreclosure, commitment to specific personal and group-defined goals, values, or beliefs without ever considering other alternatives; (b) diffusion, a lack of solid commitments or efforts to establish them; (c) moratorium, a state of crisis during which a person explores his or her life options; and (d) achieved, firm social commitments based on engaging in and resolving personally relevant life crises. This portion of his model is relevant to the issue of measurement and assessment of racial and ethnic identity because measures derived from this perpective are often used in racial/ethnic group comparison studies (see Phinney, 1990).

Nevertheless, anticipating future measurement problems, Erikson complained that identity "is used without explanation as if it were obvious what it means"; and researchers use terms such as "self-identity" as though they refer to "social roles, personal traits, or conscious self-images, shunning the less manageable and the less obscure (and often more sinister [racial]) implications of the concept" (Erikson, 1966/1976, p. 60). However, for him, identity meant "a subjective sense of invigorating sameness and continuity" (emphasis in original).

Erikson (1975) proposed that psychosocial identities in particular were characterized by an individual (i.e., intrapsychic) and a communal component. For him, the intrapsychic aspect involved the person's complex internal experiences in reaction to ingroup and outgroup socialization relative to a group. A part of this intrapsychic aspect was "a subjective sense as well as an observable quality of personal sameness and continuity, paired with some belief in the sameness and continuity of some shared world image" (p. 18). The communal component refers to the person's interpersonal relations within his or her own collective environment(s), where adequate adjustment is defined as her or his capacity to be integrated into that community by adequately fulfilling social roles given the relevant historical circumstances. Other social or collective identity theorists (e.g., Tajfel, 1978) also suggest that communality may refer to the interplay between majority-status and minority-status groups (i.e., intergroup relations) and the person's adaptation to those dynamics.

Racial identity theorists tend to emphasize the intrapersonal or intrapsychic ramifications of the person's interpersonal and intergroup conditions of oppression, whereas ethnic identity theorists tend to emphasize interpersonal (e.g, social role fulfillment) and/or intergroup dynamics (e.g., acculturation). Thus, it is reasonable to assume that racial identity theorists would choose operational definitions of identity that permit assessment of internal processes. Similarly, ethnic identity theorists seem apt to use operational definitions that assess the person's fit within his or her group(s) as well as the metacultural group.

WHAT ARE RACIAL AND ETHNIC IDENTITY?

Although Erikson (1968) perhaps introduced the notion of racial classification (specifically, membership in the "American Negro" and "white majority" groups) as critical aspects of personal identity development, he did not include it as a potential source of identity enhancement. In addition, although his theoretical framework has been used so far to discuss the conceptual difficulties in measuring and assessing racial and ethnic identity, it would be fallacious to consider his work to be a direct ancestor of most contemporary racial and ethnic identity theorists because judging from the absence of citations of his work in most of their reference lists, it is unlikely that these theorists were aware of his work. Rather, it is more appropriate to suggest that racial identity theories are in the genre of Erikson.

Be that as it may, later theorists (e.g., Cross, 1971; Thomas, 1971) began to conceptualize racial identity as a developmental process that potentially had positive as well as negative implications for visible racial/ethnic group (VREG) individuals residing in the United States as well as members of the White majority group. Originally, theorists who conceptualized racial identity as involving a developmental process used the construct of "stages" to describe the process. However, Helms (1995) has suggested that "ego statuses" be used instead because it is more consistent with theoretical descriptions of the developmental process as involving not necessarily obvious or conscious intrapsychic person-environment dynamics that are central to the person's racial self-conception. As previously mentioned, Helms (1990a; 1990b) summarizes many of these models. Also, Phinney (1990) reviewed empirical studies of racial and ethnic identity, although she does not differentiate between the two. However, the racial identity models that have generated the most measures (Helms, 1984; Helms, 1990; Helms & Carter, 1990; Parham & Helms, 1981) and measurement controversy (e.g., Ponterotto & Wise, 1987; Tokar & Swanson, 1991; Swanson, Tokar, & Davis, 1994) are those developed by Helms and her associates. Therefore, it might be useful to summarize briefly the basic principles of her racial identity conceptual models, and discuss some measurement implications for development or evaluation of the Black (Helms & Parham, 1985) and White (Helms & Carter, 1990) racial identity measures, the measures whose psychometric soundness has been challenged most frequently. Also, conceptual models and measures of ethnic identity will be briefly discussed to permit consideration of the possibility that racial and ethnic identity might be better served by different measurement models.

General Principles of Racial Identity

Racial identity theory and consequently, racial identity measurement deals with the psychological consequences to individuals of being socialized in a society in which a person is either privileged (i.e.,

White identity) or disadvantaged (e.g., Black and other People of Color identity) because of her or his racial classification. Thus, the biological or genetic realities or illusions of race are not relevant aspects of racial identity conceptualizations. Rather, the focus is on examining the person's internalized reactions to being treated as though he or she belongs to a "real" racial group. Thus, in the United States, members of the Asian, Black, Latino/a, Native, and White American groups are typically treated in society as though they belong to different mutually exclusive racial groups when such is not truly the case. Moreover, individuals who are known mixtures of more than one of these societally ascribed groups also tend to be socialized according to the physical appearance of oneself or one's presumed ancestors. Thus, racial assignment is evident in statements such as he or she "looks" Hispanic or _____ (fill in the blank).

As previously discussed, it is the case that socioracial groups (and consequently members of those groups) occupy different positions along the national sociopolitical power hierarchy such that in the U.S., Whites are assumed to define the superior group, whereas Blacks are assumed to be their opposites or the inferior group, with all other groups of color falling somewhere between the two extremes (cf. Hacker, 1992; Spikard, 1992). Moreover, differential treatment or racial discrimination is such that Whites on average occupy the top rungs of the societal sociopolitical and economic hierarchies, whereas Blacks on average occupy the bottom rungs. The other socioracial groups typically occupy intermediate rungs, although the order of their occupation may vary depending upon which dimension is being considered.

Thus, for racial identity theoretical and measurement purposes, it is assumed that lower status socioracial groups generally contrast themselves against Whites, whereas Whites generally contrast themselves against Blacks. Considerable empirical evidence exists to the effect that Whites generally consider Blacks to be their "opposites," although the term "blacks" historically was more inclusive of all groups of color than the term "Blacks" is today. Such evidence includes several decades of social distance and racial stereotype studies (Feagin, 1984; Gardner, Lalonde, Nero, & Young, 1988). Also, Gardner et al. (1988) reported that even when objective surveys of racial attitudes indicate a diminishment in such biases, more subtle forms of measurement (e.g., behavioral measures) reveal that they are still prevalent.

Unfortunately, People of Color are rarely asked about their feelings and attitudes about either other groups of color or Whites in empirical studies. Consequently, the supposition that conflictual relations with Whites define the primary racial identity themes of People of Color is based on previously cited theoretical formulations in which Whites were identified as the relevant contrast group. Most of these perspectives propose similar thematic concerns, although their concepts may be differently labeled (e.g., Atkinson, Morten, & Sue, 1989; Myers, Speight, Highlen, Cox, Reynolds, Adams, & Hanley, 1991).

Thus, Helms's Black (and People of Color) and White models differ in content so as to be consistent with relevant societal themes or, in Erikson's (1975) words, "the historical moment". However, all of Helms's racial identity models (e.g.,1989, 1990a, 1992, 1995; Helms & Piper, 1994) are based on the following underlying common racial-identity themes: (a) one's racial identity develops in comparison to one's "contrast" racial group; (b) healthy identity development involves the abandonment of societal impositions of racial-self in favor of one's own personally relevant self-definition; (c) members of all of the socioracial groups develop racial identity by means of a sequential process in which increasingly more sophisticated differentiations of the ego evolve from earlier or less mature statuses; and (d) qualitative differences in *expression* of racial identity statuses can be measured, but development must be inferred from responses to measures.

Helms uses the term ego status to refer to the cognitive-affective information-processing strategies (IPS) by which people encode, analyze, react to, and retrieve racial information. Therefore, statuses in her framework are hypothetical constructs. She uses "schema" to refer to the observable (and therefore, measurable) manifestations of statuses. Thus, existing measures of racial identity can potentially assess schema, but not statuses (or stages). As shown in Tables 2 and 3, different strategies may underlie each of the schema. Thus, two individuals governed by the same status may actually express themselves via different information processing strategies.

The extent to which statuses evolve and consequently, schema can be expressed depends, in part, on the versions of racial identity expression modeled in the environment as well as the manner in which race-related rewards and punishments are dispensed in a person's significant (that is, rewarding or punishing) environments. Therefore, an adequate measure of racial identity has to incorporate such dynamics as they presently occur in the dominant or superordinate societal environments in which respondents to such measures can be reasonably expected to have been socialized. The descriptions of the schema constitute thematic content that is presum-

Table 2. Black Racial Identity Ego Statuses, Information-Processing Strategy (IPS), and Sample Schema Items

General Principles	Black Statuses
Status 1—acceptance of societally imposed racial characterizations and rules for dispensing societal resources.	Conformity (Preencounter)—External self-definition which implies devaluation of one's own group, and idealization of Whites and White standards of merit.
IPS: denial, distancing, own-group blaming, individualism	Sample: "I feel uncomfortable around Black people."
Status 2—Confusion concerning one's racial group commitment and ambivalent racial self-definition.	Dissonance (Encounter)—Ambivalence and confusion concerning one's role relative to one's own racial group and the White group.
IPS: disorientation, repression, vacillation	Sample—"I feel guilty or anxious about some of the things I believe about Black people."
Status 3—idealization of one's group and use of external standards to define oneself, and the contrast group, resisting outgroup oppressive forces.	Immersion/Emersion—idealization of one's own racial group, denigration of that which is perceived to be White, emphasis on group empowerment.
IPS: hypervigilance, judging, dichotomizing, combative	Sample: "I frequently confront the system and the (White) man."
Status 4—resolving of intrapsychic conflict with contrast racial group and internalizing of positive racial characteristics.	Internalization—intellectualizing, capacity to objectively assess and respond to members of the White group, and use of internal criteria for self-definition.
IPS: analytic, flexible, intellectualizing	Sample: "People regardless of their race have strengths and limitations."
Status 5—questioning, analysis, and comparison of racial group status relative to other socioracial groups, universal resistance to oppression.	Integrative Awareness (Internalization/ Commitment)—Capacity to value one's own collective identities as well as recognize similarities between oneself and other oppressed people.
IPS: probing, restructuring, integrating	Sample: "I involve myself in social action and political groups even if there are no other Blacks involved."

Note: The Black racial identity statuses are listed in ascending order of evolution and complexity of expression, and are adapted from Helms (in press) and Helms and Piper (1994).

Table 3. White Racial Identity Ego Statuses, Information-Processing Strategy
(IPS), and Sample Schema Items.

General Principles	White Statuses
Status 1—acceptance of societally imposed racial characterizations and rules for dispensing societal resources.	Contact—satisfaction with racial status quo, obliviousness to racism and one's participation in it.
IPS: denial, obliviousness, naivete	Sample: "I wish I had a Black friend."
Status 2—Confusion concerning one's racial group commitment and ambivalent racial self-definition.	Disintegration—Disorientation caused by racial moral dilemmas which force one to choose between commitment to one's racial group and principles of humanity.
IPS: disorientation, suppression	Sample: "I do not feel that I have the social skills to interact with Black people effectively."
Status 3—idealization of one's group and use of external standards to define oneself, and other groups.	Reintegration—idealization of one's own racial group, denigration of other racial groups, championship of own-group entitlement.
IPS: minimization, selective perception, outgroup distortion	Sample: "I get angry when I think about how Whites have been treated by Blacks."
Status 4—"good-bad" dichotomizations of racial groups and imposition of owngroup's standards as condition for acceptance.	Pseudo-Independence—rationalized commitment to own racial group and of ostensible liberalism toward other groups.
IPS: rationalization, selective perception	Sample: "I feel as comfortable around Blacks as I do around Whites."
Status 5—questioning, analysis, and comparison of racial group status relative to other groups.	Immersion/Emersion—search for an understanding of how one benefits from and contributes to racism.
IPS: hypervigilance, probing, analyzing	Sample: "I am making a special effort to understand the significance of being White."
Status 6—self-affirming commitment to one's societally assigned racial group; flexible standards for perceiving other racial group members.	Autonomy—informed, integrated positive racial-group commitment, use of internal standards for self-definition, capacity to relinquish the privileges of racism.

(continued...)

Table 3 (continued)

General Principles	White Statuses
IPS: integrating, intellectualizing	Sample: "I involve myself in causes regardless of the race of the people involved in them."

Note: The White racial identity statuses are listed in ascending order of evolution and complexity of expression, and are adapted from Helms (in press) and Helms and Piper (1994).

ably relevant in contemporary society, but may change as the racial zeitgeist changes.

From Helms's perspective, the racial identity developmental process (that is, evolution of statuses) and expression of one's racial identity (that is, racial identity schema) are not necessarily synonomous. The process defines the sequence by which various racial identity ego statuses may become available for influencing behavior as broadly defined; expression concerns the race-related quality of the observed behavior. One can infer the presence of particular statuses from behavior samples (e.g., responses to scale items). Presumably, one cannot use a particular schema unless the underlying status has evolved to some extent. However, one cannot conclude that any single sample of race-related behavior necessarily reveals all of the statuses that are potentially accessible to the person. Because a status has differentiated to some extent in the person's ego (i.e., is present) does not mean it will necessarily govern the person's behavior. Therefore, measures of each schema ought to include more than one sample of the behavior intended to reflect a particular form of identity expression so that consistency of the person's response can be determined.

Moreover, the rate at which statuses differentiate within individuals is proposedly determined by each person's own level of cognitive-affective maturity in combination with the amount and quality of his or her race-related socialization (Helms, 1984). For measurement purposes, these idiographic aspects of racial identity may be problematic to the extent that one relies on group-level measurement principles for developing one's measures without adjusting them for person-level characteristics. Be that as it may, in general, the statuses (i.e., cognitive-affective information-processing strategies) are assumed to evolve in approximately the following sequence: (a) adaptation of societal interpetations of one's racial group(s) relative to others; (b) confusion and disorientation; (c) idealized identifying with one's own group; (d) capacity to question societal racial ascriptions with respect to one's own self relative to societal socioracial groups, and (e) internalizing of a personally affirming racial identity.

Depending on which socioracial group the person being assessed seemingly belongs to, and where the group lies in the sociopolitical power hierarchy with respect to these issues, the names given to the various statuses of the developmental process and the details of their thematic content may differ.

In Tables 2 and 3, respectively, the Black and White models of racial identity are briefly summarized for the purpose of illustrating measurement conundrums. More detailed explications can be found in Helms (in press, 1992, 1994b, 1995). In Column 1, the contents or basic themes of the expressed statuses (i.e., schema) and the cognitive-affective information processing strategies (IPS) of the statuses are described. Column 2 provides an example of relevant items from the respective identity measures.

Nevertheless, conceptually, the racial identity development process is similar. That is, regardless of the person's racial classification, the capacity to respond to racial stimuli in one's environment involves multiple intrapsychic processes that differ in the complexity of reactions to racial environmental catalysts they can generate. The process within the United States is "universal" because racial classification is omnipresent in this country, but aspects of the content of the process may be unique to groups as well as to individuals within the groups. Moreover, content may change as society changes its manner of socializing racial groups, but the process of developing racial identity should persist as long as socioracial groups are differentially valued by the society.

Black and (People of Color) Identity. In actuality, the process of racial identity development for Blacks is not incongruent with that of other disenfranchised groups of color in many respects. In fact, Atkinson et al. (1989) developed a general conceptual model of oppression to reflect their belief that "oppressed-group" identity, that is, for groups socialized under similar conditions of racial discrimination and oppression, healthy identity development requires that they resolve similar identity conflicts within themselves.

Thus, many of the theoretical issues raised with respect to Black Americans' racial identity development and expression also pertain to other groups of color. Furthermore, concerns related to the measurement of their racial identity should pertain to various VREGs to the extent that the other groups have been socialized under similar conditions of cross-generational racial oppression, and the measure purports to assess intrapsychic reactions to such oppression.

Consequently, if one is a member of the less empowered groups, then one's primary racial (social) identity issue is to overcome the internalized negative stereotyping associated with membership in such groups in order to avoid permanent psychic wounding and to form curative bonds with one's own group members. Because Blacks are a numerical and sociopolitical minority in American society, it is virtually impossible for them to exist without encountering society's pro-White/anti-Black socialization in some form. Therefore, it seems conceivable that more Blacks than not will have developed complex racial information-processing strategies at early ages because their psychological and social survival requires such adaptation.

Table 2 summarizes the basic characteristics of the ego statuses hypothesized to typify the racial identity developmental process for Black Americans. It should be noted that Helms (Helms, 1984; Helms & Parham, cited in Parham & Helms, 1981) originally used Cross's labels for the racial identity stages (now called statuses) and related subscales. However, to conform to her subsequent revisions of her conceptual models (Helms, 1995; Helms & Cook, in press), she relabeled the subscales by using a combination of Atkinson et al.'s (1989) and Cross's (1971) labels. The amalgamated labels are intended to reflect more accurately the dynamic developmental processes underlying the subscale measures. Thus, in Table 2, labels in parentheses are Cross's original names of the statuses where applicable.

White Racial Identity. If one is a member of the dominative group, one's primary racial identity issues are to (a) overcome the entitled stereotyping associated with membership in the White group, and (b) learn to appreciate one's group and oneself as a member of the White socioracial group without colluding with other group members in commandeering societal resources. Moreover, because a White person experiences majority status because he or she is a member of the White group, then the person does not have to cope with resolving issues of racial identity development unless he or she finds himself or herself in a personally relevant situation(s) that challenges his or her entitled status, and from which he or she cannot conveniently escape (Helms, 1984). In other words, if it is true that the majority of Whites do not have to contemplate their racial identity very much, then it is likely that any randomly chosen group is likely to interpret racial stimuli (e.g., race-related measure items) simplistically. Moreover, even individuals who might be predisposed to process and respond to information by means of cognitively and affectively complex statuses, might not be able to do so if White role models who can exhibit complex racial responses are not present in their socialization environments.

Implications. Perhaps it is evident from the summaries in Table 2 and 3 that major measurement dilemmas with respect to Black and White racial identity occur because each status may be expressed by means of one of several dynamic nonlinear processes. Each of the processes occurs in response to the three core components of racial identity: individual, intragroup, and intergroup. These core dimensions are defined as follows: (a) intrapsychic or personal cognitive-affective maturation processes, the extent to which a person is capable of processing racial information; (b) the manner of internalizing one's own-(racial) group affiliation (i.e., inward representations of societal messages about one's ascribed racial group as communicated by significant members of that group); and (c) the internalizing of out-group relations, intrapychic evaluations of the contrast group (e.g., Whites for Blacks) relative to one's own socioracial group.

Each of the dimensions may covary in opposite directions. Thus, for example, when a person's reactions are being directed by the Conformity (Preencounter) status, he or she may function by conceptualizing himself or herself as an individual rather than as a member of a group. Also, such a person presumably uses internalized negative stereotyping pertaining to his or her racial group to encode, interpret, and react to racial stimuli pertaining to her or his own group; but uses unrealistically positive internalized stereotyping to process racial information pertaining to Whites.

Therefore, a measure of a particular schema (i.e., manner of expressing statuses) should incorporate all three dimensions, individual characteristics, owngroup affiliation, and outgroup relations. This assertion does not mean that every item or behavior sample within a relevant measure should include all three dimensions, but rather that the collection of items or behavior samples should be at least tri-dimensional. Relatedly, the owngroup-outgroup or racial elements of each status may be inversely related (i.e., function in opposite directions), positively related (i.e., function in the same directions), or not be related at all. For example, the Dissonance (Encounter) and Disintegration statuses describe a person who is being pulled in contradictory directions, toward his or her own group as well as toward the out group. Consequently, an adequate measure of racial identity ought to include the tension of racial-group dynamics as a defining dimension.

A measurement implication of the observations concerning the potential tenuousness of White identity development and the virtually mandatory nature of Black identity development pertains to the possibility that White and Black identity when examined on a group level, may be skewed in opposite directions for the two groups. The more-or-less voluntary nature of White identity development means that the population of White people should express racial identity skewed in the direction of less mature identity statuses (positively skewed). On the other hand, the more-or-less mandatory racial identity development of Black people means the population with respect to racial identity reactions should be skewed toward more complex statuses (negatively skewed).

It has been argued (Brown & Gore, 1994; Nunnally, 1978) that a measure is more capable of differentiating among individuals if the distribution of scores underlying the measure is symmetrical (and preferably normal). Therefore, depending upon the severity of the skewness, it may be difficult to differentiate among individuals with low scores when a measure's distribution of scores is positively skewed, and among individuals with high scores when a measure's distribution is negatively skewed. Moreover, it might be difficult to develop racial identity measures or to investigate the psychometric properties of existing measures without selecting one's sample to compensate for potential skewnesses within the population under investigation.

Ethnic Identity

The informal notion of an internalized ethnic identity as a phenomenon that is influenced by a person's connectedness and interactions with primary social groups has been around at least since Freud (1959) proposed his own irresistable "attraction" to "Jewry and Jews" as an explanation for his intellectual accomplishments. Perhaps Freud also provided the initial first-person description of the psychological experience of possessing a collective identity. Here, collective identity refers to a person's internalized ascribed (societally determined) or achieved (earned) membership in social categories (e.g., racial classification, ethnic classification, gender).

Thus, Freud, who described himself as a life-long "unbeliever" and a man "without any religion," is quoted as having described his Jewish identity as follows: "[My Jewish identity consisted of] many obscure emotional forces, which *were the more powerful the less they could be expressed in words*, as well as a clear consciousness of inner identity, the safe privacy of a common mental construction. . . . [And b]ecause I was a Jew I found myself free from many prejudices which restricted others in the use of their intellect; and as a Jew I was prepared to join the Opposition and to do without agreement with the 'compact majority'" (cited in Erikson, 1976, p. 62, italics added).

Thus, from Freud's revelation, it becomes clear that as is the case for racial identity, ethnic identity can also be a nebulous motivational force that functions at the individual or person level. He also raised the notion of ethnic identity as a "mental construction," which presumably distinguishes it from an objective reality. However, in this paper, it is contended that the motivational force for ethnic identity. which distinguishes it from racial identity, is cultural in nature, and need not necessarily be "Oppositional." In fact, to be consistent, theories and measures are discussed as ethnic in focus if they incorporate group-specific culture in more than a superficial (e.g., self or theorist designation) manner, and racial if they only deal with the dynamics of in-group/outgroup opposition and conflict.

This definitional strategy excludes those theoretical models that purport to be ethnic identity models, but only deal with ethnicity in comparison to other racial (rather than ethnic) groups; or—perhaps more accurately—includes such models under the racial identity rubric. However, it includes identity (sometimes called acculturation) models that propose different styles of cultural adaptation based on inevitable metacultural acculturative or assimilative pressures toward conformity (e.g., Aboud, 1987; Aboud & Skerry, 1984). The definition also includes models that attempt to describe ethnic-group cultural affiliation or lack thereof (e.g., Bernal et al., 1990). Several measures have been developed to assess ethnic cultural characteristics for various ethnic groups. Therefore, it is probably useful to summarize some of the basic tenets of the cultural adaptation and group-affiliation perspectives.

Cultural Adaptation. Several theorists have conceptualized ethnic identity as cultural styles or patterns that groups evolve in response to metacultural pressures to relinquish traditional cultures (e.g., Aboud & Skerry, 1984; Birman, 1994; Bulhan, 1980; Ruiz & Padilla, 1977; Szapocznik, Scopetta, Kurtines, & Aranalde, 1978; Stonequist, 1937; Tajfel, 1978). Many of them propose some combination of the following patterns: (a) moving away from or relinquishment of one's traditional (ethnic) culture, (b) moving towards or internalizing the metaculture, (c) rejection of both the ethnic culture and the metaculture, and (d) moving towards or internalizing both cultures (i.e., biculturality). Thus, these conceptualizations attempt to describe differential levels of connectedness with one's ethnic group as well as the metaculture. The basic measurement task with respect to these models is to differentiate among the proposed styles.

Ethnic Group Affiliation. According to Bernal et al. (1990), ethnic identity consists of the following five components: (a) ethnic self-identification, defined as involving self-categorization and labeling of oneself as a member of the ethnic group based on "appropriate [ingroup] cues"; (b) ethnic constancy, awareness that "one's ethnic characteristics are unchanging and permanent" (p. 5); (c) performance of ethnic role behaviors, not necessarily knowledgeable use of a wide range of ethnic behaviors, values, customs, and so forth; (d) ethnic knowledge, awareness of the content (e.g., customs, behaviors, etc.) of the relevant ethnic culture; and (e) ethnic preferences and feelings, attraction toward one's ethnic group and the culture that defines the group.

This perspective does not propose specific interrelationships among the various components. Nor does it specify an ordering or sequencing of components as does racial identity developmental theory. However, Bernal et al. (1990) do speculate that children become more adept at each of the components as they age, presumably because ethnic identification is based on conceptual cues that are more subtle and, therefore, more difficult to recognize than is true of racial identity. Consequently, for measurement purposes, it does not appear that it is necessary for any single measure to evaluate all of the proposed components, although for pragmatic purposes, presumably each of them should be capable of being measured or assessed in some manner.

MEASUREMENT OF ETHNIC AND RACIAL IDENTITY

In the measurement literature, race and ethnicity generally are used interchangeably. Thus, it is often difficult to determine which construct researchers intend to quantify. Nevertheless, in general, it appears that both ethnic identity and racial identity have been measured most frequently by means of various kinds of paper-and-pencil rating scales. However, several researchers have advised that measurement of racial or ethnic identity would be improved by focusing upon the respondents' subjective experiences of race or culture, but not both in a single measure (e.g., Alba, 1990; Landrine & Klonoff, 1994). Such a differential focus would make it easier to identify measurement dilemmas that are peculiar to one form of collective identity rather than the other.

Measures of Ethnic Identity

In the identity conceptual and measurement literature, sometimes ethnic identity measures are called ethnic identity measures, and sometimes they are called acculturation measures. For the purposes of this paper, the mitigating factors that define a measure as an ethnic identity measure are that it (a) addresses some aspect of culture as defined by adaptation to a group's culture or self-reported kinship with a cultural group, (b) includes the person's subjective experience of culture or acculturation in some manner, and (c) that one's specific cultural rather than socioracial group be a central aspect of the measurement process.

Three categories of ethnic identity measures were gleaned from Atkinson and Thompson's (1992) review of racial and cultural variables in counseling. They are unidimensional, componential, and bicultural. Unidimensional scales measure the person's acquisition of the metaculture (e.g., Cuellar, Harris, & Jasso, 1980); componential scales measure the extent to which a person expresses various components (e.g., language, kinship) of her or his traditional culture (e.g., Bernal et al., 1990; Padilla, 1980); and bicultural scales measure the person's level of acclimation to the metaculture and her or his traditional culture (Szapocznik et al., 1978).

The theoretical model underlying most of these measures is either cultural adaptation or a combination of kinship and cultural adaptation. An example of a unidimensional combination scale is Cuellar et al.'s (1980) Acculturation Rating Scale for Mexican Americans (ARSMA). Respondents use 20 multiple-choice items to describe themselves with respect to (a) Spanish language facility, (b) owngroup interaction, (c) ethnic self-designation, and (d) competence in Anglo culture. Cutoff scores are used to assign respondents to one of three to five categories (very Mexican, Mexican-oriented bicultural, true bicultural, etc.). Several measures for other ethnic groups have been adapted from the ARSMA (e.g., Suinn, Rickard-Figueroa, Lew, & Vigil, 1987).

As Phinney (1990) noted, often investigators have not described the psychometric characteristics of their measures or they have relied on the measure originator's psychometric descriptions. Nevertheless, Kunkel (1990) reported a Cronbach's alpha of .92 for the ARSMA, and Suinn et al. (1987) reported an alpha coefficient of .88 for their Asian adaptation, the SL-ASIA. Such results suggest that measures of ethnic identity can be constructed in which items are highly interrelated and, perhaps, are homogeneous.

Measures of Racial Identity

In their review of measures of racial identity, Burlew and Smith (1991) classified such measures as follows: (a) developmental, focus on intrapsychic and/or psychosocial adaptations to social and environmental forces of race and racism; (b) Africentric, examine manifestations of African-oriented personality characteristics; (c) group based, emphasize level of affiliation or kinship with a racial group; and (d) racial stereotyping, evaluate the extent to which societal racial stereotypes have been internalized. Most of the racial identity measures have had Black people as their focus. The racial identity measures developed by Helms and her associates (e.g., Helms & Parham, 1985; Helms & Carter, 1990) are direct descendants of the developmental approaches of measuring racial identity (e.g., Cross, 1971).

Description. Both the Black and White racial identity measures have similar measurement dilemmas to be resolved because they are based on analogous theoretical frameworks (see Tables 2 and 3). Consequently, the subsequent observations about the psychometric properties of such measures and recommendations for resolving some of the measurement and assessment concerns generally pertain to both the Black (BRIAS) and White (WRIAS) racial identity scales, although the WRIAS will generally be used to illustrate relevant points.

Both identity scales are rationally constructed personality measures intended to quantify the level of implementation (that is, expression) of the relevant racial identity ego statuses. Because the subscales of the measures are intended to reflect the constructs of racial identity theory, they are intended to be multidimensional in nature. That is, each subscale in its entirety is intended to quantify the manner in which the respondent reacts to racial information about self relative to his or her own racial group as well as the relevant contrast group as previously discussed. Respondents use 5-point Likert scales (1=*Strongly Disagree* to 5=*Strongly Agree*) to respond to items similar to those shown in Tables 2 and 3. Primacy or strengths of schema usage are inferred from a person's racial identity subscale scores (i.e., higher scores imply stronger or more dominant schema).

The racial identity measures have face validity as attitudinal measures and were originally conceived as such. However, some evidence supports the conclusion that the items comprising the measure elicit individual interpretations of racial stimuli rather than objectively reportable attitudes or opinions. The evidence includes (a) respondents' unsolicited written interpretations of and perhaps reactions to WRIAS items (Remy, 1993), (b) the lack of substantial relationships between racial identity subscale scores and measures of social desirability (e.g., Meijer, 1993), and (c) the fluidity of racial identity subscale scores under conditions of racial stimulation (Corbett, 1994; Meijer, 1993).

Remy (1993) summarized her respondents' unsolicited written responses to WRIAS items. She noted that most of her sample either agreed or disagreed with the Contact item, "I wish I had a Black friend," as intended. However, a small (unspecified) percentage of her sample responded by reporting that they had a Black friend and chastising the researcher for accusing them of racism. Hacker (1992) contends that such testifying is typical for most White "liberals" because having a Black friend is evidence to themselves and others that they are not racists. Additionally, Remy found a variety of idiosyncratic responses to other items including drawn swastikas, musings about how Blacks might respond to the items, explanations of why the person answered as he or she did, and so forth. Interestingly, individualistic interpretations of items were even more evident on scales in which Remy replaced "Blacks" with "Asian Americans" in item stems.

Some evidence suggests that racial identity expressions may not be related to standard measures of social desirability on a group level (Meijer, 1993). The correlations shown in the diagonal of Table 6 indicate negligible correlations between the racial identity subscales and the Marlowe-Crowne Social Desirability Scale (Marlowe & Crowne, 1961), a standard measure of a social desirability response set. The sample on which the correlational analyses were conducted are from Helms and Carter (1991). Meijer also found negligible correlations ranging from -.16 (Disintegration and Reintegration) to .11 (Autonomy) for her sample of 243.

It is at least conceivable that for subscales to have strong social desirability response sets, items would need a recognizable positive direction. However, racial identity theory postulates that the social desirability of items is determined by the status the person uses in processing them.

Meijer (1993) and Corbett (1994) investigated environmental and intrapsychic conditions under which scores on WRIAS subscales vary. Meier investigated changes in psychology students' WRIAS subscale scores over a 12-week interval during which the experimental group was exposed to an introductory psychology course with a multicultural emphasis. She found that none of the racial identity expression subscale scores changed significantly except Pseudo-Independence, which decreased by the end of the interval regardless of whether respondents had participated in the course. Thus, her findings suggest that under normal circumstances, racial identity expressions measured at a group level are quite stable over time.

Corbett (1994) found that those respondents who were exposed to a role-reversal racial fantasy rather than a career fantasy expressed lower levels of Contact and Pseudo-Independence and higher levels of Disintegration, Reintegration, and Immersion/Emersion. Moreover, their racial identity expressions following the race fantasy were more predictive of dimensions of healthy and defensive narcissism than they were prior to the fantasy in directions consistent with racial identity and narcissism theories. Thus, Corbett's results support Helms's contention that racial identity expressions can be stimulated by external racial catalysts.

Consequently, when used at the group level, racial identity measures at best evaluate common reactions to the racial catalysts contained within items. However, in the absence of information about the particular racial socialization experiences of the respondents, it is not clear what subscale scores mean for or about a person's racial identity expressions at the individual level.

MEASUREMENT ISSUES AT THE GROUP LEVEL

Several explorations of the psychometric properties of the racial identity research scales have appeared in the counseling literature (e.g., Helms & Carter, 1990; Ponterotto & Wise, 1989; Swanson, Tokar, & Davis, 1994; Yanico, Swanson, & Tokar, 1994). Moreover, virtually all of the studies of other personality constructs thought to be related to racial identity schema also have included investigations of the psychometric properties of the measures to some extent (e.g., Watts & Carter, 1991; Ottavi et al., 1994), and investigators have deleted subscales on the basis of the results of these local analyses. Although investigators typically have not said so, "classical" measurement theory apparently has been the conceptual measurement model on which the psychometric explorations of racial identity measures have been based.

In classical measurement theory (i.e., "strong true score" theory), a basic measurement assumption is that every observed score (X) presumably arises from one of two sources, true score (T) or error (E). This relationship is commonly symbolized by the formula $X = T + E$. Because the value of T (the amount of the construct being measured) cannot be measured or observed directly, it is inferred from relationships among Xs (i.e., items, test scores, etc.). A number of other measurement assumptions follow from the basic true-score premise. DeVellis (1991) summarizes some of the consequent assumptions as follows:

1. The amount of error associated with individual items varies randomly. The error associated with individual items has a mean of zero when aggregated across a large number of people. Thus, items' means tend to be unaffected by error when a large number of respondents complete the items.
2. One item's error term is not correlated with another item's error term; the only routes linking items pass through the

latent variable [i.e., the true score variance], never through any error term.

3. Error terms are *not* correlated with the true score. (p. 17).

Thus, the assumptions imply that obtained interrelationships (typically expressed as correlations) among items indicate the amount of true score (e.g., racial identity) being measured rather than the amount of error. The use of correlations to indicate the amount of true score manifested in a set of items also assumes that items (or rather the true variance present in such items) are linearly related. However, there are several reasons why these basic tenets of classical measurement theory probably are not directly applicable to measurement of racial identity schema. The groundwork for most of these arguments appeared in prior sections, but it might be necessary to state the reasons more explicitly. They are as follows: (a) Racial identity theory is a description of how people process racial information at an individual level. Although the classical-measurement assumptions may be used effectively to obtain descriptive statistics for an entire group, they cannot be used to determine T and E exactly for any individual. (b) Individual differences in responding to the racial identity items are the essence of the theory, but would be considered error under the general assumptions previously cited (see Lyman, 1978). (c) Individual reactions (e.g., person-environment reactivity) to racial identity items are not proposed to be linear and consequently, relationships among items might be underestimated if one uses unadjusted linear methodologies to evaluate such relationships. These sources of incongruence between racial identity theory and the cited classical measurement assumptions also may bear on other aspects of the psychometric properties of racial identity measures.

Most efforts to evaluate the psychometric properties of racial identity measures have been studies of the reliability and/or internal structure of the measures. In these investigations, researchers have tended to treat racial identity subscales as though they were intended to be linear group-level measures, and have evaluated their psychometric properties on the basis of strict conformance to the principles of classical measurement theory as previously summarized. Consequently, the interpretations of the results obtained from such studies have contributed to the confusion regarding measurement of racial identity constructs.

Reliability

Conceptually, reliability historically has been defined as the correlation between parallel tests (DeVellis, 1991; Graham & Lilly, 1984; Nunnally, 1978). In this case, "tests" can be interpreted to mean items within subscales that are intended to measure the same process (i.e., racial identity schema). Thus, when measures are developed with classical measurement theory as their underlying measurement model, reliability coefficients describe the degree of linear interrelationship(s) among tests (or items).

In her critique of racial and ethnic identity measures, Phinney (1990) noted that reliability with respect to such measures typically is not reported or "is low enough to raise questions about conclusions based on the measure" (p. 506). Furthermore, she noted that Cronbach's alphas were the reliability coefficients usually reported by the 20% of studies she reviewed in which reliability was reported. For the various measures, she indicated that reported reliabilities have ranged from .35 to .90.

However, Helms's (e.g., Parham & Helms, 1981) Black racial identity inventory was the only measure specifically mentioned, and for this measure, Phinney (1990) cited alphas ranging from .66 to .72. Researchers subsequent to her review have reported alpha reliabilities ranging from .45 to .63 for the BRIAS (Yanico et al., 1994). For the WRIAS, the following ranges have been reported: .55 to .82 (Helms & Carter, 1990); .43 to .85 (Regan, 1992), .18 to .75 (Ottavi et al., 1994), and .61 to .84 (Tokar & Swanson, 1991; Swanson et al., 1994). In Table 4, Cronbach's (1951) coefficient alpha estimates of internal consistency reliability are reported for the WRIAS subscales corresponding to the schema described in Table 3. The range is from .54 to .79.

Table 4. Summary of Psychometric Properties of the WRIAS.

Scale	r_{xx}	Mean	SD	Range
Contact	.54	31.03	4.70	13–44
Disintegration	.76	24.38	5.45	10–39
Reintegration	.79	24.33	5.99	11–46
Pseudo Independence	.62	35.38	4.72	13–47
Autonomy	.67	34.94	4.94	16–48
Total	.37	149.35	10.54	106–182

Note. r_{xx} = coefficient alpha estimates.

Ordinarily, in constructing personality measures, internal consistency reliability is a primary issue. Nevertheless, the range of internal consistencies of subscales of well-established general identity inventories is quite variable. For example, in their analysis of the psychometric properties of seven well-known identity measures, Walsh and Betz (1985) reported internal consistency reliabilities in the .50s and .60s for the stages of Rest's (1979) Defining Issues Test (DIT), a measure of moral development; and reliabilities ranging from .45 to .78 for the Student Development Task Inventory-2 (SDTI-2; Winston, Miller, & Prince, 1979), a measure of Chickering's developmental vectors. Of the published identity measures the authors described, the DIT and the SDTI-2 were the only two by which the quality of respondents' psychosocial identity statuses is inferred from objectively scored scales rather than rater-scoring procedures.

Examination of the alpha coefficients shown in Table 4 reveals that they are not great if one uses cognitive ability tests as the standard, but that they are not bad in comparison to psychosocial identity inventories. Typically, low racial identity alpha coefficients have been interpreted to mean a lack of homogeneity among items or the presence of heterogeneity (e.g., Yanico et al., 1994). Yet at least a couple of other explanations are possible, particularly when one considers the variability of reported alphas across studies and (presumably) research sites.

An obvious explanation is that researchers may not have sampled adequately. In order to obtain high coefficient alphas, one needs to have some people who have high scores relative to some people who have low scores. If the distributions of racial identity statuses within populations are skewed, then one may need to do special sampling to include people who can express the under-represented statuses. Thus, for example, one might need to find White people who are civil rights activists to represent adequately the higher end of the Autonomy subscale. Most researchers to date have used convenience and/or regional samples, but have not selected samples who might reasonably be expected to be capable of expressing the schema under investigation.

Furthermore, under the best of circumstances, Cronbach's (1951) alpha coefficient estimates the degree of interrelationship among a set of items rather than the degree of homogeneity of scales or subscales (Green, Lissitz, & Mulaik, 1977). However, Green et al. note that alpha coefficients may underestimate the interrelatedness of items under the following conditions: (a) if items' true scores are related to one another in nonlinear ways that cannot be revealed by a correlation matrix and/or (b) items are negatively related to one another. Also, if situational variables interact with the characteristics of the person rather than being a form of random variance, then coefficient alpha might also underestimate the reliability of measures.

Ordinarily, the recommended techniques for analyzing the reliability of multifactorial scales have been split-half, alternate forms, or immediate test-retest (Cureton, 1967; Dawis, 1987). However, most of these approaches are not entirely workable for establishing the reliability of racial identity measures for a variety of reasons. Alternate form reliability will not function as a reliability-estimating approach because none of the racial identity measures has an alternate form. Immediate test-retest reliability should reveal that subscale responses are stable over short periods of time given Meijer's (1993) and Corbett's (1994) findings of stability over extended periods of time. However, although test-retest would reveal whether the processes were stable over short periods of time, it is not apparent that such procedures would reveal much about the structure of items within subscales, which presumably is the question that motivates researchers who use coefficient alpha.

Of the recommended alternative reliability procedures, split-half potentially can be adapted for assessing item structure by means of linear analysis. However, one would need to use what DeVellis (1991) calls "balanced" halves rather than the customary splitting (e.g., random, odd-even) procedures. When using a balancing procedure, halves are chosen so that items indicative of relevant item characteristics or principles are present in both halves. Thus, for example, in the present case, one might select halves according to the information-processing strategies being tapped by items, so that the strategies are equivalently represented in both halves. To date, balanced split-halves have not been used to evaluate the reliability of the racial identity subscales.

Be that as it may, due to low alpha coefficients, editors have forced researchers (e.g., Watts & Carter, 1991) to eliminate certain scales from their research as a condition for publication (Carter, personal communication). The editors contend that it is impossible to know what a scale is measuring if its coefficient alpha is low. However, given the virtual dearth of racial identity measures with a substantial history of psychometric exploration, reliance on coefficient alpha as the sole indicator of the interrelatedness of items is probably premature when the possible limitations of this approach for evaluating the reliability of racial identity measures is considered.

In addition, although sample size does generally affect the size of reliability coefficients, smaller reliability coefficients can be used to describe accurately the responses of large groups relative to small groups or individuals. Thus, for example, Thorndike and Hagen (1969) can be used to illustrate this point. They compared changes over two occasions in the rank ordering of two people's, small groups' ($N = 25$), and large groups' ($N = 100$) scores, when the initial scores placed one person or group at the 50th percentile and the other's score placed the person or group at the 75th percentile. They calculated that a reliability coefficient of .50 would result in inconsistent descriptions (i.e., a reversal in rank order) about 36.8% of the time for two people, whereas the same size coefficient would result in inconsistent descriptions of 100-person groups 1 in 2,500 (.04%) times.

It seems reasonable to infer from Thorndike and Hagen's discourse that if one uses the criteria of state-of-the-art and sample size, then even the racial identity subscale with the lowest internal consistency reliability coefficient (Contact= .54) shown in Table 4 should be suitable for describing the rank order of groups of 100 or more most of the time and smaller samples almost two-thirds of the time. Thus, for virtually all of the racial identity studies intended to examine the reliability or validity of the racial identity measures (e.g., Tokar & Swanson, 1991; Ottavi & Pope-Davis, 1994; Swanson et al., 1994), the reported internal consistency reliabilities have been adequate for describing groups according to Thorndike and Hagen's criteria, researchers' admonitions notwithstanding.

Thus, in the construct-validity literature pertaining to racial identity measures (e.g., Ottavi et al., 1994; Tokar & Swanson, 1991; Watts & Carter, 1991), alpha coefficients were used primarily to describe the subscale responses of samples of at least 100 persons. For example, even Tokar and Swanson (1991; Swanson et al., 1994), who contend that their studies demonstrate the inadequate psychometric properties of racial identity measures, used a sample consisting of 309 college students. The alpha coefficients that they obtained were adequate for the group-level statistics that they performed (multiple regressions) according to Thorndike and Hagen's criteria despite Tokar and Swanson's protestations to the contrary.

Of course, one should attempt to construct highly reliable measures, but the procedures for determining reliability should be consistent with the conceptual model on which the measure is based. Moreover, reliability should not replace validity as the indicator of a measure's psychometric merits (Ebel, 1961; Thorndike & Hagen, 1969). In those instances in which researchers obtain low alpha reliability coefficients, they should perhaps use their findings as a catalyst for considering alternative measurement models, or reconsidering the manner in which their data were collected. Moreover, low subscale coefficient alphas combined with evidence of subscale validity (e.g., significant correlations between the subscales and measures external to the identity measures) should serve as an additional catalyst for considering the applicability of one's measurement model and/or sampling procedures.

Scale Correlations

Various researchers have also used subscale intercorrelations to investigate the internal structure of racial identity measures (Ottavi et al., 1994; Swanson et al., 1994; Yanico et al., 1994). In general, subscales developmentally contiguous to one another should be correlated without being completely overlapping. Investigators of the construct validity of the subscales who use multiple regression to predict other personality variables from racial identity have been particularly concerned when moderately to highly correlated scales do not each predict the variables of interest as expected.

In this regard, Tokar and Swanson (1991) found a correlation of .66 between the Pseudo Independence (alpha=.65) and Autonomy (alpha = .71) subscales of the WRIAS. In regression analyses, they found that when Pseudo Independence was used as one of five predictors, it did not uniquely predict any of their criterion measures, but Autonomy significantly predicted inner-directedness or self-acceptance. From such findings, they concluded that "some of the [racial identity] subscale intercorrelations were so high as to suggest redundancy" (p. 299).

Although conclusions concerning redundancy of the subscales are at least debatable, it is also the case that in the absence of correlations of 1.00, correlations may not reveal much about how individuals within the sample respond. In Table 7, the subscales with the correlation between them closest to Tokar and Swanson's "redundant" correlation are Autonomy and Pseudo Independence (r = .66). Table 6 shows that most of the sample (93.5%) uses both of the two schema in statistically equivalent levels, but that approximately 4% uses Autonomy more and approximately 3% uses Pseudo Independence more. Of the two statuses, Autonomy is the more complex cognitively and affectively. Thus, at best a high intersubscale correlation can suggest the extent to which a sample uses two schemata, but it cannot reveal the ordering of the expressions within the sample.

Factor Analyses

In addition to Cronbach's alpha, exploratory factor analyses have also been used to examine the internal structure of the racial identity measures at an item level (Ponterotto & Wise, 1989; Swanson et al., 1994; Yanico et al., 1994). However, three reasons why standard factor analysis may not be the best analytic strategy for investigating Helms and her associates' (Helms & Parham, 1985; Helms & Carter, 1990) subscale items are as follows: (a) Neither racial identity subscales nor racial identity measures in their entirety are intended to be homogeneous or unidimensional; (b) the assumption of linear relationships between variables in factor analysis frequently results in a large number of dimensions (Schiffman, Reynolds, & Young, 1981); and (c) standard factor analysis cannot reveal the ordering (that is, the increasing complexity) of subscales or items within subscales.

In addition, most of the aforementioned problems have been exaggerated because contemporary researchers have performed their analyses on the entire scales rather than the individual subscales. With respect to linear relationships, researchers (e.g., Ponterotto & Wise, 1987) have reported that items reflective of transitional processes (e.g., Dissonance/Encounter) load on the same factors as the items of one or the other adjacent subscales. The general aim of such items is to pull the person in opposing directions. However, in factor analysis, items tend to be "attracted" to the subscale items with which they share the strongest linear relationships, even if those relationships are not very strong. However, such findings do not necessarily mean that nonlinear dimensions could not account for more variance, particularly if the items were analyzed within the context of their separate subscale.

Prochaska, DiClemente, and Norcross (1992) encountered the same problem with respect to continuous items intended to measure a transitional or preparatory stage of mastering addictive disorders. That is, the transitional items disappeared as a separate subscale when principal components analyses were used to examine the construct validity of their measure. They noted that abandonment of their preparatory stage in compliance with the factor analyses led them to disregard an important aspect of their population's behavior. Consequently they recommended that cluster analyses be used to find the transitional stage because such analytic procedures did consistently reveal individuals who could be classified as transitional. Cluster analytic approaches might be more appropriate than standard factor analysis for racial identity measures as well.

Also, the concept of ordering as it is used in racial identity theory may be inadequately assessed by standard factor analysis. Some of the various racial identity information-processing strategies are superficially similar in content, but not in function. For example, the denial of Contact is similar to the rationalization of Pseudo Independence. Consequently, it would not be surprising to find denial and rationalization items loading on the same factors. Yet clinicians generally consider rationalization to be a more complex mode of reacting than denial. Standard factor analysis cannot reveal this type of differential complexity.

Implications. Much of the existing literature supports the need for alternative strategies for examining the psychometric properties of racial identity scales that purport to be measures involving human judgment or perceptual processes (i.e., process measures). One set of approaches that has not received much attention in the relevant literature, but might be useful in managing the problems of nonlinearity and ordering of items within subscales is multidimensional scaling (e.g., Schiffman et al., 1981). Basically, multidimensional scaling is a statistical approach that allows one to discover the configurations among items as subjects perceive them.

Helms (1990) tried group-level multidimensional scaling to study the psychometric properties of the first 30 items of the BRIAS. She abandoned such efforts for pragmatic reasons (i.e., it was not clear that such approaches could be easily used by practitioners to assess individuals). Nevertheless, she found that four theoretically consistent dimensions accounted for 89% of the variance among items, whereas with four factors, Yanico et al. (1994) could only account for about 20% of the variance among the same items using factor analysis. Thus, this technique seems worthy of further investigation. Moreover, computer programs are now more widely available for performing multidimensional scaling on a person level than they were when Helms first tried the technique for studying racial identity rating-scale measures.

Assessment Issues

Neither the racial identity nor the ethnic identity measurement perspectives has focused much on the issue of assessing relevant constructs for practical as opposed to research (e.g., construct validity) purposes. In the absence of measures of the more psychologically complex aspects of race and culture alluded to earlier, practitioners as well as researchers have had to rely on simplistic indicators of intrapsychic and interpersonal racial and/or cultural dynamics. Thus, the most commonly used "predictor" or "measure" of racial or ethnic identity has been racial or ethnic categories as determined by surnames, self-designation, researcher categorization, and other similarly ambiguous criteria.

In general, researchers and practitioners have noted the sterility of such categorical information for describing racially or culturally related behaviors. Even when researchers (e.g., Hauser, 1972; Phinney, 1990) have used racial or ethnic group categories to compare groups' responses on general identity measures derived from Erikson's psychosocial model, the results have been less than illuminating. Categorical ascriptions per se do not reveal much about a person's intrapsychic processes, cannot discriminate among individuals within groups, and consequently, do not constitute assessment even in the narrow sense that Aftanas (1994) defines the term.

Social cognitive theorists (e.g., Gardner et al., 1988) often use the term "individual differences" to refer to assessment or measurement that occurs on an individual or person level as opposed to a "consensual" or group level. Constructs measured consensually require groups of people to respond in the same directions, whereas individualistic measurement requires description of separate persons. Most of the available racial identity measures have been investigated and interpreted by means of consensual models, which may or may not yield the same kinds of information as would individual-difference models. Nevertheless, it is possible to adapt some principles from consensual models to make racial identity measures more amenable to individual-difference interpretations.

Researchers and practitioners intending to use racial identity measures for diagnostic purposes are generally interested in discovering the extent to which individuals can be differentially described by racial identity schema. For racial identity measures to be useful, especially to practitioners, for understanding and/or communicating with their clientele about racial dynamics, practitioners need to be able to determine which schemas are dominant or recessive for each client.

Profile Error Bands

Helms (1989) recommended that when researchers are using racial identity scores whose psychometric properties have been determined by means of consensual measurement models, racial identity profiles rather than single scores should be used to describe the individual. According to previously discussed theoretical formulations, racial identity statuses (and consequently, schemas) are interrelated. Consequently, reliance on single scores risks discarding important information. Nevertheless, subscales differ in internal consistency and response variability on a consensual level (see Table 4). Therefore, subscale scores of the same numerical value might not be of the same importance in the person's overall profile.

A common adaptation of a consensual approach that is used in personality measurement to evaluate the differential significance of intra-individual subscale scores involves use of the standard error of the difference between two scores (SE_{dif}). The SE_{dif} allows one to consider variations in measurement error (i.e., reliability) between pairs of scores when interpreting intra-individual subscale score differences. It can also be used to determine whether a person's subscale scores, which appear to be different, are significantly different. By using the SE_{dif}, profile error bands or ranges can be developed to visually represent significantly different racial identity subscale scores for people on an individual level.

The ranges shown in Table 5 were calculated at the .05 level of significance using the following formula from Anastasi (1982, p. 129):

$$ SE_{dif} = SD\sqrt{2 - r_{xx} - r_{yy}} \; x \; 1.96 $$

In this usage, SD is the average standard deviation of the two subscales being compared and r_{xx} and r_{yy} are the respective subscale reliabilities.

Thus, Table 5 shows the minimum number of points by which each pair of scales must differ at the .05 level of significance. The numbers in the diagonals are the number of points by which a subscale score would have to differ from itself, as for example, in a Time 1-Time 2 testing paradigm. In case one does not have Table 5 at hand, if one uses a point spread of 9 points, then one should obtain

Table 5. Point Values For Determining Whether Subscale Scores Differ Significantly

Scale	C	D	R	P	A
Contact (C)	8.84				
Disintegration (D)	8.33	7.41			
Reintegration (R)	8.57	7.52	7.60		
Pseudo Independence (P)	8.46	7.85	7.10	8.06	
Autonomy (A)	8.40	7.69	7.87	7.97	7.86

Note. Numbers in diagonal are the minimum amount of points by which scores must differ from themselves to be significant at the .05 alpha level.

a somewhat conservative estimate of whether a person's subscale scores differ from one another at the .05 level of significance.

The reader might wish to use the SE_{dif} point-values shown in Table 5 to estimate the differential strength of individuals' responses, particularly if he or she does not have access to large samples. However, if one does have large samples (e.g., at least 100), then one might wish to calculate local values for comparative purposes.

Figure 1 uses a circular diagram to represent the schema profile bands for a person ("Sam"). The circle is used to emphasize the point

---

Figure 1. Sam's configuration of scores, C = P = =, is not an uncommon pattern (see Table 8). Moreover, in single-scale comparisons (see Table 6), approximately 36% of respondents had high Contact scores and approximately 34% had high Pseudo-Independence scores.

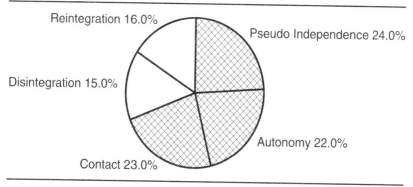

Scale	Raw Score	Strength	%ile	Comment
Contact	36	High	85	Contact is higher than Disintegration
Disintegration	23	Equal	40	Disintegration is lower than Contact and equals Reintegration
Reintegration	25	Low	60	Reintegration equals Disintegration and is lower than Pseudo Independence
Pseudo Independence	38	Equal	80	Pseudo Independence is higher than Reintegration and equals Autonomy
Autonomy	35	Equal	35	Autonomy equals Pseudo Independence and Contact
Total	157			

that although racial identity statuses may be hierarchical in the sense of reflecting ascendingly complex information-processing strategies, they are not hierarchical in the sense that the use of one necessarily precludes use of another. That is, schemas are not mutually exclusive. Proceeding clockwise around the circumference of the circle, beginning with Contact minus Disintegration, successive pairs of subscales were compared to obtain the frequencies shown in Table 6.

Table 6. Differential Frequencies of Strength of Endorsement of Pairs of Contiguous Subscales

Subscale Comparison Direction	Strength of Endorsement					
	Very High		High		Equal	
	f	%	f	%	f	%
C > D	38	8.6	161	36.3	232	52.4
D > C	4	.9	8	1.8		
D > R	1	.2	15	3.4	408	92.1
R > D	3	.7	16	3.6		
R > P	6	1.4	9	2.0	132	29.8
P > R	147	33.2	149	33.6		
P > A			12	2.7	414	93.5
A > P			17	3.8		
A > C	6	1.4	77	17.4	355	80.1
C > A			5	1.1		

Note. Very high scores differ by two or more standard errors; high scores differ by as much as one standard error; equal scores are within one standard error of each other. Scale abbreviations are C=Contact, D=Disintegration, R=Reintegration, P=Pseudo Independence, A=Autonomy.

N=443.

For this sample of 443 respondents, Table 6 shows the frequency distributions of respondents whose hypothesized developmentally adjacent (e.g., Contact versus Disintegration) subscale scores differed by one ("High"), two ("Very High"), or zero ("Equal") standard-error-difference scores. So, for example, each individual's Disintegration score was subtracted from his or her Contact scores to determine which exceeded the point spread shown in Table 5. Thus, if a person's Contact score is between 8.33 and 16.66 points higher than his or her Disintegration score, then the Contact score is "High"; a Contact score at least 16.66 higher is considered "Very High" (see Figure 1). Obviously, in this example, positive scores suggest stronger Contact reactions whereas negative scores suggest stronger Disintegration reactions.

Table 6 shows that for about half of the respondents (52.4%), Contact and Disintegration were expressed equivalently strongly (i.e., within one standard error); for about 44.9%, Contact was expressed one standard error ("High") or at least two standard errors (i.e., "Very High") more strongly than Disintegration, whereas Disintegration was expressed more or much more strongly than Contact for only 2.7% of the respondents.

A general theme evident in Table 6 for this sample is that for four of the five comparisons (Contact vs. Disintegration, Disintegration vs. Reintegration, Autonomy vs. Pseudo Independence, and Autonomy vs. Contact), more than half of the respondents' subscale scores were equivalent (range = 52.4% to 93.5%). In the remaining comparison (Pseudo Independence vs. Reintegration), Pseudo Independence was much higher (33.2%) or higher (33.6%) than Reintegration for almost as many respondents as it was equivalent (29.8%). An implication of these observations for interpreting respondents' scores is that reliance on untransformed raw score comparisons may contribute to misleading conclusions.

It is possible to obtain an individual profile by analyzing the person's five transformed (paired comparisons) scores for clusters, profiles, or patterns. Loglinear analysis was used to obtain the profiles summarized in Table 8. Of course, other clustering techniques could be used to accomplish similar effects. However, in this case, because the high versus very high categories are nominal, loglinear analysis was used to determine the number of combinations of the five (positive very high to negative very high) possible transformations per (pair of) subscale comparisons.

Although 61 (of a possible 5^5) patterns or combinations of the five transformed-comparison scores occurred, of these, only 13 were de-

Table 7. Racial Identity Subscale Correlations

Scale	C	D	R	P	A
Contact (C)	-01	-19	-39	53	39
Disintegration (D)		-08	69	-47	-59
Reintegration (R)			-03	-45	-51
Pseudo Independence (P)				-02	66
Autonomy (A)					-00

Note. Decimals omitted to conserve space. Correlations above the diagonal are intercorrelations among raw subscales. Diagonals are correlations between racial identity subscales and Marlowe-Crowne social desirability scores ($M = 5.48$, $SD = 7.21$). All values above the diagonal are significant beyond the .01 alpha level.

scriptive of as many as 10 respondents. Most respondents had comparatively high scores on at least one subscale. However, the most frequently occurring configuration (19.6%) was undifferentiated responding, meaning that none of the scales differed significantly from its neighbors.

In Table 8, the first letter of a subscale is used to indicate that it was the higher of the adjacent-scale comparisons; letters with asterisks equal very high statuses, and equal signs indicate scores were within one standard error of one another. The most frequently occurring configurations with at least 10 respondents are shown in Table 8.

Not shown in Table 8 are 28 singletons (response patterns characteristic of one person) and 11 doublets (response patterns characteristic of two persons). Naturally, scale score differences that occur infrequently in Table 6 also occur infrequently in combinations in Table 8. For example, Autonomy is only very much (two standard errors) higher than Contact for six persons (see Table 6), and four of these people were singletons when their configurations were examined.

Interpreting Response Patterns

Qualitative interpretation of personality profiles is an enduring tradition in personality psychology. Following in this tradition, qualitative interpretations of profiles presumably can be used to assist clients in exploring their own issues of racial adjustment. Thus, some suggestions as to how to use the racial identity schema profile shown in Figure 1 might be useful. The circle is a heuristic device in that it

Table 8. Summary of Frequency of Occurrence of White Identity Profile
          Error Transformations

		Comparison				
C vs D	D vs R	R vs P	P vs A	A vs C	f	%
C*	=	P*	=	=	23	5.2
C	=	P*	=	A	19	4.3
C	=	P*	=	=	56	12.6
C	=	P	=	=	60	13.5
=	=	P*	=	=	17	3.8
=	=	P	=	A	19	4.3
=	=	P	=	=	52	11.7
=	=	=	=	A	10	2.2
=	=	=	=	=	87	19.6

Note. Racial identity subscale abbreviations are C=Contact, D= Disintegration, R=Reintegration,
P=Pseudo Independence, A=Autonomy; higher subscale scores are indicated by the first letter
of subscale names. Symbols are = (within one standard error), * (at least two standard errors
difference). Only profiles with frequencies of at least 10 ($N = 443$) are reported.

symbolizes that portion of the ego that the person hypothetically
allots herself or himself for the processing of racial stimuli. Thus, in
the case of inventory measures of racial identity (e.g., the WRIAS), the
total scores might be assumed to symbolize the total space available
to the person for responding to racial stimuli. The wedges in the circle
are merely the percentages of the total scale score of each subscale.
Standard error scores determine whether or not ostensibly different
percentages of endorsement represent significantly different schema
usage, and wedges that do not differ significantly have the same
shading in the figure. Theoretically, total scores (e.g., ego space) could
range from 50 to 250 points (i.e., from strong disagreement with all
items to strong agreement). In both the case of strong disagreement
with all items and strong agreement with all items, such profiles
should be discarded for research or assessment purposes because they
indicate that the items did not elicit discriminative responses from the
respondent. Table 3 shows that for this sample, raw scores actually
ranged from 106 to 182. In Figure 1, Sam's total score (the sum of his
subscale scores) of 157 is shown on the bottom row. Sam's total score
suggests that his profile is probably interpretable.
    Ideally, each person should endorse some items strongly and
others not so strongly. However, a person with an overall score of 157
could exhibit the same patterns of subscale responses as someone

with a higher overall score. Presumably, it is primarily the subscale patterns rather than single raw subscale scores per se that reflect race-related behavior because the patterns suggest which schemas are dominant or recessive for the person.

Sam's overall profile can be described as C = P = = (that is, Contact and Pseudo Independence were higher by one standard error than their contiguous neighbor to the right). Approximately 14% of the overall sample exhibited this pattern of responding (see Table 6). In Figure 1, Sam's profile does not reveal any strong highs or lows. In fact, visually his racial identity expressions (schemas) are best described by two clusters, one described by Disintegration and Reintegration schemas, and the other described by the other three subscales (Contact, Pseudo Independence, and Autonomy). The Disintegration-Reintegration cluster appears to be a recessive set of schemas for him, whereas the Contact-Pseudo-Independent-Autonomy cluster appears to be dominant. By using the percentile (%ile) column of Sam's profile, one can get a sense of his level of expression of the schema relative to Carter's (chapter 4, this volume) consensual norms.

It is not clear what to make of Sam's profile on either an intrapsychic or consensual level. However, his high Contact and Pseudo Independence schema relative to his other subscale scores suggest that Sam uses a combination of denial, avoidance, and rationalization to cope with racial information (see Table 3). This intrapsychic interpretation is based on theoretical descriptions of Sam's highest schema. As compared to Carter's normative group, Sam also tends to express Contact (85th percentile) and Pseudo Independence (80th percentile) more strongly than most people. However, even though Reintegration is weakly expressed relative to his other schemas, it is relatively strong (60th percentile) when compared to others' expressions of the schema. Thus, again based on theoretical descriptions of the relevant schema, Sam's (presumed) denial and avoidance might be tinged with some elements of own-group superiority and outgroup inferiority.

Also, in interpreting Sam's scores, findings from consensual construct-validity studies of the racial identity variables might be of assistance in forming hypotheses about the meaning of Sam's scores. For example, Tokar and Swanson (1991) found that Contact expressions (in combination with the other racial identity schemas) were uniquely predictive of a weak inner sense of self and difficulty in developing close meaningful relationships with others. Perhaps these personality characteristics also describe Sam's characteristics with respect to members of his own and/or other racial groups. Such hypotheses would certainly be worth a clinician's exploring with him.

Conclusions and Future Research Directions

The primary theme underlying the various sections of this paper is the proposition that different measurement models—or at least more flexible usage of existing models—may be required to establish the psychometric properties of racial and ethnic identity personality inventories. Especially different models may be needed for measures intended to operationalize process models of race or culture than are needed for content models.

An implicit assumption underlying process measures is that each individual's interpretative and judgmental cognitive-affective processes are the real content of such measures. That is, the person's idiosyncratic reactions to items are a part of the measurement process. Much of what is measured by process measures is intrapsychic, and may or may not be linear in expression.

However, where cultural or racial content measures are concerned, domains of relevant values, customs, traditions, external to the person do exist, and the person may use these external criteria to make construct-relevant self-assessments. Therefore, it ought to be possible to use classical measurement theory to construct homogeneous, psychometrically sound measures of content-specific constructs such as the ethnic identity measures discussed previously. Nevertheless, the domain of behavior or other characteristics on which such measures are based rarely has been specified. Moreover, as Phinney (1990) noted, investigators have been somewhat remiss about investigating the psychometric properties of their measures.

Be that as it may, the measurement problems for racial identity process measures and ethnic identity content measures are different. In the case of ethnic identity measures as defined in this paper, many researchers have simply not provided psychometric information about their measures. Yet presumably this oversight could be easily remedied by using standard methods of exploring reliability (e.g., coefficient alpha, test-retest) and validity of measures.

However, in the case of process measures, the resolution of measurement dilemmas might not be so easily accomplished because researchers may have to become accustomed to interpreting summary test scores and items within such scores differently than they have heretofore. In their discussion of achievement tests, Snow and Lohman (1989) make a distinction between "sign-trait" and "sampling" interpretations of such devices that is seemingly applicable to process measures of racial identity. Accordingly, they suggest that those who interpret test scores have tended to regard them as "signs" of some underlying "trait" rather than as "samples" of the person's relevant mental structures or organizational processes.

When one entertains sampling as an option for explaining individuals' reactions to racial identity items, then a wide array of methodologies become candidates for developing and interpreting measures. In addition, to the alternate strategies discussed in the present paper (e.g., cluster analysis, multidimensional scaling), Snow and Lohman (1989) suggest that "any other method that sorts cognitive tasks [or racial reactions] into categories of closely related (i.e., similarly sampled) performances provides a map to guide further cognitive [affective] psychological analysis" (p. 317).

Presently, researchers seem to be fixated on coefficient alpha, inter-subscale correlations, and factor analysis as the only methodologies for developing racial identity measures and/or judging their effectiveness. This closed-minded perspective frequently has led them to discount their own findings in support of racial identity theory (e.g., Swanson et al., 1994; Yanico et al., 1994). Perhaps the issues raised in this paper can provide some directions for researchers to assess the extent to which their measurement models fit the racial or ethnic identity conceptual model being investigated.

Finally, some examples of the ways in which the racial identity measures might be used to assess respondents' quality of race-related behavior have been proposed. However, more empirical research specifically focused on patterns, profiles, or clusters of racial identity subscales and their relation to other attitudes, emotions, and behaviors is needed. This type of information would enhance the interpretative process by providing practitioners with the kinds of information that could be used to assist clients in their racial identity adjustment.

REFERENCES

Aboud, F. E. (1987). The development of ethnic self-identification and attitudes. In J. S. Phinney & M. J. Rotheram (Eds.), Children's ethnic socialization (pp. 32–55). Newbury Park, CA: Sage Publications.

Aboud, F. E., & Skerry, S. A. (1984). The development of ethnic attitudes: A cultural review. *Journal of Cross-Cultural Psychology*, 15(1), 3–34.

Aftanas, M. S. (1994). On revitalizing the measurement curriculum. *American Psychologist*, 49(10), 889–890.

Alba, R. D. (1990). *Ethnic identity: The transformation of White America*. New Haven: Yale University Press.

Anastasi, A. (1982). *Psychological testing* (5th ed.). New York: Macmillan Publishing Co., Inc.

Atkinson, D. R., Morten, G., & Sue, D. W. (1989). *Counseling American minoroties: A cross-cultural perspective*. Dubuque, IA: Brown.

Atkinson, D. R., & Thompson, C. E. (1992). Racial, ethnic, and cultural variables in counseling. In S. Brown & S. Lent (Eds.), *Handbook of Counseling Psychology* (pp. 349–382). New York: John Wiley & Sons.

Bernal, M. E., Knight, G. P., Garza, C. A., Ocampo, K. A., & Cota, M. K. (1990). The development of ethnic identity in Mexican-American children. *Hispanic Journal of Behavioral Sciences*, 12(1), 3–24.

Betancourt, H., & Lopez, S. R. (1993). The study of culture, ethnicity, and race in American psychology. *American Psychologist*, 48, 629–637.

Birman, D. (1994). Acculturation and human diversity in a multicultural society. In E. J. Trickett, R. J. Watts, & D. Birman (Eds.), *Human diversity: Perspectives on people in context* (pp. 261–284). San Francisco, CA: Jossey-Bass.

Brown, S. D., & Gore, P. A. (1994). An evaluation of interest congruence indices: Distribution characteristics and measurement properties. *Journal of Vocational Behavior*, 45, 310–327.

Bulhan, H. A. (1980). Dynamics of cultural in-betweenity: An empirical study. *International Journal of Psychology*, 15, 105–112.

Burlew, A. K., & Smith, L. R. (1991). Measures of racial identity: An overview and a proposed framework. *The Journal of Black Psychology*, 17(2), 53–71.

Casas, J. M. (1984). Policy, training and research in counseling psychology: The racial/ethnic perspective. In S. D. Brown & R. W. Lent (Eds.), *Handbook of counseling psychology* (pp. 785–831). New York: Wiley.

Corbett, M. M. (1994). *The relationship between White racial identity and narcissism*. Unpublished doctoral dissertation. College Park, MD: University of Maryland.

Cronbach, L. J. (1951). Coefficient alpha and the internal structure of tests. *Psychometrika*, 16, 297–334.

Cross, W. E., Jr. (1971). The Negro-to-Black conversion experience: Toward a psychology of Black liberation. *Black World*, 20(9), 13–27.

Cuellar, I., Harris, L. C., & Jasso, R. (1980). An acculturation scale for Mexican American normal and clinical populations. *Hispanic Journal of Behavioral Sciences*, 2, 199–207.

Cureton, E. E. (1967). The definition and estimation of test reliability. In W. A. Mehrens & R. L. Ebel (Eds.), *Principles of educational and psychological measurement* (pp. 167–186). Chicago, IL: Rand McNally and Co.

Dawis, R. (1987). Scale construction. *Journal of Counseling Psychology, 34,* 481–489.

DeVellis, R. F. (1991). *Scale development: Theory and Applications.* Newbury Park, CA: Sage Publications.

Ebel, R. L. (1961). Must all tests be valid? *American Psychologist, 16,* 640–647.

Erikson, E. H. (1963). *Childhood and society* (2nd ed.). New York: Norton.

Erikson, E. H. (1966/1976). The concept of identity in race relations: Notes and queries. *Daedalus, 95,* 145–171. (Reprinted in A. Dashefsky (Ed.), *Ethnic identity in society* (pp. 59-71). Chicago: Rand McNally College Publishing Company.

Erikson, E. H. (1968). *Identity: Youth and crisis.* New York: Norton.

Erikson, E. H. (1975). *Life History and the historical moment.* New York: Norton.

Feagin, J. R. (1984). *Racial and ethnic relations* (2nd ed.). Englewood Cliffs, NJ: Prentice-Hall, Inc.

Freud, S. (1959). Address to the Society of B'nai B'rith. Cited in A. Dashevsky (Ed.), *Ethnic identity in society* (p. 62). Chicago: Rand McNally.

Gardner, R. C., Lalonde, R. N., Nero, A. M., & Young, M. Y. (1988). Ethnic stereotypes: Implications of measurement strategy. *Social Cognition, 6,* 40–60.

Gordon, M. (1976). The subsociety and the subculture. In A. Dashefsky (Ed.), *Ethnic identity in society* (pp. 25–35). Chicago: Rand McNally College Publishing Company.

Gotunda, N. (1991). A critique of "Our Constitution is colorblind." *Stanford Law Review, 44,* 1–69.

Graham, J. R., & Lilly, R. S. (1984). *Psychological testing.* Englewood Cliffs, NJ: Prentice-Hall, Inc.

Green, S. B., Lissitz, R. W., & Mulaik, S. A. (1977). Limitations of coefficient alpha as an index of test unidimensionality. *Education and Psychological Measurement, 37*(4), 827–838.

Hacker, A. (1992). *Two nations: Black and White, separate, hostile, unequal.* New York: Charles Scribner's Sons.

Hardiman, R. (1982). *White identity development: A process oriented model for describing racial consciousness of White Americans.* Unpublished doctoral dissertation, University of Massachusetts, Amherst.

Hauser, S. T. (1972). Black and White identity development: Aspects and perspectives. *Journal of Youth and Adolescence, 1,* 113–130.

Helms, J. E. (1984). Toward a theoretical explanation of the effects of race on counseling. *Counseling Psychologist, 12,* 153-165.

Helms, J. E. (1986). Expanding racial identity theory to cover the counseling process. *Journal of Counseling Psychology, 33*, 62–64.

Helms, J. E. (1989). Considering some methodological issues in racial identity counseling research. *The Counseling Psychologist, 17*, 227–252.

Helms, J. E. (1990a). *Black and White racial identity: Theory, research, and practice.* New York: Greenwood Press.

Helms, J. E. (1990b). Three perspectives on counseling and psychotherapy with visible racial/ethnic group clients. In F. C. Serafica, A. I. Schwebel, R. K. Russell, P. D. Isaac, & L. B. Myers (Eds.), *Mental health of ethnic minoroties* (pp. 171–201). New York: Greenwood Press.

Helms, J. E. (1992). *A race is a nice thing to have: A guide to being a White person or understanding the White persons in your life.* Topeka, KS: Content Communication.

Helms, J. E. (1994a). How multiculturalism obscures racial factors in the therapy process: Comment on Ridley et al. (1994), Sodowsky et al. (1994), Ottavi et al. (1994), and Thompson et al. (1994). *Journal of Counseling Psychology, 41*, 162–165.

Helms, J. E. (1994b). The conceptualization of racial identity and other "racial" constructs. In E. J. Trickett, R. J. Watts, & D. Birman (Eds.), *Human diversity: Perspectives on people in context* (pp. 285–311). San Francisco, CA: Jossey-Bass.

Helms, J. E. (in press). An update of Helms's racial identity models. In J. Ponterotto, L. Suzuki, & C. Alexander (Eds.), *Handbook of multicultural counseling.* Newbury Park, CA: Sage Publications.

Helms, J. E. & Carter, R. T. (1990). Development of the White Racial Identity Attitude inventory. In J. E. Helms (Ed.), *Black and White racial identity: Theory, research, and practice* (pp. 67-80). Westport, CT: Greenwood Press.

Helms, J. E., & Carter, R. T. (1991). Relationships of White and Black racial identity attitudes and demographic similarity to counselor preferences. *Journal of Counseling Psychology, 38*, 446-457.

Helms, J. E., & Cook, D. A. (in press). *Using race and culture in counseling and psychotherapy: Theory and process.* Fort Worth, TX: Harcourt-Brace.

Helms, J. E. & Parham, T. A. (1985). *The development of the racial identity attitude scale.* Unpublished paper. [Available from R. Jones, Psychology Department, Hampton University, Hampton, Va.]

Helms, J. E., & Piper, R. E. (1994). Implications of racial identity theory for vocational psychology. *Journal of Vocational Behavior, 44*, 124–138.

Hutnik, N. (1991). *Ethnic minority identity: A social psychological perspective.* Oxford: Clarendon Press.

Jackson, F. (1992). Race and ethnicity as biological constructs. *Journal of Ethnicity and Disease, 2*(2), 120–125.

Johnson, S. D. (1987). "Knowing that" vs. "knowing how": Toward achieving expertise in multicultural training for counseling. *The Counseling Psychologist, 15*(2), 320–331.

Katz, J. (1985). The sociopolitical nature of counseling. *The Counseling Psychologist, 13,* 615–624.

Kunkel, M. A. (1990). Expectations about counseling in relation to acculturation in Mexican-American and Anglo-American student samples. *Journal of Counseling Psychology, 37,* 286–292.

Landrine, H., & Klonoff, E. (1994). The African American Acculturation Scale. *Journal of Black Psychology, 20,* 104–127.

Lyman, H. B. (1978). *Test scores and what they mean* (3rd ed.). Englewood Cliffs, NJ: Prentice-Hall.

Marlowe, D., & Crowne, D. P. (1961). Social desirability and response to situational demands. *Journal of Consulting Psychology, 25,* 109–115.

Meijer, C. E. (1993). *White racial identity development and responses to diversity in an introduction to psychology course and curriculum.* Unpublished doctoral dissertation. University of Maryland, College Park, MD.

Milliones, J. (1980). Construction of a Black consciousness measure: Psychotherapeutic implications. *Psychotherapy: Theory, Research, and Practice, 17*(2), 175–182.

Morris, W. (1975). *American heritage dictionary of the English language.* Boston: Houghton Mifflin.

Myers, L. J., Speight, S. L., Highlen, P. S., Cox, C. I., Reynolds, A. L., Adams, E. M., & Hanley, C. P. (1989). Identity development and worldview: Toward an optimal conceptualization. *Journal of Counseling and Development, 70,* 54–63.

Nunnally, J. C. (1978). *Psychometric theory.* St. Louis: McGraw.

Ottavi, T. M., Pope-Davis, D. B., & Dings, J. G. (1994). Relationship between White racial identity attitudes and self-reported multicultural competencies. *Journal of Counseling Psychology, 41,* 149–154.

Padilla, A. M. (1980). The role of cultural awareness and ethnic loyalty in acculturation. In A. M. Padilla (Ed.), Acculturation: Theory, models, and some new findings (pp. 47-84). Boulder, CO: Westview.

Parham, T. A., & Helms, J. E. (1981). The influence of Black students' racial identity attitudes on preferences for counselor's race. *Journal of Counseling Psychology, 28,* 250-257.

Phinney, J. S. (1990). Ethnic identity in adolescents and adults: Review of research. *Psycholgical Bulletin, 108*, 499–514.

Ponterotto, J. G., & Wise, S. L. (1989). Construct validity of the Racial Identity Attitude Scale. *Journal of Counseling Psychology, 34*, 218–223.

Ponterotto, J. G., & Wise, S. L. (1987). A construct validity study of the Racial Identity Attitude Scale. *Journal of Counseling Psychology, 34*, 218-223.

Prochaska, J. O., DiClemente, C. C., & Norcross, J. C. (1992). In search of how people change: Applications to addictive behaviors. *American Psychologist, 47*(9), 1102–1114.

Regan, A. M. (1992). *Search and commitment processes in White racial identity formation.* Unpublished doctoral dissertation. University of Maryland, College Park, MD.

Remy, L. A. (1993). *White racial identity: White college students' definition of self in relation to African-Americans, Hispanics, and Asian-Americans.* Unpublished Masters thesis. University of Maryland, College Park, MD.

Rest, J. R. (1979). *Revised manual for the Defining Issues Test.* Minneapolis: Moral Research Projects, University of Minnesota.

Rowe, W., Bennett, S. K., & Atkinson, D. R. (1994). White racial identity models: A critique and alternative proposal. *Counseling Psychologist, 22*, 129–146.

Ruiz, R. A., & Padilla, A. M. (1977). Counseling Latinos. *Personnel and Guidance Journal, 55*, 401–408.

Sabnani, H. B., Ponterotto, J. G., & Borodovsky, L. G. (1991). White racial identity development and cross-cultural counselor training: A stage model. *Counseling Psychologist, 19*, 76–102.

Scarr, S. (1981). *Race, social class, and individual differences in I.Q.* Hillsdale, NJ: Lawrence Erlbaum.

Schiffman, S. S., Reynolds, M. L., & Young, F. W. (1981). *Introduction to multidimensional scaling.* Orlando: Academic Press.

Shibutani, T., & Kwan, K. M. (1965). *Ethnic stratification.* New York: Macmillan.

Snow, R. E., & Lohman, D. F. (1989). Implications of cognitive psychology for educational measurement. In R. L. Linn (Ed.), *Educational Measurement* (3rd ed.). New York: Macmillan.

Speight, S. L., Myers, L. J., Cox, C. I., & Highlen, P. S. (1991). A redefinition of multicultural counseling. *Journal of Counseling and Development, 70*, 29–36.

Spikard, P. R. (1992). The illogic of American racial categories. In M. P. P. Root (Ed.), *Racially mixed people in America* (pp. 12–23). Newbury Park, CA: Sage Publications.

Stonequist, E. V. (1937). *The marginal man*. New York: Scribner.

Sue, S. (1992). Ethnicity and mental health: Research and policy. *Journal of Social Issues, 48*, 187–205.

Suinn, R. M., Rickard-Figueroa, K., Lew, S., & Vigil, P. (1987). The Suinn-Lew Asian Self-Identity Acculturation Scale: An initial report. *Educational and Psychological Measurement, 47*, 401–407.

Swanson, J. L., Tokar, D. M., & Davis, L. E. (1994). Content and construct validity of the White Racial Identity Attitude Scale. *Journal of Vocational Behavior, 44*, 198–217.

Szapocznik, J., Scopetta, M. A., Kurtines, W., & Aranalde, M. D. (1978). Theory and measurement of acculturation. *Inter-American Journal of Psychology, 12*, 113–130.

Tajfel, H. (1978). *The social psychology of minorities*. London: Minority Rights Group.

Takaki, R. (1993). *A different mirror: A history of multicultural America*. Boston: Little, Brown and Company.

Thomas, C. (1971). *Boys no more*. Beverly Hills: Glencoe Press.

Thorndike, R. L., & Hagen, E. (1969). *Measurement and evaluation in psychology and education*. New York: John Wiley & Sons.

Tokar, D. M., & Swanson, J. L. (1991). An investigation of the validity of Helms's (1984) model of White racial identity development. *Journal of Counseling Psychology, 38*, 296–301.

Triandis, H. C. (1994). *Culture and social behavior*. New York: McGraw-Hill, Inc.

Vontress, C. E. (1971). Racial differences: Impediments to rapport. *Journal of Counseling Psychology, 18*, 7–13.

Walsh, W. B., & Betz, N. (1985). *Tests and assessment*. New Jersey: Prentice-Hall, Inc.

Watts, R. J., & Carter, R. T. (1991). Psychological aspects of racism in organizations. *Groups and Organization Studies, 16*, 328–344.

Winston, R. B., Jr., Miller, T. K., & Prince, J. S. (1979). Assessing student development. Athens, GA: Student Development Associates.

Yanico, B. J., Swanson, J. L., & Tokar, D. M. (1994). A psychometric investigation of the Black Racial Identity Attitude Scale—Form B. *Journal of Vocational Behavior, 44*, 218–234.

Yee, A. H., Fairchild, H. H., Weizmann, F., & Wyatt, G. (1993). Addressing psychology's problems with race. *American Psychologist, 48*, 1132–1140.

Zuckerman, M. (1990). Some dubious premises in research and theory on racial differences. *American Psychologist, 45*(12), 1297–1303.

EXPLORING THE COMPLEXITY OF RACIAL IDENTITY ATTITUDE MEASURES

Robert T. Carter

Teachers College, Columbia University

In the 1970s theories of racial identity began to appear in the psychological literature. Several scholars working independently in various parts of the country introduced theories of Black racial identity development (see Helms, 1990). Since the 1970s, racial, ethnic, or minority identity theories have been introduced to include other visible racial/ethnic groups. The term "visible racial-ethnic" applies to Black, Asian, Indian, and Latino Americans; it identifies them as members of both racial and ethnic groups who are recognized by skin-color, physical features, and/or language. Ethnic or racial or cultural identity models have been proposed for Asians, Hispanics (Berry, 1980), and minorities in general (Atkinson, Morten, & Sue, 1989: Sue & Sue, 1990). In the mid 1980s Helms's White racial identity model was introduced (Helms, 1984).

Extensions and elaborations of racial identity theories have also appeared in the literature (e.g., Helms & Piper, 1994; Helms, 1994; Helms, this volume; Parham, 1989; Myers, Speight, Highlen, Cox, Reynolds, Adams, & Hanley, 1991; Sue & Sue, 1990). For instance, early models of racial identity were primarily stage models that described psychological responses to oppression. More recently, theories have evolved such that more emphasis is placed on racial identity as an aspect of an individual's psychological makeup in a race-based society (Carter, 1995; Helms, 1990; Helms & Piper, 1994). It is apparent from the growing body of theoretical activity that racial identity is becoming a major theoretical and empirical model in psychology.

Corresponding with the theoretical activity surrounding racial identity, there has been an increase in empirical investigations stimulated by the development of Black and White racial identity measures (Helms & Carter, 1990; Helms & Parham, in press). Studies have demonstrated the reliability and validity of the racial identity constructs and measures (e.g., Carter & Helms, 1992; Carter, 1990a, 1990b, 1990c; Carter, Gushue, & Weitzman, 1994: Helms & Carter, 1991; Helms & Carter, 1990; Helms & Parham, in press; & Pope-Davis & Ottavi, 1992; Tokar & Swanson, 1991; Taub & McEwen, 1992). Although there has been considerable empirical and theoretical work done with White and Black racial identity, somewhat less attention has been devoted to the underlying complexity of racial identity as reflected in the current racial identity instruments.

One purpose of this chapter is to examine the complexity of racial identity by examining scale construction. A second purpose is to examine two issues—one pertaining to how best to use raw or "scaled" scores and the other pertains to whether the scales that measure racial identity attitudes capture some of the complexity associated with identity issues as suggested by recent theory.

In the exploration of the complexity of racial identity measures, I first review the theoretical models and summarize some of the empirical support for the theories of Black and White racial identity. The reviews of research and theory are followed by descriptions of the development of the racial identity scales. After describing the measure's psychometric development, I explore the question of using raw or scaled scores (i.e., percentile scores). The description of racial identity scales is followed by a discussion about using percentile scores as one type of scaled score. The chapter ends with a conclusion and implication section.

Review of Black and White Racial Identity Theory and Research

Before describing the racial identity theories, it is necessary to clarify terminology. The clarification is needed because of advances in the theory and the varying meanings associated with the terms. In the earlier models of Black and White racial identity the process of identity development was characterized in terms of stages. Cross (1978) and Thomas (1971), two original theorists, proposed models of Black racial identity that suggested a linear progression from one stage to another. Helms's (1984) model of White racial identity also proposed a stage model. However, since then, she has revised both Black and White racial identity models and suggested that each operates as a worldview that serves as a filter for race-based information. The ego is the psychological structure that holds and transforms racial identity information. Helms has recently proposed the use of the term ego "status" to refer to the various differentiations of ego that mark more mature and complex racial identity development. I have referred to the notion of "status" by using "level" (Carter, 1995; Carter & Goodwin, 1994). So in this chapter, the terms racial identity "status" and "level" will be used interchangeably.

Racial identity involves one's psychological interpretation of the meaning of his or her race and the race of others. Models of racial identity have existed in the psychological literature for some time (e.g., Thomas, 1971; Cross, 1980). However, only a few authors (e.g. , Helms & Carter, 1990) have examined notions about racial identity through examination of how racial identity measures capture theoretical notions.

Racial identity statuses or levels (formerly stages; Helms, this volume) are composed of corresponding attitudes, thoughts, feelings, and behaviors towards both oneself as a member of a racial group and members of the dominant racial group (in this case Whites). The manner in which one's own racial identity is integrated into one's personality depends on numerous influences, such as family, society, one's own interpretive style, and the manner in which important social-political contexts influence this aspect of one's identity. The notion of status in contrast to stage suggests a model wherein a person may have as part of his or her ego structure all aspects of the racial identity statuses with one status having a predominant role in effecting one's worldview. Helms and Piper (1994) explain it this way:

> The maturation process potentially involves increasingly sophisticated differentiations of the ego, called "ego statuses." Although it is possible for each of the racial-group appropriate statuses to develop in a person and govern her or his race-related behavior, whether or not they do depends on a combination of life experiences, especially intrapsychic dissonance and race-related environmental pressures, as well as cognitive readiness the statuses are hypothesized to develop or mature sequentially. That is, statuses share space within a multilayered circle (symbolizing the ego) and the status(es) which occupies the greatest percentage of the ego has the most wide ranging influence over the person's manner of functioning. (p. 126-128).

Black racial identity. Originally presented by Thomas (1971) and expanded by Cross (1978), and later Helms (1990, also this volume), Black racial identity development consists of five levels or statuses

called Pre-encounter, Encounter, Immersion-Emersion, Internalization, and Internalization-Commitment. Each status or level of racial
identity consists of its own constellations of emotions, beliefs, motives, and behaviors, which influence its expression. The following
descriptions are drawn from recent theoretical formulations, as presented by Helms (1990; this volume).

The psychological view that is characteristic of *Pre-Encounter,* the
first level of racial identity, is the idea that race has little or no personal
or social meaning. For this person, his or her life course is determined
solely by his or her personality, ability, and effort. The belief that race has
little personal salience can be expressed in two distinct ways—passively
or actively (Helms, 1990). In the active phase, people characterized by
Pre-encounter attitudes may consciously idealize Whiteness and White
culture. They essentially want to be accepted into White society and
culture; so they strive to assimilate.

At the Pre-encounter level of racial identity one may not be
conscious of him/herself in the way described above. Such an
individual may exhibit a passive expressive mode. One accepts the
negative attributions associated with Blacks as a group and sees
Blacks in traditional societal or stereotypic ways. Consequently considerable psychic energy may be invested in maintaining distance
between him/herself and other Blacks. Passive expressions of Pre-
encounter mirror views about race common to those of the dominant
racial group in society.

Encounter. During the Encounter phase, something happens that
manages to change the person's current feeling about herself/himself as
a Black person in the United States. Encounter experiences usually
involve multiple emotional traumas that are so powerful that they begin
to weaken and break down the person's previous identity resolution.
Slowly, the meaning and significance of race is questioned and examined. Initially, as is true when one's defenses are ineffective, these
experiences are wrought with confusion and emotional turmoil. This
emotional turmoil may be acute or chronic, eventually leading to the next
level of identity. Thus, the person begins to view his/her racial identity
more positively and works to become deeply involved in learning and
experiencing the meaning and value of his or her race and unique
culture. The psychological energy used to search for a new identity or
resolve the conflict between the abandoned identity and finding something to replace it leads to the next level of racial identity.

During *Immersion-Emersion,* the individual becomes deeply involved in discovering his/her Black/African-American heritage and
has idealized images and strong emotions about Blackness. Two

phases characterize this level of identity development. The first phase of the new identity status involves *Immersion*. One feels hostile and angry toward Whites. As a consequence, the individual *immerses* himself/herself in Black experiences (e.g., clubs, groups, political organizations, etc.) and withdraws, physically when possible, and when not, psychologically, from White society as a means of discovering and affirming his/her Black identity. In general, this identity level is characterized by idealization of everything Black. His/her Black pride is strong and unquestioned, and he/she devalues anyone (including other visible racial-ethnic group people) and all things that are associated with White culture or society. These perspectives arise in part as a consequence of the newly acquired information about the experiences of Blacks. The individual at this level of racial identity development is motivated by his or her desire to embrace the culture and history once denied or withheld. In time the intensity of Immersion subsides and the person begins to *emerge*. During the *Emersion* phase of Immersion-Emersion, the emotional intensity subsides and one no longer idealizes Blackness. A more balanced view of the strengths and weaknesses of Black life and experience emerges. This leveling off leads to internalization.

The *Internalization* status is characterized by the achievement of a sense of pride regarding one's Black identity and a sense of security with respect to one's racial heritage. "The person has found resolution of conflicts between the 'old' and 'new' worldview; ideological flexibility, psychological openness, and self-confidence about one's Blackness are evident in interpersonal transactions. Anti-White feelings decline to the point that friendships with White associates can be renegotiated. While still using Blacks as a primary reference group, the person moves toward a pluralistic and nonracist perspective" (Cross, Parham, & Helms, 1991, p. 32).

The individual at this level of racial identity development is motivated by pride in his/her racial-cultural heritage and may maintain his or her positive identity privately. Helms (1990) suggests that one may also engage in an active form of Internalization that is equivalent to Cross's (1978) original fifth stage, *Internalization-Commitment*. During the Commitment mode of Internalization, the individual has adopted a behavioral style that is characterized by social and political activism.

Research Support for Black Racial Identity

Racial identity attitudes for Blacks have been found to be associated with a range of emotional, personal, and socio-cultural characteristics. Empirical support for Black racial identity supports the theoretical models have considerable merit. It is important to note that research has not kept pace with theory, so in describing the research, the term racial identity "attitude" will be used. The use of the term "attitude" reflects the fact that the racial identity measures assess attitudes that are presumed to capture important aspects of the racial identity statuses while not measuring all aspects of the statuses.

For example, Pre-encounter attitudes have been reported to be related to a preference for White counselors (Parham & Helms, 1981), high anxiety (Carter, 1991; Parham & Helms, 1985a), low self-regard, and low self-esteem (Parham & Helms, 1985a; Pyant & Yanico, 1991). Carter (1991) found that Pre-encounter attitudes were strongly related to more psychological dysfunction. Pyant and Yanico (1991) report that high Pre-encounter attitudes were related to low scores on a measure of psychological well-being and high scores on the Beck Depression scale. Watts and Carter (1991) found that adults with higher levels of Pre-encounter attitudes tended to have more favorable perceptions of the racial climate and did not perceive personal discrimination in their organization. Mitchell and Dell (1992) found that college students on the West coast who had high levels of Pre-encounter were less likely to participate in Black-oriented campus activities. Thus, high levels of Pre-Encounter attitudes seem to be associated with a low level of racial awareness and some psychological distress, as well as preferences for interactions with White people.

Encounter attitudes for college students were associated with low anxiety, high self-actualization, high self-regard, and a preference for Black counselors (Parham & Helms, 1981; Parham & Helms, 1985b). Pyant and Yanico (1991) found that non-college-students' Encounter attitudes were predictive of low psychological well-being, low self-esteem, and higher depression scale scores. Parham and Helms (1985a) found that Immersion attitudes were associated with low self-actualizing tendencies, low self-regard, and high anxiety and hostility. Martin and Nagayama-Hall (1992) found in a sample of middle-aged women that Encounter was associated with an external locus on control. The emotional turmoil believed to be characteristic of Encounter appears evident in the research findings. The seemingly conflicting findings may be the result of the two phases of Encounter. The initial stage would be more distressing than the later phase of discovery, which might be expected to be related to a greater sense of self-actualization and personal regard.

Persons with high levels of Immersion attitudes also were found to exhibit feelings of hostility. Carter (1991) reports that Immersion-Emersion attitudes were predictive of fewer memory problems and more concern about drug use. Carter (1991) found that this level of racial identity was characterized by "cultural paranoia" (p. 112) or a hypersensitivity to feelings, attitudes, and behaviors motivated by racism. Also Austin, Carter, and Vaux (1990) suggest that people with high levels of these attitudes may believe that counseling may not be effective for them. Such person's were likely to participate in Black-oriented campus activities (Mitchell & Dell, 1992); but they were less likely to endorse feminist beliefs (Martin & Nagayama-Hall, 1992). Carter and Helms (1987) found that Immersion-Emersion attitudes were predictive of Afro-centric cultural values (e.g., Harmony with Nature, Collateral or group relations, and Doing activity). The research evidence regarding Immersion-Emersion attitudes suggests that a person with a predominance of these attitudes may try to be Black in stereotypical ways, he or she may prefer a Black world, and be distrustful of Whites and white institutions.

Carter and Helms (1987) found that Internalization attitudes were predictive of Afro-centric cultural values. Helms and Carter (1991) report that Internalization attitudes were related to preferences for Black counselors. Martin and Nagayama-Hall (1992) found that Internalization was associated with an internal locus of control. People characterized by internalization attitudes seem to be able to grow and change and are aware of racism, as members identified with Black American culture.

The body of research cited above that has used the Black racial identity scale reveals the complexity of one's psychological orientation to one's racial group. Based on the research evidence, racial identity, as proposed in theory, is associated with cultural, behavioral, affective, and psychological variables. Thus, it seems reasonable to conclude that the Black Racial Identity scale (Helms & Parham, in press) shows evidence of construct and content validity. Yet some debate exists in the literature about the validity of one of the Black racial identity subscales. Ponterotto and Wise (1987) have argued that the Encounter scale should be dropped because it did not hold up in a factor analytic study. Others (e.g., Smith, 1991) argue the racial identity theory, and by implication its measures, are not useful at all. The current body of empirical literature, however, does not support these arguments. Various investigations using diverse samples have found each measured level of Black racial identity to be differentially related to a range of variables in ways consistent with theory.

White Racial Identity Theory

White racial identity theory was initially introduced by Helms in 1984. At that time she proposed a five-stage developmental (Contact,

Disintegration, Reintegration, Pseudo-Independence, and Autonomy) model in which one moved from a low level of identity development to a higher level. Most research on White racial identity has been conducted with the scale developed to measure the five-stage model (Helms & Carter, 1990). More recently, Helms (1990; 1992; this volume) has revised and expanded her model to incorporate the relationship between White racial identity and racism and she has expanded her model such that racial identity is described in terms of ego statuses.

Helms's (1990) revised theory of White racial identity development proposes a six-level or status process. Three levels or statuses—Contact, Disintegration, and Reintegration—represent the movements away from racism, and three latter levels or statuses—Pseudo-independence, Immersion-Emersion, and Autonomy—represent more complex and sophisticated ego identity statuses characterized by the eventual formation of a non-racist White racial identity.

Letting go of racism begins at the Contact level of White racial identity development. *Contact* begins when one encounters the idea or the fact of Black people. Attitudes about Blacks are usually accompanied by a lack of awareness of one's Whiteness. The person is only slightly aware of race and racial issues, and is not aware of his or her own acts of individual racism and benefits from institutional and cultural racism. People whose identity statuses are predominantly Contact usually have limited interracial social or occupational interactions with Blacks. Most interactions operate from an essentially color blind racial perspective. A person's increased cross-racial interaction will eventually result in the realization that norms do in fact govern cross-racial interaction and that Blacks are not treated the same in the U.S., no matter their accomplishments or social status.

The awareness of racial differences leads the White person to the *Disintegration* level or identity status. This level of White identity development is characterized by conscious awareness of one's Whiteness and feelings of conflict regarding that awareness. This status is accompanied by moral dilemmas. Although believing in equality, they discover that Blacks and Whites as groups, and as individuals, are not equals, regardless of statements to the contrary. What is of particular difficulty is learning the social price associated with cross-racial interactions. As a result, "the person comes to realize that they are caught between two racial groups. And that to maintain their position among Whites depends on how well they can split their personality" (Helms, 1990, p. 57).

This awareness is wrought with emotional upheavals. One experiences intense feelings of guilt, helplessness, shame, and anxiety. To reduce the emotional and cognitive confusion and conflict, one can (a) avoid Blacks altogether; (b) try to convince people that Blacks are not inferior; or (c) conclude that racism really does not exist, or, if it does, Whites today have little to do with it.

The power of group acceptance coupled with the socio-cultural depth of the beliefs in White superiority and Black and visible racial/ethnic group inferiority, makes it more likely that one would come to believe that racism does not exist or if it does it is a remnant of the past. Thus, one with these ideas enters the next level or identity status, Reintegration.

Reintegration is that level or status of White identity development where the person acknowledges that he or she is White and he or she adopts the belief in White racial superiority and Black or visible racial/ethnic group inferiority. These views may be held explicitly, as is the case with White supremacists, or implicitly as is typical of large numbers of Americans.

> He or she comes to believe that White cultural and institutional racism is the White person's due because he or she has earned such privilege and preferences. Race-related negative conditions are assumed to result from Black people's inferior social, moral, and intellectual qualities. Thus, people at this [point] tend to selectively attend and reinterpret information to conform to stereotypes common to the society. Effectively, people at this stage may feel fear and anger; however, these feelings usually are not that conscious and are seldom overtly expressed. (Helms, 1990, p. 61)

For one who holds these views passively, they may just stay as far away from Blacks and people of color as possible. American society's norms regarding race and culture make it possible for many Whites to hold Reintegration attitudes. It may take some powerful event either with Blacks or Whites for a person to question and begin to abandon this type of racial identity. The multicultural movements may be the types of events that for many White Americans trigger an examination of long-held beliefs about race and culture. This type of questioning may lead the person to abandon racism and begin the process of developing a non-racist White identity.

The process of defining a positive White identity begins at the *Pseudo-Independence* level or status of identity. The person begins to re-examine his/her ideas and knowledge about race. They question the prevailing notions about Blacks and people of color that suggest they are innately inferior or deprived, or deviant from Whites, and they begin to understand that Whites have responsibility for racism. Consequently, the individual becomes uncomfortable with being a White person and they start to alter their outlook. However, these changes are primarily intellectual. The Pseudo-Independent level is characterized by a sense of marginality. One is not as strongly identified with Whites and is not openly accepted by Blacks. The resolution is to join with other like-minded Whites, a realization that leads to the Immersion-Emersion level.

For Whites, the *Immersion-Emersion* level is distinct from the corresponding status for Blacks in that for Whites, they do not reject Blacks but embrace Whites. They change myths and misinformation about Blacks and people of color and Whites and replace them with accurate information about the historical and current significance and meaning of racial group memberships.

They also start a process of self-exploration and discovery, a process fueled by questions such as "What does it mean to be White?" and "Who do I want to be racially?" "How can I feel proud of my race without being racist?" These questions lead one to a path of learning and soul searching. Other Whites are sought out and become the source and locus for answers to the Immersion questions.

During Immersion, one may read about people who have had similar identity journeys. They may form White consciousness-raising groups. Changing Blacks or fighting for people of color is no longer their goal; they are more focused on changing Whites.

> Emotional as well as cognitive restructuring can happen during this [phase]. Successful resolution of this stage apparently requires emotional catharsis [or release] in which the person reexperiences previous emotions that were denied or distorted (cf. Lipsky, 1978). Once these negative feelings are expressed, the person may begin to feel a euphoria perhaps akin to a religious rebirth. These positive feelings not only help to buttress the newly developing White identity, but provide the fuel by which the person can truly begin to tackle racism and oppression in its various forms. (Helms, 1990, p. 65)

Autonomy is entered when the person internalizes, nurtures, and applies the new meaning of whiteness and the person does not oppress, idealize, or denigrate people based on group memberships. Because race is no longer a psychological threat, he or she is able to have a more flexible worldview, and it is possible to abandon as much as possible cultural, institutional, and personal racism. Helms suggests that the person at this level of White identity development is open to new information about race and culture and, consequently, is able to operate more effectively across races. He or she is better able to benefit from racial-cultural exchanges and sharing between members of various races and cultures. The person at this level of White identity also values and seeks out cross-racial/cultural experiences.

Research Support for White Racial Identity

Research has shown Contact attitudes to be related to low anxiety (McCaine, 1986), denial of the significance of race on the part of White women (Carter, 1990a), endorsement of racism by White men (Pope-Davis & Ottavi, 1994) social comfort with Blacks (Claney & Parker, 1988), and endorsement of traditional American cultural values (e.g., evil or mixed human nature, mastery over nature, and achievement orientation) (Carter & Helms, 1990).

People who were characterized by high levels of Disintegration attitudes were reported by Westbrook (cited in Helms, 1990) to endorse the statement "Blacks need help to graduate," and they had a hard time understanding the anger some Blacks expressed. Pope-Davis & Ottavi (1994) found that White men at this level of racial identity endorsed racist practices. Helms and Carter (1991) found that these attitudes were associated with preferences for White male and female counselors. One should note that a person at this level of White racial identity is capable of empathy when Blacks experience racial discrimination but is also unable to understand feelings of anger of Blacks. This contradiction shows how this status is characterized by confusion.

Carter (1990a) and Westbrook (cited in Helms, 1990) reported that Reintegration attitudes were related to symbolic racism. Westbrook found that people with high levels of Reintegration attitudes endorse the statement "Affirmative action gives Blacks too many jobs." Also Reintegration attitudes were predictive of racism for White males and females (Carter, 1990; Pope-Davis & Ottavi, 1994), traditional American cultural values (Carter & Helms, 1990), and low self-actualization (Tokar & Swanson, 1991). Thus, it seems that Reintegration attitudes are related to endorsement of traditional American cultural values, interpersonal discomfort, and racist and negative visions of Blacks.

Whereas Pseudo-Independent attitudes were found by Helms and Carter (1991) to be predictive of preference for White, particularly female, counselors, Westbrook (cited in Helms, 1990) reported that interracial marriage and dating were approved of by people with high Pseudo-Independence attitudes. Claney and Parker (1988) found these attitudes to be related to feeling comfortable with Blacks in various situations. Neither McCaine (1986) nor Carter (1988) found these attitudes to be associated with affect in their studies. Also

Ottavi, Pope-Davis, and Dings (1994) found these attitudes to be related to self-reported multicultural competencies. A predominance of Pseudo-Independent attitudes seems to be associated with a shift from traditional cultural values to a transitional state. The person's racial views suggest more acceptance of Blacks, but he/she still prefers Whites when help is sought. There also seems to be less emotional investment in racial issues.

Autonomy attitudes were related to support of racial integration and the belief that there were no differences in Blacks and Whites in committing crimes on campus (Westbrook, cited in Helms, 1990). Helms and Carter (1991) found no preference for White counselors among those with high Autonomy attitudes. Tokar and Swanson (1991) found that "a secure appreciation and acceptance of oneself and others [Autonomy] appears to be associated with a liberation from rigid adherence to social pressures and with a strong inner reliance (inner directedness)" (p. 299). High levels of Autonomy attitudes clearly show a qualitative difference in one's perception of race and race relations. There is less emphasis on only White relationships and the person is secure in his/her relationships. The individual also has developed a stronger self-concept.

Underlying Dimensions in Racial Identity Theory and Research

The review of theory and research involving racial identity suggests that the Black and White theories of racial identity should be discussed separately. That is, although both types of identity have to do with race, they are not similar. Also because both White and Black racial identity processes involve an understanding of both racial groups there are some interrelationships between them. But given the nature of racism and race relations in the United States, the manner of expression and maturation of racial identity are distinctly different for the two groups.

Regarding Black racial identity, the theory proposes a distinct dimension or form of expression in which race is not salient. This process is characterized primarily by a strong Pre-encounter status. The second dimension is characterized by predominance of the Encounter status that is marked by transition and confusion, and a final dimension seems to be found in the expression of intellectual and later emotional investment in racial identity. In effect, in the latter dimension, the person finds and internalizes a Black identity.

For White racial identity two dimensions are proposed. One involves abandonment of racism with a predominance of Disintegration and Reintegration Attitudes. The other dimension is associated with identity statuses that involve some type of racial acceptance. Racial acceptance may be expressed through Contact, Pseudo-Independence, and Autonomy statuses. However, the more advanced racial identity levels might predominate in a dimension associated with developing a positive White identity.

Measurement Issues

As stated above, this section reviews previous information about the racial identity instruments such as factor analytic information and psychometric data. I use this information as the first step toward exploring whether the various dimensions suggested by theory are supported psychometrically; that is, are they present in the racial identity instruments? Recall that the primary inquiry in this chapter involves the appropriate use of racial identity scale scores. That is, is it appropriate or accurate to report and use, in empirical studies, raw scores, or should raw scores be transformed? In other words, should researchers report and use racial identity scores obtained from samples in specific studies (i.e., sample raw scores) or should scores be transformed using percentile norms that best reflect the relative levels of racial identity in investigations?

These issues are explored with each racial identity instrument separately. Scale construction is reviewed. Then results of cluster analyses computed for this chapter are presented using both raw and transformed scores. These sections are followed by a discussion on implications for counseling and assessment.

Construction of The White Racial Identity Attitudes Scale

As indicated by Helms and Carter (1990), the White Racial Identity Scale consists of five subscales, each designed to measure one of the five (Contact, Disintegration, Reintegration, Pseudo-Independence, and Autonomy) levels of White racial identity. Helms and Carter (1990) reported that the scale's items were not related to social desirability as measured by Crowne and Marlowe's (1964) Social Desirability Scale.

Scoring is done by summing or averaging Likert items for each subscale. High scores reflect greater endorsement of the particular attitudinal scale. Helms and Carter recommended that it is best to use all five subscale scores like a profile rather than use a single score to assign a person to a single level. They also presented a preliminary set of percentiles ($n = 506$) that researchers can use to transform the raw scores from each scale to fit the distribution of the norm group.

However, few studies (e.g., Carter & Helms, 1992) to the author's knowledge have used the norm group to transform raw scores.

One question explored in this chapter is whether transformed scores (i.e., percentiles) or raw scores affect the interpretation of one's findings. That is, does a researcher get a different profile when using raw versus percentile scores? Helms and Carter (1990) also present both interscale correlations and the results of a factor analysis of the scale items. Following is a discussion of how the factor structure interpretation can be seen in terms of possible underlying dimensions in the overall measure.

Item Factor Analysis

To explore whether the two dimensions (i.e., abandoning racism and developing a nonracist identity) proposed by theory were discernible in the psychometric information reported by Helms and Carter (1990), I grouped the factors they reported according to racial identity scale, factor theme, and item loadings. This grouping is

Table 1. Summary of White Racial Identity Factors Reported by Helms and Carter.

Type of Factor	Racial Distance and Discomfort	
R & D	White superiority	(Factor 1; 11 positively loaded items)
C & D	Lack of awareness of race/people are people	(Factor 9; 3 items and Factor 2; 4 negative items)
D	Against cross-racial relationships	(Factor 8; 2 negatively loaded items)
D	Anxiety or insecurity	(Factor 2; 7 positively loaded items)
C	Curiosity	(Factor 3; 6 positively loaded items)
D & R	Confusion, frustration, anger	(Factor 4; 5 positively loaded items)
D & R	White racial injustice	(Factor 5; 8 positively loaded items)
C	Family taught color-blindness	(Factor 11; 4 positively loaded items)
	Racial Awareness and Acceptance	
PI & A	Racial equality	(Factor 1; 8 negatively loaded items)
PI & A	For cross-racial relationships	(Factor 8; 2 positively loaded items)
PI & A	Comfortable in racial situations	(Factor 10; 2 positively and 1 negatively loaded items)

Note: The Factor letters correspond to White racial identity scales: C=Contact, D=Disintegration, R=Reintegration, PI=Pseudo-Independence, A=Autonomy.

offered simply as a way to see how the factor analysis they conducted might reveal other aspects of the instrument. The reader might find that some items loaded on more than one factor and as a result more than 50 items appear on the table. For a more detailed discussion of the factor structure, see Helms and Carter (1990). Helms and Carter (1990) found that the 50 items comprised 11 factors. Inspection of Table 1 shows that the eleven factors, can be grouped into two distinct categories that seem to involve two primary dimensions that I have labeled racial distance/discomfort and racial awareness/acceptance.

Scale Intercorrelations

The scale intercorrelations, as shown in Table 2, reported by Helms and Carter (1990) showed that Contact was positively correlated with Pseudo-Independence ($r = .49$) and Autonomy ($r = .39$) and negatively correlated with Disintegration ($r = -.20$) and Reintegration ($r = -.32$). Disintegration and Reintegration were positively correlated ($r = .72$) with one another and negatively correlated with Pseudo-Independence ($r = -.52$) and ($r = -.55$) respectively, and Autonomy ($r = -.63$) and ($r = -.49$), respectively. According to Helms and Carter, the directions and magnitude of the interscale correlations support theoretical propositions. The directions and size of the correlations suggest that Contact, Pseudo-Independence, and Autonomy are attitudes associated with some type of racial acceptance, albeit for different reasons. The size of the correlations between Contact and Pseudo-Independence ($r = .49$) and Autonomy ($r = .39$) suggest more similarity between Contact and Pseudo-Independence and a weaker relationship with Autonomy. The interscale correlations confirm the underlying similarity of these three White racial identity attitudes and at the same time confirm some degree of independence from one another. Also the correlations suggest that each attitude represents a distinct racial identity status.

Table 2. Summary of Matrix of Correlations among the White Racial Identity Attitude Scales.

Scales	2	3	4	5
Contact (1)	-.20	-.32	.49	.39
Disintegration (2)		.72	-.52	-.63
Reintegration (3)			-.55	-.49
Pseudo-Independence (4)				.63
Autonomy (5)				

Note: Reprinted with permission from J. E. Helms and R. T. Carter (1990). Development of the White Racial Identity Inventory. In J. E. Helms (Ed.), *Black And White Racial Identity*, Westport, CT: Greenwood Press.

Similarly, the positive correlations between Reintegration and Disintegration suggest these two attitudes are related. The negative correlations between Contact, Pseudo-Independence, and Autonomy, and the former attitudes confirm, by direction and magnitude, the lack of connection between these two dimensions of racial identity. Yet the relationships also confirm that similar underlying identity dimensions are being assessed by Reintegration and Disintegration. Lastly, Pseudo-Independence and Autonomy are positively correlated indicating concordance between these closely related levels of racial identity, and at the same time, some distinctiveness.

Some (e.g., Swanson, Tokar, & Davis, 1994) argue that the scale intercorrelations between Disintegration and Reintegration suggests that the scales are not distinct and should be combined. When one considers internal consistency reliability coefficients in conjunction with interscale correlations it might seem reasonable to come to such a conclusion. However, to infer that the scales do not measure attitudes independently, solely based on one sample's reliability coefficients and interscale correlations, one must ignore three related factors. First, internal consistency reliabilities from study to study may be artifacts of the existence or the presence of attitudes in the sample or the environment rather than an artifact of the scales (Helms, 1989; this volume). Second, interscale correlations from varying samples may also reflect environmental or situational aspects of samples as is true of other developmental and personality measures. Therefore, it may be erroneous to conclude that the measures of racial identity should yield common scale scores across each sample. Third, researchers (e.g., Swanson, Tokar, & Davis, 1994; Yanico, Swanson, & Tokar, 1994) who argue that the scales do not measure distinct levels of racial identity must ignore the body of empirical research that consistently and strongly indicates that each scale of White and Black racial identity differently predicts psychological, social, and personal attributes across samples and environments in several studies. If the scales were unstable this could not be true (see the research review section).

In summary, the pattern of interscale correlations and the grouping of the factors from the item factor analysis suggests two general styles of "White racial identity attitudes might exist; one characterized by reactivity and general discomfort with racial issues and the other characterized by positivity and intellectual and emotional comfort with racial issues" (Helms & Carter, 1990, p. 72). These two dimensions seem to be consistent with discomfort with racial issues and the racial awareness and acceptance theme. One may note that the evidence of underlying dimensions for White racial identity is currently derived from the factor analysis of items previously done by Helms and Carter (1990) and is basically interpretative. The second source of evidence for underlying dimensions in the White racial identity scale is from the interscale correlations discussed above.

Cluster analyses were calculated, separately for the racial identity instruments to determine the underlying structure of the five White racial identity subscales and the four Black racial identity subscales. If, in fact, distinct dimensions exist as suggested by theory, they should be determined from the subscales. The underlying dimensions were to be derived from discrete scale sets rather than overlapping items. Once a cluster solution was found, the raw scores and percentiles were compared to explore the question of which type of score is best for interpreting the scale results and the cluster profile.

Cluster Analysis: What Does It Tell Us?

It might be helpful to clarify the distinction between cluster analysis and factor analysis, particularly because both statistical methods can be used to identify distinct structures in a data set. Both procedures are used to simplify a multivariate data set. However, factor analysis may assign a variable item to several factors. It does this because the variance is partitioned among more than one source, whereas a cluster analysis uses one source in partitioning the variance. The single source aspect of cluster analysis then creates groups of variables that can be considered discrete. The situation for factor analysis, however, where no discrete set of variables is generated makes interpreting the factors somewhat less clear (Borgan & Barnett, 1987). Therefore, cluster analyses of the Racial Identity Scales were used to explore the question of underlying dimensions.

White Racial Identity Cluster Analysis

In an effort to explore the underlying complexity of the White racial identity measure, a cluster analysis was conducted on the five White Racial Identity subscales (Contact, Disintegration, Reintegration, Pseudo-Independence, and Autonomy), using 506 white participants who were college students from large Eastern and Midwestern universities. I used the method of nearest centroid sorting cluster procedure. This method forms a partition of cases in which the cases are mutually exclusive and exhaustive (Anderberg, 1973). The cluster solutions revealed information about the underlying dimensions of the racial identity scales. (Four possible solutions were attempted— 2, 3, 4, and 5 clusters. Means, case groupings, and cluster interpretability were used to select the appropriate cluster solution.) Table 3 shows the distribution of cases for the four possible cluster solutions. Through examination of the final cluster centers and the number of cases in each cluster it was determined that a two cluster solution represented the best fit in terms of number of cases classified for the five racial identity scales.

Table 3. Summary of Distribution of Cases for Cluster Solutions for White Racial Identity Scales.

5 Groups	Cases
1	41
2	9
3	341
4	110
5	4
4 Groups	
1	4
2	349
3	8
4	144
3 Groups	
1	254
2	247
3	4
2 Groups	
1	185
2	320

I used a Cluster procedure available from SPSSX. This procedure uses a partitioning algorithm, as noted above, which creates clusters by finding cluster centers based on the values of the cluster variables (i.e., racial identity subscales). It then assigns cases to the centers that are nearest to one another. Therefore, in this procedure an initial cluster center is found. This center represents an estimate of the mean value of each variable in the cluster. For each cluster solution attempted the number of centers were specified as either 2, 3, 4, or 5. The next step involves case classification to cluster centers using the squared Euclidean distance. Finally, each case is reassigned to a cluster center that is nearest to the updated classified cluster center. These final clusters result from variable means for the cases. The five-cluster solution had 9, 4, and 41 cases in three different clusters and the remaining cases were distributed between two clusters. Similar patterns occurred for the 4- and 3-cluster solutions. The final cluster solution was determined by inspection of scale means, case groupings, and interpretability. Therefore, the two-cluster solution appeared to be the best in terms of case distribution and other criteria.

Use of Scaled Scores

Once a cluster solution was found, I determined the particular character of each cluster. In order to characterize the cluster, I examined the rank ordering of the subscale mean scores. The highest mean score was assigned the 1st rank and so on, thus generating a profile of the cluster.

The two clusters' raw scale scores were transformed to percentiles using newly developed normative tables presented in Tables 8 and 9. This way the two types (i.e., raw vs. percentile) of scale scores can be compared. Thus, each cluster can be understood as a profile in which attitudes can be seen having varying influences determined by their percentile ranking. In this way the transformed Profile Cluster, one called Racial Discomfort, is more strongly influenced by Reintegration and Disintegration Attitudes and minimally influenced by Autonomy, Contact, and Pseudo-Independence Attitudes (see Table 4). It therefore is more strongly related to what Helms calls "letting go of a racist identity" phase of white identity development. On the other hand, Cluster profile 2—Racial Acceptance—is more strongly influenced by Pseudo-Independence, Contact, and Autonomy Attitudes and less influenced by Disintegration and Reintegration. Upon inspection of Table 4, one can see that the profiles are almost opposite of one another.

Table 4. Summary of Clusters and White Racial Identity Raw and Percentile Scale Scores.

	Racial Discomfort Cluster 1 N=185				Limited Racial Acceptance Cluster 2 N=320		
Subscale	Raw Score	Scale	% ile	Scale	Raw Score	Scale	% ile
PI	32	R	85	PI	39	PI	90
R	31	D	80	A	36	C	50
D	30	PI	30	C	32	A	40
A	30	C	20	D	22	R	35
C	28	A	10	R	22	D	30

Note: The Factor letters correspond to White racial identity scales: C=Contact, D=Disintegration, R=Reintegration, PI=Pseudo-Independence, A=Autonomy.

However, inspection of Table 4 suggests that the ranking or relative influence of each racial identity score in a profile was less apparent when only raw scores were used. The raw score ranking for both clusters were somewhat different. For instance, both raw score profiles had Pseudo-Independence as the highest scale raw scores, which might suggest that it was the attitude with the greatest influence in each profile. For example, in raw score Cluster 1 Pseudo-Independence, Reintegration, Disintegration, Autonomy, and Contact followed in the enumerated order. The score distances were not large at all with only 4 points separating the highest score 32 (Pseudo-Independence) from the lowest scale score at 28 (Contact). The raw score configuration could clearly be misleading particularly when one compares the raw score with its corresponding percentile score. The percentile clearly showed that a score's meaningfulness is enhanced when the scale score is considered in light of the transformation. Other types of procedures for score transformations might also yield different configurations (see Helms, this volume).

The Racial Acceptance Cluster raw score ranking also changed when raw scores were transformed to percentiles. What became clearer is the relative contribution to the overall cluster profile of the respective scale scores. It is clear using percentiles that Pseudo-Independence had the strongest contribution. Examining the raw scores would lead one to believe that Pseudo-Independence had a slightly greater contribution in comparison to Autonomy. These findings strongly suggest that empirical investigators should begin using (where percentile is only one type of many possible alternatives) transformed data in interpreting scale scores in studies using the White racial identity scale. Otherwise the scale scores meaning may well be distorted or misleading.

Construction of the Black Racial Identity Attitudes Scale

Helms and Parham (in press) developed the Black Racial Identity Attitudes Scale to measure cognitive aspects of the racial identity worldview proposed in the descriptions of racial identity in Cross's early (1978) work.

The measure was derived in part from the Q-Sort procedures introduced by Hall, Cross, and Freedle (1972). Versions of the scale have been in existence since Parham and Helms's (1981) study on preference for counselor race. The first version of the scale (Short Form A) was used in the original study and was the version derived from Hall, Cross, and Freedle (1972).

A second version of the scale (Short Form B) was developed via factor analysis of data from Parham and Helms's (1981) and Carter and Helms's (1987) studies. The factorally derived scales were similar to the original (Short Form A). Additional items were added and a long form version was developed. In general, the internal consistency for each version of the scale has been stable.

As with the White Racial Identity Scale, each respondent has a score for each scale by adding the appropriate items or averaging by number of items for each scale. Regarding use of scale scores, Helms and Parham (in press) point out "Although some may wish to assign subjects to a single stage by using their highest scale score....[we] recommend that patterns of elevations and/or weighted linear combinations of the attitudes be used for interpretative purposes."

Helms (1990) explored the underlying structure of the Black Racial Identity Scale (Short Form B) by using a multidimensional scaling analysis. Her analysis revealed four dimensions. She named the dimensions, rational acceptance, anti-White feelings, anti-Black, and positive Black feelings. "The purpose of the analysis was to determine the nature of the structure underlying the items" (Helms, 1990, p. 38). However, it should be noted that this analysis, like factor analysis, was done on items.

Interscale Correlations

Table 5 shows a correlation matrix of the four Black Racial Identity scales from the long form version of the measure. Inspection of Table 5 shows that Pre-encounter is positively related to Immersion and negatively related to Encounter and Internalization. The correlation with Encounter is essentially zero suggesting that these phases of racial identity may be quite distinct or reflecting the transient character of Encounter. The positive, although moderate, correlation with Immersion might be somewhat puzzling, except when one considers how these levels of racial identity involve stereotypical perspectives of Blacks. Also

Table 5. Summary of Matrix of Correlations among the Black Racial Identity Attitude Scale—Long Form

Scales	2	3	4
Pre-encounter (1)	-.001	.35*	-.58*
Encounter (2)		.46*	.33*
Immersion/Emersion (3)			-.06
Internalization (4)			

Note: All significant correlations indicated by (*) are at or beyond the .01 significance level.

the small negative relationship between Immersion-Emersion and Internalization suggests that these levels of development are quite distinct.

Cluster Analysis of Black Racial Identity Scale

The long form, consisting of 39 items of the Black Racial Identity Scale, was used in this analysis. The cluster groups for the Black Racial Identity Scales are shown in Table 6. The analysis was conducted in the same way as it was for the White Racial Identity Scale. A similar procedure was used, involving inspection of scale means, case groupings, and interpretability to select the appropriate cluster solution. It seems that a three-cluster solution best fit the data. A three-cluster solution suggested that three dimensions or processes might underlie measurement of Black Racial Identity.

From a first glance at the raw scores, it appeared that the three clusters were not actually distinct from one another. Clusters 2 and 3 had the same rankings of scale scores, with highest ranks for the Internalization and Pre-encounter scales. Cluster 3 reversed the two top ranked scales, and the last two scales were similar in ranking. However, by using percentile tables (see Tables 7, 8) the ranking and profile configurations changed, suggesting distinct profiles within each cluster. The profiles seemed to indicate that the scales might actually measure three aspects or dimensions of Black Racial Identity.

Table 6. A Black Racial Identity Cluster Solutions.
        Summary of Distribution of Cases for Various Clusters

5 Groups	Cases
1	3
2	31
3	199
4	227
5	153
4 Groups	
1	427
2	141
3	3
4	42
3 Groups	
1	138
2	188
3	287
2 Groups	
1	176
2	437

These clusters seemed to capture the anti-Black pro-White or Pre-encounter dimension, the transitional phase of identity development marked by confusion, and the internalized phase of pride and personal integration of race and one's own personal style or perspective.

The first cluster called pro-White had its strongest influence from Pre-encounter attitudes followed by Immersion-Emersion, and less influence from Encounter and Internalization. It may be that those elements of Immersion that are focused on stereotypic aspects of Black life that are common in the socio-cultural folklore might contribute to Pre-encounter pro-White beliefs.

The racial confusion cluster comprises strong influences from all four racial identity attitudes. The greatest influence is from Immersion-Emersion, which represents strong idealized attitudes and feelings about race. Yet one has not quite developed a firm or consistent Black identity.

Table 7. Summary of Cluster Raw and Percentile Scores for Black Racial Identity Scales

		"Pro-White" Cluster 1	
Scale	Raw Score	Scale	% ile
PRE	41	PRE	90
INT	31	IEM	85
IEM	30	ENC	30
ENC	30	INT	20
		"Racial Confusion" Cluster 2	
INT	50	IEM	90
PRE	33	INT	85
IEM	26	PRE	70
ENC	14	ENC	70
		"Racial Pride" Cluster 3	
INT	49	INT	80
PRE	26	IEM	50
IEM	20	ENC	50
ENC	12	PRE	43

Note: PRE = Pre-Encounter, ENC = Encounter, IEM = Immersion-Emersion and INT = Internalization.

Table 8. Percentiles of White Racial Identity Scales.

		$N = 1018$ Racial Identity Attitude Scales			
Scale PercentilesM/F	Contact M/F	Disintegration M/F	Reintegration M/F	Pseudo-Independence M/F	Autonomy M/F
99	43	37	41	46	47
	(42/43.77)	(37/37.77)	(41/42.54)	(48/44.77)	(47/47)
90	37	32	32	40	43
	(37/37)	(32/32)	(33/31)	(40/40)	(43/42)
80	35	30	30	38	41
	(35/35)	(30/30)	(30/30)	(38/38)	(41/40)
70	34	28	28	37	39
	(34/34)	(28/28)	(29/28)	(37/37)	(39/39)
60	33	27	26	36	38
	(33/33)	(27/27)	(26/25)	(36/36)	(38/38)
50	32	25	24	35	37
	(32/32)	(25/25)	(24/24)	(35/35)	(37/37)
40	30	24	23	33	36
	(30/31)	(24/23)	(23/22)	(33/33)	(36/36)
30	30	22	21	32	34
	(30/30)	(23/22)	(22/20)	(32/31)	(35/34)
20	28	20	19	29	33
	(28/28)	(21/19)	(20/19)	(30/30)	(33/32)
10	26	18	17	29	30
	(27/26)	(19/17)	(18/17)	(29/29)	(30/30)

This is seen in the equally strong influences of internalization followed by equal influences from Pre-encounter and Encounter.

Last, the Racial Pride cluster seems to be mostly influenced by Internalization attitudes suggesting that this cluster represents a dimension that reflects a clear movement into an integrated sense of racial history and personality. Less influence exists from the other attitudes. Thus, as was true for White racial identity, the underlying dimensions in the Black racial identity measure seem to reflect theoretical propositions. However, the dimensions found for Black racial identity are not apparent unless raw scores are transformed to percentile scores. When the normative transformation of scores is complete the profiles and clusters reflect theoretical notions more directly.

Conclusions and Implications

The current chapter has explored the complexity of racial identity instruments and examined whether it is advisable to use raw scores or some type of score transformation (in this case percentiles). It has also offered new norm groups for both the Black and White scales (see Tables 8 and 9).

Sample Characteristics of Norm Group

The norm group used had the following demographic character-istics: Blacks (n = 557), 38% (212) male, and 62% (345) female; Ages ranged from 16-66 with a median of 20 (M = 21, $S.D.$ = 6.7); Self-reported socioeconomic status was 30% (n = 165) lower/working class, 53% (n = 293) middle class, and 18% (n = 99) upper middle/upper class. Participants came from the Midwest (28%), Northeast (30%), and the Southeast (30%) and the remainder is unspecified. Whites (n = 1,018) 39% (n = 400) male, 61% (n = 618) female; Ages ranged from 17-65 with a median of 20 (M = 21, $S.D.$ = 4.6); Self-reported socioeconomic status was 7.7% (n = 78) lower/working

Table 9. Percentiles of Black Racial Identity Scales.

	$N = 557$ Racial Identity Attitude Scales			
Scale Percentiles	Pre-Encounter M/F	Encounter M/F	Immersion-Emersion M/F	Internalization M/F
99	52 (52/52)	19 (19/19)	34 (34.91/31)	55 (55/55)
90	42 (42/41)	16 (16/16)	27 (28/26)	51 (51/51)
80	37 (37/37)	15 (15/15)	24 (25/24)	49 (49/49)
70	33 (33/33)	14 (14/14)	23 (24/23)	48 (48/48)
60	29 (29/29)	13 (13/13)	22 (23/21)	46 (45/46)
50	27 (27/27)	12 (12/13)	19 (20/19)	42 (42/43)
40	25 (25/25)	12 (12/12)	19 (20/19)	42 (42/43)
30	23 (23/23)	12 (12/11)	18 (19/17)	40 (40/40)
20	21 (21/21)	10 (11/10)	16 (17/16)	37 (36/37)
10	19 (19/19)	9 (9/9)	14 (15/13)	33 (33/33)

class, 54% (n = 546) middle class, and 39% (n = 394) were upper middle/upper class. Regions of the country were Southeast 17% (n = 176), Midwest, 30% (n = 318) , Northeast 8% (n = 80), and West 11% (n = 110) and the remainder was unspecified.

The findings presented, unlike other studies (e.g., Ponterotto & Wise, 1987; Swanson et al., 1994) involving the same racial identity measures, used the scales to determine if any distinctive dimensions could be found in the instruments. Other investigations have tended to focus on items when examining psychometric aspects of racial identity instruments. The cluster analysis at the scale level represents a more appropriate analysis because, according to racial identity theories, racial identity is differentially expressed; in part the particular expression of each level is determined by the particular configuration of the racial identity levels. Therefore, if distinct dimensions were to exist in the instruments, they should be discernible from scale configurations rather than item configurations.

The present study demonstrates that both White and Black Racial identity instruments measure distinct dimensions of racial identity. The present findings illustrate that the measures and the theories from which they were derived are congruent, particularly when one considers individual scales and corrects for local or sample effects by normalizing scale scores.

Also, the findings reported here reinforce the idea that researchers should use scale profiles rather than the single scores or stage classification procedures where participants are grouped according to highest scores. The use of profiles allows for all scores to contribute to analyses, thus, allowing the researcher to discover which racial identity attitudes are related to his or her variables of interest.

Helms (1989; this volume) raised a number of issues pertaining to methodological concerns associated with racial identity, some of which are revisited in this volume. One of these concerns had to do with the influence of local racial climates on individuals and, in turn, on group racial identity expressions. She suggested that researchers may find low scale reliability as a consequence of racial climates that might influence racial identity levels of individuals. If she is correct, then students who volunteer to participate in a study may do so on the basis of their level of racial identity. This artifact of research may also affect percentiles. However, the advantage of transforming scores even to percentiles is that the effect of climate might be reduced when raw scores are transformed. The advantage of using transformed scores would be to alleviate some of the effects of racial environment brought about by subject selection or response bias.

It is my hope that researchers will begin to attend to the complexity of racial identity as demonstrated in the instruments. The findings reported here are encouraging and reaffirming in that theorists have instruments that not only measure specific aspects of the two models but also assess underlying theoretical notions.

Future researchers should be encouraged to use the measures and to adopt the score transformation procedures proposed. Perhaps larger scale studies and longitudinal studies might be undertaken that can confirm and advance our knowledge and measurement of racial identity. It should also be noted that a new set of percentile norms are presented. These norms are based on samples twice the size of the normative samples used by Helms and Carter (1990) and Helms and Parham (in press).

The current investigation may advance the use and exploration of racial identity instruments. It also, I hope, will serve as a caution to investigators who might rush quickly to conclusions about the racial identity measures, using results typically based on a single sample (Swanson et al., 1994; Yanico, Swanson, & Tokar, 1994).

It seems imperative that consumers, practitioners, and researchers remember that racial identity is an extremely complex phenomenon. The theory suggests all people come to some racial identity resolutions. This includes researchers and practitioners. It also includes the contexts and environments in which we all work and live. The interpretation of findings when racial identity instruments are used may simply reflect the levels of complexity of the person(s) interpreting the results or the person(s) being assessed. Therefore, all people concerned or interested in the area of racial identity assessment should be mindful of the dimensions of complexity found in people as described by theory, demonstrated by research, and assessed by the instruments.

REFERENCES

Anderberg, M. J. (1973). *Cluster analysis for applications.* New York: Academic Press.

Atkinson, P. R., Morten, G., & Sue, D. W. (1989). *Counseling American minorities* (3rd ed.). Dubuque, IA: Wm. C. Brown Publishers.

Austin, L. N., Carter, R. T., & Vaux, A. (1990). The role of racial identity in Black students' attitudes toward counseling and counseling centers. *Journal of Student Development, 31*(3), 237-243.

Berry, J. W. (1980). Acculturation as varieties of adaptation In A. M. Padilla (Ed.), *Acculturation theory, models, and some new findings* (pp. 118-126). Boulder, CO: Westview Press, Inc.

Borgan, F. H., & Barnett, D. C. (1987). Applying cluster analysis in counseling psychology research. *Journal of Counseling Psychology*, 34(4), 456-468.

Carter, R. T. (1988). *An empirical test of a theory on the influence of racial identity attitudes on the counseling process within a workshop setting.* Dissertation Abstracts International, 49, 431A.

Carter, R. T. (1990a). The relationship between racism and racial identity among White Americans: An exploratory investigation. *Journal of Counseling and Development, 69,* 46-50.

Carter, R. T. (1990b). Does race or racial identity attitudes influence the counseling process in Black/White dyads? In J. E. Helms (Ed.), *Black and White racial identity attitudes: Theory, research, and practice* (pp. 105-118). Westport, CT: Greenwood Press.

Carter, R. T. (1990c). Does race or racial identity attitudes influence the counseling process in Black/White dyads? In J. E. Helms (Ed.), *Black and White racial identity attitudes: Theory, research, and practice* (pp. 145-164). Westport, CT: Greenwood Press.

Carter, R. T. (1991). Racial identity attitudes and psychological functioning. *Journal of Counseling and Development, 70,* 164-173.

Carter, R. T. (1995). *The influence of race and racial identity in psychotherapy: Toward a racial inclusive model.* New York, NY: John Wiley & Sons.

Carter, R. T., & Goodwin, A. L. (1994) Racial identity and education. *Review of Research in Education, 20,* 291-336.

Carter, R. T., Gushue, G. V., & Weitzman, L. M. (1994). White racial identity development and work values. *Journal of Vocational Behavior, 44,* 185-197.

Carter, R. T., & Helms, J. E. (1987). The relationship of Black value-orientation to racial identity attitudes. *Measurement and Evaluation in Counseling Development, 19,* 185-195.

Carter, R. T., & Helms, J. E. (1990a). The intercultural values inventory. *Test in Microfiche Test Collection.* Princeton, NJ: Educational Testing Service.

Carter, R. T., & Helms, J. E. (1990b). White racial identity attitudes and cultural values. In J. E. Helms (Ed.), *Black and White racial identity attitudes: Theory, research, and practice* (pp. 105-118). Westport, CT: Greenwood Press.

Carter, R. T., & Helms, J. E. (1992). The counseling process as defined by relationship types: A test of Helms's interactional model. *Journal of Multicultural Counseling and Development, 20,* 181-201.

Claney, D., & Parker, W. M. (1988). Assessing White racial consciousness and perceived comfort with Black individuals: A preliminary study. *Journal of Counseling and Development, 67,* 449-451.

Cross, W. E. (1978). The Cross and Thomas models of psychological nigresence. *Journal of Black Psychology, 5,* 13-19.

Cross, W. E. (1980). The Cross and Thomas models of psychological Nigrescence: A literature review. In R. L. Jones (Ed.), *Black Psychology* (2nd ed., pp. 81-89). New York: Harper & Row.

Cross, W. E. (1991). *Shades of Black.* Philadelphia: Temple University Press.

Cross, S. W., Parham, T. A., & Helms, J. E. (1991). Nigresence revisited: Theory and research. In R. L. Jones (Ed.), *Advances in Black psychology* (3rd ed., pp. 319-338). Berkeley, CA: Cobb & Henry.

Crowne, D. P., & Marlowe, D. (1964). *The approval motive: Studies in evaluative dependence.* New York: Wiley.

Hall, W. S., Cross, W. E., & Freedle, R. (1972). Stages in the development of Black awareness: An exploratory investigation. In R. L. Jones (Ed.), *Black Psychology* (1st ed., pp. 156-165). New York: Harper & Row.

Helms, J. E. (1984). Toward a theoretical explanation of the effects of race on counseling: A Black and White model. *The Counseling Psychologist, 12*(4), 153-165.

Helms, J. E. (1989). Considering some methodological issues in racial identity counseling research. *The Counseling Psychologist, 17,* 227-252.

Helms, J. E. (1990). *Black and white racial identity attitudes: Theory, research, and practice.* Westport, CT: Greenwood Press.

Helms, J. E. (1992). *Race is a nice thing to have* .Topeka, KS: Content Communications.

Helms, J. E. (1994). Racial identity and other "racial" constructs. In E. J. Trickett, R. Watts, & D. Birman (Eds.), *Human diversity* (pp. 285-311). San Francisco: Jossey-Bass.

Helms, J. E., & Carter, R. T. (1990). Development of the White Racial Identity Inventory. In J. E. Helms (Ed.), *Black and White racial identity: Theory, research and practice* (pp. 145-164). Westport, CT: Greenwood Press.

Helms, J. E., & Carter, R. T. (1991). Relationship of White and Black racial identity attitudes and demographic similarity to counselor preference. *Journal of Counseling Psychology, 38,* 446-457.

Helms, J. E., & Parham, T. A. (in press). The Racial Identity Attitude Scale (RAIS). In R. L. Jones (Ed.), *Handbook of Black personality measures.* Berkeley, CA: Cobbs & Henry, Inc.

Helms, J. E., & Parham, T. A. (in press). The development of the Racial Identity Attitude Scale. In R. L. Jones (Ed.), *Handbook of tests and measurements for Black populations.* Berkeley, CA: Cobb & Henry.

Helms, J. E., & Piper, R. E. (1994). Implications of racial identity theory for vocational psychology. *Journal of Vocational Behavior, 44*, 124-138.

Lipsky, S. (1978). Internalized oppression. *Black Reemergence*, 5-10.

Martin, J. K., & Nagayama-Hall, G. C. (1992). Thinking Black, thinking internal, thinking feminist. *Journal of Counseling Psychology, 39*, 509-514.

McCaine, J. (1986). *The relationship of conceptual systems to racial and gender identity and the impact of reference group identity development on interpersonal styles of behavior and levels of anxiety.* Unpublished doctoral dissertation. University of Maryland, College Park.

Mitchell, S. L., & Dell, D. M. (1992). The relationship between black students' racial identity attitude and participation in campus activities. *Journal of College Student Development, 33*, 39-43.

Myers, L. J., Speight, P. L., Highlen, P. S., Cox, C. I., Reynolds, A. L., Adams, E. M., & Hanley, C. P. (1991). Identity development and worldview: Toward an optimal conceptualization. *Journal of Counseling & Development, 70*, 54-63.

Parham, T. A. (1989). Cycles of psychological Nigresence. *The Counseling Psychologist, 17*, 187-226.

Parham, T. A., & Helms, J. E. (1981). The influence of black student's racial preference for counselor race. *Journal of Counseling Psychology, 28*, 250-257.

Parham, T. A., & Helms, J. E. (1985a). Attitudes of racial identity and self-esteem of Black students. *Journal of College Student Personnel, 26*, 143-147.

Parham, T. A., & Helms, J. E. (1985b). The relationship of racial identity attitudes to self-actualization of Black students and affective states. *Journal of Counseling Psychology, 32*, 431-440.

Ottavi, T. M., Pope-Davis, D. B., & Dings, J. G. (1994). Relationship between White racial identity attitudes and self-reported multicultural competencies. *Journal of Counseling Psychology, 41*, 149-154.

Pope-Davis, D. B., & Ottavi, T. M. (1992). The influence of White racial identity attitudes on racism among faculty members: A preliminary examination. *Journal of College Student Development, 33(5)*, 389-394.

Pope-Davis, D. B., & Ottavi, T. M. (1994). The relationship between racism and racial identity among white Americans: A replication and extension. *Journal of Counseling and Development, 72*, 293-297.

Ponterotto, J. G., & Wise, S. L. (1987). Construct validity study of the racial identity attitude scale. *Journal of Counseling Psychology, 34*, 123-131.

Pyant, C. T., & Yanico, B. J. (1991). Relationship of racial identity gender-role attitudes to Black women's psychological well-being. *Journal of Counseling Psychology, 38,* 315-322.

Smith, E. J. (1991). Ethnic identity development: Toward the development of a theory within the context of majority/minority status. *Journal of Counseling and Development, 70,* 180-188.

Sue, D. W., & Sue, D. (1990). *Counseling the culturally different: Theory and practice* (2nd ed.). New York: John Wiley and Sons.

Swanson, J. L., Tokar, D. M., & Davis, L. E. (1994). Content and construct validity of the White Racial Identity Attitude Scale. *Journal of Vocational Behavior, 44,* 198-217.

Taub, D. J., & McEwen, M. K. (1992). The relationship of racial identity attitudes to autonomy and mature interpersonal relationships in Black and White undergraduate women. *Journal of College Student Development, 33(5),* 439-446.

Thomas, C. W. (1971). *Boys no more.* Beverly Hills, CA: Glencoe Press.

Tokar, D. M., & Swanson, J. L. (1991). An investigation of the validity of Helm's (1984) model of White racial identity development. *Journal of Counseling Psychology, 38,* 296-301.

Watts, R. J., & Carter, R. T. (1991). Psychological aspects of racism in organizations. *Group and Organizational Studies, 16(3),* 328-344.

Yanico, B. J., Swanson, J. L., & Tokar, D. M. (1994). A psychometric investigation of the Black Racial Identity Attitude Scale—Form B. *Journal of Vocational Behavior, 44,* 218-234.

DEVELOPMENT OF THE OKLAHOMA RACIAL ATTITUDES SCALE PRELIMINARY FORM (ORAS-P)[1]

Sandra K. Choney

University of Oklahoma

John T. Behrens

Arizona State University

The attitudes one holds about oneself as a member of a specific racial or ethnic group and how those attitudes influence perceptions and behavior have been topics of increasing interest since the introduction of Cross's (1971) model of Nigrescence. However, in 1984, Janet Helms opened new vistas by urging that the racial outlook of Whites also be considered, particularly as it may affect cross-racial dyadic interactions. In addition to the potential benefits for practice, an increased understanding of White racial outlook is thought to have significant utility for both training (Sabnani, Ponterotto, & Borodovsky, 1990) and research (Atkinson & Thompson, 1992).

Although several models of White Racial Identity Development (WRID) have been proposed (Helms, 1984, 1990; Ponterotto, 1988; Sabnani, Ponterotto, & Borodovsky, 1990; Sue & Sue, 1990), the conceptual model put forward by Helms has received the most

---

[1]To request information about or permission to use the ORAS instrument address correspondence to: Dr. Mark Leach, SS Box 5025, University of Mississippi, Hattiesburg, MS 39406-5025.

attention and has been the only one with an associated assessment device, the White Racial Identity Attitude Scale (RIAS-W; Helms & Carter, 1990). However, most theoretical WRID models share certain problematic aspects: the use of oppression-adaptive models (although useful in explaining minority racial attitudes) to explain White attitudes, even though the experiential history of Whites and racial and/or ethnic minorities in the United States is radically different; the use of a developmental interpretation (with its Procrustean consequences); and the burden of additional complexity and surplus implications associated with the abstraction "identity" that result from invoking the construct of racial identity. Therefore, problems that we consider to be inherent in WRID models (Rowe, Bennett, & Atkinson, 1994) and the apparent psychometric deficiencies of the RIAS-W (Bennett, Behrens, & Rowe, 1993; Swanson, Tokar, & Davis, 1994; Tokar & Swanson, 1991) have led us to develop a pragmatic model of White racial consciousness and an associated instrument designed to assess persons on the dimensions proposed by that model.

White Racial Consciousness

The proposed model relies on the construct of racial consciousness, defined as "the characteristic attitudes held by a person regarding the significance of being White and what that implies in relation to those who do not share White group membership" (Bennett, Atkinson, & Rowe, 1993, p. 3). It is assumed that the interaction of innate attributes, particular environments, and specific learning experiences results in the acquisition of various cognitive predispositions, including racial attitudes. These attitudes, taken together, constitute the construct of White racial consciousness.

It is believed that the attitudes Whites have regarding racial and/or ethnic minorities tend to cluster into certain conglomerations and that some of these clusters can be described. Furthermore, it is thought that these descriptions can be examined and labels provided for these groupings to indicate different categories or types of racial attitudes. It is important to note that type refers to a describable set of intercorrelated attitudes and not an abstract personality configuration. This approach is regarded simply as a means of classifying people according to which type of racial attitudes best characterizes their outlook.

The types of White racial attitudes that have been proposed (Rowe, Bennett, & Atkinson, 1994) were adapted from Phinney's (1989) stages of ethnic identity. According to this model, four categories of ethnic identity were defined by the presence, absence, or consideration of two variables: exploration of one's ethnicity and commitment to one's ethnic group. In terms of White racial consciousness, one could hold attitudes that show (a) neither exploration nor commitment to racial/ethnic ideas, which is termed avoidant; (b) only commitment to some view but without meaningful exploration, called dependent; or (c) an emphasis on exploration but withholding commitment to any point of view, labeled dissonant. Each of these types of racial consciousness is considered to have an unachieved status because they are thought to be not securely integrated into one's belief structure, because they lack either one or both of the essential variables: commitment and exploration. Persons who hold attitudes that show exploration and/or commitment to racial and/or ethnic-related ideas are considered to have an achieved White racial consciousness status, and categories of achieved status have been identified and labeled conflictive, dominative, integrative, and reactive (see below for explanations).

Individuals with avoidant (av) type attitudes express a lack of interest or concern for issues that relate to racial and/or ethnic minorities. Their typical response is to ignore, minimize, or deny the existence or importance of minority concerns. Dependent (de) type attitudes are marked by the expression of dependence on others to determine one's opinions. Individuals whose attitudes are characterized by this type may "appear to have committed to some set of attitudes regarding White racial consciousness, [but] they have not personally considered alternative perspectives" (Rowe et al., 1994, p. 136). Individuals holding dissonant (di) type attitudes are uncertain about their opinions related to racial and/or ethnic minority issues. This type is considered to be transitional in nature. Individuals who express dissonant (di) attitudes appear to be searching for information that helps resolve the dissonance "generated by the conflict of previously held attitudes and recent experiential incidents" (Rowe et al., 1994, p. 137).

Achieved White racial consciousness is represented by one or more of four types of attitude clusters. Rowe and colleagues (Rowe, Behrens, & Leach, 1995; Rowe et al., 1994) have described these four types as follows:

1. Dominative type attitudes are those held by persons who have strong ethnocentric perspectives that justify the oppression of minority people by members of the White society. Ignorance about minority groups may be the core characteristic of this type, but individuals holding these kinds of attitudes seem not to make attempts to gain valid information preferring an "almost exclusive reliance on and reference to common negative stereotypes" (p. 138).

2. Conflictive type attitudes are characteristic of persons who are opposed to obviously discriminatory practices yet are also opposed to programs designed to reduce or eliminate such discrimination. Individuals with these attitudes may present reasons for their actions and attitudes that do not appear racist; however, "it might be inferred that their attitudes toward visible racial/ethnic groups have a negative valence compared to their attitudes toward Whites and whiteness" (p. 139).

3. Reactive type attitudes are those espoused by persons who recognize that White society wrongly benefits from and promotes discriminatory practices and are reacting to the inherent injustice. Individuals holding reactive type racial attitudes may be prone to overidentification with a minority group, romanticizing aspects of the minority culture, adopting a paternalistic attitude, and attempting to provide assistance based on a Euro-centric perspective.

4. Integrative type attitudes are described as those attitudes held by persons who neither idealize nor oppress minority groups and who do not respond out of anger or guilt about being White. These individuals seem "comfortable with their whiteness and comfortable interacting with visible racial/ethnic minority people" (p. 141).

Theory of Change in White Attitudes

Within the context of the model, attitude change is explained in terms of social cognitive perspectives. Although achieved attitude types are considered to be relatively stable, they are subject to change as a result of direct or vicarious experience that is inconsistent or in conflict with previously held attitudes (Bandura, 1986). This inconsistency or conflict between previous racial attitudes and recent experience, which we term dissonance, results in a lack of certainty regarding one's attitudes, and is usually seen as a precursor, if not a requirement, of changes in types of racial attitudes. It is believed that attitudes may change between those representing the avoidant or dependent types without dissonance occurring because unachieved status attitudes are not considered to be securely integrated into one's belief structure. In movement from the unachieved status to any of the achieved status types, however, an individual would be expected to experience conflict and would therefore be more likely to develop dissonant type attitudes during transition. Once attitudes are characterized by one of the four types of achieved White racial consciousness, a person is not likely to develop attitudes characteristic of another type unless he or she experiences the uncertainty associated with dissonance. Accordingly, in Figure 1, movement from one type of racial attitude to another is possible in any direction except where blocked by double lines.

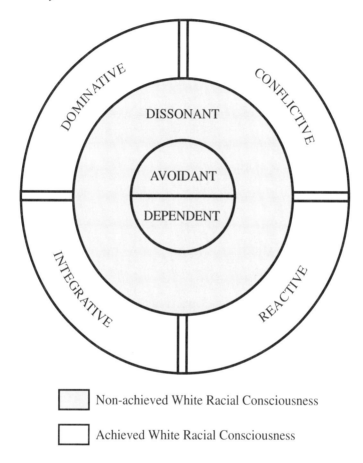

Figure 1.   Rowe, Bennet, and Atkinson's (1994) Model of White Racial Consciousness.

These propositions are necessarily speculative, but, importantly, they can be tested.   Measurement of the racial attitudes of White people will allow the empirical investigation of the construct of White racial consciousness.   Thus, the Oklahoma Racial Attitudes Scale— Preliminary Form (ORAS-P) was developed as a means of providing empirical validation for the model as well as a vehicle by which researchers, practitioners, and those involved in the training of counselors and psychologists might assess the racial outlook of White persons with whom they work.

OKLAHOMA RACIAL ATTITUDES SCALE—PRELIMINARY FORM

Items for the initial administration of the ORAS-P were developed to reflect the types of racial consciousness attitudes proposed in the theory. This approach has been called "deductive" because of its reliance on a predetermined set of constructs that the items are designed to measure (Burisch, 1984). The items included in the pool were generated in two ways. First, certain items found to measure "modern racism" and "old-fashioned racism" (McConahay, 1986) were adapted and similar items developed. Approximately 20% of the original items were developed in this manner. The remaining items (roughly an additional 80% of total items) were suggested by psychological researchers working in the field of multicultural counseling and assessment who were apprised of the dimensions of the model and by the authors of the theoretical model itself.

From this pool of over 70 items, the initial form of the ORAS-P was developed for administration. This form contained 52 items with 10 items for each of the four achieved types and four items for each of the three unachieved types. Subject-centered scaling (Dawis, 1987) that combines the Likert method using response anchors of *Strongly Disagree* and *Strongly Agree* on a 5-point scale, with the use of factor analysis was followed.

As common sense and experience with instrument development would suggest, the initial form was not completely satisfactory. Some items elicited unforeseen interpretations, reflecting subtle nuances in the original wordings. Committed to the *development*, rather than the mere *establishment*, of the instrument, we revised and re-analyzed items through five subsequent administrations conducted over 3 years. Analyses during the early administrations were heavily exploratory—not because we were without expectation concerning how we would like each item to perform, but rather because we were without experience concerning how each item would perform. Even if the theory held completely true, we were not content to believe we could simply write a complete set of flawless items to reflect this circumstance. After each administration univariate and bivariate distributions of subscale scores were viewed along with measures of internal consistency. Principal component and common factor analyses were computed over a wide range of factor numbers in search of alternate explanations. As experience with the instrument increased and consistencies across administrations were observed, development focused on the refinement of fewer and fewer items as we moved toward an instrument in which all items loaded as expected with appropriate internal consistency and presumed content validity.

Although the total number of items was only minimally reduced as development of the instrument progressed, the content of items changed through revision or complete substitution of one item for another. With each ORAS administration an average of five new items were introduced and analyzed. As of the Fall of 1993, the ORAS-P contains 42 items with 31 items measuring achieved status attitude types, 10 items measuring unachieved status types, and an initial item that is not scored. The inclusion of an unscored first item resulted from the discovery that no item, regardless of content or ability to measure a particular attitude type when placed elsewhere in the instrument, was stable in the "Item 1" position. Accordingly, the first item is considered a practice item.

Subjects

Participants for all ORAS-P administrations were White undergraduate students enrolled in a basic psychology class or in undergraduate educational psychology classes at an Oklahoma university. Four hundred ninety-six (496) participants were included in the initial analysis with 364, 479, 379, 386, and 249 included in subsequent iterations. As compensation for their participation, students received experimental credit in their respective classes.

Demographic data for participants in each administration were similar to data for the last administration of the ORAS-P, the results of which are reported below. For example, the percent of males or females fluctuated only a few percentage points across administrations (as would be expected in such large samples) and the mean age was consistently approximately 20 years. Of the 249 individuals surveyed at the administration reported here, there were 113 males with a mean age of 20.1 years and 136 females whose mean age was 20.4 years. All identified their race/ethnicity as White (Euro-American). White international students and those who self-designated themselves as any other national, racial, or ethnic category followed instructions directing them to other survey materials.

Procedure

The ORAS-P was administered in groups ranging in size from 70 to 300 subjects. In all cases, two or three graduate students (one

American Indian male, one American Indian female, and one White male) in counseling psychology along with one of the researchers (two White males, one American Indian female) were present during instrument administration. Participants were told that the purpose of the study was to measure a variety of attitudes held by students, that their responses would be completely anonymous, and that they should try to respond according to what they really think and not according to what they believe they ought to say. Participants then filled out a brief demographic questionaire that included an item requesting the student indicate their race and/or ethnicity in one of the following categories: (a) "White (Euro-American)," (b) "Black (African-American)," (c) "Hispanic-American," (d) "American-Indian/ Alaska Native," (e) "Asian American," or (f) "Other." On the basis of their self-designated race or ethnicity grouping, participants were directed to complete an appropriate survey from a packet of surveys (which included the ORAS-P) they were given upon arrival. This procedure insured that students' racial or ethnic self-designations would be confidential, and each individual has an appropriate survey to complete.

Over all administrations, less than 1% of the students chose to withdraw their participation, and less than 5% returned questionnaires that were unusable due to incomplete data or obvious lack of serious attention to the task.

Results

Table 1 outlines the theoretical statuses and types along with associated items that make up the ORAS-P with subscale scores comprising of the sum of item scores. Each item is scored on a Likert-type scale of 1 to 5; consequently the range of possible scores will be 3 to 15 for the avoidant (av) and dependent (de) scales, 4 to 20 for the dissonance (di) scale, 7 to 35 for the dominative (D) scale, and 8 to 40 for the conflictive (C), reactive (R), and integrative (I) scales. Although these raw score values may be used appropriately for certain specific purposes by future researchers, we will encourage an alternative approach to scoring discussed below.

Subscale reliability

Cronbach alphas for each subscale are presented in Table 1. As the reader may note, all values are between .72 and .82 except for a three-item scale with an alpha of .68. Test-retest reliabilities, calculated for 49 subjects with a 4-week interval between administrations, were as follows: .51 (de), .68 (av), .46 (di), .67 (D), .67 (C), .76 (R),

Table 1. Racial Attitude Statuses, Types, Subscale Items, and Cronbach Alphas For the ORAS-P

Attitude status and type	Subscale items	Range of scores	Alpha
Unachieved Status			
avoidant	av1, av2, av3	3-15	.68
dependent	de1, de2, de3	3-15	.82
dissonant	di1, di2, di3, di4	4-20	.75
Achieved Status			
dominative	D1, D2, D3, D4, D5, D6, D7	7-35	.77
reactive	R1, R2, R3, R3, R4, R5, R6, R7	8-40	.80
conflictive	C1, C2, C3, C4, C5, C6, C7, C8	8-40	.72
integrative	I1, I2, I3, I4, I5, I6, I7, I8	8-40	.79

.60 (I). The test-retest individuals were from the general psychology subject pool who had been administered the ORAS-P during a large group screening, and signed up for subsequent research participation without knowing they would be re-administered the ORAS-P.

Construct Validity

Although a combination of exploratory and confirmatory factor analyses were computed during item development on earlier versions of the instrument, here we report the results of a confirmatory factor analysis testing the factor model in which each item loads on the factor hypothesized. In this computation the four achieved types and three unachieved were specified and the Phi matrix was set to be standardized (PHI=ST) using the LISREL 7 computer package. Because of the assumption of multivariate normality underlying this model, we computed the Mahalanobis distances (analogous to multivariate z-scores) for each individual in the 41-dimension test space. Examination of the distribution of distances revealed a bump in the tail of the distribution reflecting extreme outliers. The 11 observations in this bump were further examined and determined to be different from the remaining individuals because of either very extreme patterns of responding, or patterns that were logically inconsistent (exhibiting incongruent combinations of strong dominative and integrative attitudes reflecting lack of achievement). Because these patterns suggested response bias or lack of cooperation with the task, these individuals were not used in the subsequent analyses for which the sample size was 238.

Table 2. Lisrel Loading Estimates (Maximum Likelihood)

Item	D	R	C	I	av	de	di
D!	.890						
D2	.481						
D3	.253						
D4	.646						
D5	.573						
D6	.487						
D7	.937						
R1		.389					
R2		.359					
R3		.747					
R4		.685					
R5		.551					
R6		.459					
R7		.542					
R8		.288					
C1			.377				
C2			.712				
C3			.622				
C4			.625				
C5			.722				
C6			.844				
C7			.716				
C8			.424				
I1				.483			
I2				.776			
I3				.677			
I4				.555			
I5				.535			
I6				.668			
I7				.401			
I8				.404			
av1					.458		
av2					.692		
av3					.845		
de1						.628	
de2						.709	
de3						.725	
dis1							.560
dis2							.908
dis3							.895
dis4							.703

$N = 238$

Factor loadings for each item on the appropriate factor are presented in Table 2, whereas the estimated Phi matrix (interfactor partial-correlations) is presented in Table 3. The adjusted goodness-of-fit index for this model was .77 with root means square residual of .085 and chi-square value of 1231.35 with 758 degrees of freedom. The ratio of chi-square value to degrees of freedom is 1.624—well under the moderate recommendations of 5 or 3 and below the conservative recommendation of a ratio of 2 (cf. Bollen, 1989). When examining Table 3 the reader should keep in mind that interscale correlations are likely to be larger than those for other instruments because the analysis here reports the results of examining factors after the error variance in the measurement is partialed out. This is a more precise indication of the relationship among the sets of items because of this removal of error variance.

The pattern of interfactor correlations is displayed in Table 3. The pattern is as expected, with the caveat that the correlations between dominative and integrative as well as reactive and conflictive are higher than we would like. The theory that drives the item development delinates four distinct achieved statuses, which should be distinct in this factor structure.

Thus, to test whether the four achieved scales as they presently exist could be collapsed into two bipolar scales, a confirmatory factor analysis with two achieved scales (combined dominative/integrative and combined reactive/conflictive) and the three unachieved scales was specified and computed. The fit here was worse than that of the original model with goodness of fit reduced to .75 and the chi-square value increased to 1327. This increase in chi-square residuals was significant (chi-square difference = 96.41 with 11 df., p was equal to zero at 15 decimal places). Therefore, the factor structure proposed by

Table 3. Interfactor correlation (Phi) Matrix

	D	R	C	I	av	de	di
D	*						
R	-.155	*					
C	.517	-.867	*				
I	-.826	.115	-.372	*			
av	.479	.070	.181	-.424	*		
de	.364	.133	-.010	-.520	.237	*	
di	.338	.191	.010	-.387	.301	.480	*

$N = 238$

the model is consistent with the data and leads to rejection of the notion that the achieved scales are better considered as a pair of bipolar opposites.

As shown in Table 3 the factor intercorrelation matrix reveals that dominative type attitudes are moderately related (and integrative type negatively related) to dissonance and avoidance. Dependent and dissonant types of attitudes are also shown to be moderately related.

After 3 years of development over six different rounds of administration, analysis, and revision, we are satisfied that the factoral structure of the instrument is sufficiently valid to warrant wide use in research settings while the final form of the instrument is refined. Clearly, the focus of this final period of item refinement will be the further distinction of dominative and integrative scales as well as the reactive and conflictive scales.

Discussion

The data presented here suggest that the ORAS-P exhibits a theoretically appropriate factor structure and provides good internal consistency for both achieved and unachieved status types represented by their respective subscales. The stability of scores over a brief time interval appears to be adequate, and the low test-retest coefficient reported for the dissonant scale is, in fact, consistent with the description of that racial attitude type.

In light of the analyses reported here, the instrument will continue to be refined until a final form is developed that addresses the weaknesses noted above. Above other concerns, we are working to develop items that more distinctly measure each of the four achieved status types. This is a very difficult undertaking. For example, in the case of the dominative and integrative scales, a dominative item is one people with dominative attitudes would heartily endorse. However, if it is one that an integrative person will consistently and heartily reject, then it has no additional value in describing integrative attitudes except to say that they are nondominative. The required items must tap dominative attitudes while allowing some flexibility in the responses of individuals with attitudes that predominantly fall on other scales. This subtlety of measurement is not possible to obtain without repeated refinements of an instrument. Subtle and sensitive measurement, we believe, has been missing in other racial attitudes scales of this type, and is likely the cause in previous works for items to collapse into factor structures radically different from those proposed by theory (cf. Alexander, 1992; Bennett, Behrens, & Rowe, 1993; Swanson, Tokar, & Davis, 1994).

Further comment is warranted regarding the scoring routine to be used with the ORAS-P. We propose to classify individuals according to the type of racial attitudes that best characterizes them at that time in their life. Although people are likely to hold some attitudes that represent more than one type, there is evidence (Behrens & Rowe, 1993a) that most people can be objectively classified by one of the types of White racial consciousness. Following the procedures outlined in the scoring manual (Behrens & Rowe, 1993b), subjects whose scores on the av, de, or di scales fall beyond the cutoff are identified as having racial attitudes indicating an unachieved White racial consciousness status and removed from further analysis. T-scores are computed for the remaining subjects on the C, D, I, and R scales and quantitative values or nominal categories may then be assigned.

Given the theoretical and social importance of understanding the racial attitude of White counselors and clients, quantitative instruments aimed at operationalizing a theoretical model, such as ours, should be held to the highest standards of quantitative psychology. Our work represents an effort to develop an instrument for which items are shaped both by theoretical and empirical results. It is only through the iterative process of instrument testing and revision that appropriate measures can be constructed. The practice of developing a set of items on the basis of "expert" opinion alone leaves the possibility that theoretical constructs believed to be measured by an instrument may not be the source of variation at all. This error is sometimes magnified by inappropriate use of exploratory factor analysis to try to read meaning back into the invalid items.

For example, in those cases where the empirical factor structure differs radically from the expected organization of an instrument, the appropriate conclusion is not that the instrument is "factorially complex" and the constructs are simply more complicated than originally believed. Rather, the appropriate conclusion is that there is little reason to believe that the hypothesized constructs are being measured at all. Such an assent to factorial complexity (e.g., Helms & Carter, 1990) presumes a level of validity that requires a match between the factor structure of the items and the factor structure of the concepts they are intended to measure. Such validity is by and large reached by an extensive development process. Because of the great importance of this work to the field, researchers must be held to develop instruments with specific properties, rather than establish instruments and conduct research to "discover" their properties.

Although we expect to further refine the instrument, the Oklahoma Racial Attitudes Scale—Preliminary Form, may be used for a

variety of purposes. It may be useful in assessing the racial consciousness of White clients and mental health service providers. It may also
be useful in designing individualized multicultural counseling training experiences (Sabnani, Ponterotto, & Borodovsky, 1990). In addition, a viable assessment of White racial attitudes is considered to
have significant utility as a within-group variable in multicultural
counseling research (Atkinson & Thompson, 1992). And with the
increasing emphasis on the changing racial climate in this country, the
scale may be found useful in assessing racial attitudes in public and
private industry and in educational institutions.

The ORAS-P is an instrument that would certainly benefit from
further investigation. Currently, the data available are limited to
college student samples. Consequently, results are generalizable only
to other college students attending universities similar to the Oklahoma university from which the sample was drawn. Studies that
cross-validate the factoral structure and correlational relationships of
the ORAS-P with demographically different samples would contribute an important next step. Investigations of the construct validity of
the instrument would also provide useful information. Finally, future
researchers might examine the utility of the ORAS-P in the prediction
of behavior and associated affect of White individuals toward racial
and/or ethnic minority group members.

REFERENCES

Alexander, C. M. (1992). *Construct validity and reliability of the White
Racial Identity Attitude Scale* (WRIAS). Dissertation Abstracts International, 53 (11), 3799. (University Microfilms No. AAC92-37652)

Atkinson, D. R., & Thompson, C. E. (1992). Racial, ethnic, and
cultural variables in counseling. In S. D. Brown & R. W. Lent (Eds.),
Handbook of Counseling Psychology (2nd ed.) (pp. 350-381). New York:
John Wiley.

Bandura, A. (1986). *Social foundations of thought and action.*
Englewood Cliffs, NJ: Prentice-Hall.

Behrens, J. T., & Rowe, W. (1993a). [Analysis of the ORAS scoring
program]. Unpublished raw data.

Behrens, J. T., & Rowe, W. (1993b). *Scoring the Oklahoma Racial
Attitude Scale-Preliminary Form.* Unpublished manuscript.

Bennett, S. K., Atkinson, D. R., & Rowe, W. (1993, August). *White
racial identity: An alternative perspective.* Paper presented at the
meeting of the American Psychological Association, Toronto, Canada.

Bennett, S. K., Behrens, J. T., & Rowe, W. (1993, August). *The
White Racial Identity Attitude Scale: Validity and factor structure.* Paper

presented at the meeting of the American Psychological Association, Toronto, Canada.

Bollen, K. A. (1989). *Structural equations with latent variables*. New York: Wiley.

Burisch, M. (1984). Approaches to personality inventory construction: A comparison of merits. *American Psychologist, 39*, 214-227.

Cross, W. E. (1971). The Negro to Black conversion experience: Towards a psychology of Black liberation. *Black World, 20*(9), 13-27.

Dawis, R. V. (1987). Scale construction. *Journal of Counseling Psychology, 34*, 481-489.

Helms, J. E. (1984). Toward a theoretical model of the effects of race on counseling: A Black and White model. *The Counseling Psychologist, 12*, 153-165.

Helms, J. E. (1990). Toward a model of White racial identity development. In J. E. Helms (Ed.), *Black and White racial identity: Theory, research, and practice*, (pp. 49-66). Westport, CT: Greenwood.

Helms, J. E., & Carter, R. T. (1990). Development of the White Racial Identity Inventory. In J. E. Helms (Ed.), *Black and White racial identity: Theory, research and practice*, (pp. 66-80). Westport, CT: Greenwood.

McConahay, J. B. (1986). Modern racism, ambivalence, and the modern racism scale. In J. F. Dovidio & S. L. Gaertner (Eds.), *Prejudice, discrimination, and racism* (pp. 91-126). New York: Academic Press.

Phinney, J. S. (1989). Stages of ethnic identity in minority adolescents. *Journal of Early Adolescence, 9*, 34-49.

Ponterotto, J. G. (1988). Racial consciousness development among White counselor trainees: A stage model. *Journal of Multicultural Counseling and Development, 70*, 174-180.

Rowe, W., Behrens, J. T., & Leach, M. M. (1995). Racial/ethnic identify and racial consciousness: Looking back and looking forward. In J. G. Ponterotto, J. M. Casas, L. A. Suzuki, & C. M. Alexander (Eds.), *Handbook of multicultural counseling* (2nd ed.; pp. 218–235). New York: Sage.

Rowe, W., Bennett, S. K., & Atkinson, D. R. (1994). White racial identity models: A critique and alternative proposal. *The Counseling Psychologist, 22*, 129-146.

Sabnani, H. B., Ponterotto, J. G., & Borodovsky, L. G. (1991). White racial identity development and cross-cultural training: A stage model. *The Counseling Psychologist, 19*, 76-102.

Sue, D. W., & Sue, D. (1990). *Counseling the culturally different: Theory and practice* (2nd ed.). New York: John Wiley.

Swanson, J. L., Tokar, D. M., & Davis, L. E. (1994). Content and construct validity of the White Racial Attitude Scale. *Journal of Vocational Behavior, 44*, 198-217.

Tokar, D. M., & Swanson, J. L. (1991). An investigation of the validity of Helms' (1984) model of White racial identity development. *Journal of Counseling Psychology, 38,* 296-301.

Section Three

Measurement of the Relationships of Multicultural Counseling Competencies and Counselor Training

Gargi Roysircar Sodowsky

University of Nebraska-Lincoln

Ponterotto, Sodowsky, and Pope-Davis are paying attention to the nomological net encompassing multicultural counseling competencies for definitional and utilitarian purposes. The studies reported in this section suggest that the Multicultural Counseling Awareness Scale (MCAS) and the Multicultural Counseling Inventory (MCI) are relatively reliable, valid, and pragmatic measures. Although the MCAS and MCI assess multicultural competencies, they differ in their item content, and, hence, in their operational definitions of multicultural knowledge, skills, and awareness. They have different numbers of factors. In addition, the item content of their respective factors/subscales indicates that the MCAS focuses on self-reported attitudes and the MCI on self-reported behaviors. Users need to be aware of the distinctiveness of the two measures and not treat them interchangeably. Nonetheless, one characteristic shared by the measures is their usefulness. After a decade's emphasis in counselor preparation for increased multicultural responsiveness and relevant theory-building in training, the MCAS and MCI have made available devices to assess multicultural training outcomes.

Joseph Ponterotto and his collaborators in "Development and Initial Validation of the Multicultural Counseling Awareness Scale" (MCAS) address (a) whether multicultural competence is a definable construct, and (b) whether multicultural growth acquired through training can be assessed. After defining constructs a priori on the basis of preceding landmark papers on multicultural counseling competencies, the authors show that the MCAS has two subscales, Knowledge/Skills and Awareness, with high internal consistency reliabilities for the Knowledge/Skills subscale and the full scale, a moderate alpha for the Awareness subscale, and moderate interscale correlations. The longer Knowledge/Skills subscale consistently discriminates among various criterion groups, such as individuals with a higher level of educational preparation in counseling, national experts, students with supervised minority clinical work, participant race, participant gender, and pretested-posttested students in multicultural counseling classes. However, score differences are not shown consistently and across various groups on the Awareness subscale. This difference in the ability of the two subscales of the MCAS to discriminate among groups may be due to (a) the difficulty in operationalizing and measuring sensitivity to issues of race, ethnicity, and culture; (b) the MCAS being a measure of formal learning; (c) the homogeneity of the various criterion groups in each study in terms of their multicultural awareness; or (d) the possibility that multicultural awareness is a stable attitude that is not trainable.

Ponterotto and collaborators report four studies on the MCAS for which they made strong efforts to recruit participants who were practitioners or graduate students, and who represented some diversity with regard to age, race, ethnicity, and gender. Although most of their participants were from New York City, one group of students for their pre-post training study was from New Mexico. Ponterotto et al. explain the rational-quantitative methods for the development and refinement of the MCAS, such as logically keyed item-selection, authors' card sorts, experts' content validity check, the use of a counselor-trainee focus discussion group, item analysis through the study of item correlations, item means, and score variation, and principal components factor analysis.

Low, nonsignificant correlations have been shown between the MCAS subscales and the Crowne-Marlowe Social Desirability Scale. The MCAS Knowledge/Skills subscale and LaFromboise's CCCI-R full scale are shown to have a positive, significant, moderate correlation. The MCAS Awareness subscale and Jacobson's New Racism Scale (high score indicating lower White racism towards Blacks) have a positive, significant, moderate correlation. The authors state that these correlations provide evidence for the convergent validity of the MCAS. An interesting pre-post design showed that varying subscale changes could be measured by the MCAS across three groups and for the pre-test post-test variable for each group. Such results suggest that the MCAS has great promise.

Gargi Roysircar Sodowsky in "The Multicultural Counseling Inventory: Validity and Applications in Multicultural Training" first addresses the professional, ethical, and advocacy philosophy of multicultural training. She then connects multicultural learning to the empirical need to test whether a multicultural curriculum leads to competence. This philosophical-psychometric framework is not typical in the measurement literature, but is perhaps a turn-of-the-century model that answers the values question "why have multicultural counseling competencies?" and the pragmatic question "how does one measure such competence?" Sodowsky conceptualizes that in the qualitative counseling session, validity of the data depends on the quality of the "multicultural counselor-client relationship" and on the counselor's metacognitive awareness process of "cultural self-reflexivity" and "self-monitoring." These new ideas suggest that Sodowsky is trying to understand via a wide review of conceptual and empirical literature the operationalization of competencies, as indicated by the four-factor structure of the MCI.

The instrument development methods Sodowsky and her collaborators used for the MCI were: exploratory factor analysis with a large sample of Whites from Nebraska; confirmatory factor analysis with a national sample of some diversity to test whether there were one, two, three, or four factors; higher order confirmatory factor analysis to test whether a "general" multicultural factor accounted for moderate interfactor correlations; estimates of internal consistency reliabilities and tests of factor congruence between the two samples. Thus, by using traditional measurement criteria, Sodowsky suggests a four-factor solution. She then did qualitative analyses of the Nebraskans' responses to open-ended questions. The themes that she enumerates show their concordance with at least one of the proposed four factors.

Analyses by multicultural work experience showed that those with more such experience had higher scores on Multicultural Awareness and Multicultural Counseling Relationship than those with less experience. Similar to the less experienced work group, students after taking a multicultural counseling course did not show any difference at posttest on the Relationship factor, but improved in Multicultural Counseling Skills, Multicultural Awareness, and Multicultural Counseling Knowledge, suggesting that didactic and experiential activities may show positive outcome in select competencies. Explaining the implications of students' evaluation of multicultural counseling videotapes in another study, Sodowsky proposes a possible relationship between perceived counselor credibility, as measured by the Counselor Rating Form, and counselor multicultural competencies, as measured by the MCI. Sodowsky also reports a structural equation model for the MCI from initial analyses of an ongoing study with a national sample of university counselors. This model shows the relationships of a network of variables with the MCI: multicultural training, multicultural life experience, social desirability, cultural political correctness, and feelings of social inadequacy. Sodowsky also shows a positive, significant high correlation between the MCI and D'Andrea and Daniels's MAKSS.

Donald Pope-Davis and Deanna Nielson in "Assessing Multicultural Counseling Competencies Using the Multicultural Counseling Inventory: A Review of the Research" remind readers that a debate continues regarding what should be the content and method of multicultural counseling training. They suggest that identifying specific factors that may impact the development of multicultural counseling competencies across training modalities would be helpful data. Pope-Davis and Nielson review Pope-Davis and his collaborators' survey of various training situations, using Sodowsky's MCI. This integrated review may provide additional construct validity support for the MCI, in addition to suggesting possible subscale relationships with factors external to the MCI. Pope-Davis and Nielson provide tables of the internal consistency reliabilities and interscale correlations of the MCI across a variety of studies, thus making it possible for readers to examine the stability of the MCI across administrations, time, samples, and locations.

The reported studies include graduate professional psychology students, counselors in university counseling centers, nursing students, and occupational therapists, with some subjects being recruited nationally, and others from midwestern and western states. Examples of predictor variables studied were training in counseling versus clinical psychology; completion of multicultural seminars/workshops; number of general practica; discussion of multicultural issues in clinical supervision; work with minority clients; trainees' race and ethnicity; and trainees' White racial identity attitudes, as measured by Helms and Carter's WRIAS (see Section 2 for the WRIAS). The above and other predictor variables predicted the four MCI factors variously, with Multicultural Awareness being predicted most often, followed by Multicultural Counseling Knowledge, Multicultural Counseling Skills, and Multicultural Counseling Relationship (in that order).

It is interesting to note that the MCI's Awareness subscale discriminates among groups more consistently than the MCAS' similar titled subscale. With regard to trainees not reporting competence more often in the Relationship factor, Pope-Davis and Nielson agree with Sodowsky that current training methods may not address interpersonal process issues that are involved in the multicultural client-counselor dynamics.

Although Pope-Davis and Nielson present a configuration of relationships of training variables with multicultural competencies, they comment that they did not examine the depth or content of multicultural materials used in training or the theoretical orientation of instructors and supervisors. Their suggestion is that such investigations may eventually point to a theoretical basis for the selection of experiential learning activities that would influence the development of multicultural counseling competencies.

Because Pope-Davis, Ponterotto, and Sodowsky and their respective collaborators have been doing research simultaneously on the measurement of multicultural counseling competencies, they have helped to facilitate an empirical climate much needed in the multicultural training movement for educational process and outcome evaluation. Even though they have been doing research independent of each other, the above authors have raised some similar implications in the training of psychologists and counselors to which trainers and debaters may wish to pay heed.

DEVELOPMENT AND INITIAL VALIDATION OF THE MULTICULTURAL COUNSELING AWARENESS SCALE

Joseph G. Ponterotto

Brian P. Rieger

Ann Barrett

Genevieve Harris

Rickey Sparks

Caridad M. Sanchez

Debbie Magids

Fordham University-Lincoln Center

In recent years counseling programs have devoted increasing attention to multicultural issues in the curriculum. The counseling profession's initial interest in multicultural training (or development) was buoyed by the Division of Counseling Psychology (Division #17 of the American Psychological Association [APA]) position paper on multicultural competencies (Sue et al., 1982). This position paper delineated 11 cross-cultural counseling competencies organized

Author's Note: We would like to thank the following individuals for their comments on an earlier version of this chapter: James J. Hennessy, John C. Houtz, and Mitchell Rabinowitz. We also acknowledge the assistance of Donald Pope-Davis and Rod J. Merta for their help with data collection.

within the categories of awareness (beliefs/attitudes), knowledge, and skills.

The *Awareness* category refers to the counselor's awareness of his or her own value biases and how these biases may translate into culturally insensitive counseling; to the need to check biases and stereotypes; and to the need to develop a positive orientation towards multiculturalism. *Knowledge* refers to the counselor's knowledge of his or her own worldview as well as the worldview of his or her clients; and to additional culture- specific information such as the impact of racism on clients, models of acculturation and racial identity development, and so forth. Finally, *Skills* refers to the counselor's ability to translate awareness and knowledge into culturally sensitive and relevant interventions (Pedersen, 1988; Sue et al., 1982; Sue, Arredondo, & McDavis, 1992).

Since the Sue et al. (1982) position paper was published, numerous professional preparation programs have added multicultural components to their curriculum. According to the Hollis and Wantz (1990, 1994) national surveys of counseling programs, 76 new multicultural courses were developed and added to existing curriculums from 1989 to 1991, and another 27 programs added a course from 1993 to 1995. In a survey of APA-accredited counseling psychology programs, Hills and Strozier (1992) found that 87% of the programs offered a multicultural course, and 59% of the programs required the course. Also surveying APA-accredited counseling psychology programs, Quintana and Bernal (1995) found that 73% of the programs offered at least one multicultural course and 42% required one course. In the most recent survey to date, of both APA-accredited and nonaccredited counseling psychology programs, Ponterotto (in press) found that 89% of responding programs have a required multicultural counseling course, and 58% of programs integrate multicultural issues into all courses.

However, despite the increasing attention to multicultural issues in counselor preparation, concern has been expressed that little attention has focused on the assessment of multicultural competence (Ponterotto & Casas, 1991). The question remains, "Is our current multicultural training effectively preparing practitioners and researchers for work in this area?" (Ponterotto, Rieger, Barrett, & Sparks, 1994; see also, D'Andrea & Daniels, 1991, 1995; Mio & Morris, 1990). In response to this and related concerns, the Ethnic Minority Affairs Committee of APA's Division 17 charged Derald Wing Sue with the task of forming a second national committee (Sue, Carter et al., 1992) to address the implementation and assessment of multicultural competencies in counseling preparation.   One major recommendation stemming from this report is that increased research be devoted to the development of reliable, valid, and practical assessment instruments.

The purpose of this chapter is to describe the development and initial validation of the Multicultural Counseling Awareness Scale (MCAS), a counselor self-assessment scale designed to measure multicultural awareness, knowledge, and skill. The MCAS is one of four multicultural competency instruments currently undergoing continuing validation research (see review by Ponterotto et al., 1994, and Pope-Davis & Dings, 1995). The available instruments, in addition to the current MCAS, are the Cross-Cultural Counseling Inventory-Revised (CCCI-R; LaFromboise, Coleman, & Hernandez, 1991), the Multicultural Counseling Inventory (MCI; Sodowsky, Taffe, Gutkin, & Wise, 1994), and the Multicultural Awareness/Knowledge/Skills Survey (MAKSS; D'Andrea, Daniels, & Heck, 1991). All of these instruments, with the exception of the CCCI-R, are self-report in format. Furthermore, each of these instruments utilize the Sue et al. (1982) report, to some degree, as a conceptual base for item development.

In this chapter we report the results of four studies designed to develop the MCAS and gather initial assessments of the scale's reliability, validity, and utility. Study 1 describes the development of the MCAS and examines its internal consistency, criterion-related validity, and factor structure. Study 2 focuses on assessing the convergent validity of the revised MCAS:B, and testing its potential social desirability contamination. Finally, Studies 3 and 4 utilize pretest-posttest designs to assess the instrument's ability to record change in multicultural competence as a result of specific training.

STUDY 1: SCALE DEVELOPMENT AND INITIAL VALIDATION

The purpose of this study was to develop the MCAS and examine the extent to which scores from the scale demonstrate internal consistency, content validity, criterion-related validity, and construct validity, particularly with regard to factor structure.

METHOD

MCAS Development

Scales can be classified according to the source of scale variation as either Stimulus-Centered, Subject-Centered, or Response Scales (Dawis, 1987). The MCAS was developed using Subject-Centered

Scale Methods (also called individual difference scales) where scores reflect differences among respondents in terms of their standing on the scale's dimensions. Subject-centered scales are those most frequently employed in counseling research (see Dawis, 1987, for an extensive discussion on scale construction in counseling psychology research). The MCAS was developed using the rational-empirico approach. The rational component included the initial item development and selection, a card sort procedure, a content validity check, and a focus group. The empirico component incorporated item analysis and sequenced factor analytic procedures. Each of these developments is described in subsequent sections.

Item Development

A large number of item-statements were generated from the counseling literature focusing on multicultural competence in the areas of awareness (beliefs/attitudes), knowledge, and skills (see Atkinson, Morten, & Sue, 1989; Carney & Kahn, 1984; Pedersen, 1988; Pedersen, Draguns, Lonner, & Trimble, 1989; Ponterotto & Casas, 1991; Sabnani, Ponterotto, & Borodovsky, 1991; Sue et al., 1982; Sue & Sue, 1990). The three original authors of the MCAS (Ponterotto, Sanchez, & Magids, 1991) extracted from this body of literature a total of 135 item-statements focusing on counselor multicultural awareness, knowledge, and skill. Next, the three researchers worked together to examine the respective items, check items for clarity and wording, and eliminate redundant items. As a result of this collaboration, 70 item-statements were retained. Each of the three competency areas had adequate (defined as at least 20 items per area) item representation.

Three independent card sorts were conducted by the scale developers to see if the 70 item-statements could be classified in the respective awareness, knowledge, and skill categories as originally intended. In each card sort only two categories emerged: Knowledge/ Skills combined, and Awareness. The result of this qualitative card sort procedure is not inconsistent with the validation work on the CCCI and the CCCI-R, which found only mixed support for a three-factor model through factor analysis procedures (see psychometric reviews in Ponterotto et al., 1994; Sabnani & Ponterotto, 1992).

The card sort classified this pool of 70 item-statements as 42 Knowledge/Skills items and 28 Awareness items. A 7-point Likert-type scale with responses ranging from 1 (*Not at All True*) to 7 (*Totally True*) was developed for responding to each item. The total score on the MCAS can range from 70 to 490. In developing the scale, approximately one-half of the Awareness items were recast in a negative direction to control for some forms of response bias. Clarity checks showed that Awareness items, but not Knowledge/Skills items, could be clearly recast in this way.

Content Validity Checks

Five published researchers in multicultural counseling who were not part of the research team, and who had completed at least one advanced measurement course, rated each of the 70 items on clarity (1=ambiguous/unclear to 5=clear/concise) and domain appropriateness (1=not relevant to multicultural Awareness or Knowledge/Skills to 5=most relevant to multicultural counseling Awareness or Knowledge/Skills). Any item with a mean less than 4 on both the clarity and appropriateness scale was reworded for clarity and/or domain appropriateness. The final questionnaire included the 70-item MCAS, a demographic background sheet, and the informed consent guidelines.

Focus Group

A 2-hour focus group using nine graduate students in counseling was conducted by the senior author to assess reactions to the scale format and content. The nine students comprised the total enrollment of a multicultural counseling class taught by the senior author; these students were not part of the larger development sample described below. One immediate concern identified was the length of the scale and the time necessary to complete it. Completion times ranged from 12 to 25 minutes, with the average time being 20 minutes. Respondents noted fatigue beginning around Item 50. Notwithstanding the concern for time, the respondents liked the scale, were pleased with its format and printing, and thought the items were clear and well worded. Group members also believed that the scale items served as good stimuli for discussion on multicultural issues in counseling.

Another concern expressed by the focus group was social desirability contamination. The scale instructions clearly highlighted the anonymity and confidentiality of the responses. Further, the instructions state "Base your responses on what you really feel/think at this time; do not respond as you 'think you are supposed to.' This is not a test; there are no right or wrong answers." Nonetheless, through the focus group discussion it became clear that subjects could discern socially desirable responses. Therefore, in the revised and shortened MCAS, discussed as part of the item analysis and factor analysis sections, three social desirability assessment items were added to the scale.

Participants

The total sample for Study 1 consisted of 126 counselors and counselors-in-training. No member of the previously discussed focus group or content validity assessment group was included in this sample. There were four subgroups comprising this sample: 85 graduate students representing two different counseling/counseling psychology programs in New York City; 31 full-time school counselors employed in the New York City School System (primary and secondary levels); and 10 geographically dispersed national experts ("expert" is defined in the Procedure section) in multicultural counseling. Given that the MCAS is targeted for counselors at all levels (e.g., beginning through advanced, working in a variety of counseling settings), it was important to accrue a development sample that included trainees, practicing professionals, and leaders in the field (see related discussion by Dawis, 1987).

The mean age for the full sample was 36 years (median = 34 years, $SD = 10.6$), with ages ranging from 22 to 63. There were 100 female respondents and 23 male respondents (3 individuals did not indicate gender). Racial/ethnic representation was as follows: 90 White Americans, 12 Hispanic Americans, 11 African Americans, 8 Asian American/Pacific Islanders, 1 Native American (with 2 listing "other," and 2 not reporting race/ethnicity). Highest degree held by participants included: 45 Bachelor Degrees, 43 Master's Degrees, 25 Post Masters Diplomas (N.Y. State recognizes 30-credit post masters Professional Diploma Programs), and 11 doctorates (and 2 who did not indicate their highest degree). Of those respondents currently enrolled in counseling programs, 53 were Master's Degree students, 18 were post Master's Degree students, and 25 were doctoral students.

In terms of multicultural training, 25 participants had never completed a multicultural counseling course; 40 had never completed a multicultural course *but* had covered these issues in other courses; 35 had completed one multicultural counseling course; and 23 had completed two or more multicultural classes. Of the full sample, 67 participants had attended multicultural-focused professional workshops/seminars outside of their regular academic programs. Further, 68 participants had received direct supervision of a multicultural clientele with a mean of 10 racial/ethnic minority clients seen under direct supervision.

Procedure

The graduate student samples were from counseling programs housing APA-Accredited Ph.D. Programs in Counseling Psychology.

The graduate students were enrolled in classes that were visited by the scale developers. All students in the class were invited to participate in the study and none declined. The survey was completely anonymous and participation in the study was voluntary.

The school counselor sample completed the MCAS as part of a full-day continuing education program on multicultural issues conducted by the New York City School System. All counselors attending the workshop consented to participate and completed the scale before the start of the day's activities.

The national expert sample was recruited by the senior author through personal mail invitation. These experts were not part of the content validation procedure described earlier. Eleven invitations (with the accompanying MCAS) were sent out, of which 10 were returned (response rate of 91%). Each member of the expert sample is nationally known, has published numerous articles on multicultural counseling, and has taught a multicultural counseling course. Further, all the members were involved in national committee work on minority issues for APA (Division 17) and/or the American Counseling Association (ACA). These individuals were also highly represented among a ranking of the most frequently referenced authors in the multicultural counseling literature (see Ponterotto & Sabnani, 1989). Our goal in recruiting a validation sample ranging from graduate students to distinguished national experts is consistent with the intended MCAS target audience, and allowed for predictive within-sample criterion-related validity checks.

Item Analysis

The 70-item MCAS was found to have high internal consistency (coefficient alpha = .93). The scale also produced satisfactory score variation. On this latter point, Dawis (1987) recommends that new scales achieve a coefficient of variation (standard deviation divided by the mean) in the range of 5% to 15%. The 70-item MCAS had a coefficient of variation of 11.4%.

An item analysis was conducted to empirically test the strength and relationship of the scale items to the total scale, and to identify items that were attenuating the internal consistency of the scale. It was hoped that such a procedure would identify items that could be eliminated from the scale, thus making the scale more efficient.

The following criteria were used to eliminate items:

A) Items with low corrected item-total correlations (generally defined as less than .2 for this sample/instrument, with two exceptions discussed later), or items whose elimination would raise the scale's internal consistency, were withdrawn.

B) Items with skewed means, either above 6.25 or below 1.75 on the 7-point Likert-type scale, were eliminated due to their failure to discriminate within the sample.

C) Items that did not receive responses on at least 6 of the 7 possible Likert-type selections were eliminated (see similar scale development strategies conducted by Serling & Betz, 1990).

D) Additional items were eliminated based on low factor loadings, or multiple high loadings, in a series of factor analyses described below.

MCAS Factor Structure

A principal components analysis using varimax rotation on all factors satisfying Kaiser's Criteria was performed and resulted in a 20-factor solution. A Scree test (Cattell, 1965a, 1965b), however, indicated that 4 or fewer factors would represent an optimal solution. Given the expected correlations of the scale's factors, based on the factor analytic work of LaFromboise et al. (1991) with the conceptually similar CCCI-R, we decided to use oblique rotations to examine 4-, 3-, and 2-factor extractions (as well as the 1-factor model), using the principal components method.

The four-factor extraction accounted for 37.6% of the common variance and resulted as follows: 24 Knowledge/Skills items and 3 positively worded (i.e., higher scores indicate greater awareness) Awareness items loaded highly (.35 or above) on Factor 1 (eigenvalue = 14.4). Four negatively worded (i.e., lower scores indicate greater awareness) Awareness items, 1 positively worded Awareness item, and 1 Knowledge/Skills item loaded highly on Factor 2 (eigenvalue = 5.2). One negatively worded Awareness item loaded highly on Factor 3 (eigenvalue = 3.7). Four negatively worded Awareness items and 1 Knowledge/Skills item loaded highly on Factor 4 (eigenvalue = 3.0). Importantly, the four-factor solution resulted in multiple high loadings (.35 or above on at least 2 factors) on 20 items. Further, 11 items resulted in no factor loading reaching the minimum .35 level set. It was clear that the four-factor model was not the best-fit factor solution.

The three-factor oblique solution accounted for 33.3% of the common scale variance. Thirty-one Knowledge/Skills items and 4 negatively worded Awareness items loaded highly on Factor 1 (eigenvalue = 14.4). Four negatively worded Awareness items, 1 positively worded Awareness item, and 1 Knowledge/Skill item loaded highly on Factor 2 (eigenvalue = 5.2). One negatively worded Awareness item loaded on Factor 3 (eigenvalue = 3.7). The three-factor solution resulted in 12 items with multiple high loadings, and 16 items with no high loadings. The three-factor model, which was predicated by the Sue et al. (1982) competency conceptualization, was not substantiated with the MCAS on the current sample.

The two-factor extraction accounted for 28% of the common variance. Twenty-seven Knowledge/Skills items and 3 positively worded Awareness items loaded highly on Factor 1 (eigenvalue = 14.4). Nine negatively worded Awareness items, 4 positively worded Awareness items, and 2 Knowledge/Skills items loaded highly on Factor 2 (eigenvalue = 5.2). Finally, the single factor extraction accounted for only 20.6% of the common variance and resulted in high loadings on 41 Knowledge/Skills items and 5 Awareness items.

In selecting the best factor structure, our primary criteria was the interpretability and clarity of each resulting factor in the given solution (see Ponterotto & Wise, 1987; Tinsley & Tinsley, 1987). Using this guideline it was clear that the two-factor model best represented our data base. Factor 1 represented Knowledge/Skills, and Factor 2 represented Awareness. This extraction is consistent with the pre-analysis independent card-sorts discussed earlier.

Final MCAS Version

The final MCAS scale version resulted from an examination of the item analysis results plus the factor loadings on the two-factor oblique extraction model. Initially, 31 items were eliminated using either the three item-analysis criteria specified earlier (n = 6 items eliminated) and/or through the identification of low (less than .35; n = 16 items eliminated) or multiple high factor loadings (n = 9 items eliminated) from the two-factor extraction model. Included in the final version of the scale, however, are two items that did not meet all the inclusion criteria, but were deemed by the authors and content validity evaluators to be important to our construct (see related discussion by Dawis, 1987, and Long, 1983). These items, #2 and #28, had item-to-total correlations slightly below the .20 cutoff specified in the item analysis section, but are included in the revised MCAS. Therefore, a total of 29 of the 70 items were eliminated from the prototype MCAS.

The new MCAS version (titled the MCAS Form B: Revised Self Assessment [MCAS:B], to distinguish it from the 70-item scale) consisted of 28 Knowledge/Skills items and 13 Awareness items (9 worded in a negative direction and 4 worded in a positive direction). To this pool of 41 items we added 3 social desirability items and a new awareness item. The awareness item was added to bolster this subscale; and the social desirability items were added as a potential within-scale screening caution given the socio-political sensitivity of the multiculturalism topic (see recent discussion in Ponterotto & Pedersen, 1993). We believed that the addition of 4 items would not significantly add to the amount of time required to complete the MCAS:B.

Therefore, the revised MCAS:B consists of 45 items: 41 resulting from the item analysis and sequenced factor analyses, and 4 new items. In total there were 28 *Knowledge/Skills* items, 14 *Awareness* items, and 3 Social Desirability test items. Table 1 presents these items along with factor loadings, communality estimates, and item-total correlations. The revised MCAS:B is the focus of Studies 2 through 4.

Table 1. Factor Loadings, Communality Estimates, and Corrected Item-Total
Correlations for The MCAS.

	Factor 1 Knowledge /Skills	Factor 2 Awareness	Final Communality Estimate	Corrected Item-Total Correlation
1. I am familiar with the research and writings of Janet E. Helms and I can discuss her work at length spontaneously.	.69	.20	.47	.67
a 2. I believe all clients should maintain direct eye contact during counseling.	.07	.50	.26	.19
3. I check up on my minority/cultural counseling skills by monitoring my functioning -via consultation, supervision, and continued education.	.48	.11	.23	.41
4. I am familiar with the research and writing of Derald Wing Sue and I can discuss his work at length spontaneously.	.71	.27	.51	.71

5. I am aware some research indicates that minority clients receive "less preferred" forms of counseling treatment than majority clients. .62 .32 .41 .60

6. I think that clients who do not discuss intimate aspects of their lives are being resistant and defensive. .23 .53 .29 .37

7. I am aware of certain counseling skills, techniques, or approaches that are more likely to transcend culture and be effective with any client. .44 .07 .19 .34

8. I am aware that the use of standard English with a lower-income or bilingual client may result in misperceptions of the client's strengths and weaknesses. .31 .42 .22 .40

9. I am familiar with the "culturally deficient" and "culturally deprived" depiction of minority mental health and understand how these labels serve to foster and perpetuate discrimination. .61 .25 .38 .55

10. I am familiar with the research and writings of Donald R. Atkinson and I can discuss his work at length spontaneously. .62 .08 .39 .60

b

11. I feel all the recent attention directed toward multicultural issues in counseling is overdone and not really warranted.   New Item - Awareness

12. I am aware of the individual differences that exist within members of a particular ethnic group based on values and beliefs, and level of acculturation.	.45	.31	.24	.41
13. I am aware some research indicates that minority clients are more likely to be diagnosed with mental illnesses than are majority clients.	.61	.23	.37	.57
14. I think that clients should perceive the nuclear family as the ideal social unit.	.08	.68	.48	.26
15. I believe that being highly competitive and achievement oriented are traits that all clients should work towards.	.10	.64	.42	.31
16. I am familiar with the research and writings of J. Manuel Casas and I can discuss his work at length spontaneously.	.64	.11	.42	.61
17. I am aware of my limitations in cross-cultural counseling and could specify them readily.	.42	.25	.20	.37
18. I am familiar with the research and writings of Paul B. Pedersen and I can discuss his work at length spontaneously.	.72	.23	.51	.72
19. I am aware of the differential effects of nonverbal communication (e.g. personal space, eye contact, handshakes) on different ethnic cultures.	.49	.03	.25	.34

20. I understand the impact and operations of oppression and the racist concepts that have permeated the mental health professions.	.65	.02	.45	.48
21. I realize that counselor-client incongruities in problem conceptualization and counseling goals often reduce counselor credibility.	.50	.33	.29	.42
22. I am familiar with the research and writings of Michael Santana-DeVio and I can discuss his work at length spontaneously.	New Item - Social Desirability			
23. I am aware that some minorities see psychology functioning to maintain and promote the status and power of the White Establishment.	.52	.17	.28	.55
24. I am knowledgeable of acculturation models for various ethnic minority groups.	.76	-.01	.64	.61
25. I have an understanding of the role culture and racism play in the development of identity and world views among minority groups.	.70	.12	.49	.57
26. I believe that it is important to emphasize objective and rational thinking in minority clients.	.18	.48	.23	.32
27. I am aware of culture-specific, that is culturally indigenous, models of counseling for various racial/ethnic groups.	.72	-.08	.61	.60

28. I believe that my clients should view a patriarchal structure as the ideal.	.03	.52	.29	.17
29. I am aware of both the barriers and benefits related to cross-cultural counseling.	.70	.11	.50	.58
30. At this point in my professional development, I feel very competent counseling the culturally different.	New Item - Social Desirability			
31. I am comfortable with differences that exist between me and my clients in terms of race and beliefs.	.35	.14	.12	.28
32. I am aware of institutional barriers which may inhibit minorities from using mental health services.	.72	.26	.53	.66
33. I am aware that counselors frequently impose their own cultural values upon minority clients.	.47	.32	.26	.45
34. I think that my clients should exhibit some degree of psychological mindedness and sophistication.	.23	.56	.32	.33
35. I am familiar with the research and writings of Teresa D. LaFromboise and I can discuss her work at length spontaneously.	.57	.02	.35	.53
36. I believe that minority clients will benefit most from counseling with a majority counselor who endorses White middle class values and norms.	.14	.43	.19	.28

37. I am aware that being born a White person in this society carries with it certain advantages.	.31	.54	.32	.39
38. At this point in my professional development, I feel I could benefit little from clinical supervision of my multicultural client caseload.	New Item - Social Desirability			
39. I feel that different socioeconomic status backgrounds of counselor and client may serve as an initial barrier to effective cross-cultural counseling.	.33	.40	.21	.37
40. I have a clear understanding of the value assumptions inherent in the major schools of counseling and know how these interact with values of the culturally diverse.	.72	.08	.54	.65
41. I am aware that some minorities see the counseling process as contrary to their own life experiences and inappropriate or insufficient to their needs.	.49	.34	.28	.43
42. I am aware that being born a minority in this society brings with it certain challenges that White people do not have to face.	.25	.37	.16	.31
43. I believe that clients all must view themselves as their number one responsibility.	.21	.45	.21	.32

44. I am sensitive to circumstances (personal biases, stage of ethnic identity) which may dictate referral of the minority client to a member of his/her own race/culture.	.52	.19	.28	.38
45. I am aware that some minorities believe counselors lead minority students into nonacademic programs regardless of student potential, preferences, or ambitions.	.53	.06	.29	.48
Percent of Variance	20.6	7.4		
Eigenvalue	14.4	5.2		
Coefficient Alpha	.93	.78		

Note: Items are presented to subjects on a 7-point Likert-type scale ranging from 1 (not at all true) to 7 (totally true), with 4 representing somewhat true.

a Items 2, 6, 11, 14, 15, 26, 28, 34, 36, and 43 are negatively worded and are reverse scored.

b Items 11, 22, 30, and 38 represent new scale items developed after the validation.

Internal Consistency and Subscale Intercorrelations

After selecting the 41 items through the specified elimination procedures, the data for only these 41 items were re-analyzed using the bidimensional (Knowledge/Skills, Awareness) multicultural competency construct. The coefficient alpha for the 41-item scale was .93. The Knowledge/Skills subscale had a coefficient alpha of .93; the Awareness subscale had a coefficient alpha of .78. The correlation between the Knowledge/Skills and Awareness subscales was .37, a moderate magnitude supporting the oblique nature of the two-factor model. The coefficient of variation for the 41-item MCAS:B was 17%, slightly above the 5% to 15% range deemed preferable by Dawis (1987).

Criterion-Related Validity

Using the Group-Difference approach as a measure of criterion-related validity (Walsh & Betz, 1990), we examined MCAS score differences between logical subgroups. One-way MANOVAs were used to compare the following groups on MCAS subscale scores: "experts" (n = 10) versus student (n = 11, and n = 66) and practitioner (n = 29) groups; those who had multicultural training (n = 92) in their graduate programs versus those who had no training (n = 21); and those who had seen minority clients under direct supervision (n = 62) versus those who had not (n = 47). Furthermore, MANOVAs examined the effects of race and gender because these variables have been found to be related to multicultural competency (e.g., Pope-Davis, Dings, & Ottavi, 1995; Pope-Davis & Ottavi, 1994a). Given five MANOVAs were performed, the alpha level required for significance was adjusted using the Bonferroni formula (Hays, 1981). Dividing the traditional alpha level (.05) by the number of independent MANOVAs (5), the new alpha level was set at .01.

A one-way MANOVA was performed comparing MCAS subscale scores of national experts, practicing school counselors, and two groupings of graduate students (from two separate universities). This MANOVA was significant [Wilk's Lambda $F(6, 220)$ = 8.47; p < .001]. Follow-up univariate F-tests indicated a significant effect for Subscale 1: Knowledge/Skills [$F(3, 112)$ = 15.1; p < .001] and for Subscale 2: Awareness [$F(3,112)$ = 5.4; p < .01]. A Student-Neuman-Keuls post hoc test for Knowledge/Skills indicated that the expert group scored significantly higher (p < .05) than each of the other three groups. The expert group had a mean of 6.5 (SD = .36), whereas the other three group means were between 4.54 (SD = .67) and 4.64 (SD = .96). The post-hoc tests for Awareness found the expert group (Mean = 5.85; SD = .26) to be significantly higher (p < .05) than each of the other groups: school counselors (Mean = 4.88; SD = .84), graduate student group one (Mean = 5.33; SD = .69), and graduate student group two (Mean = 5.11; SD = .62). Furthermore, graduate student group one scored significantly higher (p < .05) than the school counselor group.

A one-way MANOVA was used to compare those subjects who had never had a multicultural counseling course with subjects who had either had one or more courses or who had multicultural issues covered in other classes. This MANOVA reached the traditional required alpha level [Hotellings $F(2, 110)$ = 3.99; p < .05], but not our Bonferroni adjusted requirement, and therefore will be interpreted as not significant.

Subjects who had worked with minority clients under supervision scored significantly higher [Hotellings $F(2, 106)$ = 7.4; p < .001] than subjects who had not counseled minority clients under direct supervision. Univariate follow-up tests found a significant effect only for Knowledge/Skills [$F(1, 107)$ = 14.9; p < .001]; with the mean for supervised subjects being 5.17 (SD = .83) and the mean for the comparison group 4.496 (SD = .98).

Given the relatively small samples of men and non-Whites in the study, a race-by-gender factorial comparison was not feasible (e.g., there were only four non-White males in the study). Therefore two separate one-way MANOVAs were conducted. With regard to the race of the respondent, minority subjects (all minority groups combined for adequate sample size, n = 32) did score significantly higher than did White subjects (n = 82) [Hotellings F(2, 111) = 6.0; p < .01]. Follow-up univariate tests showed that there was a significant difference on Knowledge/Skills scores only [F(1, 112) = 6.5; p < .05]. On this *Knowledge/Skills* subscale minority subjects scored a mean of 5.13 (SD = .98) whereas White respondents scored a mean of 4.62 (SD = .94). Finally, although the mean score for women (Knowledge/Skills = 4.8 [SD = 1.01], and Awareness = 5.29 [SD = .73]) appeared slightly higher than the score for men (Knowledge/Skills = 4.6 [SD = .84], and Awareness = 5.07 [SD = .72]), the magnitude of the difference was not statistically significant.

DISCUSSION

The MCAS is a subject-centered (Dawis, 1987) self-report instrument developed using a rational-empirico approach. The instrument is designed to operationalize aspects of the "multicultural competency" construct deemed central to preparation in counseling psychology (Atkinson et al., 1989; Pedersen, 1988; Sue et al., 1982; Sue, Carter, et al., 1992). A 70-item MCAS prototype was developed and piloted on a diverse counselor sample.

Using factor-analytic and qualitative (i.e., card sorts) procedures, Study 1 found a two-factor solution to best represent "multicultural competence" as defined by the MCAS items. Specified item-analysis and factor-analysis procedures led to the elimination of 29 items from the prototype MCAS. The 41-item MCAS was conceptualized as a bi-dimensional instrument consisting of a *Knowledge/Skills* subscale and an *Awareness* subscale. Both subscales were found to have adequate internal consistency, and there was a moderate interscale correlation between the two subscales, supporting the bidimensional, oblique nature of the MCAS.

Incorporating the Walsh and Betz (1990) Group Differences Approach to criterion-related validity, we found that, as expected, the national "expert" subsample scored significantly higher than the comparison groups on both subscales. Interestingly, this series of comparisons also indicated that a graduate student subsample scored higher on the Awareness subscale than did a full-time practicing school counselor subsample.

The fact that the "expert" group scored higher on both subscales is not surprising, given the selectivity of this subsample. However, it is interesting to consider the higher Awareness scores of one graduate student subsample over the practicing professionals. One explanation could center on the fact that many of the school counselors were trained a number of years ago when multicultural issues were not regularly integrated into counseling curricula. The graduate student sample, however, was attending a program with a multicultural emphasis, where three of the five core faculty specialize in this area, and where cultural issues are often discussed and explored. The small sample sizes of the cohorts, however, caution against more detailed interpretation of these findings at this time.

Study 1 also found that subjects who had worked with minority clients under clinical supervision scored higher on Knowledge/Skills. This finding is consistent with previous related research (e.g., Ottavi, Pope-Davis, & Dings, 1994; Pope-Davis & Ottavi, 1994a; Sodowsky, this volume).

Finally, the race and gender MANOVAs indicated only a significant effect for race, with non-Whites scoring higher than Whites on Knowledge/Skills. The race comparison is consistent with previous findings (e.g., Pope-Davis & Ottavi, 1994a; Sodowsky, this volume). The lack of a gender effect contradicts findings reported in Pope-Davis and Ottavi (1994b) and Pope-Davis et al. (1995). One of the limitations of this study, however, was the small sample of men.   Clearly, more systematic research with larger and more balanced (by gender) samples is needed to tease out the mixed findings.

It is interesting to explore the root of the varied findings for the Knowledge/Skills and Awareness subscales.   Knowledge/Skills differences were more readily picked up by the MCAS. Research is needed to examine whether the Awareness subscale, measuring awareness, sensitivity, and subtle racial bias, is more stable and immutable to change, and therefore less sensitive to experience (courses, supervision), or whether the MCAS Awareness subscale is not effective in measuring "real" differences. Notwithstanding the need for further research, the group-differences approach incorporated in this study lends some support to the criterion-related validity of the MCAS.

An important limitation of this study is the relatively small sample size. Although perhaps adequate for our item analysis and factor analysis (see empirical work of Arrindell and Van der Ende, 1985 who found that smaller sample sizes, with at least 20 subjects per factor, can yield stable factor solutions), larger national samples are needed to further explore the factor structure of the MCAS. Notwithstanding the limitations of the present study, the overall results indicate that the MCAS had enough reliability and validity support to warrant additional research. Studies 2 through 4 expand the critical assessment of the MCAS using the revised (MCAS:B) 45-item version (the four new items were specified earlier and are listed in Table 1).

STUDY 2: TESTS OF CONVERGENT VALIDITY AND SOCIAL DESIRABILITY CONTAMINATION

The purpose of Study 2 was to examine the convergent validity and the potential social desirability of the MCAS:B and to gather additional indices of homogeneity (assessing internal consistency using the coefficient alpha). In selecting instruments to administer with the MCAS:B we considered those that would have hypothesized relationships to our theoretical construct and that were empirically reliable and valid. Three small correlational studies were conducted with separate samples and incorporating the following three instruments: the Cross-Cultural Counseling Inventory-Revised (CCCI-R; LaFromboise et al., 1991), the New Racism Scale (NRS; Jacobson, 1985); and the Marlowe-Crowne Social Desirability Scale (SDS; Crowne & Marlowe, 1960). The latter instrument was incorporated to examine the potential social desirability contamination of the MCAS:B. We were further interested in an examination of the three-item social desirability check added to the MCAS:B, as this item cluster is considered a unique aspect of the MCAS:B relative to other self-report multicultural competency assessments (see Pope-Davis & Dings, 1995).

Our hypothesis was that MCAS:B Knowledge/Skills subscale scores would correlate positively and significantly with scores on the CCCI-R (a general multicultural knowledge instrument). We further expected the MCAS:B Awareness subscale to correlate significantly with scores on the NRS, as both measure racial/ethnic awareness, sensitivity, and bias.

Samples

Three samples were employed in the present study. No participants in this study were involved in Study 1. Each sample was recruited from two separate graduate courses in counseling or counseling psychology (the later program is APA-Accredited) from an urban university in the Northeast. This university was one of the two described in Study 1.

Sample 1 included 72 graduate students (two participants were counselor educators) who ranged in age from 22 to 61, with a mean age of 34.69 (*SD* = 10.2). The demographic breakdown was as follows: 20 males, 52 females; 48 White participants, 24 minority participants (12 African Americans, 9 Hispanics, plus other); 32 held the Bachelor's Degree, 38 a Master's Degree, and 2 a Doctorate. Twenty-one participants had received no prior academic coursework (complete course[s] or parts of a course) in multicultural counseling, and 51 had some prior coursework. Finally, 47 participants had completed no separate workshop exercises in multicultural counseling, whereas 25 had taken such workshops.

Sample 2 included 42 graduate students (one participant was a counselor educator) who ranged in age from 21 to 56, with a mean age of 30.71 (*SD* = 8.5). The demographic breakdown was as follows: 5 males, 37 females; 35 White participants, 7 minority participants (3 Asian Americans plus other); 30 participants held the Bachelor's Degree, 11 a Master's Degree, and 1 a doctorate. Eighteen participants had received no prior academic coursework in multicultural counseling, and 24 had some prior coursework. Finally, 34 participants had completed no separate workshop experience in multicultural counseling, whereas 8 had taken such workshops.

Sample 3 included 45 graduate students (two participants were counselor educators) who ranged in age from 22 to 50, with a mean age of 31.11 (*SD* = 8.9). The demographic breakdown was as follows: 15 males, 30 females; 36 Whites, 9 minority persons (5 African Americans, plus other); 34 participants held the Bachelor's Degree, 9 a Master's Degree, and 2 a doctorate. Twenty-two participants had received no prior academic coursework in multicultural counseling, and 23 had some prior coursework. Finally, 35 participants had completed no separate workshop experience in multicultural counseling, whereas 9 had taken such workshops.

Procedure

Instruments were distributed to full classes by one of the seven authors. In each case, arrangements were made with the course professor to allow a researcher into the classroom to administer two instruments, and then provide a debriefing period and a guest lecture/ discussion on multicultural issues. The research team felt it was important that the subjects receive something tangible for their participation in the study, and because we did not pay them, we gave them a full class lecture. In this regard we followed the stringent ethical recommendations for multicultural research set forth by Ponterotto and Casas (1991).

Sample 1 completed the MCAS:B and CCCI-R, Sample 2 completed the MCAS:B and NRS, and Sample 3 completed the MCAS:B and SDS. Each pair of instruments (the MCAS:B with each of the three instruments described below) was counterbalanced and given to two counseling classes. Classes were selected based on availability, and all were visited during the same academic year. In total, six counseling courses (of varying topics) on two of the University's three campuses were involved. No prospective subjects declined to participate in the study.

Instruments

Cross-Cultural Counseling Inventory-Revised (CCCI-R). The CCCI-R (LaFromboise et al., 1991) is a 20-item instrument designed to measure the 11 competencies set forth in the Sue et al. (1982) Position Paper. The CCCI-R is completed by an evaluator or supervisor observing a counselor (or counselor-trainee) engaged in a cross-cultural counseling situation. Using a 6-point Likert-type response format (where 1 = *Strongly Disagree* and 6 = *Strongly Agree*), the evaluator indicates the extent to which the items describe the observed counselor. A sample CCCI-R item is "Counselor demonstrates knowledge about client's culture." Scores range from 20 (little multicultural knowledge/skill) to 120 (high levels of multicultural knowledge/skill).

In the present study the CCCI-R was adapted for use as a counselor self-report instrument. This was done by asking subjects to rate themselves on the items. This modification was pilot tested among the research team and found to be meaningful and understandable. It is important to note that the CCCI-R items are similar in content, focus, format, and wording to items on the MCAS Factor 1 and to items on other multicultural competence self-report instruments (see review in Ponterotto et al., 1994), and therefore, it is not surprising that this adaptation proceeded smoothly.

The CCCI-R is the longest standing, and at the time this study began, the most researched multicultural competency scale. The subject of periodic psychometric reviews (Ponterotto et al., 1994; Sabnani & Ponterotto, 1992), the CCCI-R has very good internal consistency (coefficient alpha = .95; LaFromboise et al., 1991), satisfactory interrater reliability, and adequate indices of content and criterion-related validity. Although conceptualized as a tridimensional construct (consistent with the Sue et al., 1982 report), it is recommended that the scale be used as a unidimensional (single Total Score) measure

(T. LaFromboise, personal communication, December 3, 1990), given its mixed factor analytic results (Ponterotto et al., 1994).

The New Racism Scale (NRS). The NRS was developed by Jacobson (1985) and is a modification of the older Modern Racism Scale (McConahay & Hough, 1976). The scale is designed to measure White people's racism toward Blacks. The NRS includes seven multiple-choice items, with each item having either three or four response choices. Scale scores range from 7 to 26. In the present study the items were coded so that low scores indicate higher levels of racism. A sample stimulus question is as follows: "Would it upset you personally if Blacks moved into your neighborhood?"

The NRS has satisfactory internal consistency: Coefficient alphas across three respective studies were .70 (Jacobson, 1985), .62 (Carter, 1990), and .62 (Pope-Davis & Ottavi, 1992). Given the brevity of the NRS, these moderate coefficients support the internal consistency of the scale. Three studies provided evidence of convergent and discriminant validity for the NRS through its expected relationship with various levels of White Racial Identity Development (Carter, 1990; Pope-Davis & Ottavi, 1992; Pope-Davis & Ottavi, 1994b).

Social Desirability Scale. The Marlowe-Crowne Social Desirability Scale (SDS) consists of 33 true-false items measuring one's need to seek approval by responding in a culturally appropriate and acceptable manner. Crowne and Marlowe (1960) report the internal consistency of the SDS to be .88, and they report a one-month test-retest stability coefficient of .89. The SDS is a frequently used social desirability scale and has strong indices of validity (Crowne & Marlowe, 1964).

RESULTS

Table 2 presents coefficient alphas for the CCCI-R, NRS, SDS, and MCAS:B subscales (including the three-item social desirability cluster) across the three samples. Table 3 presents the results of Pearson correlations of MCAS:B subscale scores with the CCCI-R, NRS, and SDS. The MCAS:B Knowledge/skills subscale correlated positively and significantly ($r = .44$; $p < .001$) with the CCCI-R as hypothesized. The MCAS:B Awareness subscale correlated positively and significantly ($r = .49$; $p < .001$) with the NRS as hypothesized. These significant correlations in the expected direction provide some evidence for the convergent validity of the MCAS:B. (Note: These findings also support the construct validity of the MCAS:B using the criteria specified by Tinsley, 1992). Finally, the correlations between the Knowledge/Skills subscale and the Awareness subscale across the three samples were .45, .35, and .47, respectively.

Table 2. Coefficient Alphas for the MCAS:B Factors, CCCI-R, NRS, and SDS
          Across Three Samples.

	CCCI-R	NRS	SDS	MCAS:B Knowledge/ Skills Subscale	MCAS:B Awareness Subscale	MCAS:B Social Desirability Cluster
Sample 1 (N=72)	.93			.93	.81	.43
Sample 2 (N=42)		.65		.91	.76	.15
Sample 3 (N=45)			.83	.93	.78	.02

Note: MCAS:B = Multicultural Counseling Awareness Scale: Form B
       CCCI-R = Cross Cultural Counseling Inventory—Revised
       NRS = New Racism Scale
       SDS = Social Desirability Scale

Table 3. Pearson Correlations of MCAS:B Factor Scores with the CCCI-R,
          NRS, and SDS Across Three Samples; and Correlations Between
          MCAS:B Factor Scores Acrosss Samples.

	MCAS:B Knowledge/ Skills Subscale	MCAS:B Awareness Subscale	Correlations Between Knowledge/Skills and Awareness Subscales
(Sample 1: N=72) CCCI-R	.44**	.15	.45**
(Sample 2: N=42) NRS	.16	.49**	.35*
(Sample 3: N=45) SDS	.22	.00	.47**

Note: MCAS:B = Multicultural Counseling Awareness Scale: Form B
       CCCI-R = Cross-Cultural Counseling Inventory—Revised
       NRS = New Racism Scale
       SDS = Social Desirability Scale
       * = $p < .05$
       ** = $p < .001$

DISCUSSION

The coefficients in Table 2 demonstrate that the internal consistency of the MCAS:B Knowledge/Skills and Awareness subscales were satisfactory and were similar to the results found in Study 1. Coefficient alphas for the MCAS:B three-item social desirability test cluster were lower and more variable. Given only three items, one would expect to find low internal consistency. Another possible explanation is that the three items were measuring different types of social desirability. For example Item #22, "I am familiar with the research and writings of Michael Santana-DeVio and I can discuss his work at length spontaneously," clearly measures faking for there is no such person. However, the other two social desirability items (#30 and #38; see Table 1) may be more a measure of naiveté or ignorance than purposeful faking. This possible distinction could have affected the overall homogeneity of the cluster (personal communication, Jonathan G. Dings, University of Iowa, February 24, 1993). Regardless of the explanation for lower coefficient alphas on this cluster of items, it would be wise not to use them for any interpretive purposes. This topic will be covered further in this chapter's Integrative Discussion.

The present study found the coefficient alphas for the comparison instruments, the CCCI-R, NRS, and SDS to be quite similar to their previous use reported in the Instruments section. The magnitude of these correlations led us to conclude that these instruments were valid for use in the present study. It should be highlighted that although the NRS coefficient alpha was somewhat low (.65), the instrument includes only seven items.

The CCCI-R did not correlate significantly with the MCAS:B *Awareness* subscale ($r = .16$), as expected. Furthermore, the MCAS:B *Knowledge/Skills* subscale did not correlate significantly ($r = .16$) with the NRS, also as predicted. The pattern of correlations provides some additional evidence that although moderately correlated, the *Knowledge/Skills* and *Awareness* subscales are measuring unique aspects of multicultural competence (see discussion by Long, 1983). Finally, with regard to possible social desirability contamination of the MCAS:B, the results show minimal and nonsignificant correlations between the SDS and the MCAS:B subscales.

In summary, Study 2 indicated that the MCAS:B subscales maintained satisfactory internal consistency across new, yet smaller, samples. Furthermore, the pattern of correlations with theoretically linked instruments supports the convergent validity of the MCAS:B subscales. Finally, this study provides some evidence that the MCAS:B subscales are not subject to social desirability contamination, at least as measured by the Social Desirability Scale (Crowne & Marlowe, 1960).

STUDIES 3 AND 4

The purpose of Studies 3 and 4 was to examine the sensitivity of the MCAS:B in recording changes as a result of multicultural training. In Study 3, the MCAS:B was used as a pre-/post-test measure in a single multicultural counseling course. Study 4 replicated Study 3 using tighter experimental controls and geographically dispersed samples. These studies were designed to further test the criterion-related and construct validity (in that multicultural competence is a construct that can be taught and developed) of the MCAS:B [see *Standards for Educational and Psychological Testing* (American Educational Research Association, American Psychological Association, & National Council on Measurement in Education, 1985), Tinsley (1992), and Walsh and Betz (1990) for guides we used to distinguish types of validity].

STUDY 3

Sample and Procedure

This sample consisted of 19 graduate students enrolled in a multicultural counseling class. Sample demographics are very similar to the samples described fully in Study 2. The MCAS:B was administered on the first and last days of the semester. Participation was voluntary and anonymous. No student declined to participate in the study.

Results

A one-way MANOVA was performed with time of test (pre or post) serving as the grouping variable, and the two MCAS:B subscale scores as the dependent variables. Post-test scores were significantly higher [Hotelling $F(2, 35) = 22.1; p < .001$] than pre-test scores. Univariate follow-up tests indicated a significant effect for Knowledge/Skills [$F(1, 36) = 45.1; p < .001$]. The mean at pre-test was 3.88 ($SD = .70$) and at post-test the mean was 5.39 ($SD = .68$). The Awareness subscale mean rose from 6.0 ($SD = .54$) at pre-test to 6.25 ($SD = .41$) at post-test, but the increase was not enough to reach significance ($p = .1$).

Discussion

This pilot study indicated that the MCAS:B was sensitive to measuring a post-course increase in multicultural knowledge/skills. With regard to the *Awareness* subscale, either the course was not successful in raising multicultural awareness to a significant degree, or the MCAS:B was not sensitive enough to measure an increase. This pilot study had obvious limitations, the most blatant being that the study had no control group, and the course instructor was one of the MCAS developers (creating a possible course content bias). Study 4 addressed these concerns through a more sophisticated design.

STUDY 4

Given the obvious limitations of Study 3, in Study 4 we administered the MCAS:B as a pre- and post-test measure in three courses during a single semester. Course 1 was the multicultural course described in Study 3, taught again by the senior author one year later. Course 2 served as a control group; this course was a general developmental counseling course offered by the instructor of Course 1. Course 3 was a multicultural counseling course offered at a university in the state of New Mexico.

The expectations of this study were as follows. Course 1 and Course 3 would both result in significant improvement on MCAS:B scores at post-test. Assuming that multicultural competence is a definable construct (Sue et al., 1982; Sue, Carter et al., 1992) and that the MCAS:B effectively measures this construct, then score improvements should result, regardless of the professor or university where the content is taught (assuming that both professors are knowledgeable of the construct). Course 2, the control, would not show significant improvement at post-test. It is important to note, however, that at the university where Course 1 and Course 2 are taught, multicultural issues are integrated into all coursework (so the control nature of Course 2 is in reality only a partial control), and for this reason some gain in post-test scores would not be surprising even for Course 2.

Sample

Course 1 was a multicultural counseling course offered by the senior author. There were 8 students (out of 10) who were present for both the pre-test and post-test. The student demographic profile was similar to that described in Study 2.

Course 2 was a developmental psychology course (with a counseling emphasis) taken by 30 students (30 of whom completed the pre-test and 24 the post-test) in the same counseling program described above. Although multiculturalism is not the focus in this course, the topic is integrated to some degree into the curriculum. Student demographics were similar to those described fully in Study 2.

Course 3 was offered at a university in New Mexico. Twenty-nine students were enrolled, 26 completed the pre-test and 29 the post-test. The content, structure, and format of this class is similar to that of Course 1 and many multicultural courses in counseling programs (see discussion by Mio & Morris, 1990). This sample ranged in age from 21 to 61, with a mean age of 37.38 (*SD* = 11.3). The demographic breakdown was as follows: 10 males, and 19 females; 21 White participants, 8 minority participants (5 Hispanics plus other); 25 participants held the Bachelor's Degree and 4 the Master's Degree.

Procedure

The MCAS:B pre-test was group-administered the first day of class for each course. As noted previously, the first page of the MCAS:B includes informed consent guidelines and specific directions for completing the instrument. No student declined participation in the study. The MCAS:B post-test was completed during the last or next to last class of the semester (depending on the professor's timetable). In Course 1 and Course 2, the post-test was again group administered. In Course 3, however, the professor was short on time and asked students to complete the MCAS:B at home and return it the following week. This alteration of the testing situation was unfortunate and presents a methodological limitation of the study.

Results

To examine the equivalency of MCAS:B scores across the three courses at pre-test, a one-way MANOVA was performed with the course as the grouping variable and MCAS:B subscale scores as the dependent variable. This MANOVA was not significant and suggested score equivalency across courses. Pretest and post-test means and standard deviations for all three courses are presented in Table 4.

A one-way MANOVA at post-test (again with course as the grouping variable) resulted in a significant overall effect (Wilk's Lambda: $F(4, 114) = 6.87, p < .001$). Follow-up univariate F-tests found a significant effect for the Knowledge/Skills subscale ($F[2, 58] = 13.92$, $p < .001$) and for the Awareness subscale ($F [2, 58] = 4.20, p < .05$). Given there were three levels of the grouping variable, Neuman-Keuls post hoc tests were conducted for each subscale. For the Knowledge/Skills subscale, Course 1 (New York multicultural course) post-test scores were significantly higher than Course 2 (New York partial control course) post-test scores and Course 3 (New Mexico multicultural course) post-test scores. Furthermore, Course 3 scores were significantly higher than Course 2 scores.

Table 4. MCAS:B Pretest, Posttest, and Change Scores for Course 1, Course 2, and Course 3.

	Pretest		Posttest				Change	
	K/S	A	K/S		A		K/S	A
	M (SD)	M (SD)	M	(SD)	M	(SD)		
Course 1	4.0 (.98)	5.8 (.66)	5.7	(.73)	6.3	(.70)	1.7	0.5
Course 2	3.5 (.98)	5.4 (.81)	4.2	(.84)	5.5	(.83)	0.7	0.1
Course 3	3.8 (.58)	5.3 (.81)	4.8	(.67)	5.9	(.63)	1.0	0.6

Note: K/S = Knowledge/Skills Subscale; A = Awareness Subscale

With regard to the post hoc tests for the *Awareness* Factor, Course 1 post-test scores were significantly higher than Course 2 scores; and Course 3 scores were also significantly higher than Course 2 scores (see Table 4).

We were further interested in isolating the effects of the semester's experience on the individual courses. Separate MANOVAs were conducted for each course, with the MCAS:B pre-test versus post-test serving as the grouping variable. The Bonferroni formula was used to control for inflated alpha, with a new alpha set at .017.

For Course 1 (New York multicultural) the MANOVA was significant: Hotellings F (2, 13) = 7.28, $p < .01$. Follow-up univariate tests revealed that the Knowledge/Skills subscale was significantly higher at post-test than at pre-test. Subscale 2, Awareness, approached but did not reach significance ($p = .17$). Course 2, the partial control, approached but did reach the Bonferroni adjusted alpha: Hotellings F [2, 51] = 4.4, $p < .05$.

Finally, for Course 3 (New Mexico multicultural) there was a significant main effect on the MANOVA: Hotellings F [2, 52] = 21.57, $p < .001$. Follow-up univariate tests resulted in significant effects for both subscales. The Knowledge/Skills subscale at post-test was significantly (F [1, 53] = 33.73, $p < .001$) higher than at pre-test. The Awareness subscale also reached significance (F [1, 53] = 9.7, $p < .01$).

Discussion

The results of Study 4 provide further evidence that the MCAS:B is sensitive to growth in multicultural competence. An important component of this study was that MCAS:B scores rose significantly in a multicultural counseling course taught by a professor in a distant (from New York) state. This result presents additional evidence for the content and construct validity of the MCAS:B. That is, the construct of "multicultural competence," as envisioned by two separate instructors in the field, is being reliably measured by the MCAS:B.

Given a number of limitations, this study needs to be interpreted with caution. First, the sample size for Course 1 was quite small. Second, the developmental counseling course served only as a partial control, and not as a "true" control group. It would be valuable to incorporate a true control group where multicultural issues are not discussed or covered at all. However, at the institution where Courses 1 and 2 were offered, all courses incorporate multicultural issues, including measurement courses. Third, the professor of Course 3 modified the procedure for collecting the post-test data. The lack of procedural consistency across the three courses raises concern. Clearly, more carefully controlled pre-post course assessments are needed.

INTEGRATIVE DISCUSSION

This chapter reports the results of four studies designed to develop and psychometrically evaluate the Multicultural Counseling Awareness Scale. The rationale and need for instruments such as the MCAS stems from over a decade of conceptual work on the construct of "multicultural competence" (Pedersen, 1988; Ponterotto & Casas, 1991; Sue et al., 1982; Sue, Carter et al., 1992). Utilizing both qualitative and quantitative procedures, Study 1 found the MCAS subscales to be face- and content-valid, to possess a satisfactory level of internal consistency, and to have moderate levels of criterion-related and construct validity.

Importantly, Study 1 indicated that the MCAS items are best represented by two correlated subscales—Knowledge/Skills and Awareness. This finding is somewhat at odds with initial (Sue et al., 1982) and subsequent (Pedersen, 1988; Sue, Arredondo et al., 1992; Sue, Carter et al., 1992) conceptualizations, which define multicultural competence as a tripartite model. Two explanations for the disparate findings are that (a) multicultural competence is best conceptualized by two factors; that is, given that counselor needs knowledge to implement a skill, knowledge and skill items are indistinguishable and thus represent one subscale whereas awareness represents the second; or (b) the MCAS (self-report) items are not sensitive enough to distinguish between counselor knowledge and skills.

Study 2 examined the relationship of MCAS:B subscale scores to conceptually linked constructs measured by the validated Cross-

Cultural Counseling Inventory—Revised (CCCI-R) and the New Racism Scale (NRS). Correlations were in the predicted direction and demonstrated adequate levels of convergent validity for both the Knowledge/Skills and Awareness subscales. Low and nonsignificant correlations between the MCAS:B subscales and the Social Desirability Scale (SDS) provided evidence that social desirability contamination is not a problem with the MCAS:B.

Studies 3 and 4 demonstrated the MCAS:B's utility as a pre-post measure in multicultural development. Theoretical models of multicultural development (e.g., Carney & Kahn, 1984; Sabnani et al., 1991) suggest that competence is attainable through programmed learning (e.g., a multicultural course). This multicultural "growth" was documented in these studies, therefore providing some support for the construct of "multicultural competence" generally, and the MCAS:B's content and construct validity specifically.

Many of the limitations of the four studies were highlighted earlier, and therefore we would like to conclude the chapter with recommendations for needed research. First, and foremost, large sample research is needed to further examine the factor structure of the MCAS:B. It will be interesting to see whether the two-factor oblique model proposed here is replicable across additional samples. Clearly, additional exploratory as well as confirmatory analytic procedures are needed in this regard.

Immediate research is also needed to correlate the MCAS:B subscales with comparable self-report instruments, namely the Multicultural Counseling Inventory (MCI, Sodowsky et al., 1994) and the Multicultural Awareness/Knowledge/Skills Survey (MAKSS, D'Andrea et al., 1991). Initial work has begun in this area with the multitrait-multimethod (Campbell & Fiske, 1959) study by Pope-Davis and Dings (1994). Incorporating the MCAS and MCI, these authors found that the two instruments differed in their assessment of dimensions of self-reported multicultural counseling competency, with the MCI focusing on behavioral aspects of perceived competency, and the MCAS:B focusing on attitudinal aspects. The authors also conclude that both instruments are useful tools in assessing multicultural counseling competencies.

As a result of the focus group run in Study 2, we added three social desirability test items to the MCAS:B. This cluster was intended as an auxiliary measure of desirability contamination. As might be expected with three items, the cluster had a low coefficient alpha. Future research on the MCAS:B should address this cluster. One consideration might be to drop this cluster, given the MCAS:B has little social desirability contamination, at least as measured by the Social Desirability Scale (SDS; Crowne & Marlowe, 1960). However, given that the SDS is not without limitation, another option would be to build the three-item cluster into a legitimate MCAS subscale. Some multicultural experts who have studied the MCAS (e.g., Pope-Davis & Dings, 1994; Pope-Davis & Dings, 1995) support the latter recommendation as they see the cluster adding a unique dimension to multicultural competency assessment.

It is hoped that the present study will stimulate both quantitative and qualitative research into the measurement of multicultural counseling competence. Recent authors have emphasized the need to augment quantitative, paper-and-pencil focused research in multiculturalism with more descriptive qualitative methods (Ponterotto & Casas, 1991). For example, using participant observation, unstructured interviews, and/or case studies to study acknowledged experts in multicultural counseling practice might be one promising direction for "competency" research.

Generally, counseling programs have not been vigilant in implementing and evaluating the outcomes of multicultural development, despite the position of APA generally and Division 17 specifically (see Ponterotto & Casas, 1991; Sue, Carter et al., 1992). As the clientele of counseling psychologists becomes increasingly heterogeneous along cultural lines, the need for accountability in multicultural development grows increasingly clear (see related discussions in Ponterotto, Casas, Suzuki, & Alexander, 1995). As highlighted in the separate Discussion sections of the four studies comprising this report, the MCAS:B is certainly not without limitation. The instrument, however, does appear to have promise for meaningful use in multicultural development, and it is hoped that the research on this instrument and comparable ones will continue.

REFERENCES

American Educational Research Association, American Psychological Association, & National Council on Measurement in Education. (1985). *Standards for educational and psychological testing.* Washington, DC: American Psychological Association, Inc.

Arrindell, W. A., & Van der Ende, J. (1985). An empirical test of the utility of the observation-to-variables ratio in factor and component analysis. *Applied Psychological Measurement, 9,* 165-178.

Atkinson, D. R., Morten, G., & Sue, D. W. (Eds.). (1989). *Counseling American minorities: A cross-cultural perspective* (3rd ed.). Dubuque, IA: W.C. Brown.

Campbell, D. T., & Fiske, D. W. (1959). Convergent and discriminant validation by the multitrait-multimethod matrix. *Psychological Bulletin, 56*, 81-105.

Carney, C. G., & Kahn, K. B. (1984). Building competencies for effective cross-cultural counseling: A developmental view. *The Counseling Psychologist, 12*, 111-119.

Carter, R. T. (1990). The relationship between racism and racial identity among white Americans: An exploratory investigation. *Journal of Counseling and Development, 69*, 46-50.

Cattell, R. B. (1965a). Factor analysis: An introduction to essentials: I. The purpose and underlying models. *Biometrics, 21*, 190-215.

Cattell, R. B. (1965b). Factor analysis: An introduction to essentials: II. The role of factor analysis in research. *Biometrics, 21*, 405-435.

Crowne, D. P., & Marlowe, D. (1960). A new scale of social desirability independent of psychopathology. *Journal of Consulting Psychology, 24*, 349-354.

Crowne, D. P., & Marlowe, D. (1964). *The approval motive.* New York: John Wiley & Sons.

D'Andrea, M., & Daniels, J. (1991). Exploring the different levels of multicultural counseling training in counselor education. *Journal of Counseling and Development, 70*, 78-85.

D'Andrea, M., & Daniels, J. (1995). Promoting multiculturalism and organizational change in the counseling profession: A case study. In J. G. Ponterotto, J. M. Casas, L. A. Suzuki, & C. M. Alexander (Eds.), *Handbook of multicultural counseling* (pp. 17-33). Thousand Oaks, CA: Sage.

D'Andrea, M., Daniels, J., & Heck, R. (1991). Evaluating the impact of multicultural counseling training. *Journal of Counseling and Development, 70*, 143-150.

Dawis, R. V. (1987). Scale construction. *Journal of Counseling Psychology, 34*, 481-489.

Hays, W. L. (1981). *Statistics* (3rd ed.). New York: Holt, Rinehart, and Winston.

Hills, H. I., & Strozier, A. L. (1992). Multicultural training in APA-approved counseling psychology programs: A survey. *Professional Psychology: Research and Practice, 23*, 43-51.

Hollis, J. W., & Wantz, R. A. (1990). *Counselor preparation 1990-92: Programs, personnel, trends* (7th ed.). Muncie, IN: Accelerated Development Inc.

Hollis, J. W., & Wantz, R. A. (1994). *Counselor preparation 1993-95 Volume II: Status, trends, and implications* (8th ed.). Muncie, IN: Accelerated Development Inc.

Jacobson, C. K. (1985). Resistance to affirmative action: Self-interest or racism. *Journal of Conflict Resolution, 29,* 306-329.

LaFromboise, T. D., Coleman, H. L. K., & Hernandez, A. (1991). Development and factor structure of the Cross-Cultural Counseling Inventory—Revised. *Professional Psychology: Research and Practice, 22,* 380-388.

Long, J. (1983). *Factor analysis.* Newbury Park, CA: Sage.

McConahay, J. B., & Hough, J. C. (1976). Symbolic racism. *Journal of Social Issues, 32,* 23-45.

Mio, J. S., & Morris, D. R. (1990). Cross-cultural issues in psychology training programs: An invitation for discussion. *Professional Psychology: Research and Practice, 21,* 434-441.

Ottavi, T. M., Pope-Davis, D. B., & Dings, J. G. (1994). Relationship between racial identity attitudes and self-reported multicultural counseling competencies. *Journal of Counseling Psychology, 41,* 149-154.

Pedersen, P. B. (1988). *A handbook for developing multicultural awareness.* Alexandria, VA: American Association for Counseling and Development.

Pedersen, P. B., Draguns, J. G., Lonner, W. J., & Trimble, J. E. (Eds.). (1989). *Counseling across cultures.* (3rd ed.). Honolulu, HI: University of Hawaii Press.

Ponterotto, J. G. (in press). Multicultural counseling training: A competency model and national survey. In D. B. Pope-Davis & H. L. K. Coleman (Eds.), *Multicultural competencies: Education, training, and supervision.* Thousand Oaks, CA: Sage.

Ponterotto, J. G., & Casas, J. M. (1991). *Handbook of racial/ethnic minority counseling research.* Springfield, IL: Charles C. Thomas.

Ponterotto, J. G., Casas, J. M., Suzuki, L. A., & Alexander, C. M. (Eds.) (1995). *Handbook of multicultural counseling.* Thousand Oaks, CA: Sage.

Ponterotto, J. G., & Pedersen, P. B. (1993). *Preventing prejudice: A guide for counselors and educators.* Thousand Oaks, CA: Sage.

Ponterotto, J. G., Rieger, B. P., Barrett, A., & Sparks, R. (1994). Assessing multicultural counseling competence: A review of instrumentation. *Journal of Counseling and Development, 72,* 316-322.

Ponterotto, J. G., & Sabnani, H. B. (1989). "Classics" in multicultural counseling: A systematic five-year content analysis. *Journal of Multicultural Counseling and Development, 17,* 23-37.

Ponterotto, J. G., Sanchez, C. M., & Magids, D. M. (1991, August). *Initial development and validation of the Multicultural Counseling Awareness Scale (MCAS).* Poster presented at the annual meeting of the American Psychological Association, San Francisco.

Ponterotto, J. G., & Wise, S. L. (1987). Construct validity study of the Racial Identity Attitude Scale. *Journal of Counseling Psychology, 34*, 218-223.

Pope-Davis, D.B., & Dings, J.G. (1994). An empirical comparison of two self-report multicultural counseling competency inventories. *Measurement and Evaluation in Counseling and Development, 27*, 93-102.

Pope-Davis, D. B., & Dings, J. G. (1995). The assessment of multicultural counseling competencies. In J. G. Ponterotto, J. M. Casas, L. A. Suzuki, & C. M. Alexander (Eds.), *Handbook of multicultural counseling* (pp. 287-311). Thousand Oaks, CA: Sage.

Pope-Davis, D. B., & Dings, J. G., & Ottavi, T. M. (1995). The relationship of demographic and educational variables on multicultural counseling competencies. *The IOWA Psychologist, 40* (1), 12-13.

Pope-Davis, D. B., & Ottavi, T. M. (1992). The influence of white racial identity attitudes on racism among faculty members: A preliminary examination. *Journal of College Student Development, 33*, 389-394.

Pope-Davis, D. B., & Ottavi, T. M. (1994a). Examining the association between self-reported multicultural counseling competencies and demographic variables among counselors. *Journal of Counseling and Development, 72*, 651-654.

Pope-Davis, D. B., & Ottavi, T. M. (1994b). The relationship between racism and racial identity among white Americans: A replication and extension. *Journal of Counseling and Development, 72*, 293-297.

Quintana, S. M., & Bernal, M. E. (1995). Ethnic minority training in counseling psychology: Comparisons with clinical psychology and proposed standards. *The Counseling Psychologist, 23*, 102-121.

Sabnani, H. B., & Ponterotto, J. G. (1992). Racial/ethnic minority instrumentation in counseling research: A review, critique, and recommendations. *Measurement and Evaluation in Counseling and Development, 24*, 161-187.

Sabnani, H. B., Ponterotto, J. G., & Borodovsky, L. G. (1991). White racial identity development and cross-cultural counselor training: A stage model. *The Counseling Psychologist, 19*, 76-102.

Serling, D. A., & Betz, N. E. (1990). Development and evaluation of a measure of fear of commitment. *Journal of Counseling Psychology, 37*, 91-97.

Sodowsky, G. R., Taffe, R. C., Gutkin, T., & Wise, S. L. (1994). Development of the Multicultural Counseling Inventory: A self-report measure of multicultural competencies. *Journal of Counseling Psychology, 41*, 137-148.

Sue, D. W., Arredondo, P., & McDavis, R. J. (1992). Multicultural counseling competencies and standards: A call to the profession. *Journal of Multicultural Counseling and Development, 20*, 64-88.

Sue, D. W., Bernier, J. E., Durran, A., Feinberg, L., Pedersen, P. B., Smith, E. J., & Vasquez-Nuttal, E. (1982). Position paper: Cross-cultural counseling competencies. *The Counseling Psychologist, 10*(2), 45-52.

Sue, D. W., Carter, R. T., Casas, J. M., Fouad, N. A., Helms, J. E., Ivey, A. E., LaFromboise, T. D., Manese, J. E., Ponterotto, J. G., & Vasquez-Nuttall, E. (1992, August). *Cross-cultural counseling competencies: Revised*. Symposium presented at the annual meeting of the American Psychological Association, Washington, DC.

Sue, D. W., & Sue, D. (1990). *Counseling the culturally different: Theory and practice* (2nd ed.). New York: John Wiley.

Tinsley, H. E. A. (1992). Psychometric theory and counseling psychology research. In S. D. Brown & R. W. Lent (Eds.), *Handbook of counseling psychology* (2nd ed.) (pp. 37-70). New York: John Wiley.

Tinsley, H. E. A., & Tinsley, D .J. (1987). Uses of factor analysis in counseling psychology research. *Journal of Counseling Psychology, 34*, 414-424.

Walsh, W. B., & Betz, N. E. (1990). *Tests and assessment* (2nd ed.). Englewood Cliffs, NJ: Prentice-Hall.

THE MULTICULTURAL COUNSELING INVENTORY: VALIDITY AND APPLICATIONS IN MULTICULTURAL TRAINING[1]

Gargi Roysircar Sodowsky

University of Nebraska-Lincoln

Counseling professionals in the United States (U.S.) realize that they live in a multicultural, multiethnic, and diverse socioeconomic society. The complexity of this society challenges the counselor ("counselor" is used to include all psychological service providers) to revise and relearn the help-giving process. This challenge has been taken up by multicultural training (MCT). MCT's challenge is professional, philosophical, and political in nature.

Professional mandates of the American Association for Counseling and Development (AACD, 1988) (now called American Counseling Association [ACA]) and the American Psychological Association (APA) (APA, 1992; APA Office of Ethnic Minority Affairs, 1993) that influence university accreditation and provide professional ethics are one reason for including MCT in master's and doctoral training.

[1]This project was supported by a grant from the Teaching Council, UN-L, and by funds provided by Dr. James O'Hanlon, Dean of Teachers College, UN-L. The assistance and encouragement of Dr. James O'Hanlon are deeply appreciated. Special thanks are extended to counseling and school psychology students at UN-L for their participation in the various studies.

There is another motivation for MCT that is less pragmatic and more implicit than professional guidelines. It is the philosophical ideology of wanting respect for differences of cultural groups and of envisioning multiculturalism as a peaceful process to co-existence in the 21st century. The third motivation has led to a political or advocacy mission that redresses the conditions of under-representation, racism, and inequity in U.S. institutions.

MCT is being increasingly provided via either university course work or topic-focused continuing education workshops. Consequently, there is a need to evaluate MCT (D'Andrea, Daniels, & Heck, 1991; Ponterotto et al., Chapter 7 this volume; Pope-Davis, Chapter 9 this volume; Ridley, Mendoza, & Kanitz, 1994; Sodowsky & Taffe, 1991). The Multicultural Counseling Inventory (MCI) (Sodowsky, Taffe, Gutkin, & Wise, 1994a), a self-report measure, was developed for two purposes: to offer philosophical support to MCT and to present a robust instrument to measure multicultural counseling competencies, an expected outcome of MCT.

There are four parts to this chapter. In Part I, literature on multicultural counseling competencies, pertinent to the contents of the MCI instrument, is reviewed. This section also addresses the philosophical underpinnings of MCT and its outcome, multicultural counseling competencies. In Part II, the development and psychometric properties of the MCI (Sodowsky et al., 1994a) are summarized. In Part III, two additional studies, called Study 3 and Study 4, assess via the MCI different aspects of multicultural learning of counseling psychology and school psychology students at the University of Nebraska-Lincoln. In Part IV, initial results of an ongoing study, called Study 5, inform about the MCI's relationships with other variables, including MCT, with regard to issues of convergent, discriminant, and predictive validity, as well as social desirability and cultural political correctness.

PART I:
WHY HAVE MULTICULTURAL COUNSELING COMPETENCIES?

The need to develop competencies in multicultural counseling is an issue of a pluralistic philosophy of life. It is also a matter of professional ethics, as stated by professional organizations such as APA and ACA. Ethical Standard 1.04(c) (under *Boundaries of Competence*) of the *Ethical Principles of Psychologists* (APA, 1992) states, "In those emerging areas in which generally recognized standards for preparatory training do not exist, psychologists nevertheless take reasonable steps to ensure the competence of their work and to protect patients, clients . . ." (p. 1600). Thus the responsibility falls upon the individual counselor to seek out MCT. It is also reasonable for counselors to expect that the course work and/or workshops they attend will at the minimum educate them on basic multicultural competencies so that they can work with a diverse population. Ethical Standard 2.04(c) (under *Use of Assessment . . . With Special Populations*) (APA, 1992) states, "Psychologists attempt to identify situations in which particular interventions or assessment techniques or norms may not be applicable or may require adjustment in administration or interpretation because of factors such as individuals' . . . age, race, ethnicity, national origin, religion . . . language, or socioeconomic status" (p. 1603). Using this standard as an educational objective, MCT needs to make available the prerequisite knowledge, skills, and applications, so that one can do multiculturally competent intake, assessment, and counseling.

MCT includes an experiential learning process, so that a counselor at a self-monitoring level becomes aware of his or her silent, private reactions to counselor-client interactions involving issues of cultural and ethnic identities, racism, and sociopolitical constructions of race and ethnicity (Sodowsky, Kuo-Jackson, & Loya, in press). Cultural self-reflexivity means reflective evaluation of oneself as well as a questioning orientation to one's views of culture, race, and professional discipline and practice (Sodowsky et al., in press). According to Berg and Smith (1988), in the qualitative clinical interview, validity of the data depends critically on the quality of the interviewer-interviewee relationship, reflexivity on the part of the person conducting the interview, and a willingness to modify perceptual schemata and theories in accordance with the evolving pattern of understanding. Hoshmand (1991) states that a relationship of reciprocity with the interviewee decreases reactivity and superficial reports of data, and cognitive attention to personal epistemology or personal ways of knowing (that is, reflexivity) increases alertness to personal biases and overinvolvement with the interviewee.

Cultural self-reflexivity (Sodowsky et al., in press) is related to the multicultural competence of cultural awareness, helping the counselor to be respectful of the differences of a minority client. General Principle D: *Respect for People's Rights and Dignity* (APA, 1992) exhorts, "Psychologists are aware of cultural, individual, and role differences, including those due to . . . age, race, ethnicity, national origin, religion . . . language, and socioeconomic status . . . . [and] try to eliminate the effect on their work of biases based on those factors, and do not knowingly participate in or condone unfair discriminatory practices" (p. 1599-1600). Standard B.19. (under *Counseling Relation-ship*) of the *Ethical Standards of AACD* (1995) states that a counselor must ensure that members of various ethnic/racial, religious, disability, and socioeconomic groups have equal access . . ." (p. 5).

Professional standards of APA and ACA are helpful in guiding and, in some cases, enforcing standard professional behaviors. However, what is of even greater import than the listed standards per se, for which the purpose at the most basic level is to prevent client harm, is the implicit morality behind the standards. The moral is the belief that multiculturalism is more than understanding cultural differences, or communicating in a civil manner, or respecting an individual because he or she is a human being and shares some panhuman similarities with all people. A problem underlying suitable behaviors of communication (as mandated by APA and ACA ethics) is that the person who is behaving correctly may continue to believe in the superiority of one's own culture or race and give silent consent to the practices of institutional and social racism. A deeper, moral reason for cross-cultural respect is that a person needs to honor those who are different. It is not just a matter of accepting differences or looking beyond differences.

If counselors fail to integrate into their philosophy the value of honoring a client's cultural differences, they are, then, guilty of "cultural oppression" (Sue et al., 1982, p. 46), and they violate the principle of maintaining client integrity (Cayleff, 1986). Additionally, the counselor's socioeconomic status and employment with the establishment place the counselor, relative to that of the racial or ethnic minority client, in a more powerful position (Cayleff, 1986). Therefore the counselor needs to give to the client gifts of hopefulness (Sue & Zane, 1987), affirmation, consent, and sharing. The counselor must consciously distance himself or herself from the power, privilege, racism, and silent consent for racism associated with most U.S. institutions.

Sue et al. (1982) argued that it is critical to reprogram counselor understanding to a recognition that for one to be different does not mean to be "deficient," "deprived," or "disadvantaged" (p. 46). Therefore, counselor interventions must not consist of remediation aimed at producing homogeneity of behavior, performance, and motivation. Differences could be reconceptualized as strengths and results of one's groundedness in one's origins, socialization, or varied experiences (Sue et al., 1982); immutable aspects of one's worldviews (Kwan, Sodowsky, & Ihle, 1994); mutations of the biculturally driven acculturation and ethnic identity processes (Sodowsky, Lai, & Plake,

1991; Sodowsky, Kwan, & Pannu, 1995); and minority coping strategies for survival (Osvold & Sodowsky, in press; Zimmerman & Sodowsky, 1993).

Katz (1985) asserted that "White culture serves as a foundation for counseling theory, research, and practice" (p. 615). For example, Western psychological theories depend heavily on low-context abstractions (e.g., the constructs of intelligence and ego), cause and effect relationships (e.g., use of schedules of reinforcement), linear analytic thinking (e.g., use of interval scales in assessment), and deductive and inductive reasoning (e.g., hypothesis testing and hypothesis building). On the other hand, many people who come from collectivistic cultures (see Triandis [1990] for an explanation of the term), such as new Asian immigrants, think contextually or cyclically, repeat the thoughts of sages, find causes in historical events or the supernatural, are field dependent, and find motivations in their religions (Sodowsky et al., 1995). Thus, behavioral manifestations (e.g., linear problem-solving skills) that counseling researchers investigate, the independent variables they control or manipulate (e.g., low self-efficacy versus high self-efficacy), and the interpretations they give their findings are intimately linked to their Euro-American value-based research paradigms.

Even when culture is the focus of discussion in a counseling case, it is typically framed according to the White dominant culture's views of mental health, such as the cognitive development of the individual person, client independence, internal locus of control, personal responsibility, self-concept, self-esteem, assertiveness, self-efficacy, career interests, decision-making skills, heterosexual love, intimacy, happiness, or life satisfaction. The counselor assesses, whether quantitatively, diagnostically, or qualitatively, how the minority individual functions in such dimensions in reference to the average functioning of the White normative group. Then the counselor tends to see how different or how many standard deviations from the mean the minority individual's performance is and finds stereotypical answers in the client's culture.

However, the relationship between the minority individual's personality and the influence of his or her ingroup, such as natural support systems, or hierarchically positioned reference groups (e.g., elders, the family, a religious body, and extended kinship), all important anchors of mental health for many non-White American cultures, is not included in the assessment of a racial or ethnic or culturally different client (Sodowsky, 1991; Sodowsky & Taffe, 1991). Almost all the data of psychology come from individualistic cultures, such as that of the U.S., although 70% of the population of the world lives in collectivistic cultures (Triandis, 1990). It could be argued that human nature is not necessarily individualistic, but U.S. psychologists assume it so. Therefore, if psychology does not account for "human nature" but rather reflects psychologists' values (Triandis, 1990), then multicultural counseling needs to expand the epistemology of counseling.

Counseling practice evolving from the above-described mainstream American psychology is inevitably narrow. Counseling professionals are trained to serve middle class White Americans (Sue et al., 1982); thus, their class- and culture-specific interventions could be variables affecting the high underutilization and early termination of mental health services by some American ethnic minority groups (Sue, 1977). Given the stronghold of Euro-American psychological practice, counselors may find it difficult to create, self-monitor, and maintain an implicit and personally meaningful pluralistic philosophy, motivating them to voluntarily seek multicultural competencies, a concept that is new to one's profession and to one's personal meanings about knowledge.

Dimensions of Multicultural Counseling Competencies

The two main literature sources for multicultural counseling competencies have been the following: a position paper by Sue et al. (1982), who comprised the Education and Training Committee of APA's Division of Counseling Psychology (Division 17); and the theoretical expansion of this position paper 10 years later by Sue, Arredondo, and McDavis (1992), who comprised the Professional Standards Committee of the Association for Multicultural Counseling and Development.

Sue et al. (1982) presented 11 "minimal" characteristics (p. 49) of a culturally skilled counselor, which were conceptualized within three broad dimensions. (a) *Skills*, covering the behavioral domain, are proficiencies gained through active participation in multicultural clinical work and through experiences in diverse populations. (b) *Cultural self-awareness and other-awareness* (called beliefs-attitudes by Sue et al., 1982), covering a cognitive-affective domain, encompass the counselor's attitudes toward one's own culture and to differences of others in cultural, racial, and sociopolitical terms. And (c) *knowledge*, covering the domain of learning, involves knowing theory, research, and cross-paradigmatic approaches to understanding cultural diversity.

Ten years later, Sue et al. (1992) introduced three specific counselor characteristics: (a) counselor's awareness of their own assumptions, values, and biases; (b) counselor's understanding of the worldview of the culturally different client; and (c) the counselor's development of appropriate intervention strategies and techniques. By cross-classifying the newly proposed counselor competencies with the previously proposed general competencies, Sue et al. (1992) presented a 3x3 matrix of nine competency areas indicating 31 skills. Generally speaking, the focus of the three counselor characteristics appears to be on the counselor's awareness of his or her own worldview and the client's worldview.

The recently evolved emphasis on the interaction of counselor worldview and client worldview (Ihle, Sodowsky, & Kwan, 1996; Sodowsky, Maguire, Johnson, Ngumba, & Kohles, 1994; Sue et al., 1992) may correct a limitation of MCT that has emphasized the acquisition of knowledge and skills. What is lacking is education on how counselor racial attitudes, worldviews, and values about acculturation impact counselor-client interactions.

According to McRae and Johnson (1991), "Aside from understanding one's self as a racial-ethnic and cultural being, it is important for counselors to examine the dynamics of the counselor-client relationship" (p. 131), "which includes examining the therapeutic relationship between counselors and clients with similar and different cultural values, racial identity attitudes, [and] issues of power, control, and oppression" (p. 135). Thus, Sodowsky et al. (1994a) have proposed a fourth counselor dimension that reflects the human factor in counseling: (d) *multicultural counseling relationship*. The multicultural counseling relationship stands independent of Sue et al.'s (1992) proposed competencies of counselor's awareness of counselor worldview and client worldview and counselor intervention strategies, although all are characteristics of the multicultural counseling process.

Thus, the four competency areas, with permeable boundaries, are not mutually exclusive. For instance, awareness indirectly affects both knowledge and skills but can be separate from both because it implies insightful understanding as well as an emotional component, whereas knowledge and skills are more declarative in nature. Below, each dimension is mostly elaborated on the basis of conceptual thoughts expressed by trainers in multicultural counseling. Reference is also made to some empirical studies.

Skills

Sue et al. (1992) specifically added the new counselor characteristic of the counselor developing appropriate intervention strategies and techniques. McRae and Johnson (1991) stated that "there is a need to design training strategies that would move trainees from 'knowing that' cultural differences exist to helping them to 'know how' to conduct therapeutic sessions with clients from diverse cultures" (p. 133). The competent counselor also questions, reinterprets, and adapts previously learned skills so that assessment is culturally sensitive, and counselor language and strategies are within the worldview of the client (Sue, Akutsu, & Higashi, 1987). Of utmost importance is the counselor's ability to match interventions with the expectations of the client (Lefly, 1987).

Competent counselors interface with the client's natural support system, realizing the benefits of an easily accessed source of assistance to discover the cause or the remedy of a problem (Pearson, 1987). At times, innovative culturally consistent strategies are needed (Sue et al., 1987). The counselor may need to consider action to change the system and its services rather than to change the client to fit the system (Pedersen, 1987a). Pedersen (1987a) stated that the more alternatives or strategies the counselor possesses, the more choices the counselor has for dealing with the client and the environment, and the greater is the counselor's flexibility for responding with increasingly complex strategies. The culturally competent counselor proceeds with caution when using standardized instruments with minority populations, realizing the inherent probability of profile misinterpretations and the barriers of language and reading levels that go along with mainstream assessment devices (Ibrahim & Arredondo, 1986).

Cultural Self-Awareness and Other-Awareness

The first broad theme is one of intrapersonal awareness. This is accomplished through a systematic examination of one's own beliefs and attitudes and is primarily done through introspection, self-monitoring, and reflective self-evaluation. Espin (1987) noted that if counselors were aware of the influences of their race or ethnicity on their own personality and interpersonal styles, then they would be better able to recognize the ways in which culture and ethnicity influence client behaviors, interactions, values, and life goals. Cayleff (1986) recommended that counselors be aware of the influence of their own sociocultural characteristics (e.g., gender and/or social economic status) on their perceptions of, responses to, and labeling of client problems. Pedersen (1987a) described counselors as culturally competent when they can look at their own culture by stepping outside of it, a self-monitoring action. Wrenn (1962) suggested that counselors need to realize that something they feel very strongly about may be completely irrelevant to others. Smith (1982) noted that:

> Racial differences between client and counselor do constitute formi-
> dable but not insurmountable barriers in the counseling relation-
> ship. Differences in race per se should not preclude the possibility
> of ethnic minority clients and majority counselors working together
> effectively. The really important factor is how people feel about
> racial differences. (p. 63)

Another broad theme is exposure-oriented awareness, which is increased through an external route such as by working with minority clients (Sue et al., 1987); by participating in sensitivity training programs such as the Pedersen triad training method (Pedersen, 1988), the cultural assimilator (Fiedler, Mitchell, & Triandis, 1971), and the Intercultural Sensitizer (Leong & Kim, 1991); and by acknowledging and integrating into counselor interventions what has been called the client's natural support system (Pearson, 1987). This type of awareness involves the counselor's experiences of the contrasts and conflicts between cultures. Additionally, Cayleff (1986) and Casas, Ponterotto, and Gutierrez (1986) noted that the ethical counselor is aware of the negative impact of racial and sexual stereotyping and discrimination. Through this awareness the counselor upholds the principle of beneficence and guards the client's rights and dignity. Drapela (1987) stated that the counselor needs to display a willingness to use available cultural resources to learn about specific interpersonal skills that are necessary when interacting with and serving a culturally different client.

Knowledge

Having intercultural sensitivity and being trained in culture-specific techniques do not qualify one as a counselor. To be a qualified professional, a counselor needs to have theoretical knowledge to justify the counselor's intercultural sensitivity and cultural techniques.

Several trainers stress that counselors need to have multicultural pedagogical competencies to be culturally effective. Leong and Kim (1991) state that "Increasing counselors' cultural sensitivity without providing some tentative culture-specific information about interventions would invite frustrated paralysis on the part of these counselors (i.e., 'I know I need to be sensitive to my client's cultural background but what am I supposed to do')" (p. 113).

Additionally, knowledge of racial and cultural variables such as racial identity, ethnic identity, acculturation, worldviews, sociocultural influences, and value differences, and their respective influences on clients are factors that competent therapists address in their conceptualization of client problems, intervention strategies, and goals

(Sodowsky & Taffe, 1991). Knowledge of sociocultural characteristics that distinguish between and within cultural groups contributes to implementing culturally relevant and effective strategies (Casas et al., 1986; Sodowsky et al., 1991).

With certain minority clients, counselor competence involves honoring folk belief systems that are an integral part of the client's psychological being (Cayleff, 1986). A cross-paradigmatic framework for drawing and synthesizing information from several disciplines enables the competent counselor to question psychology's set concept of "normal behavior" (Pearson, 1987; Pedersen, 1988). Arredondo (1987) proposed a psycho-historical approach to assessment, which requires that counselors look at biographical and clinical data from the perspective of contextual factors (e.g., history, politics, family systems, and the effects of institutional role) as well as from the perspective of individual factors (e.g., age at the time of immigration, generational status, number of years in the U.S., gender, role identification, education, immigration entry status, and goals of sojourners; see Sodowsky et al., 1991; Sodowsky & Lai, in press). Culturally sensitive counselors also emphasize individual differences within a cultural group; in other words, they do not apply knowledge about the group without considering the particular client (Sue et al., 1987).

Sue and Zane (1987) hypothesized that the application of cultural knowledge to counseling tasks, such as conceptualization of the client problem, treatment strategies, and counseling goals, facilitates the counseling process. When Sodowsky (1991) and Sodowsky and Taffe (1991) examined the above hypothesis with international and White American student groups and a sample of Midwestern counseling trainees, they found significant effects for multiculturally knowledgeable counseling tasks on subjects' perceptions of counselor expertness and trustworthiness.

Multicultural Counseling Relationship

In the counselor-client relationship, the counselor models multicultural attitudes and behaviors, develops within oneself positive racial or ethnic identity, shows adjustment by accommodating mainstream counseling theory and practice to diversity needs, creates a bicultural-multicultural counseling relationship process, and fosters positive racial or ethnic identity and collective self-identity in minority clients. In addition, the competent therapist communicates respect, shows personalized perceptions and knowledge, displays empathy, tolerates ambiguity, and demonstrates reciprocal concern (Pedersen, 1987b). Although true of any client-therapist relationship, these relationship conditions may be difficult to observe with a culturally different client with whom it is not easy to communicate or relate.

Pedersen (1987b) pointed out that the cross-cultural adjustment process of the minority person relies more heavily upon acceptance and support from those within the host or dominant culture than upon information provided by the host or dominant group. In many cases, the therapist will be a significant representative of the host or dominant group; therefore, the therapist's openness and warmth will be critical to the client's adjustment and overall attitude toward the counseling process (Pedersen, 1987b).

Wrenn (1962) stated that the therapist's job is to support the client in becoming his or her person rather than becoming the therapist's pygmalion. He added that clients need to develop their integrity even if it may be different from that of the therapist. Pedersen (1987b) identified the following key personality variables in competent multicultural counselors: sociability, high self-esteem and a positive self-concept, and an ability to solve problems in unfamiliar settings.

LaFromboise and Dixon (1981) showed that counselor trustworthy behaviors and not counselor ethnicity had a significant effect on Native American high school students' perceptions of counselor trustworthiness, and Vontress (1971) stressed that African-American clients would be self-disclosing if their White therapists could be convincing as people of goodwill and trust. Sodowsky (1991) demonstrated that an Asian-Indian international student group considered counselor trustworthiness significantly more important than client-counselor similarity. Sue and Zane (1987) have theorized that the counseling process characterized by ascribed counselor credibility and achieved counselor credibility may be of primary importance when doing therapy with Asian Americans.

PART II
THE MULTICULTURAL COUNSELING INVENTORY (MCI): TWO INITIAL STUDIES[2]

Summary of Previously Reported Research

None of the major instruments commonly used for counseling process and outcome research presently include a component for assessing multicultural competence (Ponterotto & Furlong, 1985). For example, although the Counselor Effectiveness Rating Scale (CERS;

---

[2]This section summarizes the results of two initial studies of the MCI. Some of this material has been reported in detail elsewhere (Sodowsky, Taffe, Gutkin, & Wise, 1994a), and some are reported here for the first time.

Atkinson & Wampold, 1982) and the Counselor Rating Form (CRF; Barak & LaCrosse, 1975) have been used in racial/ethnic minority studies (Atkinson, Maruyama, & Matusui, 1978; Atkinson, Ponce, & Martinez, 1984, LaFromboise & Dixon, 1981; Ponce & Atkinson, 1989; Sodowsky, 1991; Sodowsky & Taffe, 1991), neither of these instruments has a component for assessing multicultural counseling competencies. Neimeyer and Fukuyama (1984) used the Cultural Attitudes Repertory Techniques (CART) for counselor-trainees' self-examination of their personal subjective constructs regarding different cultures. However, the CART does not assess how multiskilled the counselor is in working with minority individuals. Because the literature on multicultural counseling competencies has proposed several constructs, the author developed the multidimensional Multicultural Counseling Inventory (MCI), a self-report measure.

Along with the MCI, three other multicultural competency instruments in counseling, the Cross-Cultural Competency Inventory-Revised (CCCI-R; LaFromboise, Coleman, & Hernandez, 1991), the Multicultural Awareness-Knowledge-Skills Survey (MAKSS; D'Andrea, Daniels, & Heck, 1991), and the Multicultural Counseling Awareness Scale (MCAS; Ponterotto et al., Chapter 7, this volume) cover conceptually similar domains (see Sodowsky et al.'s [1994a] review of the instruments). However, the MCI's presentation of more than three factors indicates greater diversity of structure than the other three scales. Sue et al.'s (1992) revised theoretical hypothesis also suggested the potential for more constructs. Additionally, the MCI underwent developmental procedures that were different from those of the other three scales.

The MCI was developed empirically using exploratory factor analysis (EFA) (n = 604 from a Midwestern state), confirmatory factor analysis (CFA) (n = 350 from APA-approved university counseling centers in the U.S.), and tests of factor congruence across the two samples (i.e., the factor structure of the second sample obtained through an EFA was correlated with the factor structure of the first sample). The two samples consisted of student trainees (n = 115) and long-standing practitioners (n = 839) in the mental health professions. Mailing lists or addresses were obtained from university departments and state professional associations. The MCI questionnaire was mailed along with a demographic questionnaire, a request for open-ended responses to three questions on MCT in the instrument that the subjects would have previously answered, and a letter that described the purpose of the study. Subjects were requested to give anonymous, voluntary responses.

The EFAs and CFA resulted in four multicultural counseling factors, with moderate to moderately high internal consistency reliabilities (see Table 1) and moderate interfactor correlations. The three factors of the MCI—Multicultural Counseling Skills, Multicultural Awareness, and Multicultural Counseling Knowledge—were comparable in substance to the three broad competencies defined by Sue et al. (1982; i.e., skills, beliefs-attitudes, and knowledge). One additional factor, Multicultural Counseling Relationship, reflected the interpersonal process of multicultural counseling. This dimension, although given limited attention by MCT, has been pointed to by Sue et al.'s recent revision (1992) and by Pedersen (1987a, 1987b).

Multicultural Counseling Skills (Factor 1) includes five multicultural counseling skills items, referring to success with retention, recognition of and recovery from cultural mistakes, use of nontraditional methods of assessment, counselor self-monitoring, and tailoring structured versus unstructured therapy to the needs of minority clients. Six general counseling skills items are also included, such as observing congruence, being focused, using concise reflections, and doing crisis intervention—skills that also apply to multicultural counseling. *Multicultural Awareness* (Factor 2) consists of 10 items, suggesting proactive multicultural sensitivity and responsiveness, extensive multicultural interactions and life experiences, broad-based cultural understanding, advocacy within institutions, enjoyment of multiculturalism, and an increase in minority case load. *Multicultural Counseling Relationship* (Factor 3) consists of eight items referring to the counselor's interactional process with the minority client, such as the counselor's trustworthiness, comfort level, stereotypes of the minority client, and worldview. *Multicultural Counseling Knowledge* (Factor 4) consists of 11 items, referring to culturally relevant case conceptualization and treatment strategies, cultural information, and multicultural counseling research.

The MCI Instrument

The MCI consists of 40 self-report statements rated on a 4-point Likert scale (4 = very accurate, 3 = somewhat accurate, 2 = somewhat inaccurate, 1 = very inaccurate). Items are so worded that a score of 1 indicates low multicultural competence and a score of 4 indicates high multicultural competence; seven items are presented in reverse to reduce the effects of a response set. Items are behaviorally stated, including the attitudinal and sensitivity items (e.g., statements begin with expressions such as "I am able to," "I use," "I am skilled at," "I am effective with," "I am comfortable," "I make," "I recognize," and

"I am successful at"). A summary of the MCI item contents, loadings on the four factors, and related psychometric information for Studies 1 and 2 are shown in Table 1.

Factor correlations were as follows. In Study 1, Skills correlated .22 with Awareness, .41 with Relationship, and .41 with Knowledge; Awareness correlated .21 with Relationship and .39 with Knowledge; Relationship correlated .18 with Knowledge. In Study 2, Skills correlated .17 with Awareness, .31 with Relationship, and .31 with Knowledge; Awareness correlated .17 with Relationship and .28 with Knowledge; and Relationship correlated .16 with Knowledge. In Study 2, CFA of the 4-factor oblique model proposed through EFA methods showed much higher correlations among the factors: For Skills the correlations were .30, .62, and .58; for Awareness the correlations were .47 and .56; and for Relationship the correlation with Knowledge was .47. These moderately high CFA factor correlations, along with the evidence of high interscale correlations of the CCCI-R, MAKSS, MCAS, as well as of general credibility-effectiveness scales in the counseling literature, led the authors to test higher order models in the CFA to investigate whether there was a higher order factor accounting for the correlations among the factors.

The relationships between the EFA factor structures obtained from the two samples (the state sample and the national sample) indicated coefficients of factor congruence ranging between .75 and .87, showing that the factor loadings of the EFA on the instrument development sample were relatively generalizable to the national sample. As shown by Table 1, the factor structures, eigenvalues, and internal consistency reliabilities of the MCI across the two samples were fairly similar.

In Study 2, using the national sample, CFA procedures examined the relative adequacy of models reflected in the literature: a unitary factor model discussed as a possibility by LaFromboise et al. (1991) and also implied by the very high correlation shown by J. Ponterotto (personal communication, 1995) between the first subscale and the full scale of the MCAS; a 2-factor model (Ponterotto et al., chapter 7 this volume); a 4-factor model (D'Andrea et al., 1991; LaFromboise et al., 1991; Sue et al., 1982); and a 3-factor model, as indicated by Study 1 of the MCI. Two higher order or second order models, one for the 3-factor structure and one for the 4-factor structure shown by EFAs of Study 1 were also tested to investigate whether a higher order factor accounted for the correlations among the factors. The first step in the higher order model was proposed to have separate factors, that is, the first order factors, and the second step was proposed to have one independent general factor, that

Table 1. MCI Summarized Items, Factor Loadings for Studies 1 (N = 604) and 2 (N = 350), and Coefficients of Internal Consistency and Factor Congruence.

Items	Factors							
	Skills		Awareness		Relationship		Knowledge	
	Study 1	Study 2	Study 1	Study 2	Study 1	Study 2	Study 1	Study 2
1. client mistrust of racially different counselor	.00	.00	.17	.18	.53	.62	.10	.16
2. counselor overcompensation, oversolicitation, and guilt	.07	.00	.11	.14	.49	.60	.12	.12
3. case conceptualizations not stereotypical or biased	.02	.08	.07	.02	.42	.48	.10	.22
4. differences between counselor worldviews and client worldviews	.02	.02	.04	.04	.61	.63	.01	.02
5. cognitive differences make communication difficult	.05	.08	.09	.14	.55	.59	.01	.06
6. understanding the effects of age, gender roles, and socioeconomic status	.16	.14	.08	.11	.05	.07	.35	.40
7. innovative concepts and treatment methods	.25	.02	.02	.15	.14	.09	.30	.59
8. a "world-minded" or pluralistic outlook	.03	.08	.21	.09	.01	.09	.30	.48
9. self-examination of counselor cultural biases	.15	.12	.00	.09	.03	.06	.37	.38
10. minority clients compared with majority group members	.12	.12	.01	.09	.53	.57	.12	.10
11. research on minority clients' preferences applied	.14	.11	.07	.06	.05	.15	.63	.68
12. aware of the changing practices, views, and interests of people	.03	.03	.10	.19	.16	.15	.41	.42
13. the range of differences within a minority group considered	.08	.02	.08	.05	.20	.25	.40	.44

Table 1. (continued)

Items	Factors							
	Skills		Awareness		Relationship		Knowledge	
	Study 1	Study 2	Study 1	Study 2	Study 1	Study 2	Study 1	Study 2
14. referrals and consultations on the basis of clients' minority identity development	.08	.17	.06	.01	.13	.16	.51	.50
15. self-examination of personal limitations shakes counselor confidence	.19	.15	.06	.02	.38	.45	.07	.05
16. counselor defensiveness is self-monitored and corrected	.26	.23	.04	.02	.10	.16	.30	.32
17. the sociopolitical history of the clients' respective minority groups is applied	.00	.03	.13	.11	.07	.12	.54	.67
18. 50% of clients seen more than once	.37	.35	.01	.00	.10	.25	.05	.04
19. client differences causing counselor discomfort	.11	.07	.13	.13	.38	.49	.05	.03
20. cultural mistakes quickly recognized and recovered	.34	.34	.03	.01	.17	.23	.11	.14
21. use of several methods of assessment	.33	.38	.01	.05	.08	.00	.20	.17
22. solving problems in unfamiliar settings	.24	.27	.33	.42	.17	.17	.02	.11
23. understanding client's level of acculturation	.08	.06	.00	.11	.02	.03	.49	.64
24. counselor philosophical preferences are understood	.30	.32	.02	.06	.03	.02	.21	.28
25. having an understanding of specific racial and ethnic minority groups	.13	.12	.52	.59	.04	.02	.11	.10
26. able to distinguish between those who need short-term therapy and long-term therapy	.46	.54	.03	.02	.04	.03	.11	.09

Table 1. (continued)

Items	Factors							
	Skills		Awareness		Relationship		Knowledge	
	Study 1	Study 2	Study 1	Study 2	Study 1	Study 2	Study 1	Study 2
27. understanding the importance of the legalities of immigration	.00	.06	.39	.51	.07	.00	.09	.02
28. extensive professional or collegial interactions with minority individuals	.02	.05	.77	.79	.00	.02	.03	.02
29. multicultural case load has doubled in the past year	.16	.21	.54	.55	.03	.03	.01	.06
30. interactions with people of different cultures are enjoyable	.03	.00	.36	.32	.24	.24	.16	.23
31. involved in working against institutional barriers for minority services	.01	.02	.60	.66	.10	.10	.12	.03
32. well-versed with nonstandard English	.10	.12	.55	.53	.05	.06	.08	.06
33. extensive life experiences with minority individuals	.16	.15	.70	.68	.01	.01	.10	.00
34. frequently seek consultation and attend multicultural workshops or training sessions	.08	.10	.58	.59	.07	.07	.16	.18
35. effective crisis interventions	.59	.64	.12	.16	.03	.04	.06	.06
36. various counseling techniques and skills used	.56	.63	.01	.03	.04	.01	.02	.01
37. concise and to the point in verbal skills	.62	.68	.01	.03	.11	.19	.04	.00
38. comfortable exploring sexual issues	.49	.48	.00	.02	.05	.12	.06	.10
39. effective in getting a client to be specific	.65	.65	.12	.09	.02	.09	.12	.12

Table 1. (continued)

Items	Factors							
	Skills		Awareness		Relationship		Knowledge	
	Study 1	Study 2	Study 1	Study 2	Study 1	Study 2	Study 1	Study 2
40. compatible nonverbal and verbal responses	.51	.61	.00	.07	.08	.06	.05	.03
Alphas of subscales	0.83	0.81	0.83	0.80	0.65	0.67	0.79	0.80
Eigenvalues	8.30	7.62	3.18	3.03	2.34	2.41	1.69	1.77
% Variance Explained	19.30	18.10	7.40	7.20	5.50	5.70	3.90	4.20
Coefficients of factor congruence for factor structures of Study 1 and Study 2	.87		.80		.78		.75	

Note. Underlined loadings indicate the items that are strong measures of each factor. These items have factor loadings of .30 or above. Skills has 11 items, Awareness has 11 items, Relationship has 10 items, Knowledge has 8 items, and Knowledge has 11 items. The items listed in this table are summarized, conveying the general meaning of the items.

The MCI is copyrighted by the author, from whom the instrument may be obtained.

is, a second order factor. Conceptually, each item was viewed as an indicator of one of the first order factors; then the first order factors were considered to be indicators of the higher order factor. Thus, each item was examined to determine its relationship to the first order factors; then the first order factors were examined to assess whether there was a higher order factor.

Whether or not the MCI is a unitary or a multidimensional scale needed to be addressed at the MCI's development stage. Whether the MCI is influenced by a higher order factor also needed to be examined. CFA tests whether actual data fit an identified model. It tests whether specific items of a measure define a prespecified latent factor. Rotation is not used, and a solution is directly given and is based on a model that was previously constructed through EFA or through conceptual modeling. Thus, the CFA study of the data from the national data was concerned with assessing the relative fit of six competing factor models. All of the confirmatory indexes of this study indicated that the oblique four-factor model had the best fit to the data, including tests of significant chi-square difference for this model in relation to the other five models. Some of the relatively strong indexes for the 4-factor oblique model were: goodness-of-fit index, GFI = .84; adjusted GFI (i.e., a predicted value if the identified model was tried on another sample) = .81; the ratio of the chi-square goodness-of-fit to its degrees of freedom, X^2:df = 1.99 (the ratio should be below 2); root-mean-square residual, RMR = .024 (should be low); normed index of fit or delta (evaluation of the fit of a proposed model relative to a logical worse case, that is, the null model) = .80, and significant t values for all standardized loadings. These and other indexes met the rule-of-thumb acceptance levels suggested by Bollen (1989).

The 4-factor higher order model, which was the second best model, indicated worse indexes of fit and lower standardized factor loadings than did the 4-factor oblique model. However, the first order factors had high loadings on the higher (second) order factors, ranging between .51 and .77; 82% of the variance accounted for by the first order model was accounted for by the higher order model. In addition, as stated earlier, CFA indicated moderately high to high correlations among the factors of the 4-factor oblique model, ranging between .30 and .62. Thus, there was some weak empirical evidence of a higher order factor model.

In conclusion, two levels of factors may be conceptualized for the MCI. First, there are the four relatively specific factors indicated empirically. Second, there is some evidence to suggest a general multicultural competency factor that reflects counselors' evaluations of themselves as being a multicultural counselor, without reference to any specific dimensions. Counselors' overall self-evaluation of being a

multicultural counselor affects the evaluation of their particular competencies, thus affecting factor correlations.   In reference to the
conceptualization of the 4-factor oblique model as well as the higher
order model, it is suggested that the subscales as well as a total score (i.e.,
the full scale) of the MCI be scored when evaluating counselor competencies in training and applied settings.

Additional Analyses of Data from the Midwestern State Sample of Study 1

In order to understand the influence of multicultural counseling
experience on the competencies of the Study 1 sample (n = 604) from the
Midwestern state, a multivariate analysis of variance (MANOVA) was
performed in which the dependent variables were the four MCI subscales
and the independent variable was the amount of respondent work in
multicultural services, as reported by the subjects in the demographic
section. Multicultural services included minority client contact as well as
community work, outreach, teaching, and political activities related to
racial and ethnic minority issues. Such services reported were catego-
rized as being either less than 50% or more than 50% of one's work in
multicultural services, hereafter referred to as the less than 50% work
group and the more than 50% work group. In order to have equal cell
sizes, 82 subjects were randomly chosen from the less than 50% work
group because the more than 50% work group consisted of 82 subjects.
A significant MANOVA was followed up by univariate analyses
(ANOVAs) to isolate the source of the significance. An ANOVA was also
performed using the full scale MCI score as the dependent variable and
the work groups as the independent variable.

In addition, responses to three open-ended questions that followed
the Likert-type MCI items of Study 1 were content analyzed (Altheide,
1957) to identify recurring themes for each question across all subjects
who answered the open-ended questions. Question 1 was answered by
206 individuals. Question 2 had responses from 197 individuals, and
Question 3 received 487 responses. The proportion of subjects expressing each theme or issue was determined for each question.

Results

Differences between multicultural work groups. Homogeneity of
variance/covariance matrices (Box M) was not violated (p > .20). A
significant MANOVA, $F(4,157)$ = 14.82, p < .001, was followed by
significant ANOVAs for Multicultural Awareness, $F(1,160)$ = 51.60,
p < .001, and Multicultural Counseling Relationship, $F(1,160)$ = 5.32,
p < .02. Nonsignificant ANOVAs were found for Multicultural Counsel-

ing Skills, $F(1,160) = 3.66$, $p < .06$, and for Multicultural Counseling Knowledge, $F(1,160) = 2.30$, $p < .13$. An ANOVA on the full scale indicated a significant difference between the two groups, $F(1,162) = 24.50$, $p < .001$. For all significant differences, the more than 50% work group obtained higher competency scores. Table 2 reports means, standard deviations, and ANOVAs of the two groups on the MCI subscales.

The significantly higher scores of the more than 50% work group on Multicultural Awareness and Multicultural Counseling Relationship may point to the effectiveness of actual multicultural work on proactive multicultural sensitivity, outreach, and advocacy and on enhanced multicultural client-counselor relationship. The nonsignificant findings for skills and knowledge lend support to Sue et al.'s (1992) expanded counselor constructs regarding awareness of self and others, and to Sue and Sue's (1990) assumption that sole emphasis on knowledge and skills may be a limitation in MCT that may not differentiate between counselors. What distinguishes a multicultural counselor, as indicated by the initial study of the MCI, are the additional awareness and relationship variables. These findings also confirm the importance placed by trainers (e.g., Sue et al., 1987) on obtaining clinical and practicum experiences with minority clients. In their responses to open-ended questions (see below), subjects also gave important meaning to their contacts with culturally diverse clients or their need or lack of such clinical experiences.

Content Analysis of Open-ended Questions. A total of 493 (82%) subjects answered at least one of the open-ended questions in the MCI. The first question regarding the subjects' strengths in multicultural counseling was answered by 206 respondents. Seven recurring themes were found for the first question. Subjects felt that (a) their strengths were derived from contact with specific culturally diverse individuals or clients or from experiences (25%); (b) their strength consisted of knowledge gained from working with specific cultures (24%); (c) the inventory covered their multicultural strengths (20%); (d) their knowledge was gained through multicultural workshops/courses/readings (15%); (e) client race or ethnicity was not an issue for them because they treated all clients as equals (7%); (f) their strength was their curiosity for learning about different cultures or new culture-based counseling methods (5%); and (g) their strength was their use of culture-based counseling techniques (4%).

The second question concerning areas in multicultural counseling in which subjects believed they needed to improve was answered by 197 subjects. Seven recurring themes were found for this question. Subjects felt that (a) they needed more experiences with minority indi-

Table 2. Means, Standard Deviations, and ANOVAs for the More Than 50% Multicultural Work Group and the Less Than 50% Multicultural Work Group on the MCI.

Subscales	More than 50% Work			Less than 50% Work			Hyp MS	Error MS	F	p
	n	M	SD	n	M	SD				
Multicultural Counseling Skills	82	3.5	.33	82	3.4	.35	.42	.12	3.7	.06
Multicultural Awareness	82	3.1	.54	82	2.4	.53	14.71	.29	51.60	.001***
Multicultural Counseling Knowledge	82	3.2	.44	82	3.1	.44	.45	.20	2.30	.13
Multicultural Counseling Relationship	82	3.3	.43	82	3.1	.46	1.06	.20	5.32	.02*
Full Scale	82	3.3	.31	82	2.9	.34	19.55	.12	24.50	.001***

* p < .05
*** p < .001

viduals (20%); (b) they needed a more general awareness about multicultural issues (19%); (c) they needed more multicultural training (18%); (d) the inventory covered important multicultural topics (15%); (e) they needed more self-awareness regarding their own cultural context (10%); (f) they were unsure about needed self-improvements as they rarely worked with racial or ethnic minority clients (10%); and (g) they needed more information about specific areas across cultures (e.g., working with adolescents from different cultures, understanding family structures across different cultures, etc.) (8%).

The third question regarding the subjects' reactions to the inventory was answered by 437 subjects. Nine recurring themes were found for this question. Subjects felt that (a) the inventory was too long (20%); (b) their answers reflected a lack of multicultural experience (18%); (c) the MCI or similar instruments were needed for the future (15%); (d) the MCI was comprehensive (10%); (e) their experience of responding to the questionnaire was negative (10%); (f) their multicultural awareness was raised by the MCI (8%); (g) their answers were the result of specific multicultural experiences (e.g., work with a particular client, life experiences, work with a specific population, etc.) (7%); (h) their suggestions or questions about the development of the scale needed to be addressed (7%); and (i) their experience of responding to the questionnaire was positive (5%).

All of the themes elicited by the first open-ended question were in concordance with at least one of the four subscales, except for the opinion that ethnicity and race were not issues for counselors because all clients are treated as equals. This opinion did not fit with the view of MCT that inequity prevails in counseling theory, research, and practice with regard to minority clients. The MCI did not reach the level of specificity and specialization desired by some of the subjects because the MCI purports to measure broad multicultural counseling competencies. Some subjects noted that responding to the scale was a negative experience, which could have been a realistic reaction because the MCI assesses cultural biases and nonmainstream competencies. Many subjects, however, also expressed a desire for MCT, indicating an increasing acceptance of multicultural issues by counseling professionals and students.

PART III
USE OF THE MCI TO EVALUATE COUNSELING TRAINING:STUDIES 3 AND 4

After initial development of the MCI, it was administered to graduate students in counseling and school psychology at the University of Nebraska-Lincoln who took the one-semester Multicultural Counseling course between 1990 and 1993. These students did not participate in the instrument development Studies 1 and 2; nor did they participate in more than one study. The general objective of Studies 3 and 4 was to examine whether MCT could be related to the outcome of perceived competencies (Study 3), as measured by the MCI, and whether students could assess simulated counseling video-tapes, applying the constructs of multicultural counseling competencies, as operationalized by the MCI (Study 4). The two MCT-related studies were as follows.

STUDY 3: A PRE-TEST AND POST-TEST STUDY

Ponterotto and Casas (1987) found that variability in the depth and scope of training was notable even among programs singled out by training directors of counseling psychology programs as being in the forefront of multicultural training. These authors further noted the lack of conclusive data that these special programs produced multiculturally competent counselors. A competency-based training approach to multicultural counseling has been proposed by several authors. Ivey (1977) presents a taxonomy linking cultural skills with communication and states that one who has cultural expertise is able to communicate. Arredondo-Dowd and Gonzales (1980) presented a schema of multiple competencies as a means of preparing culturally effective counselors. Casas's (1982) competency-based model proposes an outline of courses, practica, and workshops within a multicultural counseling specialty. Finally, Sue and Sue (1990) stated that cross-cultural counseling programs must relate "race and culture-specific incidents and counseling skills" (p. 14). Owing to the strong recommendation that MCT should result in skills and competencies, the MCI was used to test whether there were any differences between the competencies of students at the beginning and end of a multicultural counseling course. This course is required for all master's and doctoral students in counseling psychology and is strongly recommended for students in school psychology at the University of Nebraska-Lincoln. The course presents theories, research, practice, professional issues, and challenges of multicultural counseling. In addition, experiential activities, such as the Pedersen Triad Training Model, critical incident exercises, videotape viewings and analyses, ethnographic interviews, case presentations, and small group process, facilitate affective learning and the development of self-monitoring strategies needed for enhanced cultural and racial self-awareness.

Method

Subjects. Second year master's students and doctoral students who took the Multicultural Counseling course were administered the MCI. MCI data were collected from 42 students over a period of three semesters. Students were informed that they were participating in research investigating a multicultural instrument, and all enrolled students voluntarily participated. Although at the same university, these students had not participated in Study 1.

Data Analysis. Student responses to the MCI administered on the first day of a multicultural counseling course were compared with their responses on the last day of the course, using a repeated measures multivariate test, followed by repeated measures dependent *t*-tests performed on the four MCI subscale scores and the full scale. A significance level of .05 was used for all analyses.

Results

A significant multivariate repeated measures test, $F(4,37) = 5.97$, $p < .001$, was followed by three significant repeated measures dependent *t*-tests. The pretest means for Multicultural Counseling Skills, Multicultural Awareness, and Multicultural Counseling Knowledge were significantly lower ($p < .01$) than the posttest means for the same subscales. The full scale pretest score was significantly lower ($p < .001$) than the full scale posttest score. There was no significant difference for Multicultural Counseling Relationship. Table 3 reports the means, standard deviations, and *t*-tests of the pre-post tests.

Discussion

The author acknowledges that a pre-test and post-test design that lacks a control group does not take into account competing explanations for score change, such as pre-test sensitization of students and general maturation over time. However, this initial effort assessing the outcome of MCT related to specific competency objectives was an important source of information for the author, among various other standard course evaluation data, to examine the effects of MCT course work.

Scores on the MCI reflected competency change between the time the course began and the time it ended. Perhaps self-reported higher ratings for awareness, knowledge, and skills (placed in rank order) suggested that the predominant components of didactics, research, writing, experiential activities, case interviews, and case presentations in the Multicultural Counseling course taught at the University of

Table 3. Repeated Measures Dependent *t*-tests for Pretest and Posttest MCI Scores of Students in a Multicultural Counseling Course in Three Different Semesters

Subscales	*n*	Pretest		Posttest				
		M	*SD*	*M*	*SD*	*t*	*df*	*p*
Skills	42	2.9	.44	3.2	.54	-2.94	41	.005**
Awareness	42	3.0	.48	3.4	.53	-4.54	41	.001***
Knowledge	42	2.3	.71	2.6	.52	-3.15	41	.003**
Relationship	42	2.7	.44	2.8	.49	-0.73	41	.460
Full Scale	42	2.8	.39	3.0	.43	-3.87	41	.001***

** $p < .01$
*** $p < .001$

Nebraska-Lincoln may be related to only three competency dimensions. Thus, formal coursework may not affect the multicultural counseling relationship, which perhaps results only from actual work experiences with minority clients, as implied by the differences between the more than 50% work group and the less than 50% work group of Study 1. It is also possible that training, as pointed out by Sue and Sue (1990), traditionally emphasizes skills, awareness, and knowledge, while being less attentive to the dynamics of the interpersonal process between the counselor and client.

STUDY 4: COUNSELOR TRAINEES' MCI RATINGS OF CASE CONCEPTUALIZATION, INTERVENTIONS, AND COUNSELING GOALS

A line of inquiry that lends itself readily to MCT and to investigating the multicultural competencies of a counselor is studying the effects of a culturally consistent counseling perspective versus a culturally discrepant counseling perspective (with regard to a client's cultural upbringing and values) on perceptions of counselor multicultural competencies. Sue and Zane (1987) argued that to enhance the multicultural counseling process, cultural knowledge needs to be incorporated into counseling tasks such as (a) conceptualization of the client problem, (b) treatment strategies, and (c) counseling goals. Discrepancy between such counseling tasks and what is culturally appropriate for the client could negatively affect perceived counselor characteristics.

Sodowsky (1991; see also: Sodowsky & Parr, 1991; Sodowsky & Taffe, 1991) made two treatment videotapes of a simulated intake interview carried out by the same counselor with the same client. The above mentioned counseling tasks were culturally consistent with the client's cultural upbringing in one tape and culturally discrepant with the client's cultural upbringing in the other tape (this tape showed mainstream counseling practice). As reported in Sodowsky (1991), Sodowsky and Parr (1991), and Sodowsky and Taffe (1991), the counseling perspectives in the two tapes were significantly different. The two counseling perspectives also differed for perceived counselor credibility, which covers the domains of expertise, attractiveness, and trustworthiness. Thus, Sodowsky called one tape culturally consistent and the other tape culturally discrepant.

The principal objective of Study 4 was to examine whether the counselor using culturally consistent counseling tasks, perceived to be significantly more credible, would be evaluated as being more multiculturally competent than the counselor using culturally discrepant counseling tasks. The following is a description of the two counseling perspectives.

Treatment Videotapes

The first 15 minutes of both tapes depicted the same simulated counseling intake involving a White male counselor doing an intake with a male Asian-Indian international student. Scene 1 of both tapes was identical. The counselor was played by an actor who was unaware of the study's purpose. An international student, who was also unaware of the purpose of the study, played the role of a student in computer science.

In Scene 1, the international client wished to change the academic major his parents in India and uncle and aunt in the United States had chosen for him. The client expressed several family-related concerns: chief among them were his boredom with computer science, in which he was relatively competent; his growing interest in the social sciences; his sense of duty to his parents, who spent their savings and also borrowed money to provide him with a technological education in the United States; his obligations to this uncle and aunt in the United States, who supported him emotionally and physically, so that he could have a degree in an area that had family consensus and that also promised employment prospects benefiting the client's parents, siblings, and extended family; his feelings of shame for seeking help from a counselor, an outsider to his family and friends; and his belief that expressing private feelings and thoughts is a weakness.

The counselor followed the client-counselor dialogue (Scene 1) with a 15-minute monologue (Scene 2, in which the client was not present), wherein he described his three counseling tasks. The contents of Scene 2 in the two tapes differed from each other. In the culturally consistent tape, the counselor tailored the tasks to be consistent with the cultural values and upbringing that the client referred to at the intake. For instance, he considered the client's role in maintaining structural balance in his family and extended kinship and his role in enhancing his family honor through future professional and monetary success. The counselor wanted to prevent a confrontation between the client and his relatives because of the client's strong respect for his family seniors and their judgment and his affiliation to some traditional values. Specifically, the counselor said the client was to be encouraged to seek assistance from his natural support system, such as a co-national faculty member and his uncle, who could become intermediaries, helping to resolve the client's differences with his parents. The client's feelings of guilt regarding wanting something different from what his parents wanted were to be acknowledged, but no attempt would be made to alleviate his guilt.

In the discrepant tape, the counselor did not tailor the tasks to be congruent with the client's cultural values and upbringing. The counselor said he planned to encourage the client to be assertive with his parents and uncle and aunt and to recognize and satisfy his career needs and interests. The counselor considered the advice of family seniors as restricting for the client. He planned to help the client explore his guilt, self-concept, self-esteem, and cognitive set and their effects on his functioning. The counselor considered the client's difficulties as developmental issues related to his personal identity development and to making choices about his adult vocation. The counselor planned strategies to enable the client to develop an attitude of responsibility to himself and to adopt an independent lifestyle. He also planned to give the client career and vocationally oriented personality tests. In the discrepant tape, to generalize across some common counseling theories, concepts from developmental, humanistic, and cognitive-behavioral theories were integrated in an eclectic manner considered structurally coherent and professionally acceptable. The actor playing the counselor was instructed to be equally enthusiastic and to maintain the same posture and gesture in both tapes. Both tapes had the same office setting.

Method

Subjects. Master's and doctoral students in counseling psychology and school psychology taking a multicultural counseling course during two different semesters at the University of Nebraska-Lincoln volunteered for the study. Although drawn from the same university as the subjects in the previous MCI studies, these students did not participate in any other studies with the MCI.

Procedures. Four class periods of 1 hour and 20 minutes each were spent discussing readings on multicultural competencies and MCT. Then students in each class were randomly assigned to watch one of the two tapes. There were 38 participants, 18 who viewed the culturally consistent counselor and 20 who viewed the culturally discrepant counselor. Equal numbers did not view the two tapes because the enrollment in the two classes differed. The students rated the counselor they viewed on the MCI. The use of the first person in the self-report statements of the MCI was substituted by the third person; that is, "I" was replaced with "the counselor"; and subject-verb agreements were accordingly changed.

Data Analysis. Using subscale scores as multiple dependent variables, a MANOVA was performed to test for differences between the ratings on the MCI given to the culturally consistent counselor and those given to the culturally discrepant counselor. Homogeneity of variance/covariance matrices (Box M) was not violated ($p > .20$). Subsequently, ANOVAs were performed on the four MCI subscales, and a t-test was performed on the full scale. A significance level of .05 was used for all analyses.

Results

A significant MANOVA was found, $F(4,33) = 254.87$, $p < .001$. This significant MANOVA was followed by significant ANOVAs on all four subscales, Multicultural Counseling Skills: $F(1,36) = 291.20$, $p < .001$; Multicultural Awareness $F(1,36) = 945.14$, $p < .001$; Multicultural Counseling Relationship: $F(1,36) = 223.94$, $p < .001$; and Multicultural Counseling Knowledge: $F(1,36) = 337.82$, $p < .001$; A t-test on the full scale indicated significant differences between the two counseling perspectives, $t(36) = 28.8$, $p < .001$. For the subscales and the full scale, the culturally consistent counseling tasks had higher means than the culturally discrepant counseling tasks, indicating greater multicultural counseling competencies in the culturally consistent counseling. Table 4 reports means, standard deviations, and ANOVA and t-test results.

Discussion

Both counseling perspectives were considered equally plausible in a previous study (Sodowsky & Taffe, 1991), but the culturally consistent perspective had the additional characteristics of multicultural counseling knowledge, specific multicultural counseling skills, and sensitivity to a client's family relationships that were representative of the client's culture. The MCI identified these differences, indicating the superior multicultural competencies of the culturally consistent counselor. It is interesting that students in Study 3 did not perceive themselves to have greater multicultural relationship characteristics at the end of a multicultural course, but students in Study 4 were able to recognize and assess this competency or lack of it in another counselor who presented a culturally sensitive perspective versus a culturally insensitive perspective.

This study helps to provide evidence to support a hypothesis that the MCI might be able to show a relationship between perceived multicultural counseling competencies and perceived counselor credibility, as measured by a credibility measure. (Previous studies with the videotapes indicated that the culturally consistent counseling was also viewed as more credible.) In previous studies (e.g., Sodowsky, 1991; Sodowsky & Taffe, 1991), some items that showed the greatest

Table 4. Means, Standard Deviations, and ANOVAs on the MCI Subscales for the Culturally Consistent and Culturally Discrepant Tapes as Rated by Students in a Multicultural Counseling Course.

Subscales	Culturally Consistent Tape			Culturally Discrepant Tape			Hyp MS	Error MS	F	p
	n	M	SD	n	M	SD				
Multicultural Counseling Skills	18	3.4	.24	20	1.9	.32	24.00	.08	291.20	.001***
Multicultural Awareness	18	3.5	.20	20	1.3	.24	45.52	.05	945.14	.001***
Multicultural Counseling Knowledge	18	3.4	.31	20	1.4	.34	36.44	.12	337.82	.001***
Multicultural Counseling Relationship	18	3.7	.28	20	1.9	.44	31.15	.14	223.94	.001***

*** $p < .001$

difference in perceived counselor credibility were unbiased-biased, informed-uninformed, respectful-disrespectful, insightful-insightless, selfless-selfish, expert-inexpert, responsible-irresponsible, experienced-inexperienced, and competent-incompetent. These credibility characteristics, although related to general counseling practice, also have powerful meaning for multicultural counseling competencies, as discussed by the author in the literature review in Part 1. The viewing of the tapes, discussions about the two perspectives in counseling, and their respective evaluations on the MCI educated the students on multicultural counseling competencies. This training exercise also provided additional validation evidence for the MCI.

PART IV
A PREDICTION MODEL FOR MULTICULTURAL TRAINING (MCT) AND THE MULTICULTURAL COUNSELING INVENTORY (MCI)

The MCI is being researched nationally and internationally by graduate students, professors, and clinicians. Recently, investigations into the MCI's relationships with professional training (e.g., nursing, psychology, and K-12 teaching), white racial identity attitudes, and other multicultural competency instruments have appeared in *The APA Monitor, Journal of Counseling Psychology, Journal of Counseling and Development, Measurement and Evaluation in Counseling and Development, Journal of Nursing Education*, etc. It appears that the MCI is a promising tool for the evaluation of training and for process and outcome research in help-giving services.

After developing and studying the psychometric properties of the MCI, the author began investigating the MCI's relationships with predictors. Reported below are initial results from an on-going study that was initiated with collaborators (Sodowsky, O'Dell, Hagemoser, Kwan, & Tonemah, 1993). Early results from this study, called Study 5, may give readers a broader picture of the MCI in terms of its relationships with (a) scales measuring racist attitudes, rigidity, cultural political correctness, and social desirability and (b) another multicultural competency instrument and MCT. Knowing how the MCI relates to other variables would increase the meaningfulness of the MCI to its users.

Letters were written to the directors of all APA-approved university counseling centers in the nation, requesting them to release the names of their staff psychologists, counselors, predoctoral psychology interns, and graduate practicum students. Out of a list of 450 names thus acquired, 300 subjects were randomly chosen to receive mailed questionnaires that included the MCI. The response rate was 67%, consisting of 201 anonymous, volunteer respondents with approximately equal numbers of staff psychologists, counselors, predoctoral interns, and graduate practicum students. The age range was between 25 and 60, and there were 115 women and 86 men. The subjects of Study 5 differed from the previously mentioned instrument development sample of Study 2, which also consisted of university counseling center subjects.

The package of materials sent to each person in the sample consisted of: a demographic sheet that had questions on subjects' MCT experiences (e.g., number of multicultural courses, research, theses, dissertations, workshops, specialization; also reading and/or speaking a Third World language), multicultural life experiences (e.g., living in integrated and/or ethnic neighborhoods, working in inner city schools, having racial and ethnic minority friends and family, volunteering in community organizations serving low SES people, foreign travel, foreign work, and foreign living experiences), racial and ethnic self-designation, geographic location, etc.; items on cultural political correctness (CPC, created by the author and her collaborators), measuring a preference to make a good impression on others regarding cultural and racial matters (e.g., one's work-related involvements with regard to diversity, evaluation of people of diverse racial, ethnic, and cultural backgrounds, social experiences in the context of race and culture, race-based humor); a measure of a sense of social inadequacy or low social self-esteem that consisted of the Revised Janis-Field Scale (Eagly, 1973); the Social Desirability (SD) Scale (Crowne & Marlowe, 1973); the Multicultural Awareness-Knowledge-Skills Scale (MAKSS; D'Andrea, Daniels, & Heck, 1991); a measure of a racist orientation towards African Americans (Gurin, Gurin, Lao, & Beattie, 1973); a measure of rigidity (Wesley, 1953); a measure of intolerance for ambiguity (Budner, 1973); and the MCI.

Certain demographics appeared to be related to subjects' self-reported competencies. Practitioners located in western, eastern, and southern regions reported significantly higher competencies than those in the midwest and mountain regions in multicultural skills, multicultural awareness, and multicultural relationship. There was no difference in multicultural knowledge. American racial and ethnic minorities and international subjects reported significantly higher scores than their White colleagues on the above subscales as well as on the fourth dimension, multicultural knowledge. No effects were identified on the MCI for such demographics as educational degrees, years of professional experience, and gender.

The full scales of the MCI and MAKSS showed a moderately high correlation of .68. Variables such as attributing blame to African

Americans, rigidity, and intolerance for ambiguity did not appreciably correlate with either the MCI ($r = -.12$; $r = -.07$; $r = -.04$, respectively) or the MAKSS ($r = -.15$; $r = -.04$; $r = .01$, respectively). The correlations of social desirability (SD) and cultural political correctness (CPC) with the MCI were .27 and .19, respectively. The correlation between SD and CPC was .32. A stepwise multiple regression, with SD and CPC as predictor variables and the MCI total score as the criterion variable, revealed that SD accounted for 7% of the variance of the MCI, and CPC did not enter into the model because it did not account for any additional variance. In a full multiple regression model where SD and CPC were entered as a block, they together accounted for 8% of the variance. Thus, neither scale was a strong predictor of the MCI, suggesting that the MCI may not strongly elicit diverse social desirability response sets.

A structural equation model was tested. Multicultural training (MCT) and multicultural life experiences (MClife) were theoretically proposed to be related to the MCI. Social desirability (SD) was also placed in the model, with the expectation that it would not be related to the MCI. An additional hypothesis was that two counselor characteristics, cultural political correctness (CPC) and a sense of inadequacy in social situations (SOCINAD) would affect MCT rather than the MCI, with MCT being directly linked to the MCI. See Figure 1 for the structural model of the hypothesized relationships and the obtained path coefficients.

To test the above model, Lisrel 7 (Jöreskog & Sorbom, 1988) analysis was used, following the maximum likelihood estimation procedure. (See Part III for an explanation of CFA indexes of fit.) Very strong goodness-of-fit indexes were indicated for the hypothesized model of Study 5: GFI = .95, AdjGFI = .94, chi-square = 1.70, $p = .79$, (a nonsignificant chi square indicated that the hypothesis that the proposed model and the actual data were not different was tenable—suggesting a good fit), chi square: df = .43, and RMR = .02. MCT and MClife indicated significant standardized path coefficients and t-scores in their respective relationships with the MCI. In addition, CPC and SOCINAD had significant standardized path coefficients and t-scores, negative in direction, in their respective relationships with MCT.

The results suggest that MCT and multicultural life experiences may be related to multicultural counseling competencies, as measured by the MCI. General social desirability, as conceived by Crowne and Marlowe, had no direct relationship with the MCI. However, trainers may need to be attentive to such characteristics in

Figure 1. Structural Relationships of Observed Variables with the MCI.

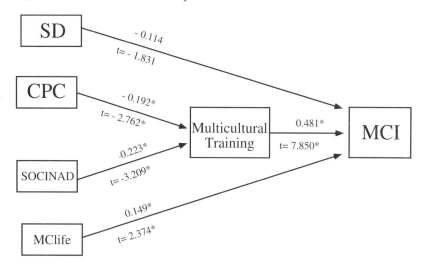

Note: *Significant correlations and *t* scores; SD = social desirablilty, CPC = cultural political correctness, SOCINAD = sense of social inadequacy, and MClife = multicultural life experiences.

their students as a tendency for cultural political correctness and feelings of social inadequacy. They may need to explain to their students how these two processes may not facilitate multicultural training. For instance, students practicing cultural political correctness may not allow themselves to self-monitor and reflect (i.e., learning how to learn) about their cultural biases and racial stereotypes. A lack of self-monitoring and self-reflexivity skills will prevent one from learning cultural and racial self-awareness, which is an important component of MCT. Also students need to feel confident about themselves and their abilities in diverse social settings because their professional work will take them to strongly heterogeneous and pluralistic settings.

In summary, the convergent validity of the MCI was supported by a moderately high correlation of the MCI and MAKSS full scales. The low correlations of the MCI with racist attributions to African Americans, rigidity, and intolerance for ambiguity suggest that the latter constructs are conceptually different from the pluralistic philosophy of the MCI. Using the MCI as a dependent variable, the author was able to show two significant components of an MCT model: the actual training itself and multicultural life experiences.

CONCLUSION

A series of five studies addressed the development and validity of the MCI, a self-report instrument, designed to measure multicultural counseling competencies. Initial scale development involved exploratory factor analyses (EFAs) on data from a midwestern state sample. These analyses were followed by: an examination of the Pearson correlations of the EFA factor structures of the two samples, the state sample and a national sample; confirmatory factor analysis on data from the national sample; multivariate tests comparing practitioners with high levels of multicultural practice and those having less multicultural practice; and content analyses of open-ended responses given by subjects after answering the MCI. The MCI was administered in two different training conditions (pre-post evaluation of multicultural counseling classes; and viewing of two simulated counseling videotapes) in a multicultural counseling course, using different samples of students; results indicated that the MCI can be applied meaningfully when evaluating different multicultural learning. Initial findings of an ongoing study indicate relationships of the MCI to other measures with regard to issues of convergent, discriminant, and predictive validity, as well as measures of social desirability and cultural political correctness. A conceptual model of the structural relationships of multicultural training (MCT), including its components, with the MCI was shown to have good fit with actual data.

Results from all the studies were supportive of the MCI, demonstrating it to be a psychometrically robust instrument, measuring distinct, yet interrelated dimensions and also to have potential for measuring multicultural training processes. The author proposes that the MCI constructs are consistent with general graduate training contexts and with objectives and training outcome criteria in counselor training programs. Because operationalizing training objectives is uncommon in MCT, the author has attempted to formulate training objectives in measurable terms, making it likely that evaluation of MCT will be carried out. That is, the MCI may serve as a measure directly linked to certain training objectives. The MCI could provide the necessary feedback loop with respect to a program's ability to achieve certain proposed training objectives.

With the ever-increasing multicultural population in the U.S., "the issues surrounding ethnic-minority populations can no longer be viewed as minor or peripheral to the concerns of the nation" (Sue et al., 1987, p. 276). Thus, although the provision of multiculturally competent counseling may result from the counseling profession's enlightened and pragmatic self-interest (Casas, 1987), it is even more important to recall that in 1973 APA suggested that counseling or therapy that was conducted without cultural considerations would be considered unethical (APA Follow-up Commission, 1973). Finally, the study of multicultural counseling competencies as an effect of training will provide a more complete and balanced perspective to the scientist-practitioner approach of education in professional psychology, which until a few years ago concerned itself only with general competencies, as defined by mainstream training theories and previous APA guidelines.

REFERENCES

Altheide, D. L. (1957). Ethnographic content analysis. *Qualitative Sociology, 10*(1), 65-77.

American Association for Counseling and Development. (1988). Ethical standards of the American Association for Counseling and Development (3rd revision, AACD Governing Council, March 1988). *Journal of Counseling and Development, 67*, 4-8.

American Psychological Association (APA). (1992). Ethical principles of psychologists. *American Psychologist, 47*, 1597-1611.

APA Conference Follow-Up Commission. (1973, September). *National conference on levels and patterns of training in professional psychology.* Report from the meeting of the American Psychological Association, Vail, Colorado.

APA Office of Ethnic Minority Affairs. (1993). Guidelines for providers of psychological services to ethnic, linguistic, and culturally diverse populations. *American Psychologist, 48*, 45-48.

Arredondo, P. (1987). Cross-cultural counselor education and training. In P. Pedersen (Ed.), *Handbook of cross-cultural counseling and psychotherapy* (pp. 281-289). New York: Praeger.

Arredondo-Dowd, P., & Gonzales, J. (1980). Preparing culturally effective counselors. *The Personnel & Guidance Journal, 59*, 376-378.

Atkinson, D. R., Maruyama, M., & Matusui, S. (1978). Effects of counselor race and counseling approach on Asian Americans' perception of counselor credibility and utility. *Journal of Counseling Psychology, 25*(1), 76-83.

Atkinson, D. R., Ponce, F. Q., & Martinez, F. M. (1984). Effects of ethnic, sex, and attitude similarity on counselor credibility. *Journal of Counseling Psychology, 31*(4), 588-590.

Atkinson, D. R., & Wampold, B. E. (1982). A comparison of Counselor Rating Form and the Counselor Effectiveness Rating Scale. *Counselor Education and Supervision, 22*, 25-36.

Barak, A., & LaCrosse, M. B. (1975). Multidimensional perception of counselor behavior. *Journal of Counseling Psychology, 22,* 471-476.

Berg, D. N., & Smith, K. K. (1988). The clinical demands of research methods. In D. N. Berg & K. K. Smith (Eds.), *The self in social inquiry* (pp. 21-34). Newbury Park, CA: SAGE.

Bollen, K. A. (1989). *Structural equations with latent variables.* New York: Wiley.

Budner, S. (1973). Intolerance of ambiguity. In J. P. Robinson & P. R. Shaver (Eds.), *Measures of social psychological attitudes* (pp. 401-408). Ann Arbor, MI: Survey Research Center Institute for Social Research.

Casas, J. M. (1982). *Complementary cross-cultural counseling model for the 80s.* Unpublished manuscript.

Casas, J. M., Ponterotto, J. G., & Gutierrez, J. M. (1986). An ethical indictment of counseling research and training: The cross-cultural perspective. *Journal of Counseling and Development, 64,* 347-349.

Cayleff, S. E. (1986). Ethical issues in counseling gender, race, and culturally distinct groups. *Journals of Counseling and Development, 64,* 345-347.

Crowne, D., & Marlowe, D. (1973). Social desirability scale. In J. P. Robinson & P. R. Shaver (Eds.), *Measures of social psychological attitudes* (pp. 727-732). Ann Arbor, MI: Survey Research Center Institute for Social Research.

D'Andrea, M., Daniels, J., & Heck, R. (1991). Evaluating the impact of multicultural training. *Journal of Counseling and Development, 70,* 143-150.

Drapela, V. J. (1987). International and comprehensive perspectives in counselor education. In P. Pedersen (Ed.), *Handbook of cross-cultural counseling and psychotherapy* (pp. 291-298). New York: Prager.

Eagly, A. (1973). Revised Janis-Field scale. In J. P. Robinson & P. R. Shaver (Eds.), *Measures of social psychological attitudes* (pp. 79-80). Ann Arbor, MI: Survey Research Center Institute for Social Research.

Espin, O. M. (1987). Psychotherapy with Hispanic women: Some considerations. In P. Pedersen (Ed.), *Handbook of cross-cultural counseling and psychotherapy* (pp. 165-171). New York: Praeger.

Fiedler, F. E., Mitchell, T., & Triandis, H. C. (1971). The culture assimilator: An approach to cross-cultural training. *Journal of Applied Psychology, 55,* 95-102.

Gurin, P., Gurin, G., Lao, R. C., & Beattie, M. (1969). Multidimensional IE scale. In J. P. Robinson & P. R. Shaver (Eds.), *Measures of social psychological attitudes* (p. 218-221). Ann Arbor, MI: Survey Research Center Institute for Social Research.

Hoshmand, L. L. T. (1991). Clinical inquiry as scientific training. *The Counseling Psychologist, 19*, 431-453.

Ibrahim, F., & Arredondo, P. M. (1986). Ethical standards for cross-cultural counseling: Counselor preparation, practice, assessment, and research. *Journal of Counseling and Development, 64*, 349-351.

Ihle, G. M., Sodowsky, G. R., & Kwan, K. L. (1996). Worldviews of women: Comparisons between White-American clients, White-American counselors, and Chinese international students. *Journal of Counseling and Development.*

Ivey, A. E. (1977). Cultural expertise: Toward a systematic outcome criteria in counseling and psychological education. *The Personnel & Guidance Journal, 55*, 296-302.

Jöreskog, K. G., & Sorbom, D. (1988). *LISREL 7: A guide to the program and applications.* Chicago: SPSS.

Katz, J. H. (1985). The sociopolitical nature of counseling. *The Counseling Psychologist, 13*, 615-624.

Kwan, K. L., Sodowsky, G. R., & Ihle, G. M. (1994). Worldviews of Chinese international students: An extension and new findings. *Journal of College Student Development, 35*, 190-197.

LaFromboise, T. D., Coleman, H. L., & Hernandez, A. (1991). Development and factor structure of the Cross-Cultural Counseling Inventory—Revised. *Professional Psychology: Research and Practice, 22*, 380-388.

LaFromboise, T. D., & Dixon, D. N. (1981). American Indian perceptions of trustworthiness in a counseling interview. *Journal of Counseling Psychology, 28*, 135-139.

Leong, F. T. L., & Kim, H. H. W. (1991). Going beyond cultural sensitivity on the road to multiculturalism: Using the Intercultural Sensitizer as a counselor training tool. *Journal of Counseling and Development, 70*, 106-111.

Lefly, H. P. (1987). Mental-health training across cultures. In P. Pedersen (Ed.), *Handbook of cross-cultural counseling and psychotherapy,* (pp. 259-266). New York: Praeger.

McRae, M. B., & Johnson, S. D. (1991). Toward training for competence in Multicultural Counselor Education. *Journal of Counseling and Development, 70*, 131-135.

Neimeyer, G. J., & Fukuyama, M. (1984). Exploring the content and structure of cross-cultural attitudes. *Counselor Education and Supervision, 23*, 214-224.

Osvold, L., & Sodowsky, G. R. (in press). Eating attitudes of Native American and African American women: Differences by race/ethnicity and acculturation. *Explorations in Ethnic Studies.*

Pearson, R. E. (1987). The recognition and use of natural support systems in cross-cultural counseling. In P. Pedersen (Ed.), *The handbook of cross-cultural counseling and psychotherapy*, (pp. 299-306). New York: Praeger.

Pedersen, P. (1987). Ten frequent assumptions of cultural bias in counseling. *Journal of Multicultural Counseling and Development*, 16-24.

Pedersen, P. (1987b). Intercultural criteria for mental health training. In P. Pedersen (Ed.), *Handbook of cross-cultural counseling and psychotherapy* (pp. 315-321). New York: Praeger.

Pedersen, P. (1988). *A handbook for developing multicultural awareness*. Alexandria, VA: American Association for Counseling and Development.

Ponce, F. Q., & Atkinson, D. R. (1989). Mexican-American acculturation, counselor ethnicity, counseling style, and perceived counselor credibility. *Journal of Counseling Psychology, 36*, 203-208.

Ponterotto, J. G., & Casas, J. M. (1987). In search of multicultural competence within counselor education programs. *Journal of Counseling and Development, 65*, 430-434.

Ponterotto, J. G., & Furlong, M. J. (1985). Evaluation of counselor effectiveness: A critical review of rating instruments. *Journal of Counseling Psychology, 32*, 597-616.

Ridley, C. R., Mendoza, D. W., & Kanitz, B. E. (1994). Multicultural training: Reexamination, operationalization, and integration. *The Counseling Psychologist, 22*, 227-289.

Smith, E. J. (1982). Counseling psychology in the marketplace: The status of ethnic minorities. *The Counseling Psychologist, 10*(2), 61-68.

Sodowsky, G. R. (1991). Effects of culturally consistent counseling tasks on American and international student observers' perception of counselor credibility. *Journal of Counseling and Development, 69*, 253-256.

Sodowsky, G. R., Kuo-Jackson, P. Y., & Loya, G. J. (in press). Outcome of training in the philosophy of assessment: multicultural counseling competencies. In D. Pope-Davis & H. Coleman (Eds.), *Multicultural counseling competencies: Assessment, education and training, and supervision*. Newbury, CA: SAGE.

Sodowsky, G. R., Kwan, K. L., & Pannu, R. (1995). Ethnic identity of Asians in The United States. In J. G. Ponterotto et al. (Eds.), *Handbook of multicultural counseling* (pp.123-154). Thousand Oaks, CA: SAGE.

Sodowsky, G. R., & Lai, E. W. M. (in press). Asian immigrant variables and structural models of cross-cultural distress. In A. Booth (Ed.), *International migration and family change: The experience of U.S. immigrants*. Hillsdale, NJ: Lawrence Erlbaum Associates.

Sodowsky, G. R., Lai, E. W. M., & Plake, B. (1991). Moderating effects of sociocultural variables on acculturation attitudes of Hispanics and Asian Americans. *Journal of Counseling and Development, 70,* 194-204.

Sodowsky, G. R., Maguire, K., Johnson, P., Ngumba, W., & Kohles, R. (1994b). World views of White American, Mainland Chinese, Taiwanese, and African students: An investigation into between-group differences. *Journal of Cross-Cultural Psychology, 29,* 309-324.

Sodowsky, G. R., O'Dell, J., Hagemoser, S., Kwan, K. L., & Tonemah, D. (1993, August). *Symposium: Investigating multicultural counseling competencies: Training and service relevance.* Paper presented at the annual meeting of the American Psychological Association, Toronto, Canada.

Sodowsky, G. R., & Parr, G. (1991). Cultural consistency and counselor credibility. *Journal of Texas Personnel and Guidance Association, 19*(1), 33-38.

Sodowsky, G. R., & Taffe, R. C. (1991). Counselor trainees' analyses of multicultural counseling videotapes. *Journal of Multicultural Counseling and Development, 19*(3), 115-129.

Sodowsky, G. R., Taffe, R. C., Gutkin, T. B., & Wise, S. (1994a). Development of the Multicultural Counseling Inventory: A self-report measure of multicultural competencies. *Journal of Counseling Psychology, 41,* 137-148.

Sue, D. W., Arredondo, P., & McDavis, R. J. (1992). Multicultural competencies and standards: A call to the professional. *Journal of Counseling and Development, 70,* 477-486.

Sue, D. W., Bernier, J. E., Durran, A., Feinberg, L., Pedersen, P., Smith, E. J., & Vasquez-Nuttall, E. (1982). Position paper: Cross-cultural counseling competencies. *The Counseling Psychologist, 10*(2), 45-52.

Sue, D. W., & Sue, D. (1990). *Counseling the culturally different: Theory and practice* (2nd ed.). New York: John Wiley & Sons.

Sue, S. (1977). Community mental health services to minority groups: Some optimism, some pessimism. *American Psychologist, 32,* 616-624.

Sue, S., Akutsu, P. D., & Higashi, C. (1987). Training issues in conducting therapy with ethnic-minority-group clients. In P. Pedersen (Ed.), *Handbook of cross-cultural counseling and psychotherapy* (pp. 275-280). New York: Praeger.

Sue, S., & Zane, N. (1987). The role of culture and cultural techniques in psychotherapy. *The American Psychologist, 42,* 37-45.

Triandis, H. C. (1990). Cross-cultural studies of individualism and collectivism. In R. A. Dienstbier & J. J. Berman (Eds.), *Cross-cultural perspectives* (pp. 41-133). Lincoln, NE: University of Nebraska Press.

Vontress, C. E. (1971). Racial differences: Impediments to rapport. *Journal of Counseling Psychology, 18,* 7-13.

Wesley, E. (1973). Rigidity scale. In J. P. Robinson & P. R. Shaver (Eds.), *Measures of social psychological attitudes* (pp. 397-400). Ann Arbor, MI: Survey Research Center Institute for Social Research.

Wrenn, C. E. (1962). The culturally encapsulated counselor. *Harvard Educational Review, 32,* 444-449.

Zimmerman, J. E., & Sodowsky, G. R. (1993). The influence of acculturation on Mexican American drinking practices and implications for counseling. *Journal of Multicultural Counseling and Development, 21,* 22-35.

ASSESSING MULTICULTURAL COUNSELING COMPETENCIES USING THE MULTICULTURAL COUNSELING INVENTORY: A REVIEW OF THE RESEARCH

Donald B. Pope-Davis

The University of Maryland

Deanna Nielson

The University of Iowa

Since the publication of the position paper on cross-cultural counseling competencies of the Education and Training Committee of the American Psychological Association's Division of Counseling Psychology (Division 17; Sue, Bernier, Durran, Feinberg, Pedersen, Smith, & Vasquez-Nuttall, 1982), a great deal has been written about the need for increased training in cross-cultural counseling. Many textbooks and journal articles on multicultural[1] counseling theories and techniques have been published to provide guidance to trainers (e.g., D'Andrea, Daniels, & Heck, 1991; Leong & Kim, 1991; Pedersen, 1987, 1988; Sue & Sue, 1990) in the provision of services to counselor trainees. As a result, there seems to be some general agreement that

---

[1]As stated in Ponterotto, Rieger, Barrett, and Sparks (1994), although some authors have made a distinction between the terms *multicultural* and *cross-cultural* (e.g., Casas, 1984), they are used interchangeably in the area of counseling assessment and will be used interchangeably throughout this chapter.

all multicultural counseling training programs should provide experiences that allow trainees to develop competencies in three broad areas identified by Sue et al. (1982): (a) beliefs–attitudes, (b) knowledges, and (c) skills. More recently, these competency areas have been further elaborated by Sue, Arredondo, and McDavis (1992) to include (a) counselors' awareness of their own assumptions, values, and biases; (b) an understanding of the worldview of the culturally different client; and (c) the development of appropriate intervention strategies and techniques.

Together with the interest in theory and practice of multicultural counseling training is a growing interest in assessment of training effectiveness. It is within the three broad areas of awareness, knowledge, and skills that the majority of work in multicultural counseling competency assessment has been directed. Ponterotto, Rieger, Barrett, and Sparks (1994) reviewed four assessment instruments currently in use, identifying the strengths and limitations of each from a psychometric perspective. Three of the instruments (Cross-Cultural Counseling Inventory–Revised, LaFromboise, Coleman, & Hernandez, 1991; Multicultural Counseling Awareness Scale–Form B, Ponterotto, Sanchez, & Magids, 1991; Multicultural Counseling Inventory, Sodowsky, Taffe, Gutkin, & Wise, 1994) are based explicitly on the cross-cultural competencies identified by Sue et al. (1982), whereas the fourth (Multicultural Awareness-Knowledge-and-Skills Survey, D'Andrea et al., 1991) assesses competencies in these three broad categories without specific reference to the position paper. Yet, despite the specification of broad competency areas and the focus on assessment of multicultural competencies within these areas, "there is no clear consensus as to what constitutes a good multicultural training program and how the effects of such training are to be empirically assessed" (Ponterotto et al., 1994, p. 316).

While the debate regarding content and method of multicultural counseling training continues, there is a need to identify specific factors that may impact the development of multicultural competencies of trainees across training modalities. Utilizing survey methods, Pope-Davis and his colleagues have attempted to identify such factors across a variety of training situations using the Multicultural Counseling Inventory (MCI). The remainder of this chapter will examine the MCI as a tool for measuring multicultural counseling competencies based on results from the Pope-Davis studies. First, reliability of the MCI will be examined in comparison to the original Sodowsky et al. (1994) data. Next, results from the studies will be examined to identify variables associated with self-reported multicultural competencies. The chapter will then conclude with a discussion of implications for training and education as well as suggestions for future research.

RELIABILITY OF THE MCI

Pope-Davis and his colleagues have used the Multicultural Counseling Inventory (MCI) to examine the self-reported multicultural competencies of psychology graduate students (Ottavi, Pope-Davis, & Dings, 1994; Pope-Davis, Reynolds, Dings, & Nielson, 1995), counselors affiliated with university counseling centers (Pope-Davis & Ottavi, 1994), nursing students (Pope-Davis, Eliason, & Ottavi, 1994), and occupational therapists (Pope-Davis, Prieto, Whitaker, & Pope-Davis, 1993). The graduate student and counselor samples were obtained through national surveys. The sample of university center counselors (Pope-Davis & Ottavi, 1994) is a subsample of the group reported in Study 2 by Sodowsky et al. (1994). The nursing students were all enrolled in the same course at a midwestern university. The occupational therapists represent one western and two midwestern states (See Table 1).

Coefficient alpha reliabilities obtained in all the Pope-Davis studies are similar to those reported by Sodowsky et al. (1994), ranging from a low of .65 for the Relationship subscale (Pope-Davis et al., 1993) to a high of .82 for Skill (Pope-Davis et al., 1995). Thus, these studies provide further validation of the reliability of the MCI subscales (see Table 2).

Initial interscale correlational evidence reported by Sodowsky et al. (1994) suggested that the MCI subscales are relatively independent. However, in the Pope-Davis studies the interscale correlations among the four MCI subscales are somewhat higher overall than those reported by Sodowsky et al. (1994) with the exception of the Relationship subscale (see Table 3). Looking across all the Pope-Davis studies, the intercorrelations of Awareness with Skills (range: .37 to .50) and Knowledge (range: .36 to .68) are moderately higher, as is the intercorrelation between Skills and Knowledge (range: .46 to .65). These findings suggest that the four factors of the MCI are measuring different, but related constructs. This should not be surprising in that one's awareness of personal assumptions, values, and biases are generally believed to arise from exposure to different perspectives in these realms, which implies some level of understanding other worldviews. Further, the belief that an individual has awareness and knowledge of other cultures may lead a person to believe, whether rightly or wrongly, that he or she has some skill in working with others from different cultural backgrounds.

Table 1. Summary of MCI Studies.

MCI STUDIES	SAMPLE	VARIABLES MEASURED	SIGNIFICANT FINDINGS
Sodowsky, Taffe, Gutkin, & Wise (1994)	Study 1: statewide sample, 604 psychology students, counselors, & psychologists (95% White) Study 2: nationwide sample, 320 university center counselors (68% White)	Study 1: age; gender; ethnicity; degree held; years of mental health service; percentage multicultural work Study 2: age; ethnicity; degree held	Study 1: respondents who worked 50% or more in the MC area scored significantly higher on the Awareness & Relationship than respondents with less that 50% minority service (reported in Ponterotto et al. and Pope-Davis & Ottavi)
Ottavi, Pope-Davis, & Dings (1994)	128 White counseling graduate students; nationwide sample	age; gender; degree program; year in program; practicum; course work; workshop; supervision; WRIAS	demographic variables did not account for significant variance for any MCI subscales Awareness: course work, workshop, minority client hours, number of practica Skills & Knowledge: course work WRIAS Pseudo-Independence w/ALL; Autonomy w/Knowledge
Pope-Davis & Ottavi (1994)	220 university center counselors (76.8% White); nationwide sample	age; gender; ethnicity; highest degree held; minority group worked with most; percentage of work done in multicultural counseling	ethnicity influenced Knowledge, Awareness, and Relationship Asian Americans & Hispanics scored higher than Whites on Knowledge; African, Asian, & Hispanic Americans scored higher than Whites on Relationship
Pope-Davis, Reynolds, Dings, & Nielson (1995)	344 clinical and counseling psychology students; nationwide sample Clinical: 185 (81% White) Counseling: 159 (72% White)	age; gender; ethnicity; highest degree held; year in program; course work; workshop; practicum; supervision; minority client hours	Counseling: Awareness influenced by ethnicity; practicum, workshop & culturally diverse client contact Knowledge influenced by culturally diverse client contact Relationship influenced by ethnicity Clinical: Awareness influenced by ethnicity; course work, workshop, & mc supervision Knowledge influenced by ethnicity; course work & supervision Relationship influenced by ethnicity
Pope-Davis, Eliason, & Ottavi (1994)	120 undergraduate nursing students in a single course (96% White)	age; gender; ethnicity; class standing; course work; work experience	those with work experience scored higher on Knowledge & Skills
Pope-Davis, Prieto, Whitaker, & Pope-Davis (1993)	94 occupational therapists from three states (87% White)	age, gender, ethnicity, degree held, months of work experience, course work, workshop, minority client hours	more multicultural course work, workshop participation, minority client hours scored higher on Awareness highest degree held predictive of Knowledge

Table 2. Coefficient Alpha Reliabilities for the MCI Subscales by Study.

Study	Skill	Knowledge	Awareness	Relationship
Sodowsky, Taffe, Gutkin, & Wise (1994)				
(Study 1)	.83	.79	.83	.65
(Study 2)	.81	.80	.80	.67
Ottavi, Pope-Davis, & Dings (1994)	.77	.76	.70	.78
Pope-Davis & Ottavi (1994)	.81	.80	.80	.67
Pope-Davis, Reynolds, Dings, & Nielson (1995)	.82	.80	.77	.68
Pope-Davis, Eliason, & Ottavi (1994)	.81	.74	.76	.69
Pope-Davis, Prieto, Whitaker, & Pope-Davis (1993)	.77	.78	.78	.65

It is particularly interesting to examine the correlations reported in Study 2 of Sodowsky et al. (1994) and in Pope-Davis and Ottavi (1994), which is a subsample of the Study 2 data. The interscale correlations reported by Pope-Davis and Ottavi (1994) are higher, suggesting greater overlap in the subscales. However, Pope-Davis and Ottavi (1994) reported that 76.8% of their sample identified themselves as White, whereas Sodowsky et al. (1994) reported 68% White counselors for the larger sample. Although no other distinctions between the samples are reported, these results suggest the possibility that there may be different patterns of responding with regard to self-reported competencies related to the racial and ethnic background of the respondent. In other words, the higher correlations found in the Pope-Davis studies could be related to the greater homogeneity of the sample group. Further studies of the MCI with racially and ethnically diverse groups are needed to verify this hypothesis.

Although the results of the Pope-Davis studies generally support the validity of the MCI subscales, the higher reported interscale correlations lend support to the suggestion made by Ponterotto, Rieger, Barrett, and Sparks (1994) that the four-factor solution proposed by Sodowsky et al. (1994) may not provide the ideal solution. Sodowsky et al. (1994) also reported in the confirmatory factor analysis of Study 2 data moderately high to high correlations (.30 to .62) among the factors of a proposed higher order four-factor oblique model. They conclude "It is not clear whether the responses on the MCI are driven by a general, higher order factor rather than by four specific factors" (p. 146). They also add that "until further research

Table 3. MCI Subscale Intercorrelations Reported by Study.

Study	Subscales	Skill	Knowledge	Awareness	Relationship
Sodowsky, Taffe, Gutkin, & Wise (1994)					
Study 1: counseling, school, & clinical psychology students; psychologist and counselors	Skills	-			
	Knowledge	.41	-		
	Awareness	.22	.39	-	
	Relationship	.41	.18	.21	-
Study 2: counselors affiliated with university counseling centers	Skills	-			
	Knowledge	.31	-		
	Awareness	.17	.28	-	
	Relationship	.31	.16	.17	-
Ottavi, Pope-Davis, & Dings (1994) graduate psychology students	Skills	-			
	Knowledge	.65	-		
	Awareness	.50	.50	-	
	Relationship	.40	.18	.28	-
Pope-Davis & Ottavi (1994) counselors affiliated with university counseling centers	Skills	-			
	Knowledge	.49	-		
	Awareness	.37	.56	-	
	Relationship	.43	.27	.51	-

Table 3. (continued)

Study	Subscales	Skill	Knowledge	Awareness	Relationship
Pope-Davis, Reynolds, Dings, & Nielson (1995) counseling psychology students (data obtained from the authors; not previously reported)	Skills	-			
	Knowledge	.57	-		
	Awareness	.38	.50	-	
	Relationship	.31	.20	.27	-
clinical psychology students	Skills	-			
	Knowledge	.46	-		
	Awareness	.42	.68	-	
	Relationship	.38	.17	.31	-
Pope-Davis, Eliason, & Ottavi (1994) nursing students	Skills	-			
	Knowledge	.52	-		
	Awareness	.42	.36	-	
	Relationship	.24	.18	.17	-
Pope-Davis, Prieto, Whitaker, & Pope-Davis (1993) occupational therapists	Skills	-			
	Knowledge	.51	-		
	Awareness	.37	.47	-	
	Relationship	.29	.02	.13	-

clarifies this issue, subscales as well as the full scale of the MCI should be scored in training and applied settings" (p. 146). Further factor analysis with larger, heterogeneous samples may be necessary to test the factor structure of the MCI.

Although the correlational evidence from these studies does not clearly substantiate the four-factor solution proposed by Sodowsky et al. (1994), this does not preclude the examination of the relationship between the MCI subscales and other factors believed to influence perceptions of one's own multicultural competencies. To explore factors that may be related to multicultural counseling competencies, Pope-Davis and his colleagues have looked primarily at demographic, educational, and clinical variables. Additionally, Ottavi et al. (1994) have examined racial identity attitudes of White counseling psychology graduate students as they relate to the multicultural counseling competencies as measured by the MCI. Findings from these various studies will be reviewed within these broad categories before presenting an overall summary of findings.

DEMOGRAPHIC VARIABLES

Gender, age, and ethnicity were assessed in all studies reported by Pope-Davis and his colleagues. No gender or age differences in self-reported competencies were found in any of these studies. However, Pope-Davis and Ottavi (1994) and Pope-Davis, Reynolds, Dings, & Nielson (1995) reported significant differences in some MCI subscale scores based on reported racial and ethnic affiliation of the participants.

Pope-Davis and Ottavi (1994) surveyed 220 counselors affiliated with university counseling centers throughout the United States. Racial and ethnic group affiliation reported by respondents included African American (11.8%), Asian American (6.8%), Hispanic (4.5%), and White (76.8%). Using multivariate analyses of variance, a significant main effect was found for ethnicity. Follow-up ANOVAs on the individual subscales revealed significant overall ethnicity effects for the Knowledge [$F(3,216) = 5.21, p <.01$], Awareness [$F(3,216) = 20.23, p <.0001$], and Relationship [$F(3,216) = 10.71, p <.0001$] subscales. Tukey pairwise comparison indicated that Asian-American and Hispanic counselors scored significantly higher on the Knowledge subscale than did White counselors. African-American, Asian-American, and Hispanic counselors scored significantly higher on the Awareness and Relationship subscales than did the White counselors. Mean subscale scores and standard deviations of the four groups are reported in Table 4.

Table 4. MCI Subscale Means and Standard Deviations Reported by Study.

Study	Sample	Skill	Knowledge	Awareness	Relationship
Ottavi, Pope-Davis, & Dings (1994) graduate psychology students	Total	3.30 (.32)	3.09 (.39)	2.41 (.49)	2.88 (.45)
Pope-Davis & Ottavi (1994) counselors affiliated with university counseling centers	White	3.52 (.29)	3.15 (.38)	2.65 (.50)	2.95 (.41)
	African-American	3.57 (.29)	3.31 (.35)	3.16 (.41)***	3.28 (.45)***
	Asian-American	3.45 (.32)	3.40 (.29)*	3.24 (.34)***	3.30 (.34)***
	Hispanic	3.61 (.21)	3.48 (.41)*	3.45 (.36)***	3.29 (.35)***
Pope-Davis, Reynolds, Dings, & Nielson (1995) graduate psychology students	Counseling Psych.	3.35 (.35)*	2.67 (.48)**	3.20 (.38)**	2.99 (.43)
	Clinical Psych	3.25 (.34)	2.42 (.60)	3.03 (.49)	3.00 (.45)
	Total	3.29 (.35)	2.54 (.56)	3.11 (.45)	2.99 (.44)
Pope-Davis, Eliason, & Ottavi (1994) nursing students	No work experience	2.39 (.33)	2.79 (.38)	2.32 (.45)	3.06 (.41)
	With work exper.	3.21 (.40)**	3.00 (.38)**	2.34 (.57)	3.07 (.49)
	Total	3.06 (.37)	2.86 (.39)	2.32 (.49)	3.06 (.43)

$* p < .05$ $** p < .01$ $** p < .0001$

Counselors in all racial and ethnic minority groups reported high levels of skill in working with minority clients. Given the variability in self-assessed Awareness, Knowledge, and Relationship it is curious that there is no similar variability in perceived skill. It may be that counselors believe they possess a sufficiently diverse repertoire of techniques which are appropriate with clients from a variety of backgrounds. A second explanation may be that the counselors have over-rated their multicultural counseling skills. If awareness and knowledge of cultural differences precede development of appropriate skills, as is implied in the literature, this explanation seems plausible. Alternatively, it may be that the items of the MCI intended to assess multicultural counseling skills are not being interpreted by participants in the way intended by the authors, or that the skills items are more general counseling competencies and not specifically related to work with culturally diverse clients. Finally, because these are practicing counselors, it may be that the respondents have received feedback from clients, supervisors, and colleagues indicating that they are effective with their culturally diverse clients. Thus, the self-ratings could be an accurate reflection of their counseling skills regardless of their multicultural awareness and knowledge.

In the only other study to report differences in MCI subscales, Pope-Davis, Reynolds, Dings, and Nielson (1995) surveyed 344 graduate students in APA-affiliated counseling and clinical psychology programs nationwide. Racial and ethnic group affiliation reported by participants for the total sample was African American (10%), American Indian (1%), Asian American (5%), Hispanic (5%), and White (77%). Subscales, however, were only reported by program area.

In this study, data were analyzed separately for counseling and clinical psychology students. A significant main effect for program affiliation was found [$F(4,331) = 5.18$, $p < .001$]. Follow-up analysis revealed significant program effects for Skills [$F(1,341) = 6.88$, $p < .01$], Knowledge [$F(1.336) = 11.76$, $p < .001$], and Awareness [$F(1,340) = 17.02$, $p < .0001$]. T-test comparisons indicated that counseling psychology students scored significantly higher than clinical psychology students on these three subscales (Table 4).

Pope-Davis et al. (1995) were also interested in exploring variables predictive of multicultural counseling competencies. Hierarchical regression analyses were used to determine variability accounted for in prediction of each MCI subscale score within each program (counseling and clinical). Age, gender, and racial and ethnic group affiliation were the demographic variables assessed. Racial and ethnic group affiliation was the only significant demographic predictor for either group. Among counseling psychology students, racial and ethnic affiliation was a unique predictor of scores for Awareness ($t = 3.03$, $p < .01$) and Relationship ($t = 4.08$, $p < .001$). Together with age and gender, these demographic variables accounted for a statistically significant amount of the variance observed in subscale scores for Awareness [8%; $F(3,131) = 4.75$, $p < .01$] and Relationship [11%; $F(3,131) = 6.25$, $p < .01$]. For clinical psychology students, racial and ethnic affiliation predicted scores for Knowledge ($t = 3.42$, $p < .001$), Awareness ($t = 5.74$, $p < .001$), and Relationship ($t = 2.63$, $p < .001$). Demographic variables accounted for a statistically significant portion of the variance only for the Knowledge [5%; $F(3,163) = 4.00$; $p < .01$] and Awareness [16%; $F(3,163) = 11.35$, $p < .001$} subscales.

In both studies (Pope-Davis & Ottavi, 1994; Pope-Davis et al., 1995), racial and ethnic affiliation was significantly related to scores on the Awareness, Relationship, and, in some cases, Knowledge subscales. Pope-Davis and Ottavi (1994) is the only study to examine specific racial and ethnic group affiliation of respondents as it relates to self-reported multicultural competencies. However, given the similar pattern of findings in Pope-Davis et al. (1995), it is reasonable to suggest that non-White counselors and trainees generally perceived themselves as having greater awareness and knowledge of cross-cultural factors that may affect their racially and ethnically diverse clients and be more comfortable with managing issues of culture as these may affect the counseling relationship. More research with diverse counselors and trainees is needed to replicate and extend these findings.

EDUCATIONAL AND CLINICAL VARIABLES

The growing body of literature on teaching theory and methods in multicultural counseling assumes that education can have an effect on developing appropriate awareness, knowledge, and skills among trainees. Along with formal course work, counselor training occurs in seminars and workshops and includes practical training such as practica and supervision in clinical settings. Work experience itself provides yet another opportunity for obtaining "on the job" training.

Completion of multicultural course work and seminars/workshops were assessed in all of the Pope-Davis studies reported with the exception of Pope-Davis and Ottavi (1994). Practica and clinical supervision were assessed among graduate students by Ottavi et al. (1994) and Pope-Davis et al. (1995). Other educational and experiential variables assessed included highest degree held (Ottavi et al., 1994; Pope-Davis & Ottavi, 1994; Pope-Davis et al., 1995; Pope-Davis et al., 1993), year of study in current degree program (Ottavi et al., 1994; Pope-Davis et al., 1995), work with minority clients (Pope-Davis & Ottavi, 1994; Pope-Davis et al., 1995; Pope-Davis et al., 1993), and length of work experience (Pope-Davis et al., 1994; Pope-Davis et al., 1993).

The only study to obtain significant findings regarding degree status was Pope-Davis et al. (1993). Highest degree held was the only significant predictor of scores on the Knowledge subscale among a sample of occupational therapists, accounting for 10% of the score variability (F Change = 9.91, p <.01). Correlations indicated that occupational therapists who held higher degrees reported more knowledge of racial and cultural variables and their influences on patients.

Likewise, Pope-Davis et al. (1994) was the only study to report significant findings related to general work experiences (not necessarily with minority clients). Nursing students who had some work experience reported higher levels of multicultural Skills and Knowledge than students with no work experience (See Table 4). "Students with work experience reported more skills in interpersonal communication, cultural consideration, and knowledge of cultural factors and appropriateness when interacting with minority clients" (Pope-Davis et al., 1994, p. 33). No other significant findings were reported for this study.

The major findings with regard to educational/clinical variables and multicultural competencies related to multicultural course work, workshops and seminars, practicum and supervision, and experience with minority clients. Results in these four areas will be examined across all studies in which the variables were assessed. Implications of the findings and suggestions for future research are presented.

MULTICULTURAL COURSE WORK

In all the studies cited, multicultural course work was assessed using four categories of response: (a) never had a course in which multicultural issues were covered; (b) had multicultural issues covered in other counseling courses; (c) completed one course in multicultural counseling; and (d) completed two or more courses in multicultural counseling. Multicultural course work was predictive of MCI subscale scores in three studies (Ottavi et al., 1994; Pope-Davis et al., 1995; Pope-Davis et al., 1993) with higher subscale scores obtained by participants reporting more multicultural course work.

Ottavi et al. (1994) reported course work was a uniquely significant predictor of Skills ($t = 3.87$, p <.01), Knowledge ($t = 3.94$, p <.001), and Awareness ($t = 4.10$, p <.001) scores among their sample of White counseling graduate students. Pope-Davis et al. (1995) found that multicultural course work was a significant predictor for clinical psychology graduate students on the Knowledge ($t = 2.95, p < .01$) and Awareness ($t = 3.44, p < .001$) subscales, but not a uniquely significant predictor of scores for counseling psychology students on any subscale. Pope-Davis et al. (1993) reported that multicultural course work contributed significantly toward predicting variance accounted for on the Awareness subscale beyond that accounted for by percentage of minority patients worked with for occupational therapists (10%; F Change = 16.98, $p < .001$).

The categorical way in which completion of multicultural course work was assessed in these studies provides no information regarding such important factors as the length, content, depth of coverage, setting, or orientation to multicultural counseling provided in the courses completed by participants. Thus, it is difficult to generalize from these findings with regard to the specific effects of course work on developing multicultural competencies. However, at a minimum it seems that completion of some multicultural course work had a positive effect on developing multicultural sensitivity, interactions, and advocacy in general life experiences and professional activities of the participants (assessed by the Awareness subscale). Future studies should attempt to assess specific information regarding the multicultural course work completed by participants, such as content areas covered, orientation of the course (e.g., culture-specific or culture-general; skills-based; overview/survey), depth of coverage, and length of the experience (e.g., contact hours).

MULTICULTURAL WORKSHOPS/SEMINARS

Workshops and seminars are another common means for providing training, particularly among practicing professionals. They are also typically more time-limited, yet they may provide an opportunity for more focused study and/or discussion of issues on a specific topic or within a limited scope as compared to course work. Thus, the effect on development of multicultural competencies attributable to participation in workshops or seminars may be unique.

Participation in multicultural workshops or seminars, assessed in the same three studies (Ottavi et al., 1994; Pope-Davis et al., 1995; Pope-Davis et al., 1993), again related to scores on the Awareness subscale. Ottavi et al. (1994) reported that the number of workshop hours uniquely predicted Awareness among White graduate counseling students ($t = 2.51, p < .05$). Using a categorical variable of participation in multicultural workshops or seminars, Pope-Davis et al. (1995) reported similar findings on the Awareness subscale for counseling (t = 2.59, p <.05) and clinical (t = 2.13, p <.05) psychology graduate students. Pope-Davis et al. (1993) reported that participation in multicultural workshops or seminars accounted for an additional 5% of the variance accounted for in the Awareness subscale scores of occupational therapists (F Change = 5.33, p <.05).

These results demonstrate more clearly that participation in time-limited training experiences such as multicultural workshops and seminars only impacted areas related to increasing multicultural Awareness of the participants. These time-limited training strategies may not be sufficient for imparting more in-depth knowledge or skills related to multicultural competency development. Again, the specific content and intent (e.g., developing awareness vs. skill development) of workshops and seminars completed could be assessed in future research to determine the effectiveness of these methods of presenting multicultural information.

PRACTICA AND CLINICAL SUPERVISION

Practica and supervision provide a distinct type of educational experience combining instruction, practice, and evaluative feedback. Ideally, practica provide an opportunity for the trainee to use the knowledge obtained from course work in the discipline and to practice the skills being developed. Thus, practica provide a unique opportunity to develop multicultural skills and to "test" developing awareness and knowledge as these relate to work with racially and ethnically diverse clients. Practicum experience and clinical supervision were assessed in the studies of graduate students (Ottavi et al., 1994; Pope-Davis et al., 1995).

Ottavi et al. (1994) found that the number of practica completed uniquely and significantly predicted scores on the Awareness subscale (t = -2.02, p <.05) among White counseling graduate students. Similarly, Pope-Davis et al. (1995) reported participation in practica was a uniquely significant predictor of Awareness scores among counseling psychology graduate students (t = -2.17, p <.05), but not among clinical psychology students. Practicum experience was not predictive of scores on any other subscales in either study.

Discussion of multicultural issues in supervision was predictive of Awareness (t = 2.75, p <.01) and Knowledge (t = 3.04, p <.01) subscale scores among clinical psychology graduate students. However, it was not found to be a significant predictor of multicultural competencies among counseling psychology students by either Pope-Davis et al. (1995) or Ottavi et al. (1994).

It is difficult to interpret these findings given the limited information available regarding participants' involvement in practica and supervision. As with course work, workshops, and seminars, too little is known about the definitions, focus, length, or setting of the practica and supervision experiences of the participants. Additionally, these experiences occur within a more comprehensive training program, which includes other forms of instruction. It may be feasible to speculate that there is greater variability between clinical and counseling psychology programs than there is within these program areas; this may account for the differential findings in the types of educational experiences that impact development of multicultural counseling competencies. However, not enough data exist to support this generalization. At best, these results suggest an avenue for further exploration.

EXPERIENCE WITH MINORITY CLIENTS

It is not unreasonable to expect that experience with minority clients may itself lead to greater multicultural competence. Three studies (Ottavi et al., 1994; Pope-Davis et al., 1995; Pope-Davis et al., 1993) reported a relationship between work with minority clients and MCI subscale scores.

Ottavi et al. (1994) found that contact hours with racial and ethnic minority clients was a uniquely significant predictor of Awareness ($t = 2.41$, $p < .05$) for counseling psychology students. Likewise, Pope-Davis et al. (1995) reported contact hours with minority clients was a unique predictor of Awareness ($t = 4.52$, $p < .001$) and Knowledge ($t = 2.59$, $p < .05$) for counseling psychology students. However, this result did not follow for clinical psychology students, who reported fewer contact hours with minority clients. Pope-Davis et al. (1993) reported that, of all demographic and educational variables assessed among their sample of occupational therapists, proportion of minority patients worked with (reported as percentage of total patients) accounted for the most variance in predicting multicultural Awareness (40%; F Change = 58.43, $p < .001$).

These results suggest that experience with racial and ethnic minority clients may influence multicultural Awareness, but is less predictive of development of other multicultural competencies. Thus, it could be hypothesized that competencies in the other three areas—Knowledge, Skills, and Relationship—require other educational interventions.

RACIAL IDENTITY ATTITUDES

In addition to demographic, educational, and clinical variables hypothesized to relate to multicultural counseling competencies, Ottavi et al. (1994) examined the relationship between scores on the MCI and White racial identity attitudes of counseling psychology graduate students. Sabnani, Ponterotto, and Borodovsky (1991) suggested that students' White racial identity development strongly influences the attainment of multicultural counseling competencies. Ottavi et al. (1994) used the White Racial Identity Attitude Scale (WRIAS; Helms & Carter, 1990) to assess the stages of racial identity attitudes as proposed by Helms (1984). The authors were interested in determining if White racial identity attitudes could account for additional variance in self-reported multicultural counseling competencies beyond that accounted for by demographic and educational variables.

The Pseudo-Independence subscale of the WRIAS had a significant effect on prediction of all the MCI subscale scores even when demographic and educational variables had already been entered into the regression equation (Skills: $t = 3.07$, $p < .01$; Knowledge: $t = 2.05$, $p < .05$; Awareness: t = 3.21, $p < .01$; Relationship: $t = 4.29$, $p < .001$). In addition, the Autonomy subscale was a unique predictor of the Knowledge subscale score ($t = 2.46$, $p < .05$). In each case, the WRIAS accounted for 11% to 19% additional variance in the prediction of MCI subscale scores beyond that attributable to demographic and educational variables. These findings substantiate the Sabnani et al. (1991) model of multicultural counseling competency development and suggest that further study of racial identity attitudes may be an important area for future research in the assessment of multicultural counseling competencies.

SUMMARY AND DISCUSSION

Results from the educational and clinical data reported by Pope-Davis and his colleagues provide further evidence of the predictive validity of the MCI. In each case where significant effects were reported, results were in the expected directions. More multicultural course work, workshop and seminar participation, practicum and supervision experience, and minority client contact were associated with greater assessed multicultural competence. Additionally, the findings based on the ethnicity of participants suggest that racial and ethnic minority participants reported higher levels of multicultural competencies, a finding that could be expected given their life experience.

The educational and clinical variables assessed were most often predictive of scores on the multicultural Awareness subscale. Awareness was influenced by amount of multicultural course work, participation in workshops and seminars, work with minority clients, and to some extent by participation in practicum and supervision. Knowledge competencies were primarily influenced by greater participation in multicultural course work and by ethnicity of the participant. Participant ethnicity was the only variable found to predict Relationship competencies, suggesting that current training methods do not help trainees address cross-cultural counseling process issues involved in working with minority clients. Only two studies (Ottavi et al., 1994; Pope-Davis et al., 1994) reported significant findings related to multicultural Skills, both in the predicted direction.

In all studies for which mean scale scores are reported, self-reported Skills received the highest competency rating of the four subscales (except Pope-Davis et al. [1994] nursing students with no work experience). This result is somewhat surprising given that, based on models of multicultural development, multicultural skills are hypothesized to result from increased multicultural awareness and knowledge (Carney & Kahn, 1989; Pedersen, 1988). It is the possible that participants answered these questions based on anticipated rather than actual behavior. It is also possible that participants have developed some level of skill in working with people from diverse backgrounds, but lack self-confidence in their cross-cultural knowledge and awareness. A similar explanation is that participants had not received any feedback to suggest they are less effective with minority clients, and thus assume that they are highly competent in providing service to these clients in spite of the counselors' less-well-developed multicultural awareness and knowledge. Alternatively, the Skills items of the MCI may have been interpreted differently by participants than was intended by the authors of the instrument.

Multicultural educational and clinical experiences are expected to influence the acquisition of competencies in knowledge, awareness, and skills related to cross-cultural counseling. However, none of the reported studies examined such factors as depth and content of material covered or length of courses, workshops, and seminars; educational and clinical settings; theoretical orientation of instructors and supervisors; and other life experiences that may influence cross-cultural competencies (e.g., knowledge of other languages, time spent living within a cultural environment different from one's childhood background). The lack of consensus as to what constitutes a good multicultural training program, as well as the lack of a clear theoretical basis for the selection of other experiential variables that may influence development of multicultural competencies limit the current study of multicultural competency assessment.

The work of Pope-Davis and his colleagues has provided a needed beginning in the assessment of multicultural competencies and suggested fruitful directions for future research. In addition, these studies have implications for the training of psychologists and mental health counselors.

REFERENCES

Carney, C. G., & Kahn, K. B. (1989). Building competencies for effective cross-cultural counseling: A developmental view. *The Counseling Psychologist, 12,* 111-119.

Casas, J. M. (1984). Policy, training, and research in counseling psychology: The racial and ethnic minority perspective. In S. D. Brown & R. Lent (Eds.), *Handbook of counseling psychology* (pp. 785-831). New York: Wiley.

D'Andrea, M., Daniels, J., & Heck, R. (1991). Evaluating the impact of multicultural training. *Journal of Counseling and Development, 70,* 143-150.

Helms, J. E. (1984). Toward a theoretical model of the effects of race on counseling: A Black and White model. *The Counseling Psychologist, 12,* 153-165.

Helms, J. E., & Carter, R. T. (1990). Development of the White Racial Identity Inventory. In J. E. Helms (Ed.), *Black and White racial identity: Theory, research, and practice* (pp. 67-80). Westport, CT: Greenwood Press.

LaFromboise, T. D., Coleman, H. L. K., & Hernandez, A. (1991). Development and factor structure of the Cross-Cultural Counseling Inventory—Revised. *Professional Psychology: Research and Practice, 22,* 380-388.

Leong, F. T. L., & Kim, H. H. W. (1991). Going beyond cultural sensitivity on the road to multiculturalism: Using the Intercultural Sensitizer as a counselor training tool. *Journal of Counseling and Development, 70,* 112-118.

Ottavi, T. M., Pope-Davis, D. B., & Dings, J. G. (1994). Relationship between White racial identity attitudes and self-reported multicultural counseling competencies. *Journal of Counseling Psychology, 41,* 149-154.

Pedersen, P. (1988). *A handbook for developing multicultural awareness.* Alexandria, VA: American Counseling Association.

Pedersen, P. (1987). *Handbook of cross-cultural counseling and psychotherapy.* New York: Praeger.

Ponterotto, J. G., Rieger, B. P., Barrett, A., & Sparks, R. (1994). Assessing multicultural counseling competence: A review of instrumentation. *Journal of Counseling and Development, 72,* 316-322.

Ponterotto, J. G., Sanchez, C. M., & Magids, D. M. (1991, August). *Initial development and validation of the Multicultural Counseling Awareness Scale (MCAS)*. Paper presented at the annual meeting of the American Psychological Association, San Francisco, CA.

Pope-Davis, D. B., Eliason, M. J., & Ottavi, T. M. (1994). Are nursing students multiculturally competent? An exploratory investigation. *Journal of Nursing Education, 33*, 31-33.

Pope-Davis, D. B., & Ottavi, T. M. (1994). Examining the association between self-reported multicultural counseling competencies and demographic variables among counselors. *Journal of Counseling and Development, 72*, 651-654.

Pope-Davis, D. B., Prieto, L. R., Whitaker, C. M., & Pope-Davis, S. A. (1993). Exploring multicultural competencies of occupational therapists: Implications for education and training. *American Journal of Occupational Therapy, 47*, 838-844.

Pope-Davis, D. B., Reynolds, A. L., Dings, J. G., & Nielson, D. (1995). Examining multicultural counseling competencies of graduate students in psychology. *Professional Psychology: Research and Practice, 26*, 322-329.

Sabnani, H. B., Ponterotto, J. G., & Borodovsky, L. G. (1991). White racial identity development and cross-cultural counselor training: A stage model. *The Counseling Psychologist, 19*, 72-102.

Sodowsky, G. R., Taffe, R. C., Gutkin, T. B., & Wise, S. L. (1994). Development of the Multicultural Counseling Inventory: A self-report measure of multicultural competencies. *Journal of Counseling Psychology, 41*, 137-148.

Sue, D. W., Arredondo, P., & McDavis, R. J. (1992). Multicultural counseling competencies and standards: A call to the profession. *Journal of Counseling and Development, 70*, 477-486.

Sue, D. W., Bernier, J. E., Durran, A., Feinberg, L., Pedersen, P. B., Smith, E. J., & Vasquez-Nuttall, E. (1982). Position paper: Cross-cultural counseling competencies. *The Counseling Psychologist, 10*, 45-52.

Sue, D. W., & Sue, D. (1990). *Counseling the culturally different: Theory and practice*. New York: Wiley.

Epilogue

The book has shown the use of a combination of approaches to understand the nature of a problem: traditional diagnosis and standardized assessment, cultural and racial explanations as alternative hypotheses, clinical judgement based on a decision-tree involving cross-cultural and indigenous frameworks, quantitative-qualitative methods of data analyses, and the use of multicultural paper-and-pencil and projective tests. The attitudes and cognitive-affective tests presented or referenced in the book, in addition to being formally administered, could be used as springboards for collaborative discussions with clients and psychology trainees in order to gain a better understanding of their values and assumptions and, by inference, their modes of problem-solving in a multicultural society. We look forward to these new instruments' future refinements, psychometric enhancements, and diverse sampling of subjects.

The measurement of acculturation attitudes is important in counseling and clinical psychology. Its importance to applications has been affirmed by the 1994 *Diagnostic and Statistical Manual of Mental Disorders* (DSM-IV), and the 1993 *APA Guidelines for Service Providers to Ethnic, Linguistic, and Culturally Diverse Populations*, the latter stating that psychologists must document culturally relevant factors in client records, including number of generations in the country, number of years in the country, fluency in English, community resources, level of education, and level of stress related to acculturation. Because a multicultural book is incomplete without addressing issues of acculturation, Appendices A and B provide measurement and research information on acculturation scales. Appendix A summarizes select psychometric properties of and predictions for frequently referenced acculturation scales developed for Hispanic/Latino and Asian groups in the U.S. Appendix B summarizes select counseling psychology studies showing the effects of acculturation on client reactions. At the end of each Appendix is a reference list of the authors of the instruments and related research studies.

We hope this work, *Multicultural Measurement in Counseling and Clinical Psychology*, will add to the long and colorful history of psychological assessment.

> Gargi Roysircar Sodowsky
> James C. Impara
> University of Nebraska-Lincoln
> Spring 1996

Appendix A
Acculturation Instrumentation
Edward Wai Ming Lai and Gargi Roysircar Sodowsky

Table 1

14 Acculturation Scales: Information about Respondents, Administration Procedures, Initial Scale Development, Reliability, and Validity

| Authors | Respondents | | | | | Scale Development | Reliability (rel.) | Validity |
	Ethnicity	Size	Age	Sampling	Geograp. Location	Characteristics			
Burnam et al. (1987) LAECA N of items =26	Mexican Americans	1245	18 or older	Random sampling	California	General population	Factor analysis Internal consistency test Subscales: 1) Language 2) Social Activities 3) Ethnic Background	Coefficient alpha=97 Corrected item-total correlations ranged from .41 to .92	Criterion-related validity: 1) differentiation by generation 2) age and sex had complicated relations with acculturation Respective factor variances=62%, 6%, & 5% Factor loadings ranged from .43 to .93
Cuellar et al. (1980) ARSMA N of items =20	Mexican Americans, Mexicans, & Anglos	192 17 13 T=222	M=32	Recruitment	Mainly Texas	Psychiatric patients, hospital staff & students	A priori Factor analysis Internal consistency test Subscales: 1) Language 2) Ethnic Identity & Generation 3) Cultural Heritage & Exposure 4) Ethnic Interaction	Coefficient alphas=.88 & .81 Test-retest rel.=.72 & .80 Rater rel.=.89	Criterion-related validity: differentiation by staff ratings, language tests, and generation. Concurrent validity: 1) Correlation with Behavioral Acculturation Scale (rho=.76) 2) Correlation with Biculturation Inventory (rho=.77) Respective factor variances= 64.6%, 18.9%, 11.4%, & 5.2% Factor loadings ranged from .50 to .91

Table 1 continues

Table 1 continued.

Authors	Ethnicity	Size	Respondents Age	Sampling	Geograp. Location	Characteristics	Scale Development	Reliability (rel.)	Validity
Deyo et al. (1985) N of items =4	Mexican Americans, & Anglos	1782 1103 T=2885	25-64	Random sampling & recruitment	Texas	Medical patients & general population	Scalogram analysis Scale: 1) Language	Guttman coefficient of reproductivity=.97, .97, & .96 Coefficient of scalability= .89, .90, & .81	Construct validity: Correlation between language scores and interviewers' rating is .79 Criterion-related validity: Differentiation by ethnic groups, country of birth, generation, and ethnic density of neighborhood
Garcia & Lega (1979) CBIQ N of items =8	Mainly Cubans & non-Cuban Hispanics	210 62 T=272	M=37.3 & 32.8	Recruit-ment	Florida, New Jersey	General population	Pilot study Expert rating Factor analysis Internal consistency test Scale: 1) Cuban Ethnic Identity	Coefficient alpha=.84	Criterion-related validity: Differentiation between Cuban and non-Cuban on the item of Cuban identity Factor variance=48.8% Factor loadings ranged from .24 to .81
Lang et al. (1982) GAS N of items =9	Latino	270	25-75	Random sampling	California	General population	A priori Subscales: 1) Generation 2) Years of Education 3) Percent of life in U.S. 4) Language	Not reported	Not reported
Marin et al. (1987) N of items =12	Hispanics Anglos	363 228 T=691	M=31.2 M=38.8	Recruit-ment	California	General population	Factor analysis Internal consistency test Subscales: 1) Language & Ethnic Loyalty 2) Media 3) Ethnic Social Relations	Coefficient alphas=.92, .90, .86, .78	Criterion-related validity: Differentiation by generation, length of residence in the USA, self-rating, ethnic groups, and age. Respective factor variances=54.5%, 7%, & 6.1%

Table 1 continues

Table 1 continued

Authors	Respondents						Scale Development	Reliability (rel.)	Validity
	Ethnicity	Size	Age	Sampling	Geograp. Location	Characteristics			
Mendoza (1989) N of items =not reported	Mexican Americans, Anglos	Varied at different phases of the study	not reported	not reported	not reported	A priori Pilot study Expert ratings Factor analysis Cluster analysis Subscales: 1) Intra-Family Language 2) Extra-Family Language 3) Social Affiliation & Activities 4) Cultural Familiarity & Activities 5) Cultural Identification & Pride	Coefficient alphas=87, .91 .89, .84, & .84 Test-retest rel=.91, .88, .95 Parallel form equivalence= .80 & .77	Criterion-related validity Differentiation by generation, exposure to the mainstream culture, temporary/permanent residence, and observer rating
Olmedo & Padilla (1978) N of items =20	Chicanos, Anglos	254 670 T=924	not reported	Recruit- ment	California	High school students	A priori Factor analysis Subscales: 1) Nationality-Language 2) Socioeconomic Status 3) Semantic	Test-retest rel=.84, .89, .66	Employed a double cross- validation regression procedure, yielding stability of .66 & .80 Respective factor variances=50.8%, 29%, & 20.2%
Padilla (1980) N of items =185	Mexican Americans	381	18-70	Recruit- ment	California	General population	A priori Factor analysis Cluster analysis Subscales: A) Cultural Awareness has 4 factors 1) Cultural Heritage 2) Spouse's Cultural Heritage 3) Parent's Cultural Heritage & Pride 4) Perceived Discrimination B) Ethnic Loyalty has 4 factors 1) Language 2) Cultural Pride & Affiliation 3) Cultural Identification & Preference 4) Social Behavior Orientation	Coefficient alpha=90	Respective factor variances=89% & 11%

Table 1 continues

Table 1 continued

Authors	Ethnicity	Respondents			Geograp. Location	Characteristics	Scale Development	Reliability (rel.)	Validity
		Size	Age	Sampling					
Sodowsky & Plake (1991) AIRS N of items =34	International people	606 335 (pilot study) T=941	M=28 M=26	Recruit-ment	Nebraska Texas	College students, faculty, & staff	Factor analysis Internal consis-tency test Content analysis Subscales: 1) Perceived Prejudice 2) Social Customs 3) Language	For pilot study Coefficient alphas=.77 to .87 and Spearman-Brown split half rel=.75 to .82 For final study coefficient alpha=.89, .88, .79,& .82	Similar factor analysis results for both studies Respective factor variances= 20.6%, 8.1%, & 5.6% Factor loadings=.33 to .83 Criterion-related validity Differentiation by nationality group, residence status, years of residence, & religion.
Sodowsky et al. (1991) MMRS N of items =38	Hispanics, Asian Americans	133 149 T=282	M=24	Recruit-ment	Nebraska	College students, faculty, & staff	Confirmatory Factor analysis Test of generalizability Internal consis-tency test Subscales: 1) Perceived Prejudice 2) Social Customs 3) Language	Coefficient alphas=.95, .92, .89, & .94	For generalizability study, coefficients of factor congruence between MMRS and AIRS= .86, .54, & .80 Goodness of fit index of con-firmatory factor analysis =.73 Criterion-related validity: Differentiation by ethnic group, Asian culture subgroups, immigration status, religion, & generation
Sodowsky & Lai (In press) MMRS N of items =38	Asian Americans	200 T=282	M=27	Recruit-ment	Nebraska	College students, faculty, & staff	Internal consis-tency test Same subscales as above	Coefficient alphas=.89, .88, .79, .82	Structural equation modeling: GFI=.87; Adj GFI=.85; nonsignificant chi square (as required); significant path coefficients and t scores for extent of ethnic friendships, years of U.S. residence, and age at immigration, with acculturation as dependent variable; significant path coefficient and t score for acculturation, with acculturative distress as dependent variable

Table 1 continues

Table 1 continued

Authors	Ethnicity	Size	Respondents		Geograp. Location	Characteristics	Scale Development	Reliability (rel.)	Validity
			Age	Sampling					
Osvold & Sodowsky (In press) MMRS *N* of items =38	Native Americans, African Americans	34 28 T=62	*M*=25	Recruit-ment	Nebraska	High School students, human service professionals, & home makers	Internal consistency test Same subscales as above	Coefficient alphas=.82, .77, & .70	Criterion-related validity: Differences between more and less acculturated women on problematic eating attitudes and behaviors
Suinn et al. (1987) SL-ASIA *N* of items =21	Asian Americans	82	*M*=19	Recruit-ment	Colorado, California	College students	Internal consistent test Subscales: 1) Language 2) Ethnic Identity & Generation 3) Cultural Heritage & Exposure 4) Ethnic Interaction	Coefficient alpha=.88	Criterion-related validity: Differentiation by generation, length of residence in the USA, and self-rating
Suinn et al. (1992) SL-ASIA *N* of items =21	Asian Americans	284	*M*=24.4	Recruit-ment	Colorado	College students	Internal consistency test Principal Components Factor analysis 1) Reading/Writing/Cultural Preference 2) Ethnic Interaction 3) Affinity for Ethnic Identity and Pride 4) Generational Identity 5) Food preference	Coefficient alpha=.91	Concurrent validity: Significant correlations with years in U.S. school, age of entering U.S. school, length of residence in the USA, years lived in non-Asian neighborhood; significant effect of English as first language Factorial validity: Factors 1, 2, and 4 similar to ARSMA factors 2, 3, and 4 Self-rated acculturation related to language preferences and ethnicity of friends

Table 1 continues

Table 1 continued

| Authors | Respondents | | | | | | Scale Development | Reliability (rel.) | Validity |
	Ethnicity	Size	Age	Sampling	Geograp. Location	Characteristics			
Szapocznik et al. (1978) BAS N of items =24 VAS N of items =10	Cubans Anglos	265 201 T=466	14-85	Recruit- ment	Florida	General population	A priori Factor analysis Discriminant item validity Subscales: 1) Behavioral Acculturation Dimension 2) Relational Value Acculturation Dimension	Coefficient alpha=.97, .77 Parallel language forms (r=.88, .46) Test-retest rel=.96, .86	Criterion-related validity: Differentiation by years in the USA, age, and gender. Respective factor variances=48.1%, 13.5%, 13.4%, & 12.9% Items significantly discriminated between Cubans and non-Cubans and between high and low acculturated Cubans
Wong-Reiger & Quintana (1987) MAS N of items =21	South East Asians, Hispanics, & Anglos	170 174 90 T=434	Not reported	Recruit- ment	Oklahoma	General population	Pilot study Subscales: 1) Voluntary Behavior 2) Involuntary Behavior 3) Cognitions 4) Self-Identity	Not published	Criterion-related validity Differentiation between Canadian and foreign born students Concurrent validity Correlation with 2 acculturation scales (information unpublished)

REFERENCES

Burnam, M. A., Hough, R. L., Telles, C. A., Karno, M., & Escobar, J. I. (1987). Measurement of acculturation in a community population of Mexican Americans. *Hispanic Journal of Behavioral Sciences, 9,* 105-130.

Cuellar, I., Harris, L. C., & Jasso, R. (1980). An acculturation scale for Mexican American normal and clinical populations. *Hispanic Journal of Behavioral Sciences, 2,* 199-217.

Deyo, R. A., Diehl, A. K., Hazuda, H., & Stern, M. P. (1985). A sample language-based acculturation scale for Mexican Americans: Validation and application to health care research. *American Journal of Public Health, 75,* 51-55.

Garcia, M., & Lega, L. I. (1979). Development of a Cuban ethnic identity questionnaire. *Hispanic Journal of Behavioral Sciences, 1,* 247-261.

Lang, J. G., Munoz, R. F., Bernal, G., & Sorensen, J. L. (1982). Quality of life and psychological well-being in a bicultural Latino community. *Hispanic Journal of Behavioral Sciences, 4,* 433-450.

Marin, G., Sabogal, F., Marin, B. V., Otero-Sabogal, R., & Perez-Stable, E. (1987). Development of a short acculturation scale for Hispanics. *Hispanic Journal of Behavioral Sciences, 9,* 183-205.

Mendoza, R. H. (1989). An empirical scale to measure type and degree of acculturation in Mexican-American adolescents and adults. *Journal of Cross-Cultural Psychology, 20,* 372-385.

Olmedo, E. L., & Padilla, A. M. (1978). Empirical and construct validation of a measure of acculturation for Mexican Americans. *Journal of Social Psychology, 105,* 179-187.

Osvold, L., & Sodowsky, G. R. (In press). Eating attitudes of Native American and African American women: Differences by race/ethnicity and acculturation. *Explorations in Ethnic Studies.*

Padilla, A. M. (1980). The role of cultural awareness and ethnic loyalty in acculturation. In A. M. Padilla (Ed.), *Acculturation: Theory, models and some new findings* (pp. 47-84). Boulder, CO: Westview Press.

Sodowsky, G. R., Lai, E. W. M. (In press). Asian immigrant variables and structural models of cross-cultural distress. In A. Booth (Ed.), *International Migration and Family Change.* Hillsdale, NJ: Lawrence Erlbaum.

Sodowsky, G. R., Lai, E. W. M., & Plake, B. S. (1991). Moderating effects of sociocultural variables on acculturation attitudes of Hispanics and Asian Americans. *Journal of Counseling and Development, 70,* 194-204.

Sodowsky, G. R., & Plake, B. (1991). Psychometric properties of the American-International Relations Scale. *Educational and Psychological Measurement, 51*, 207-216.

Suinn, R. M., Ahuna, C., & Khoo, G. (1992). The Suinn-Lew Asian Self-Identity Acculturation Scale: Concurrent and factorial validation. *Educational and Psychological Measurement, 52*, 1041-1046.

Suinn, R. M., Rickard-Figueroa, K., Lew, S., & Vigil, P. (1987). The Suinn-Lew Asian Self-Identity Acculturation Scale: An initial report. *Educational and Psychological Measurement, 47*, 401-407.

Szapocznik, J., Scopetta, M. A., Kurtines, W., & Aranalde, M. A. (1978). Theory and measurement of acculturation. *International Journal of Psychology, 12*, 113-130.

Wong-Rieger, D., & Quintana, D. (1987). Comparative acculturation of Southeast Asian and Hispanic immigrants and sojourners. *Journal of Cross-Cultural Psychology, 18*, 345-362.

Appendix B
Acculturation Effects on Client Reactions
Edward Wai Ming Lai and Gargi Roysircar Sodowsky

Table 2

Summary of Select Acculturation Research Related to Counseling

Authors	Subjects Ethnicity	Size	Instruments	Independent Variables	Dependent Variables	Main Effects	Interaction Effects
Atkinson & Gim (1989)	Chinese A. Japanese A. Korean A.	263 185 109	1) Suinn-Lew Asian Self-Identity Acculturation Scale (SL-ASIA) 2) Attitudes Toward Seeking Professional Help Scale (ATSPHS)	1) Respondent acculturation (low, medium, & high levels) 2) Respondent ethnicity 3) Respondent sex	Four ATSPHS subscales: Need, Stigma, Openness, & Confidence	1) Acculturation effect (H > M > L on Need, Stigma, & Openness) 2) Insignificant gender & ethnicity effects	1) no significant interaction effects
Atkinson et al. (1990)	Chinese A. Japanese A. Korean A. Filipino A. South East Asian A.	268 151 108 186 103	1) SL-ASIA 2) Help providers ranking list (11 helpers)	1) Respondent acculturation (low, medium, & high levels) 2) Respondent ethnicity 3) Respondent gender	1) Help provider rankings	1) Acculturation effect (H > L on ratings for mother & friend, L > H on ratings for oldest person, teacher, & counselor/psychologist) 2) Gender effect	1) Acculturation X Gender (on ratings for father) effect

Table 2 continues

Table 2 Continued

Authors	Subjects Ethnicity	Size	Instruments	Independent Variables	Dependent Variables	Main Effects	Interaction Effects
Gim et al. (1990)	Chinese A. Japanese A. Filipino A. Korean A. South East Asian A.	268 151 186 108 103	1) SL-ASIA 2) Personal Problems Inventory (PPI)	1) Respondent acculturation (low-medium & high levels) 2) Respondent ethnicity 3) Respondent gender 4) 8 personal concerns	1) 2 dimensions of PPI: ratings for severity of concern and willingness to see a counselor	For severity ratings, 1) acculturation effect (L-M > H on mean ratings across all concerns) 2) Ethnicity effect 3) Concerns effect For willingness to see a counselor, 1) acculturation effect (L-M > H on willingness to see a counselor) 2) Gender effect 3) Concerns effect	For severity ratings, 1) Acculturation X Concerns effect (L-M respondents rated financial problems first & academic problems second whereas the order was reversed for H respondents) 2) Ethnicity X Concerns effect For willingness to see a counselor, no significant effects
Gim et al. (1991)	Chinese A. Japanese A. Filipino A. Korean A. South East Asian A.	36 24 22 14 8	1) SL-ASIA 2) Cross-Cultural Counseling Inventory (CCCI) 3) Counselor Effectiveness Rating Scale (CERS)	1) Respondent acculturation (low & high levels) 2) Counselor cultural sensitivity (sensitive vs blind) 3) Respondent ethnicity 4) Respondent gender	1) CCCI scores 2) 4 CERS subscales: Expertness, Trustworthiness, Attractiveness, & Willingness to see a counselor	For CCCI, 1) nonsignificant acculturation effect 2) significant counselor cultural sensitivity effect 3) significant counselor ethnicity effect For CERS, same as 1), 2), 3)	For CCCI, 1) Cultural Sensitivity X Ethnicity effect 2) Cultural sensitivity X Ethnicity X Gender effect For CERS 1) Acculturation X Cultural Sensitivity X Gender effect

Table 2 continues

Table 2 Continued

Authors	Subjects Ethnicity	Size	Instruments	Independent Variables	Dependent Variables	Main Effects	Interaction Effects
Hess & Street (1991)	Mexican A.	48	1) Acculturation Rating Scale for Mexican Americans (ARSMA) 2) CERS	1) Respondent acculturation (high-bicultural & low-bicultural) 2) Counselor ethnicity (Anglo vs Mexican A.) 3) Respondent sex	1) Ratings of 4 subscales: Expertness, Trustworthiness, Attractiveness, & Willingness to see a counselor	1) no significant main effect	1) no significant interaction effect
Kunkel (1990)	Mexican A. Anglo A.	213 137	1) ARSMA 2) Expectations About Counseling-Brief Form (EAC-B)	1) Respondent acculturation (Mexican-oriented bi-cultural (M-O), true bicultural (B), Anglo-oriented bi-cultural (A-O) & very Anglicized (VA) levels) 2) Respondent ethnicity 3) Respondent gender 4) Respondent experience with counseling (yes vs. no)	1) EAC-B 17 subscale scores	1) Acculturation effect (M-O > B > VA > A-O on Directness & Empathy) 2) Gender effect 3) Counseling experience effect	1) Acculturation X Counseling Experience effect
Pomales & Williams (1989)	Puerto Ricans Mexican A.	85 9	1) ARSMA 2) Acculturation Rating Scale for Puerto Ricans (ARSPR) 3) Counselor Rating Form-Short Version (CRF-S) 4) Counselor Effectiveness Rating Scale (CERS)	1) Respondent acculturation (high, medium, & low levels) 2) Counseling styles (directive vs nondirective) 3) Respondent gender	1) 3 subscales of CRF-S: Expertness, Attractiveness & Trustworthiness 2) 5 items of CERS knowledge of psychology, ability to help, willingness to help, understanding problems & willingness to see a counselor	For CRF-S, 1) Acculturation effect on trustworthiness but not on attractiveness or expertness (H > M & L on trustworthiness) For CERS, 1) nonsignificant acculturation effect 2) Style effect	For CRF-S, 1) no interaction effect For CERS, 1) Acculturation X Counseling Style effect on counselor understanding 2) Gender X Counseling Style effect

Table 2 continues

Table 2 continued

Authors	Subjects Ethnicity	Size	Instruments	Independent Variables	Dependent Variables	Main Effects	Interaction Effects
Ponce & Atkinson (1989)	Mexican A.	169	1) ARSMA 2) CERS 3) PPI	1) Respondent acculturation (high, medium, & low levels) 2) Counselor ethnicity (Anglo, Mexican A.) 3) Counseling style (directive vs nondirective)	1) 3 subscales of CERS: Expertness, Trustworthiness, & Attractiveness 2) 2 dimensions of PPI: ratings of severity of problems and willingness to see a counselor	For CERS, 1) nonsignificant acculturation effect 2) Ethnicity effect 3) Counseling style effect For PPI, same as 1), 2), & 3)	For CERS, 1) Ethnicity x Counseling Style effect For PPI, same as 1)
Sanchez & Atkinson (1983)	Mexican A.	109	1) Cultural Commitment item 2) Preference for seeing culturally similar counselor 3) ATSPHS	1) Respondent cultural commitment (com.) level (strong com. to Anglo culture (SA), strong com. to Mexican American culture (SM), strong com. to both cultures (SB), & weak com. to both cultures (WB) 2) Respondent sex	1) Counselor ethnicity 2) 4 ATSPHS subscales: Need, Stigma, Openness, & Confidence	For counselor ethnicity, 1) Cultural com. effect (SM > SB > WB > SA on choosing a Mexican A. counselor) For ATSPHS, 1) Cultural com. effect on Openness (WB > SM on using professional counseling services)	1) No interaction effects

REFERENCES

Atkinson, D. R., & Gim, R. H. (1989). Asian-American cultural identity and attitudes toward mental health services. *Journal of Counseling Psychology, 36,* 209-212.

Atkinson, D. R., Whiteley, S., & Gim, R. H. (1990). Asian-American acculturation and preferences for help providers. *Journal of College Student Development, 31,* 155-161.

Gim, R. H., Atkinson, D. R., & Whiteley, S. (1990). Asian-American acculturation, severity of concerns, and willingness to see a counselor. *Journal of Counseling Psychology, 37,* 281-285.

Gim, R. H., Atkinson, D. R., & Kim, S. J. (1991). Asian-American acculturation, counselor ethnicity and cultural sensitivity, and ratings of counselors. *Journal of Counseling Psychology, 38,* 57-62.

Hess, R. S., & Street, E. M. (1991). The effect of acculturation on the relationship of counselor ethnicity and client ratings. *Journal of Counseling Psychology, 38,* 71-75.

Kunkel, M. A. (1990). Expectations about counseling in relation to acculturation in Mexican-American and Anglo-American student samples. *Journal of Counseling Psychology, 37,* 286-292.

Pomales, J., & Williams, V. (1989). Effects of level of acculturation and counseling style on Hispanic students' perceptions of counselor. *Journal of Counseling Psychology, 36,* 79-83.

Ponce, F. Q., & Atkinson, D. R. (1989). Mexican-American acculturation, counselor ethnicity, counseling style, and perceived counselor credibility. *Journal of Counseling Psychology, 36,* 203-208.

Sanchez, A. R., & Atkinson, D. R. (1983). Mexican-American cultural commitment, preference for counselor ethnicity, and willingness to use counseling. *Journal of Counseling Psychology, 30,* 215-220.

Author Index

Subject Index